GOVERNING THE TONGUE

GOVERNING THE TONGUE

The Politics of Speech

in Early New England

JANE KAMENSKY

Oxford University Press • New York Oxford

Oxford University Press

Oxford   New York
Athens   Auckland   Bangkok   Bogotá   Buenos Aires   Calcutta
Cape Town   Chennai   Dar es Salaam   Delhi   Florence   Hong Kong   Istanbul
Karachi   Kuala Lumpur   Madrid   Melbourne   Mexico City   Mumbai
Nairobi   Paris   São Paulo   Singapore   Taipei   Tokyo   Toronto   Warsaw

and associated companies in
Berlin   Ibadan

First published in 1997 by Oxford University Press, Inc.
198 Madison Avenue, New York, New York 10016

First issued as an Oxford University Press paperback, 1999

Oxford is a registered trademark of Oxford University Press

Library of Congress Cataloging-in-Publication Data
Kamensky, Jane.
Governing the tongue : the politics of speech in early New England/
Jane Kamensky.
p. cm.
Includes index.
ISBN 0–19–509080-2; ISBN 0–19–513090-1 (pbk.)
1. English language—Political aspects—New England.   2. New England—History—Colonial period,
ca. 1600–1775.   3. English language—Early modern, 1500–1700—History.
4. English language—Religious aspects—Christianity.   5. English language—Spoken English—
New England.   6. Language and culture—New England—History.   7. Oral communication—
New England—History.   8. English language—18th century—History.
9. Americanisms—New England—History.   10. Puritans—New England—Language.   11. Women—
New England—Language.   12. Authorship—Sex differences.   I. Title.
PE2906.K36 1997
420'.974—dc21   97-10595

Portions of chapter 5 appeared in somewhat different form, in Robert Blair St. George, ed., *Possible
Pasts: Becoming Colonial in Early America* (Cornell, forthcoming) and are reprinted here with permission.

1 3 5 7 9 8 6 4 2

Printed in the United States of America
on acid-free paper

For Dennis

ACKNOWLEDGMENTS

Like all scholarly voyages, mine has been a collaborative path from first to last. Standing at the finish line, it is a joy at last to recognize some of the people and institutions whose support—financial, intellectual, and emotional—has made the journey always feasible, often bearable, and sometimes even delightful.

When this book was in its infancy as a dissertation, I benefited from the generosity of the Andrew W. Mellon Foundation, whose Fellowship in the Humanities underwrote my graduate education. Brandeis University helped to nurture the project through its stormy adolescence. Part of that help came in the form of a grant from the Mazer Fund for Faculty Research, which provided needed funds at a critical juncture. Even more important has been the institution's unwavering support for the growth and development of junior faculty, without which I might not have become either an effective teacher or a productive scholar. As the book approached its adulthood, I benefited from a year of uninterrupted research leave granted by Brandeis and funded by a National Endowment for the Humanities Fellowship for University Teachers (grant number FA-34093–96), a Faculty Fellowship from the Program in Religion and American History of the Pew Charitable Trusts, and a Fellowship from the Mary Ingraham Bunting Institute of Radcliffe College.

No less essential to this enterprise were the sometimes heroic efforts of archivists and librarians at a number of institutions, including the

Sterling and Beinecke Libraries of Yale University; the Widener and Houghton Libraries of Harvard University; the Goldfarb and Farber Libraries of Brandeis University; the Massachusetts Historical Society in Boston; the James Duncan Phillips Library of the Peabody-Essex Museum in Salem, Massachusetts; the Connecticut State Library in Hartford; and the Massachusetts State Archives in Boston. Together, these institutions and their staffs have provided the building blocks that made this project possible, and I remain in their debt.

Of course, a scholar's obligations take other forms, too; intellectual debts run every bit as deep as material ones. Each chapter that follows has been improved by the attention of generous colleagues. For their incisive comments on the parts of this work that were presented at various conferences and colloquia, I would like to thank Susan Amussen, Richard Bauman, Ruth Bloch, Tim Breen, Peter Burke, Jon Butler, Jonathan Chu, Cornelia Dayton, Richard Fox, Richard Gildrie, Thomas Haskell, Carol Karlsen, Mary Kelley, Bob St. George, and Robert Westbrook. Numerous others have read draft chapters, shared their own unpublished work, and passed along stray bits of early New England speech. For such service above and beyond the call, I thank Frank Bremer, Fran Dolan, Edward Gray, Sue Juster, Merja Kytö, Mark Peterson, Lizzie Reis, and Bernie Rosenthal. One of the delights of this project has been seeing some of my graduate students become my teachers. I am grateful to Dana Comi, Jenny Pulsipher, Chris Sterba, and Richard Rath for sharing their wit and wisdom and work on the politics of language, and for letting loose their red pens on drafts of various of my chapters and essays. The contributions of Jennifer Ratner run much deeper. As an indefatigable and meticulous researcher, a careful reader, and an enthusiastic cheerleader from the sidelines, she has left her mark on every page of this book.

I am blessed to count as colleagues and friends a number of people who have seen this project through from beginning to end, reading the entire manuscript—some of them, many times. As members of the dissertation committee that supervised the book's initial stages, Nancy Cott and Harry Stout were peerless mentors. Bob St. George, whose knowledge of symbolic communication in colonial America is so extensive as to be frightening, has served as a generous colleague-in-absentia for nearly a decade. Cornelia Dayton, Richard Godbeer, Susan Juster, Laurel Ulrich, and an anonymous reviewer for Oxford University Press read the manuscript and offered wise counsel about revisions large and small. Sheldon Meyer and Thomas LeBien offered editorial wisdom of the very best sort. Always eager, responsive, and interested in the book, they allowed me the latitude to pursue my own detours and to make my own mistakes. Others at Oxford University Press *kept* me from making my own mistakes whenever possible. Jessica Ryan calmly and capably steered the manuscript through the maze of production, and copy editor Eric Edstam's eagle eyes spotted in the text flaws that had long since become invisible to its author. Rudy Binion and David Fischer, colleagues in the Department of History at Brandeis, read the manuscript from cover to cover and responded with particularly detailed suggestions, many of which they will see reflected in what follows. From its inception as a paper in a research seminar under his tutelage in 1988, this project has had the good fortune to count John Demos as its patient, wise, and dedicated midwife. His faith in this book has at times been more unwavering than my own; his friendship has been equally unstinting. I hope he will find both to be in some measure rewarded here.

Finally, it is my sincere privilege to thank several people whose support has been so vital that without it, this book would not exist. Ruth Sedlock, Susan Bers, and especially Meg Turner gave me the voice with which to explore the politics of language. Cathy Corman has read and heard more about Puritan understandings of speech than anyone could reasonably be asked to bear. Her comments are always both rigorous and kind, but that is the very least of what her friendship gives me. Dennis Scannell's affection is the very soil in which this project, and nearly everything else of worth in my life, has taken root. He has done many things to assist in the birth of this book, for which I have already applauded him. Here, I thank him for what matters.

A NOTE ON THE TEXT

In order to preserve as closely as possible the integrity of early New Englanders' voices, I have retained original spellings and punctuation when quoting from their records, with the exception of following modern usage for the letters *u, v, w, j,* and *i,* and expanding archaic contractions. Where erratic spellings or punctuation made meanings unclear, I have bracketed small editorial changes. I have also modernized dates throughout, starting each year on 1 January rather than on 25 March, as New Englanders did under the Old Style, or Julian, calendar, which prevailed in the British colonies until 1752.

CONTENTS

GOVERNING THE TONGUE

INTRODUCTION

I f you want to understand what the act of speaking meant to the men and women who lived in early New England, start with Cotton Mather's diary. A would-be minister plagued throughout his childhood with a debilitating stutter, Mather conceded that the whole issue of speech was "a matter of more than ordinary Thoughtfulness unto me."[1] But if Mather wrote a good deal more about the spoken word than did most of his contemporaries, he was hardly alone in his fascination with the promise and perils of the human tongue, a topic that intrigued most English people in his day and was a matter of particular concern to Mather's "Puritan" coreligionists. Let us allow him, then, to act as a translator of a sort, giving written expression to the deep concern with speech and its consequences that so many of his unlettered neighbors voiced in other ways, chiefly through their interactions with kin, friends, and those in authority. Consider, for example, the following scenes:

The first takes place in June 1681, when Mather—usually an anxious young man, even by Puritan standards—appears uncharacteristically exuberant. The reason for his delight is clear. During the previous winter, his twentieth, he has with great effort overcome the crippling speech defect that had earlier caused him to fear that he lacked the "necessary Supplies of *Speech*" to embark upon a successful "Ministry." Now that his tongue is finally "untyed," Mather dares to hope that he will become a preacher of great skill, capable of using a combination of his own words

and God's Word to melt the hearts of even the most sinful listeners. Three years out of Harvard, he may yet prove himself worthy of
his linguistic patrimony, inheriting the voice of his preacher father, Increase Mather, or perhaps even echoing that of his maternal grandfather,
John Cotton, renowned as one of the greatest Puritan orators. At long
last, Mather imagines, he might fulfill one of the reformed Protestant's
fondest dreams: the dream of speaking, without fetters, both to and of
God; the dream of simple prayer, unimpeded by popish forms and unmediated by priestly meddlers. With a heart full of "*Gratitude* unto the
Lord," young Mather retires to his prayer closet, where he cries out in
thanks for his newfound voice: "How *Miraculous* a Thing is the *Freedom of Speech* . . . !"[2]

Skip ahead to the following spring. The delight Mather's "freedom of
speech" brought him the previous June has been supplanted by anxiety.
Now, instead of agonizing over the physical impediments to his tongue's
liberty, Mather frets about his *lack* of restraint in speaking. Perhaps his
unaccustomed fluency has suddenly made him aware of something virtually every early modern Englishman and Englishwoman already knows:
that the hot passions of the tongue more often cause words to flow too
freely than not freely enough—particularly, it seems, in New England.
Has not the history of the Massachusetts Bay Colony's first half century,
a history that includes both the inspiring oratory of John Cotton and the
"infectious" heresies of Anne Hutchinson, proved the truth of the popular maxim stating that "the tongue is every man's best or worst"?[3]

Whatever the reason, just months after reveling in his "freedom of
speech," Mather sets out to define, and refine, and *confine* his verbal
liberties. He begins in his diary a list of what he calls "*Rules of right
Speaking*," precepts for the proper "*Government of the Tongue*" to which
he will refer throughout his preaching life. Having at last taught himself
to speak freely, he now reminds himself also to speak "*cautiously, moder-
ately, deliberately*," and rarely. In order to sound like a godly man, Mather
writes, he must "*take heed that hee sinned not with His Tongue*."[4] He tells
himself, in short, that free speech is not enough. Or, more precisely, he
cautions himself: free speech is sometimes too much.

And so, in the coming years, Mather will use his own, carefully cultivated, free public voice to urge others—especially women, especially
children—to govern theirs. In 1692, he will caution the pious matrons
whom he calls the "daughters of Zion" to remember the words "of the
Psalmist, *I will take heed unto my ways that I sin not with my Tongue; I will
keep my Mouth with a Bridle*."[5] Several years later, he will warn the youth
of the rising generation about the dangers of speaking against their parents.[6] Until the end of his life, Mather will persist in preaching "against
the Sins of *Evil-Speaking*," hoping always that he "might fully come at
the *Sins of the Tongue*, with a Cure for them."[7] His very last major work,
a lengthy medical treatise which will not see print during his lifetime,
will continue the fight, repeatedly enjoining readers against "trespassing

on the Holy Rules of Speech"—rules that, Mather would come to feel, were the backbone of a godly society; rules that, he would lament, too often were honored in the breach.[8]

MATHER'S VIRTUAL OBSESSION with speech and its attendant joys and dangers raises a number of questions about the culture of early New England, questions that this book is dedicated to exploring. We have to wonder, first, about the sheer quantity of his musings on the subject. Why did he devote so much time and energy not only to speaking per se, but, more particularly, to what ethnographers today would call "meta-linguistics"—that is, to "speaking of speaking"?[9] In Mather's case, the psychological scars left by years of stammering are part of the explanation, but not the whole of it. The reasons that speech mattered in early New England are rooted in collective experience as well as in individual biography.

Mather's neighbors shared his concern with the nature, and quality, and power of the spoken word. The twin desires to promote godly speech and to prevent what one scholar calls "heated" utterances lay at the very center of New England's culture. Wherever people came together—in parlors, fields, taverns, and milk yards; in churches, courtrooms, town meetings, and other arenas of law and politics—the power of talk was a favorite subject of conversation.[10] In seventeenth-century parlance, the word "conversation" referred both to verbal exchange in particular and to human conduct in general. This definition surely made sense to New Englanders; for them, speech was conduct and conduct was speech. In their worldview, "conversation"—in both of its contemporary meanings—amounted to nothing less than the whole "way or course of a mans life."[11]

Why speech came to assume such prominence in the thinking of people such as Cotton Mather, and how such beliefs about the power of the spoken word in turn shaped the history of early New England, are the central questions of my study. The answers are complex, for as we shall see, the significance of speech in that place and time had numerous causes and myriad consequences. Some of the causes are quite generic, part of the dynamics of face-to-face communities in which the small scale of daily life makes words loom large.[12] Others are more specific to New England—to the particular nexus of beliefs and material conditions that prevailed there. In Mather's world, more than in most small societies, ideology and circumstance combined to elevate the attention paid to speech.

The contributions of Puritan theology are essential to recognize in this regard. Like so many other Christian reformers before them and since, English nonconformists in the sixteenth and seventeenth centuries made the relationships between Word and flesh, words and deeds, central tenets of their faith. In their religious beliefs as well as in their social and spatial arrangements, early New Englanders were not simply people of words but, more pointedly, people of the Word. The reformed Protestant emphasis on Scripture, sermons, and free-form prayer held out new possibilities for speech to ministers and also to layfolk, who were urged to address God directly. But if Puritan thought increased the value of prayerful words, it also raised the cost of deviant speech—making blasphemy, for example, an unforgivable (and, in New England, a capital) offense. Just as nonconformists argued that speech could do more good than most people in the early modern world tended to recognize, so they also feared that words could do more harm than the Church of England was likely to admit.

Living as colonials at the far western edge of a metropolitan culture further complicated the meaning of speech among early New Englanders. The tension between godly words and deadly words would have been difficult enough to resolve had Puritan precepts been tested in an environment that held constant everything else in English culture. But New England was not such a place. In the Puritans' "new world," old markers of status and power carried diminished importance. Where the institutions of authority (government, law, schools, parishes, and trading empires) were in their infancy, leaders had to find new means by which to articulate their places in the world, a world that now also included new and different peoples to define oneself *against*.

Taken together, the dislocations of colonialism, the dictates of Puritan belief, and the mundane realities of village life created an environment in which such people as Mather found themselves compelled to invest the spoken word with special powers and special dangers. This is not to say, of course, that speech mattered *only* in New England, but rather to suggest that words carried particular weight there. Precisely how much additional weight is a question that this study—which attempts a thick description of New England's economy of speaking in the seventeenth century—cannot address. I hope that close, comparative analysis of my findings by future scholars may reveal the relative "exceptionalism" of New England in this respect.

In addition to exploring the volume of attention New England Puritans paid to speech, this book also strives to understand the particulars of what they said about the spoken word. Here, too, Mather offers a useful starting point, for many of the seeming contradictions that emerge in his writings on the matter resonated widely in the discourse of ordinary folks, as well as in the printed debates of his peers in the ministry and the civil government. Like Mather, most New Englanders prized speech that was "free" and yet "governed," unfettered and yet orderly. To us, the notion may sound paradoxical; freedom and restraint have, over the past two centuries, come to seem like natural enemies. To the Puritans, the reverse was true; in their world, verbal liberty and verbal government were necessary allies, essential partners in the creation of a godly society.

Thus as early as 1641, Massachusetts law granted ordinary men (and men alone) "full freedome" to voice "any advise, vote, verdict, or sentence in any Court, Counsell, or Civill Assembly" so long as they articulated their opinions "orderly and inofensively," "Christianlie and respectively," and "in convenient time" and "due order."[13] Yet at the same time that they endorsed this ambivalent sort of verbal freedom—which was exceptionally broad by the standards of the day—New England magistrates regularly punished offenders who used any of literally dozens of types of deviant speech. In Massachusetts, court dockets were crowded with presentments for crimes of the tongue: varieties of misspeaking ranging from the capital (including blasphemy and, as this book will demonstrate, witchcraft), to the serious (contempt of authority, for example), to the relatively trivial (such as profane swearing). Magistrates in Essex County tried an average of thirteen cases for criminal speech every year between 1636 and 1686.[14]

The courts were not alone in their campaign against "heated" utterances. Common people, too, embraced a doubled vision of verbal freedom. Zealous in asserting their privilege to speak in court, in town meetings, and especially in their churches, villagers were equally devoted to reigning in the loose tongues of their neighbors. Defending their good names against the hard words of their detractors, men and women in Essex County brought, on average, more than seven slander suits per year throughout the half century before 1686.[15] Like their preachers and magistrates, ordinary litigants argued that it was one thing, as Boston merchant Robert Keayne noted, to voice one's "protestation of dissent . . . modestly and without provoking expressions." But it was quite another to speak "as if men had the liberty of their tongues to reproach any that were not beneficial to them."[16] The Good Neighbor, many said, was "one of few words." Which meant that the Bad Neighbor often had to be reminded to "cary a good tounge in your head, & . . . know to whom you speake."[17] Understanding the logic behind this tight pairing of verbal freedom with verbal restraint in the minds of early New Englanders is another major objective of this book.

Of course, as Mather would have been the first to point out, the definition of "a good tongue" varied with the social position of a given speaker. The deliberate, public, authoritative style that counted as "right speaking" when employed by the heads of a godly community (Mather himself included) might sound quite different—and much less "right"—when used by other members of the body politic. When a son spoke out against his father, he could not claim "freedom" for his voice, any more than could a yeoman who denounced the wisdom of his social betters. And when a witch cursed her neighbors, or a daughter of Zion such as Anne Hutchinson claimed the right to explicate doctrine before a large audience, it became clear that women in New England possessed a lot less verbal license than did their husbands, fathers, brothers, or sons.

Indeed, the "freedom of speech" claimed by some depended upon the *lack* of freedom imparted to others. New Englanders' concept of right speaking thus required a double balancing act, demanding that all speakers seek an equilibrium between freedom and restraint in their utterances, while insisting that the proper ratio of speech to silence was different in every case. The ways in which status, age, race, and, especially, gender shaped New Englanders' concepts of right speaking are a major focus of the chapters that follow.

The precarious balance between free speech and right speech in Mather's New England varied in another important way: over time as well as from speaker to speaker. When Mather took to his closet to shout out the virtues of his own "freedom of speech" in 1681, English colonists in the region had already spent some sixty years battling over definitions of right speaking, with no end in sight. At times, the issue had seemed particularly urgent, for reasons the present study seeks to explain. In the early years of white settlement, for example, the vulnerability of new plantations to rumors and other ill words made the government of the tongue a matter of pressing, official concern. Likewise, Anne Hutchinson's challenge to a nascent Massachusetts orthodoxy in the mid-1630s forced New Englanders to refine further their notions of who should say what to whom, where, and in what manner. During the 1650s and early 1660s, the deaths of many of New England's founding orators, together with the threat of the new linguistic order promoted by itinerant Quakers, once again made verbal governance one of the highest priorities of clerical and civil leaders. Finally, barely a decade after Mather expounded upon the glories of his own, newly liberated tongue, the words of Salem's alleged "witches" and their "afflicted" accusers would again bring the power of the spoken word to the forefront of the public discourse of Massachusetts. In this last and most explosive of seventeenth-century New England's conversations about conversation, earlier notions of whose tongues deserved to command the public ear would be turned upside down, much to the peril of everyone involved. Only after 1692, with the widespread repudiation of the Salem trials and the imposition of a new, royal charter mandating religious tolerance in the Bay Colony, would the tension between New England's twin demands for free speech and "governed" speech begin to be resolved in favor of the former.

Of course, in each of these instances (and, indeed, in all "metalinguistic" encounters), it was not only the act of speaking in general but also the *content* of certain utterances in particular that concerned authorities in New England. When Anne Hutchinson explicated doctrine, for example, orthodox clergy considered *what* she said—her articulation of a piety without preachers and a godliness without earthly rules—to be as menacing as the mere fact of her public voice. In fact, the threat of Hutchinson's ideas and the dangers of her speech reinforced one another; in her case as in so many others, expressed content and expressive form were interdependent.[18] Thus exploring New Englanders' "rules for right speaking" requires that we pay attention to what was said as well as to who was talking, how much, and when. By examining the particular words and thoughts that, such men as Mather argued, were best left unsaid, we begin to glimpse in the negative some of New England's most closely held and often unspoken values.

Throughout the seventeenth century, then, rules for right speaking were not simply Cotton Mather's personal precepts. They were New England's rules: rules about social power as well as about manners and politeness. The work of "governing the tongue," as so many seventeenth-century experts called it, was central to the work of governing families, neighborhoods, towns, and even empires. To understand the importance of right speaking in Mather's world is thus to glimpse New England in the making: to apprehend some of the ways in which Puritan leaders and common men and women together constructed the fragile social order to which they clung so tenaciously, long after the voices of their founding generation had grown faint.

If understanding the meaning of speech teaches us something essential about early New England, it should also teach us something about ourselves. For in many respects, this story does not—and cannot—stop in the seventeenth century. Today, no less than in Mather's lifetime, we are engaged in wars over words: struggles to understand the relationships between language and experience, and between speech and power. Can words harm, and even kill? Is so-called hate speech talk, or action? Where lies the proper balance between our individual desires for expressive liberty and our societal need for order? And how can we keep the freedom accorded to some speakers from stilling the voices of others? It goes almost without saying that our own social agendas are markedly different from those of New England's seventeenth-century settlers. But in modern American democracy much as in Puritan oligarchy, the connection between speech and society remains a vital and tangled one. Thus in various arenas of our contemporary public discourse, we continue to debate some of the thorny questions about the nature of language that once vexed Cotton Mather.

In scholarly circles, too, words continue to matter. Indeed, perhaps more than ever before, the meaning of language has become a central concern in many areas of academic inquiry. In philosophy, the problem is an old one; scholars working in that discipline have long paid close attention to the bonds between words and what they name.[19] In recent years, linguists, anthropologists, cultural critics, and historians have followed the philosophers' lead, taking what some have labeled a "linguistic turn" in their explorations of particular times and places. This means that instead of treating language as a window through which distant realities can be glimpsed naked and entire, we have begun to imagine it as a densely woven fabric that is sometimes translucent and sometimes opaque. Rather than simply a mode of communication, speech thus becomes a cultural system whose meanings take their shape from a nexus of persons, places, and times.[20] So, too, scholars have started to think about the *social* laws governing discourse, exploring the extent to which knowing a language—or, more properly, belonging to a "speech community"—means learning culture as well as grammar.[21] We have begun, in short, to pay heightened attention to the interdependence of language and society. Instead of supposing a one-directional relationship between words and their speakers—a monologue in which people have power over words—we now think in terms of the dialogue through which cultures create the languages that create cultures. In such a schema, speech emerges both as a mirror of existing social relations and as a force that continually shapes and re-shapes a given society.[22]

With these insights in mind, my study of early New England takes as its point of origin the belief that language—in this case, the spoken variety—cannot merely be something we see *through*. It must also, for reasons my story will dramatize, be something we are prepared to *see,* full on, as a subject worth studying in its own right. About this, early New Englanders would surely have agreed. Indeed, their "cooperation," in this sense, is critical to the present study. Exploring the speech codes espoused at any given moment in time becomes a worthy and feasible project precisely because ordinary speakers in the past were themselves often aware—even acutely so—that their ways of speaking had "social meaning."[23] A language-centered approach to New England's history, therefore, is not an exercise in grafting a contemporary theoretical framework onto past experience. To the contrary, by examining the ways Mather's contemporaries used and understood speech, we begin to uncover something of how they conceived of themselves. We begin, that is, to *hear* their history: to restore the voices, the silences, and the clamor amid which people in that distant world made sense of their lives, day by day.

IN ITS QUEST to understand the meaning of speech in the culture of early New England, this book is an exercise in historical eavesdropping, an attempt to listen in on the everyday conversations of people in the seventeenth century. Yet a reader may well wonder how it is possible to overhear the utterances of people long dead. Speech, after all, is ephemeral stuff, vanishing for all intents and purposes at the moment it comes into being. (Indeed, we shall see, the fleeting nature of the spoken word—the fact that promises, threats, insults, and rumors lived only in the memories of their speakers and hearers—was a vital component of its power in early New England.) How, then, do those same words become accessible to the prying ears of the historian working nearly four centuries after the fact? What "speech" survives, and how authentically "spoken" is it?

Without exception, spoken utterances from the seventeenth century survive only in written form. Inevitably, therefore, the caprices of human memory and the strictures of written syntax have rearranged every extant "conversation." The snippets of talk that appear in early New England court records, letters, sermons, and diaries have been sifted at least twice: through the screen of recollection, and through the filter of writing. Moreover, the speech represented in these records is anything but a random sample. People recorded spoken exchanges that stood out in some way from the seamless fabric of daily talk, which means that deviant or "heated" words are far more likely to reach our ears than are unobjectionable ones. To these biases of syntax and survival, we must add yet another source of distortion of the voices of our early New England informants: the social bias of the recorders themselves. For the most part, the transcribers of speech in seventeenth-century New England came from a different social stratum than those whose words they entered into the written record. The utterances of women, children, and Native Americans, as well as the words of the poor, the elderly, the illiterate, and the discontent: all of these were preserved for posterity almost exclusively by the pens of white, literate, enfranchised, Puritan men.[24]

As any ethnographer could point out, from a social-scientific standpoint, such data barely passes muster. And think of what else we lack: There are no audio recordings from which to assess the social power of speakers by tracking their use of interruptions, angry tones, or supplicant inflections. There are no videotapes to offer us glimpses of talkers from the past: their physical postures; the distance between speakers of different sexes, ages, races, or ranks; their use of the language that is gesture; or the changes in their affects over the course of a conversation. The historian finds herself without even that most ambiguous technique in the anthropologist's bag of tricks: the ability to enter a community of discourse as a participant-observer, the chance to *ask*, face-to-face, the questions to which she wants answers. What is available to the student of colonial speech communities is, instead, a rather motley assortment of thirdhand conversational fragments collected for purposes other than, if not at odds with, the mission of analyzing the social relations of talk. A linguist invested in the scientific niceties of modern-day ethnography might well throw up her hands and ask, how can we know *anything* of the relationship between speech and power in early New England?

I can offer two answers to this question, the first of which concerns the constraints of history as a discipline. Historical evidence is *always* inadequate, never more so than when the subject under investigation lies in the distant past. Striving to re-create vanished worlds from the bits and pieces that happen to survive, historians practice the art of making do. Like the drunk in the old joke, who hunts for his lost keys under the glare of a nearby street lamp all the while knowing that he lost them in a dark alley two blocks away, we are stuck looking where the light is best. Thus while I confront, here and elsewhere, the limits of the existing data, I must also dedicate myself to interpreting, as faithfully, fully, and creatively as possible, the imperfectly recorded oral milieu that Cotton Mather and his contemporaries have left behind. It is a legacy of surprising depth and fullness. In fact, given the evanescence of speech, the constraints of writing, and the vagaries of time, it is more remarkable that we can reconstruct even part of the web of talk in colonial New England than that the voices we hear are faint and sometimes muffled.

Indeed, the most important answer to the question, how can we know? is provided by the Puritans themselves. We can recover a great deal about what speaking meant in seventeenth-century New England because the people who lived there cared so much about the social meanings of language. The white inhabitants of Massachusetts imbued the act of speaking with dramatic and fearful power: power to symbolize and to shape the relationships that made up their daily lives. Because they did so, they invested a great deal of energy not merely in communicating with one another, but also in recounting, evaluating, and otherwise exploring the meaning of their spoken exchanges.

They did so, first and foremost, in their own everyday behaviors, particularly in their diligent listening to what others said. To a significant degree, the vaunted "watchfulness" of New England towns was really "hearfulness": an ethos of keeping one's ears peeled for loose talk.[25] Proficient eavesdropping was one of the skills that made and unmade reputations in early New England. In this face-to-face world, stories about one's neighbors constituted a vital form of social currency. Only through what period vernacular referred to as careful "ear-witnessing" could a person accumulate a store of this currency. One was obliged, therefore, to listen attentively to what others said, whether one came upon their words by happenstance (when stumbling "accidentely" into a "disscorseing"), or by design (when asked "to take notis" of what a neighbor was about to say).[26] At times, neighborly hearfulness could be hard work, as Salem's Joanna Curtis well knew. Anxious one night because she heard her daughter and son-in-law "talke but could not understand what thay sayd," mother Curtis "layed [her] heed off from the bed upon the flower" until she could make out the details of the conversation unfolding in the chamber below.[27] This brazen feat of ear-witnessing did not endear Joanna Curtis to her son-in-law, about whose impotence she later told the local magistrates. But her unashamed hearfulness surely earns the gratitude of the historian, whose own eavesdropping Curtis so ably abets.

Still, hearfulness alone could not ensure the survival of seventeenth-century speech. Memory was the next ingredient necessary to transform the ephemera of the spoken into the permanence of the written. If building a stock of stories about one's neighbors hinged on careful listening, trading shares of this story wealth required both a knack and a willingness accurately to restate what one had heard. This early New Englanders did with a level of precision that strikes a modern reader as astonishing.[28] It was not unusual for neighbors' recollections of what they had said and heard to reach back some "twentie years agoon" and more. Then as now, human memory was imperfect; on occasion a witness admitted that he was "uncertaine," after many years, of who had said what to whom.[29] But failure to remember the tiniest detail, the precise setting, or the exact words of an encounter was a fault many deponents before early New England magistrates deemed worth noting.[30] In the absence of such disclaimers, we can assume that those who came before the bar trusted their memories. Moreover, the infrequency of disputes among litigants and witnesses about what they had said suggests that such recollections were dependable indeed.

Alert ears and keen memories may have been all New Englanders needed to transact the daily business of building and policing their "common fames." But fortunately for the historian of communication, devoted hearfulness and flawless recall were not enough for colonial officials. New England culture, especially its legal culture, did still more to ensure the survival of its spoken utterances. It is the industriousness of the secretary of the Essex County courts, as much as the studious listening of Joanna Curtis, that allows us to "hear" the results of her eavesdropping. His care with her words belongs to a more generalized concern on the part of colonial authorities with ensuring that their business was "exactly recorded, & kept for publike use." From the very beginnings of white settlement in Massachusetts, laws required that all court proceedings be faithfully transcribed, going so far as to specify the kinds of materials ("four large paper books, in folio, bound up with velum & past[e]board") in which clerks were to record the court's work "in some alphabeticall or methodicall way." To safeguard the records whose accuracy so concerned them, the members of the General Court passed additional acts, including provisions to secure extra copies of their work, and an order committing any individual convicted of being a "DEFACER OF RECORDS" to two months in prison or two hours in the pillory.[31]

The goal, as the court made clear, was to produce, insofar as it was possible to do so, "a perfit record"—free of "mistakes" and misrepresentations—of the "verball testimonyes" offered in connection with any given case.[32] For only when ear-witnesses' exact words were accurately restated, closely examined, and carefully weighed could the true aim of Puritan jurisprudence be accomplished. Only then could the voices contending over a given instance of civil litigation or a particular criminal "presentment" find resolution in the one, authentic voice that was God's truth. It was for this reason, too, that the language of New England's courts in the seventeenth century was itself a straightforward vernacular, largely uncluttered by the "legalese" that characterizes English legal records of the period. Like Puritan preachers, godly magistrates favored a "plain style": an official discourse that approximated ordinary speech. Avoiding much of the common law's arcane rhetoric, jurists in New England presided over plainspoken courts in which godliness was the overarching goal of all proceedings. Their devotion to conversational substance over legal form means that what these courts recorded comes very close to reproducing what witnesses actually *said*, particularly in the many cases in which speech itself was at issue.[33] In this respect, once again, the linguistic priorities of the latter-day historian work in tandem with those of Puritan elites.

The hearfulness and long memories of ordinary folks, the devotion of legal authorities to careful record keeping, and the preference of both preachers and magistrates for a written style that closely resembled speech—each of these tendencies among early New Englanders accomplished part of an act of translation, the depiction of speech as writing. Thus each of these habits helped to produce the data that is essential to this project—and that was essential, as well, to New Englanders themselves. Such acts of translation lay at the very core of their culture, a world that existed at the crossroads of speech and print.

Today, we often treat speaking and writing as distinct acts—almost as different languages. Moreover, we tend to rank the two, privileging printed words over spoken ones. Speech, in this modern understanding, is primitive; writing, evolved. Speaking is what children do; writing is for grown-ups. Speaking is for low, unmediated, unreasoned thoughts; writing is the stuff of sober reflection, high culture, great literature.[34] The boundaries were fuzzier three centuries ago. Early New Englanders conceived of speech and script as interdependent, overlapping, virtually contiguous.[35] True, the white settlers of the region, people who made a written text—the Bible—their script for living, inhabited a world suffused by print. But Scripture offers a perfect example of the ways in which the spoken and the written intertwined in Puritan culture. Although New Englanders were (as historians have long maintained) people of the Book, they conceived of the Bible more as oral performance than as written text. Much, if not most, Bible reading was done aloud—as befitted the texts that were believed to represent God's *spoken* Word. As such, godly men and women read *and listened* to it closely. Preachers were its public performer-interpreters. Print was only the technology that made it audible to mere mortals.[36] The book, in this sense, was but the servant of the living Word. Surely, this is what Cotton Mather meant when he rhymed his thanks for his "*Employment,* with Free *Speech* and *Fame,* And *Books* to feed the Same."[37] Early New England, in other words, was the very essence of what philosopher of language Walter J. Ong labels a "residually oral" culture, a milieu at once literate and speech centered.[38] While English settlers there made spoken exchanges the center of their daily lives, they also devoted themselves to rendering many of those exchanges in written form.

This book, then, relies on the careful work of two kinds of listeners-turned-speakers-turned-writers. Cotton Mather is an example of the first type, which I'll call the metalinguist. A leading man who rendered in print both his delight in and his anxiety about the spoken word, Mather has much to tell us about the impact of speech on the inner life of the Puritan elite. And, along with others in positions of religious and civil authority, he described and prescribed the contours of correct speech, reminding his reader-listeners about the boundaries separating godly words from dangerous words. Yet like statutes and case law governing the tongue, Mather's counsel about rules for right speaking can tell us only so much about the verbal component of New England's culture. It is the ear-witnessing of a second sort of translator that allows us to set such prescriptions in context.

If Cotton Mather represents the verbal lawgiver who articulated what *should* be said in early New England, Robert Keayne exemplifies the transcriber who brings alive what *was* said. On most Sundays and Thursdays for nearly two decades after his admission to membership in 1636, Keayne sat attentively in his assigned seat in Boston's First Church listening—and writing. Covering each page with his tiny, cramped script, Keayne filled three substantial notebooks with transcriptions of sermons, disciplinary proceedings, and other church business. Poring over his notes to correct mistakes that crept in during the haste of taking down what he heard, Keayne worked diligently to produce a faithful record of what his fellow church members had said. Nearly four centuries later, a computer-assisted "factor analysis" of his notebooks suggests that he succeeded. Linguist Merja Kytö, an expert on Keayne's writings, concludes that his "scribal interference" in the speech he recorded was minimal; Keayne, she argues, "did not put words into the mouths of his speakers."[39] In this dedication to capturing the exact words of his neighbors, Keayne was hardly alone. The verbatim transcripts he and others labored to produce offer twofold evidence of the linguistic priorities of early New England. They provide a record, accurate given its limits, of what was said so long ago. Equally important, they demonstrate how very much the give-and-take of every conversation meant to ordinary speakers living in that place and time.

"STICKS AND STONES will break my bones, but names will never hurt me!" To our ears, the phrase is familiar, even hackneyed—a weapon each of us likely mustered in our own defense at some point during childhood, perhaps as a charm to ward off the hard words of a schoolyard bully. But the saying, first recorded by folklorists in the late nineteenth century, is also a distinctly modern one, as is the sentiment behind it.[40] Nobody in early New England would have believed any such thing. In fact, their incantation on the subject said nearly the opposite: *"a soft tongue breaketh the bone"* was the equivalent in early modern folk wisdom.[41] This study places that wisdom at the center of New England's history, and invites readers to travel the imaginative distance between our own culture, which often trivializes the power of speech, and that of the Puritans, who fetishized it.

Each of the following chapters investigates a particular facet of the relationship between verbal order and social order in early New England. Organized around a series of episodes from the 1620s through the 1690s in which the government of the tongue assumed momentous public significance in Massachusetts, the narrative moves both topically and chronologically. The story begins in England, with a chapter exploring the assumptions about speech that white New Englanders brought with them across the Atlantic. Their inheritance, the chapter explains, was an ambiguous one. In early modern England, preachers and magistrates worked to eradicate what William Perkins called the "lamentable and fearefull . . . abuse of the tongue among all sorts and degrees of men every where."[42] At the same time, however, dissenters from the Church of England advanced a new and less constrained economy of speaking, one that prized speech as the medium through which laypeople could interact directly with the Word of God. Migration across the Atlantic sorely tested the degree of verbal license granted by this ideal, as chapter 2 demonstrates. As emigrating Puritans quickly discovered, setting up house in New England meant transforming an ideology of dissent into a new orthodoxy, and coming to terms with the radically different understandings of "governed" speech exhibited by the region's native inhabitants.

The next two chapters center on episodes that revealed New England's evolving ideals of governed speech in the breach. Chapter 3 considers the "misgoverned" words of two prominent Boston women (Anne Hutchinson and Ann Hibbens) and investigates the impact of disorderly female speech early in New England's history. Through the story of John Porter Jr., who, in the mid-1660s, became the only New Englander ever tried under laws making filial rebellion—by word as well as deed—a capital offense, chapter 4 investigates the contested verbal domains of parents (particularly fathers) and children (especially sons). In addition to charting the relationship between the growing silence of the founding generation and the rising voices of their children at midcentury, this chapter explores the gendered constraints governing male speech.

Chapter 5 steps back from the chronological march of the previous four chapters to analyze the ritual of public apology, a preferred remedy for the damage caused by heated words. Why, this chapter asks, did some victims of harsh words take comfort from a ceremony during which the remarks that had so wounded them were restated? Finally, chapter 6 looks at words that could not be retracted: threatening female voices as incarnated in the speech of "witches" and the devil's "possessed" victims. This most serious of speech offenses all but disappeared (as an official, legal entity) after the infamous trials at Salem in 1692. Thus the exploration of witchcraft-as-speech-crime points toward an epilogue touching upon the very different economy of speaking ushered into being by the changing world of eighteenth-century America.

THE SWEETEST MEAT,
THE BITTEREST POISON

Its author claimed that the story was as old as history, if not as old as speech itself. Once upon a time in an ancient land, the sovereign, King Amasis, directed his young manservant to "goe into the market and to buy the best and profitablest meat he could get." When the boy returned to the palace bearing a parcel of "nothing but tongues," the disappointed king "asked him the reason why he bought no other meat." The servant, one Lyas, readily replied: "I was commaunded to buy the best meate, and from the tongue come many good and profitable speaches." Logical enough, to be sure. But Amasis, still craving variety for the royal table, decided to try once more. This time, he dispatched the youth to "buy the worst and unprofitablest meat." And again, the hapless servant "bought nothing but tongues." When the astonished king "asked him the reason," the boy offered an impeccable answer. Tongue was indeed the least palatable of meats because "from nothing . . . commeth worse venome then from the tongue," particularly from "such tongues" as "most women have." The hungry king had learned his lesson. Both delectable and poisonous, the tongue was a model paradox, at once the finest and the basest human instrument.[1]

Joseph Swetnam used this parable of the wise peasant and the carnivorous king to illustrate the dangers of a particular type of speech: scolding by "froward" women. But readers of his enormously popular tract, which saw ten printings between 1615 and 1634, must have sensed a broader meaning.[2] For the tale, with its emphasis on the primacy and the perils of the spoken word, captured the very essence of contemporary fears about speaking. Indeed, Swetnam's tract was but one item in a veritable canon of prescriptive literature about ungoverned speech that flourished in England during the seventeenth century. In the dense leather-bound treatises favored by learned theologians, and in the cheap ephemeral pamphlets penned by such bawdy secularists as Swetnam, the fruits of the human tongue were weighed, measured, dissected, and examined. The results of such appraisals spanned the gamut from high drama to low comedy. But all of them shared a fascination, bordering on obsession, with the influence words exercised over human relations.

The power of speech, as Swetnam himself suggested, was a most unpredictable sort of power. Like the servant in Swetnam's little fable, advice writers in early modern England cast the tongue as a creature of opposites, an organ that "knows nothing but extremes."[3] On one hand, the capacity for speech distinguished men and women from the lesser orders of being, allowing them dominion over the creatures of the earth and linking them with their creator. As one authority on preaching put it, "Man alone is endowed" with speech, "an Instrument suitable to the Excellency of his Soul." Was not the ability to speak the one respect "wherein *Man* did most resemble *Angels*"?[4] But if the sounds that emanated from the human tongue were sometimes "exceedingly good," Puritan cleric Thomas Adams noted, they just as often proved "excessively evil." "Than a good tongue, there is nothing better; than an evil, nothing worse," he explained.[5] And the worst was very bad indeed. Capable of destroying as well as of creating "humane Societies," the tongue was seen as an author of the disorders that plagued England's ruling elite. It would be no exaggeration, Anglican prelate George Webbe supposed, to account that *"Halfe the sinnes of our life . . . are committed by the tongue."*[6] Unchecked speech, Webbe and others warned, caused not just irritation but also real danger.

The precise nature of the threat depended upon one's place in society. Leading men—the authors of books inveighing against loose words—worried that the "ungoverned" tongue endangered social order. In a world in which it was widely assumed that "inferiours" of every sort "ought to submit themselves to their superiors," the orderly flow of conversation from those below to those on top was a matter of signal importance.[7] To elite ears, respectful speech represented nothing less than the hierarchy of "human relations turned into sound."[8] In contrast, many readers of the period's numerous tracts about governed speech—ordinary men and women living in face-to-face villages across England—probably worried less about the links between speech and large-scale disorder than they did about the more mundane threats that words posed to their households and neighborhoods. From hard experience, they knew that speech both by and about an individual affected the price of that most crucial of all commodities in small societies: personal reputation.[9] The court of everyday life offered ample proof of the Bible's maxim stating that "a good name is better than precious ointment."[10] And was a good name ever more vulnerable than when it was invoked in the loose talk of others? Thus for ordinary folks and cultural elites alike, talk was anything but cheap, and words were to be taken seriously indeed.

Which is the reason, no doubt, that the precise nature of the damage sharp words could inflict was so often a favored theme of English moralists and their audiences. It was not enough simply to classify the tongue as "man's worst." What George Webbe called "the faults of an evill tongue" had to be "opened"—searched, classified, and elaborated upon—before appropriate "remedies" could be "prescribed."[11] Chief among those faults was the tendency of speech to resist fetters. Lamenting the difficulty of "taming" the tongue, many authors punned on its "mere animal" qualities, comparing ill words to stinging serpents, nipping curs, and raging lions.[12] In addition to evoking the baseness of the animal kingdom, unchecked speech mimicked other forces of nature. Disease, for one: ill words had been known to fester like an insidious "Gangrene."[13] Or catastrophe: heated words might engulf society with the force of "a torrent . . . which must and will flow," and incinerate the common peace with the speed of a firebrand touched to "a heap of combustible matter."[14] Such depictions of words as natural calamity emphasized the uncanny ability of the tongue—that notoriously "unruly member"—to elude control and run amok.[15] Damaging talk could, in seventeenth-century parlance, "break out" with no warning, and spread almost of its own accord. Yet if contemporary authors tended to cast the tongue as an agent in its own right for dramatic effect, they knew that it was not in fact an independent actor. Words did not wound blindly, unwittingly. Instead, like the arrows, razors, and other "sharpe weapons" to which it was often compared, speech was a marvelous instrument of purposeful, all-too-human destruction.[16] Wrongful words thus amounted to the worst possible mix of the natural with the cultural, the unthinking with the intentional. Possessing both the unbridled savagery of brute creatures and the murderous agency of human actors, speech could turn society into a "wild bedlam" where people acted like animals.[17]

These sins of the tongue were generically human. As advice-book writers and ordinary men and women could attest, the perils of misspeaking could befall anyone at any time. Still, some people seemed particularly inclined to exploit the tongue's malign potential. Women were thought to be chief among such habitual offenders. Speech might be, as Thomas Adams wrote, "every *man's* best or worst." But it was more often *woman's* worst than her best. "Woman, for the most part, hath the glibbest tongue," Adams conceded. Few living in his place and time would have disagreed.[18] Concern about the special dangers posed by female speech had been around, many writers suggested, literally since the beginning of time—since Genesis. Evil speaking was a primordial feminine transgression. "By the *tongue* of the *Serpent* was *Eve* seduced, and her *tongue* did seduce *Adam*," Webbe explained.[19] Although the verbal treachery of Eve had been a favorite literary theme since biblical times, anxiety about women's voices reached a fever pitch during the century before the English Civil War. From roughly 1560 to 1660, evidence ranging from drama, to theological treatises, to local court records betrays a virtual obsession with "scolding" women.[20]

What made a scold? What, precisely, did women *say* to leave their mates in a state Joseph Swetnam described as one of "terror and utter confusion"?[21] One central feature of the scold's speech was that there was simply too much of it. Well-known quips held that women were "Word-mad": temperamentally incapable of keeping quiet.[22] Indeed, from the scold's perspective, the tongue's tendency to excess was a virtue. Or so one popular pamphlet imagined in purporting to depict a scold's advice to her daughter about how to catch a man. "[W]ith the Clapper of your tongue," the fictional mother advised, you must "ring him a perpetuall peale. . . . noise him, rowze him, torment and torture him with your tongue, that he shall have no minde either to eate or sleepe."[23] This railing, chattering woman was such a stock figure that authors could summon her with a kind of shorthand. John Taylor suspected that every man knew a *"Tabitha Turbulent," a "Franke Froward,"* an *"Ellen Ever-heard,"* a *"Parnell Prate a pace,"* or a *"Rachell Raile at him."* But how many had married a *"Sissy Sweet-lips"* or a *"Margery Quiet"*? Few indeed, Taylor supposed. "Theres many men who live unquiet lives," he mused, "Would spare that bitter member of their wives."[24]

Did ordinary men—and perhaps women—hear in these rough, noisy parodies echoes of their real-life marital distress? The extreme popularity of such works as Taylor's and Swetnam's reveals that satiric meditations on the "woman question" found a large readership, if not widespread assent. Full of lively doggerel, crude in meter and construction but vivid, easy to remember, and eminently quotable, such pamphlets were part of a national conversation about the dangers of women's voices. Surely there were many taverns in which common men, lubricated with drink, toasted their wives by bellowing the simple rhymes of "The Husband's Wish":

> Bedlam, God blesse thee,
> Thou wants naught but wit,
> Which being got, from
> whipping thou art quit.
>
> As for thee Bridewell,
> I cannot much dispraise thee,
> For thou feedest the hungry,
> And dost firke the lazy.
>
> And for thee Newgate, I can
> not much complaine

For once a month thou
ridst men out of paine.

But from a wicked womans
tongue, God defend me,
To Bedlam, Newgate, Bridewell
rather send me.

For there in time Wit,
Worke, or Law sets free,
But from a womans malice,
neither wit, worke, nor
Law gives libertie.[25]

With colorful images of prison, asylum, and workhouse, ditties of this
sort must have been part of ordinary people's store of knowledge about
relationships between women and men. In fiction, at least, wives were
verbal predators and husbands their unwitting prey. Propped up by an
extensive lexicon of aphorisms, drawings, limericks, and rituals, the trope
of women's scolding earned the status of folk wisdom so deep it took on
the proportions of myth.[26]

But there was more to scolding than mere chatter. For as elite and
popular writings alike made clear, the real danger of "Female Gossiping"
lay less in the unquiet household than in the unquiet society.[27] The scold
spoke not only too *much*, but also—more important—too *publicly*. Like
the gadders of Scripture, whom Paul condemned for "wandering about
from house to house . . . speaking things which they ought not," the
scold, as John Taylor reported, loved "to make debate abroad" as well as
"to be unquiet at home."[28] By reporting her husband's shortcomings to
her "Gossips," a "nimble-tongued Wife" effectively "published" his failure
for "all the Town" to hear.[29] And "publishing," as every Englishwoman
knew, was men's business. Men, cultural norms held, were speakers—
"publishers," in period parlance. Obedient women were listeners. Yet
such distinctions meant nothing to the scold, who cared little for the
conventional markers distinguishing "male" from "female." All the more
reason to fear that these boundaries, so vital to the right ordering of
society, were under siege. One anonymous pamphleteer bemoaned that
"since the days of Adam women were never so Masculine . . . from bold
speech to impudent action." There still lived, of course, "good women,
modest women, true women . . . ever chaste, ever glorious," ever silent.
But increasingly, it seemed, these quiet paragons risked being drowned
out by a new breed of "Masculine women" who eagerly "buried silence
to revive slander." Said to appear male in dress, hairstyle, and gesture,
the notorious "Man-Woman" confirmed her pretensions to authority by
speaking in public. To seventeenth-century ears, the "vile and horrible
profanations" of such women's "tongues" made them "deformed," "man-
like," even "monstrous."[30] What could have been less "quiet"?

In the end, then, women's speech served as a particularly trenchant example of the threat posed by all ungoverned words: an unwelcome reminder that nature might yet trump culture, that the superficial trappings of civility were no match for humanity's underlying barbarism. Print debates about the special perils of female speech thus belonged to the intense anxiety about disorder and instability that beset English authorities in the sixteenth and seventeenth centuries. To clerical and civil leaders convinced (rightly, as it would turn out) that their world lay in imminent peril of being "turned upside down," women's disorderly speech indicated gender treachery. Gender treachery promised the subversion of marriage. And the undermining of marriage portended the dissolution of state and society. The scold who, with her voluble tongue, "matched and over-matched" her husband was, therefore, a political as well as a domestic troublemaker—in period vernacular, a *"home-rebell,* a *house-traitor."* [31] The ungoverned tongue, George Webbe reminded his readers, was the author of myriad varieties of social chaos. Words could "breaketh the peace betweene neighbours," breed "quarrels among servants," and even turn "shrewd wives . . . against their husbands." [32] Once such damage had been done, could the wholesale dismantling of society be far behind?

THE DANGERS OF SPEECH, then, were easy for anyone to hear. A thornier question was: What was to be done about them? Given prevailing assumptions about the power of the spoken word, it was clear that wrongful speaking—be it the scold's railing against her husband at home, or a rebel's words against the king in a public square—could not be dismissed as a private failing, a breach of manners. But how was it possible to prevent unregulated speech from turning what was supposed to be an orderly ladder of superiors and inferiors into an antisociety of contentious neighbors, rebellious servants, undutiful children, and "shrewd," imperious wives shouting down their husbands? Burlesques lampooning women's tongues suggested one possible answer. From Shakespeare to street performers, English dramatists promised that scolding shrews could be "tamed" by (male) physical force. But if using fists, knives, and "scold's bridles" to still disorderly tongues made for good theatricals, it was in everyday life a partial solution at best. [33] Not every man, woman, and child whose words threatened the social order could literally be gagged into submission. People needed to *speak*—and to do so in a socially acceptable fashion.

But what was to keep them from speaking wrongfully? Although words came naturally to humans, there was nothing automatic about *proper* speaking. Quite the reverse; the scold's renowned volubility demonstrated the tongue's instinctive tendency to disorder. Not even the exemplar of orderliness whom George Webbe dubbed the "quiet man" was by nature *"slow in speaking, meeke in speech, sober in censuring, soft in answering: mild in reproving, . . . and fearefull of offending."* He *became* so by deliberate effort. His tongue was "kept in as with a bridle, that his mouth should not offend."[34] Even for the best of men, ideal or "quiet" habits of speaking had to be cultivated, if not explicitly imposed. If the tongue was notoriously capricious, the trick was to play to its best and downplay its worst: to instill an appreciation for orderly talk and a disdain for heated words.

Discovering how seventeenth-century English folk went about this task presents formidable obstacles. It goes almost without saying that historians have little access to the most mundane, frequent, and, therefore, powerful mechanisms by which ordinary people governed everyday talk in the remote past. Today, the borders between the (socially as opposed to grammatically) correct and incorrect in our own conversations are most often policed with barely audible sanctions: an interruption, a facial tic, a change in tone of voice. A dramatic breach of verbal etiquette might draw a spoken rebuke: "Don't use that language with me!" But even such extreme responses are rarely recorded. Although the subjects of this study doubtless governed their day-to-day discourses in much the same way, few traces of their having done so remain in the historical record. We "overhear" only the truly exceptional: written encomiums to the virtues of governed speech, legal mechanisms called upon when socialization failed. We cannot equate printed prescription with spoken reality. Still, the various kinds of "laws" early modern English people constructed to govern the ungovernable tongue tell us much that is valuable.

The best sort of "law" for controlling speech, George Webbe argued, was moral suasion. "[I]n all Ages, & among all Nations, there have ever beene sharpe punishments provided against shrewd Tongues," he reminded his readers. But "all the policy in the world" could not "prevent . . . the lash of an evill tongue."[35] A more formidable weapon was that yielded by Webbe himself: exhortation. Authorities including Webbe drew on historical precedents reaching all the way back to Scripture. Was not a harsh tongue one of the seven things designated "an abomination unto" God? Proverbs warned: "the froward tongue shall be cut out." But Scripture also held out glorious rewards for pious speech. It was said that "the tongue of the just is as choice silver"—as precious, but not, it was hoped, as rare.[36] The mission of authors of didactic literature, most of whom were clerics, was to help readers cultivate such tongues of silver. Doing so was essential to the efforts of European elites to comport themselves in ways that distinguished humans from animals, cultured peoples from "savages," highborn from lowborn, men from women, and adults from children. It was a project accorded special urgency amidst the social chaos of the early modern period.[37]

The goal of English prescriptive writings on speech was not to promote stimulating conversation—witty, sophisticated, and urbane—but rather to proscribe dangerous words.[38] In the service of this goal, virtually all prescriptive literature on the subject outlined two fundamental principles: "First, Meditation before we speake: secondly, Moderation" in both the quantity and quality of one's words. If the tongue innately tended to extremes, governing talk meant striving for a golden mean. And where speech was too often unmediated—a spontaneous impulse that traveled from heart to mouth and thence to a listener's ears—regulating verbal interactions meant learning to "premeditate" one's every utterance.[39] It is because of these twin principles that images of forcible restraint so dominate prescriptive writings on well-ordered speech. To control the tendency of speech to take "undue liberties," Richard Allestree recommended keeping a "strict watch" over one's words. Like an animal that needed to be corralled and tamed, the tongue would try to wander "thro . . . its wild rambles." But the quiet man would "bring home his stray" and erect stout fences so that "it break not loose again."[40] Wild rambling versus bridled, domesticated pasture life, undue liberty as opposed to strict watch: prescriptions for right speaking sought to impose human order on organic chaos.

The battle to bring order to the tongue's "wild rambles" ideally began in childhood. As embryonic social creatures—learning to be cultural rather than natural beings—children were especially prone to the sins of an ungoverned tongue. Sources ranging from textbooks on rhetoric, to sermons on family duty, to manuals on proper deportment schooled children to play their proper parts in the community's discourse. That role, for young boys and girls alike, was one of respectful submission to superiors at home and in the church, the school, and the commonwealth. Children, in sum, were rather seen than heard. As one popular English authority put it, all young *"Discoursers . . . should rather be given to heare than speake."* Before they could learn the art of conversation, young people were instructed to "learne the art of silence."[41]

The "art of silence," however, meant different things for different children. For proper speaking was not only a cultural "age way," differentiating adults from youths, but also an important component of English "rank ways" and "gender ways."[42] The privileged little tyke to whom Richard Brathwait directed *The English Gentleman* would balance speech and silence differently from either his sister or lower status boys. For one thing, the gentleman-in-training would likely be formally schooled in the art of rhetoric. The classical paradigm held that good orators made sound and moral leaders. Thus humanistic scholars of the day led their pupils through declamations in Latin and Greek.[43] If the God-given "habite of Speech" naturally lifted humans above "all other Creatures of the earth," the learned "Art" of Latin grammar—which amplified "the grace and eloquence" of speech, making it a "more excellent and rare benefite"— exalted some humans above others.[44] For simple "Countrey" lads, in contrast, it was deemed sufficient to acquire "a good Stile" in their native tongue. Why "perplex them many Years with Latine," one writer wondered, when the real goal of their education was to "fit [common] Boys for Apprenticeships"?[45] Instead, their training was focused on the kinds of conversational skills their station demanded: clear pronunciation, good penmanship, and respectful communication with their journeymen-masters.

Boys of higher status were groomed for loftier speaking parts. The pupil who studied one widely used Latin grammar learned to be "prepared upon all occasions [to] useth the ministery of the Tongue to unfold" his opinions.[46] To do so without giving offense, young gentlemen were advised to overcome the *"hotnesse"* that tended to make youths "unmeasurably passionate in any argument." Hence Brathwait instructed gentlemen-in-training "not to give their opinions in any matter of State in publike places" where they might expose their rashness and ignorance. But in time, he implied, voicing opinions on public matters in public places would *become* their rightful province—provided, that is, that they learned well the paradoxical lessons of their privileged childhoods: to "[s]peake freely, yet with reservation." Learned young men knew that their speech should be "sober" and that "moderation of the tongue is . . . an absolute virtue."[47] But they were also entrusted to develop mature public voices, both spoken and written.[48] This free-but-restrained style of speaking would serve boys well when they became adults. As men, they would need to exercise their tongues as well as to govern them.

Prescriptions for girls' speech were less equivocal. Authorities dating back to Aristotle had counseled that "[s]ilence is a woman's glory" but "not equally the glory of a man." A woman, it was said, "would be thought loquacious if she imposed no more restraint on her conversations than the good man."[49] Instead, the best public voice for women was, effectively, no voice at all. In this regard, exemplary women shared the same linguistic imperatives as children. Richard Brathwait made the similarity between the proper voice of the girl-child and that of the "English Gentlewoman" explicit: "what is spoken of [young] Maids," he cautioned, is "properly applyed . . . to all women: *They should be seene, and not heard.*" Where the young "English Gentleman" was readied for a voice in the world of affairs, his sister learned that to "discourse of State-matters" would "not [ever] become" her province. Nor, as Saint Paul had mandated, should she "dispute high poynts of Divinity." Hence, most authorities on female education agreed, training even aristocratic girls in rhetoric was a useless vanity if not a dangerous folly. Ill suited to the "Art" of "a Rhetoricall tongue," the gentlewoman's "best Rhetoricke" consisted of "maiden blushes, and bashfull smiles."[50] For boys, mute deference was but a temporary stopping point on the road to a full adult voice. But silence was more than a stage in the female life course; it was the ideal woman's perpetual lot. In this sense, Brathwait's "Gentlewoman" had more in common with ordinary girls than she did with high-status men.

In the early modern English worldview, this was logical enough. Grown men might embrace callings as disparate as their varying ranks and stations. But virtually all women aspired to the same vocation: to be a "meete help" to their husbands. This calling meant that women also shared a *location* for speaking: the household. Where the fabled scold might seek "to live amongst men, or speak abroad," the Christian woman was content "to be *at home within* and unknown to other folks."[51] A good wife knew "not to speak many words but in her Husbands presence."[52] She knew, likewise, that such verbal "modesty" amounted to more than feminine politeness. It was testimony to another key element of the female vocation: sexual chastity. Simply put, a loose tongue made a loose woman. "[T]here is scarce anything looks more indecent, than to see a young maid too forward and confident in her talk," warned Richard Allestree.[53] One Italian author, whose directives English authorities eagerly translated, was more literal. "Speech in public, especially with strangers, is not suitable for women," he noted flatly. Women's public "voice is not less to be dreaded than their [public] nakedness," which it symbolically evoked.[54]

Yet if her fabled loquaciousness symbolized woman's "lightness," attaining the prescribed degree of verbal reticence would only half redeem the daughters of Eve. For although gadding and gossiping invited scorn, homebound silence did not purchase public respect. Too-frequent speech "enricheth, and corrupteth" a woman's character, yet "Silence is poor," conceded one advice giver.[55] Prescriptions for female speaking thus asked women to choose among imperfect options. One sixteenth-century reformer's treatise on education for women, still popular in Stuart England, spelled out the inadequate alternatives: "If thou talke little in company folks think thou [know] but little good; if thou speak much they reckon thee light. If thou speak uncunningly, they count thee dull witted; if thou speak cunningly thou shalt be counted but a shrew."[56] From the perspective of the seventeenth century, this "double bind" was exactly as it should be.[57] Neither maidenly silence nor licentious chatter gave women credible, public voices in the community's affairs. Girls were not reared to have such voices. English authors laying down rules for right speaking made clear that the social landscape upon which women could speak not just acceptably, but *commandingly*, was almost invisibly small.

The trouble, as we have seen, was that real women did not quietly embrace such prescriptions. Among women in particular as well as among English folk in general, exhortation had, in the end, limited success against the overwhelming force of the spoken word. In an ideal world, merely delineating the social geography of proper speech—men's as well as women's—would be enough to order a community's conversation. In an ideal world, women and men would—perhaps with the aid of sermons and inspirational tracts on the subject—train themselves to speak in ways that articulated their respective places. In an ideal world, people would learn, in effect, to govern their own tongues. But the real world was a fallen world. And in a fallen world, muscle was sometimes needed to enforce the boundaries between decorous and wrongful speech.

Where moral suasion and self-control failed, the law interceded to curb the excesses of the tongue.

Two essential principles informed the body of customary and substantive rules for controlling speech that English legal authorities had amassed by the beginning of the seventeenth century. The first derived from the Roman-law concept of *injuria* (literally, insult), which encompassed both physical and verbal assaults. English jurists drew on this concept of verbal "injury" to express their belief that heated words, in and of themselves, could cause hurt that required legal redress: hurt that imperiled the commonweal as well as the names and fortunes of individuals. Thus the early modern English legal system treated disorderly speech as both a vital interpersonal issue (a civil matter) and a concern of broad significance for the functioning of the state (a crime).[58] The second major principle underpinning English law on speech declared the state's compelling need to protect itself against the *injuriae* the tongue could inflict. In the sixteenth and early seventeenth centuries, an era that accepted social hierarchy as necessary and unquestionable, the state saw its right to circumscribe harmful speech as virtually absolute. Indeed, the competing claim—the need to protect subjects' expressive liberties—was seldom advanced at all. Overzealous restraint, authorities reasoned, was not nearly so dangerous as an overabundance of verbal freedom. In criminal cases even truth was no defense. That a "scandalous" utterance might be correct in point of fact was less important than the disruptive potential of *any* words against the social order.[59]

The body of law codifying these principles was a tangled mass that grew over centuries. Of pivotal importance in this dense web of local custom, common-law precedent, ecclesiastical-court doctrine, and substantive legislation was the 1275 statute that proscribed the crime of *scandalum magnatum*, literally "the scandal of magnates." Enacted during a period of intense concern over political instability, this measure defined "scandalous" words by their targets as much as by their substance. According to the statute, any words against the "great men of this realm"— regardless of their truth—were seeds from which "discord . . . may grow between the king and his people." Such words were thus more properly a matter for political and legal concern than for private redress.[60]

By the early modern period, the law against *scandalum magnatum* was one of the few constants in an area of law that was very much in flux. Cases adjudicating heated words came before any and every authority; although the task of punishing civil and criminal misspeakers fell increasingly to common-law tribunals, ecclesiastical courts and local, manorial officers continued to hear enormous numbers of complaints. Indeed, as legal historian James Sharpe has written, legal remedies for wrongful words "proved almost embarrassingly popular" in the sixteenth and seventeenth centuries. In the church courts of Chester, for example, the volume of suits for defamation grew fourfold between 1544 and 1594.

Judicial bodies reaching from borough courts to Star Chamber witnessed a similar explosion.[61]

As English people began to look more often to the courts than to the sword to avenge verbal wrongs, some jurists sought to stem the rising tide of prosecutions over speech. As John March noted in his tract on speech offenses, punishing wrongful speech at the bar was supposed to "deterre men from words, which are but winde." Yet somehow the reverse was happening: instead of law deterring speech, speech was deterring justice as suits over harmful words clogged the dockets. Such "Actions were very rare in our old bookes," March claimed. But by the seventeenth century, fighting over words brought more "Grys[t]e to the Mill" of the courts "then any one [other] branch of the Law whatsoever."[62] This overwhelming growth in the volume of slander litigation under the Tudors and the Stuarts led March and other legal thinkers to narrow their definitions of legally "actionable" speech. The emphasis, increasingly, was on specificity and precision, on distinguishing civilly or criminally wrongful words from day-to-day verbal rancor. Henceforth, charging someone with the commission of a felony, accusing a person of carrying an infectious disease, attacking a man's professional competence, or threatening the title to an inheritance were to be the only kinds of words meriting common-law prosecution.[63]

But narrowing the inlet to the courts failed to dam the rising tide of heated words. As Swetnam's King Amasis could have predicted, the poisons of the tongue kept right on flowing. England was losing the battle, March lamented, to "manage that . . . little member" that proved both "the greatest good" and "the greatest evil to most men." The "tongues of men" had been "set on fire," and the law had become little more than a "Bellowes to blow the Coles."[64] March was scarcely exaggerating. As Sharpe has quipped, archival evidence confirms that where crimes of the tongue were concerned, the Cassandra-like rhetoric of seventeenth-century English elites was well founded; they really *did* live "in the worst of all possible worlds."[65] A plague of words was sweeping the country, infecting people from the top to the bottom of the social ladder. Easily overcoming the strongest barriers that law, education, and persuasion could erect, the tongue was all but ungovernable. In the minds of most English folk, speech—especially female speech—seemed chiefly a malign force, growing more so by the day.

But the migrants who left England for New England in the early seventeenth century were not just any English folk. The religious dissidents among them, at least, were not only different from their neighbors, but self-consciously so. In an era of "great overturning, questioning," and "revaluing," they were among the overturners, the questioners, the revaluers: the *challengers* of received wisdom more than its guardians.[66] And, although historians continue to debate the extent of the differences between "godly" New England migrants, their stay-at-home counterparts, and English émigrés to other parts of the globe, this much, at least, is clear: if the cultural baggage "New England's generation" brought with them was, in the broadest sense, generically English, it was also, in many important ways, specifically "Puritan."[67] This was true in matters of law and faith, and in the arenas of custom and daily life. It was also notably true in matters of *speech*. All seventeenth-century English people knew speech as a malign, potentially ungovernable force. But Puritans had other understandings of words—and of the Word—as well.

YOU COULD *hear* a Puritan coming. About that if about nothing else the reformers and their opponents agreed. From the perspective of the dissenters who agitated, beginning in the late sixteenth century, against the status quo in matters religious, this new manner of speaking was laudable—indeed godly. Like the fathers of the early Church, such dissenters as John Field and Thomas Wilcox sought to set themselves apart "*by voice*, learning and doctrine" rather than by the "cap, gowne, [and] tippet" that marked their nondissenting brethren. There was a new sweetness as well as a new weightiness to Protestant sermonizing, they argued. For what could more delight the ear and inflame the mind than "preaching of the worde purely"?[68] "[W]e are commaunded to cry out," proclaimed Thomas Cartwright. "Crye out and cease not, lift up thy voice like a trumpet."[69]

A trumpet, indeed! Defenders of the Elizabethan settlement of 1559, which established a rather tepid and formalist brand of Protestantism as the English state religion, thought Puritan speech was distinctive enough, to be sure. But instead of the clarion call of Gabriel's trumpet, they heard the rancorous words of "*unnaturall subjects, seditious persons, troublesome and unquiet spirites, members of Sathan.*" The dissenters claimed to have "framed [their] wordes" in a decorous and appropriate manner, but the defenders of England's faith knew otherwise. Puritans, Richard Bancroft believed, were "murmurers, complayners, [and] mockers" who went about the country "rayling, libelling, and lying," attempting to seduce wayward believers with their "*trayterous, seditious, and contumelious words.*" When confronted with their "shamelesse and slaunderous discourses," Bancroft advised, "her majesties faithfull subjectes should learne to . . . stop their eares."[70] When an Elizabethan pamphleteer opined that Puritans were "[t]he hotter sort of protestants," he was referring to the temperature of their discourse.[71]

Consensus, then, on one score: if there existed a single entity that we can call English Puritanism, it existed as a tissue of words. (Even the name "Puritan"—not a self-selected label, but rather an epithet hurled at the dissenters by their detractors—belonged to this war of words.)[72] The Puritan impulse was, among other things, a fundamental redefinition of both the spiritual and the social meanings of speaking. It was also, as we will see, a Janus-faced impulse, propounding at once new freedoms for the tongue and new demands for its government. On the one hand, Puritan thinkers sought to remove the fetters that choked off true communication within the Church of England. At the same time, however, they invested the medium of speech with a new gravitas, effectively raising the standards by which every utterance would be judged. In the realm of the sacred and in the arenas of everyday life, speaking would count for more among the Puritans than it did among English folk more broadly. And among those for whom modes of speaking marked the boundary between the godly and the reprobate, certain kinds of misspeaking would be judged more harshly as well.

This emphasis on speaking resonated strongly in Puritan sacred life. In their religious practices, English reformers strove for spareness. For leanness. Intent upon paring away bankrupt traditions, priestly trappings, and corrupt structures of authority, nonconformists sought to return to barest essentials, to first principles: to God's Word. His *spoken* Word. An overly literal rendering of Calvin's translation of John emphasized the primacy of speech at the dawn of creation: "In the beginning was Speech, and Speech was with God; and Speech was God." "God, *by speaking*, was the Creator of the universe," Calvin explained, and his speech continued to have "solid and abiding essence."[73] If the spoken Word was the engine that animated the world, it was also the only authority to which Puritans admitted allegiance. "[W]e say the worde is above the church . . . surely it is above the Englishe churche," wrote Cartwright.[74] Thus reforming the church, for Calvin and for his English disciples, centered above all on finding new and better ways to speak and to listen.

In Scripture, Calvin noted, the phrase "to hear" was virtually synonymous with "to believe." Since biblical times, knowledge of the divine had come first and foremost through the ear. But no believer could "hear [God's] voice" over the din of the unreformed church, with its babbling sophists, formulaic masses, and diverting rituals.[75] Indeed, from the Puritan perspective, everything about the "popish" mass seemed deliberately to draw the ears of the faithful *away* from God's voice. Reformer John Foxe argued that the visual pageantry of the Church of Rome and its English analogue—so "visible and glorious in the eyes of the world, so shining in outward beauty"—was but a clever mask for the inner bankruptcy of popish worship. With the Scripture imprisoned in ancient languages, God's Word was incomprehensible to the great majority of worshipers. Latin liturgical forms were little more than mimetic aids to piety. The "clear sunshine of God's Word," nonconformists proclaimed, had been so "overshadowed with mists and darkness" that awe, not understanding, had become the goal of devotional exercises. Even in the so-called reformed churches of the Tudors, the dissidents alleged, glittering chalices, priestly vestments, and elaborate paintings drew the attention of the faithful away from the ignorance and corruption of their priests. Outside church walls, the vivid images presented in supposedly "religious" plays, in cheap picture books, and in popular ritual kept ears

closed to the sacred and eyes focused on the profane.[76] The first generation of English Protestants had borrowed and transmuted many of these
traditional forms, using the medieval visual language of the sacred to
pronounce new meanings. But the accommodation between Protestant
content and Catholic forms proved short-lived. By the 1580s, most visual
representations of the Word looked positively idolatrous to the reformers.
The logocentric ethos of Calvin admitted little ornament. Plays, statues,
and paintings had come to be seen as dangerous distractions from the
only proper object of devotion: the intonation of Scripture.

From the late sixteenth century on, then, Puritan spirituality was an
affair of the mouth and the ear. The eye, with its tendency to mistake
graven idols for God himself, and to confuse passion plays with Scripture,
could not be trusted. "[H]owever fitting it may be for man seriously to
turn his eyes to contemplate God's works," Calvin explained, "it is [still
more] fitting that he prick up his ears to the Word, the better to
profit."[77] Of course, we cannot minimize the importance of *reading*
among the English devotees of Calvin. The advent of the vernacular
Bible was a cultural watershed of the absolute highest order, and its widespread distribution was a necessary and perhaps even a sufficient precon-
dition to Protestantism throughout Europe. It was no accident that Calvin so often referred to God as "author," or that English dissidents,
including John Foxe, put such faith in the ability of the press to "speak"
for them.[78] But reading and speaking were not nearly so distinct in the
early modern period as we tend to assume. Far from being what one
scholar has termed a "privatised mental discipline," the transmission of
information from the printed page to the believer's mind and heart was
often a social occasion. That is, a great many more people *heard* books
than *read* them.[79] Reading thus engaged the tongue as well as the eye, as
theologian John Cotton suggested when he quipped, "I love to sweeten
my mouth with a piece of Calvin before I go to sleep."[80]

The close connection between reading and speaking is particularly
evident when we consider that Book of all books: the Bible. Although
knowledge of Scripture was communicated through the printed page, its
oral performance dominated public worship among the English Puritans.
Scripture was not mere text; it was the instrument through which God
"opens his own most hallowed lips." "[T]rue doctrine," Calvin had written,
began with "a prompt eagerness to hearken to God's voice."[81] The Puritan worship service was designed to satisfy this yearning. So it was that
a particular kind of spoken form—the sermon—came to occupy the absolute center of the Puritans' sacred world. Sermons were the preeminent
medium through which ministers engaged the Word and through which
lay believers made sense of their lives. Indeed, after the clutter and
clamor of popish practices had been cleared away, little remained *but* the
doctrine delivered: God's voice intoned and interpreted by his ministers.
Puritan services were designed so that the Word and only the Word need

command the attention of the faithful. No set forms of prayer or liturgical formulas, no "carnal sacrifices" or "golden cup[s]," no false sacraments
or images of saints: nothing could stand in the way of the Word.[82]

This is not to suggest, however, that Puritan preachers were "Dumme
Doggs" who simply mouthed Scripture or other preset prayers.[83] Indeed,
they proclaimed, the reverse was true. Reformed Protestant theology emphasized not only the centrality of God's Word, but also the need to
interrogate, dispute, digest, and otherwise wrestle with biblical texts. The
ministers whose dissenting voices were nurtured in the spiritual hothouse
of late-sixteenth-century Cambridge University were trained to engage
Scripture rather than merely to parrot it. Studying in "conferences," they
eschewed the rote learning of classical forms and instead devoted their
energies to debating and interpreting points of doctrine.[84]

Despite their awe in the presence of the unmediated Word of God,
the tone these reformed ministers strove for in their sermons was interrogative, argumentative—indeed, conversational. In the Church of England, one Elizabethan pamphleteer noted, preaching was but "bare reading": "service saying" from the Book of Common Prayer. But where
"popishe priestes" drew their homilies "oute of their Portuise [breviary],"
regenerate or truly pious ministers relied on another source: the Word of
God, filtered through the searching of their hearts.[85] The resulting style
was famously plain, stripped of the "magic incantation[s]," "mumbled
. . . words," and Latinate mysteries of Rome.[86] But the mood created by
their discourses could be ecstatic and rapturous as well as reverent and
somber. Instead of paintings, incense, and passion plays, the reformers
offered their listeners "verbal pictures . . . mental images." The Puritan
sermon was sound, sight, and sense to its hearers.[87]

It could also be, in a way, their salvation. For while good preaching
could not ensure an experience of divine grace, conversion was unlikely
to happen without it. Thus William Perkins reminded his audience that
"hearing the word preached is the means of the new birth." True, there
was more to it than that; ultimately, salvation depended on what Perkins
called "special faith," inborn and predestined. But "special faith requires
a special word"—Scripture—which "being otherwise general is made special by application." And what was application but "the ministry of the
word"? It was the sermon, then, that watered "the immortal seed" of
grace, without whose flowering one "cannot enter into the kingdom of
heaven."[88] Ample reason, in an age of nearly universal belief, to listen
carefully.

Yet Puritan precepts did not cultivate passive lay hearers any more
than they esteemed ministers who were "bare readers." If, in moments of
public worship, the minister took the main speaking part, ordinary men
and women possessed plenty of opportunities for speech in their private
devotions. In fact, it was considered *imperative* that they speak. Just as
the preacher was called upon to articulate the unmediated Word of vernacular Scripture, laymen and laywomen were urged to address God di-

rectly, giving voice to their innermost thoughts and feelings. Prayerful speech was not only desirable, Calvin had written, but absolutely necessary. The point lay not so much in the hearing (who could be so vain as to suppose that God was "sleeping until . . . aroused by our voice?") as in the saying.[89] Indeed, Puritans believed, God had given people the ability to speak so that they might pray. "The tongue is man's clapper," Thomas Adams argued, "given him that he may sound out the praise of his Maker." Words of prayer were the tongue's glory, justifying its claim to be (on occasion) "man's best."[90]

Moreover, there was something natural, artless, uncultivated about prayerful speech. Sincere, effective prayer did not require education. To address God, one needed no fancy syllogisms or elaborate forms. Thus even "infants, while they nurse at their mothers' breasts, have tongues . . . eloquent to preach [God's] glory." Even the Lord's Prayer, the one written supplication Calvin deemed a "necessary help for us," was important for its content rather than for its form. The pious would truly *speak* to God, not recite a script. It was for this reason that all prayer had to be "in the language of the people." Latinate mumblings represented "the tongue without the mind." While no one should address God in an "undisciplined" or "irreverent" manner, the discipline required was strictly internal; a properly reverent state of mind would all but ensure that one's words resonated with the desired humility. The reverse was also true. A properly penitent frame of mind would virtually impel prayerful speech. Although "the best prayers are sometimes unspoken," Calvin argued, "when feelings of mind are aroused" toward God, "unostentatiously the tongue breaks forth into speech." For once, such verbal outbreaks were all to the good. "[D]are" to "call upon him as Father," Calvin enjoined.[91]

It would seem, in this sense, that reformed Protestant theologians called for a new kind of expansiveness where speech was concerned, an expansiveness that flew in the face of prevailing mores. The Puritan emphasis on the sermon and on prayer held out to ministers and lay-folk alike new possibilities for speaking both to and of God. If "mediation" was the overarching principle by which the tongue was to be governed in seventeenth-century England, the Puritans were advancing, in some respects, a much less mediated speech order. Where Scripture was concerned, they preached a new directness, extolling the necessity of encountering and responding to God's Word without fetters or barriers.

Yet the Puritan legacy is considerably more complicated than this. For neither Puritan theologians nor their followers actually *lived* in the Word; they lived in the world—in social as well as sacred space and time. Along with their less zealous neighbors, they inhabited a landscape of overlapping authorities and dependencies. And in this more mundane landscape of meetinghouse, neighborhood, and household, the license Puritan theology granted the tongue was often problematic.

The reformers' ideals fostered confusion, for example, about the relationship between the minister and his followers. In many respects, Puritan thought enhanced the voices of laypeople along with those of their preachers. Following the most radical precepts of Calvin and his ilk, godly men and women might well argue that layfolk and preachers were equally suited to dispute the fine points of scriptural interpretation. After all, wasn't Protestantism *about* doing away with the caste of priestly intermediaries who stood between God and people? And yet, in a place and time where social order was imagined to be essentially vertical, there was something intolerably horizontal about this logic. Who was to speak and who was to listen? Who was to lead and who was to follow? In heaven, all men and women would praise God with one voice. But here on earth, in the decorous fellowship of the meetinghouse speech community, didn't somebody's voice have to come out on top?

Implicitly, at least, Puritan theologians hinted at an answer to this question. If the leveling impulses of the Reformation elevated both the voice of the minister and the voice of the layperson, they lifted the minister's voice a bit higher. Thus tracts instructing ministers in the art of reformed preaching emphasized not only the authority of God's Word, but also that of its earthly interpreters. Manuals taught preachers how to persuade, captivate, and otherwise command their congregations as well as how to honor God. A treatise on preaching by William Perkins, for example, divided the preacher's task into two main parts. Understanding the substance of God's Word was an essential starting point, but scholarly hermeneutics were not sufficient for what Perkins called "the arte of prophecying." "Uttering . . . the Sermon" in the most effective possible style was a discipline in itself, equally important for the edification of the faithful. A preacher's interpretation had to be performed in a way that would move a given audience—a congregation likely to be composed of the elect and the unregenerate alike. This meant that the minister's way of speaking had to be carefully cultivated. Although he might rely on his learning in "the artes, philosophie, and varietie of reading" while "framing his sermon," Perkins warned, the preacher "ought in publike to conceale all these from the people," employing no "words of arts, nor Greeke and Latin phrases and quirks" in his homilies. Because any public display of erudition on the minister's part could alienate ordinary listeners, his "speech" and "gesture" had to be "*spirituall* and *gracious*" but also "moderate and plaine."[92] Thus the legendary Puritan "plain style" was a tactic self-consciously aimed at audience persuasion.

Audience persuasion was also, in a very real sense, audience control—something that reformers since Calvin had known was not to be taken for granted. The preacher had to earn the dutiful "obedience" of his hearers. And so, from the tempo of his delivery, to the tone of his voice, to his choice of literary tropes, he used his voice to enhance his spiritual *and earthly* authority. True preachers were, as Calvin had written, "interpreters from whose lips the people might" discern the "true meaning" of

Scripture. Ministers spoke "just as if [God] himself spoke"—and deserved just as careful a hearing.[93]

The reason preachers like Perkins and Calvin took such care in cultivating the authority of their own voices was simple enough: reformist zealots were a tough lot to impress. Protestantism spurred the faithful to ignore one set of ruling voices. How could it impel them to obey another? Did it ring false when Calvin, having spent hundreds of pages denigrating the teachings of Rome in the most daring language possible, told his readers that they "owe[d]" an "attitude of reverence and therefore of piety toward all our rulers . . . whatever they may be like"?[94] How could the movement's leaders inspire in their followers "an attitude of reverence" toward some people (notably themselves), and an attitude of deliberate *irreverence* toward others?

Speech, both to and from lay audiences, was the fulcrum upon which this delicate balance rested. Thus Thomas Adams exhorted his listeners to use their voices to ring out God's praises and, at the same time, urged them to erect a "double fence" around their tongues: to make their words "few, true, [and] weighty."[95] In a similar vein, William Perkins, who outlined such an authoritative speaking role for ministers, allotted a more limited voice to laypeople. For them, the "holy usage of the Tongue according to GODS Word" meant "Modestie, Meeknesse," and especially "Reverence"—both toward God and toward those men "above us in age, gifts, authoritie."[96] Given the layperson's much-touted prerogative to speak to God, such prescriptions sound anxious indeed—and for good reason. A theology with such verbally expansive tenets made clashes between religious leaders and the faithful all but inevitable.

Likewise, the ambiguities of Protestant notions of right speaking also paved the way for conflicts between godly Puritans and "reprobate" English authorities. From roughly 1570 to 1640, Puritan rhetoric was a rhetoric of dissent: an attack on the status quo in matters religious. And, under prevailing English law, virtually all attacks on the status quo— verbal, written, and printed—were expressly forbidden. Ever tighter controls on freedom of expression dating from the late sixteenth century meant that it was perhaps easier to speak seditiously during Elizabeth's reign than at any other moment in English history.[97] Simply by promoting their alternative theology, therefore, the reformers were claiming greater expressive liberties than most of their countrymen thought necessary or desirable.

While all nonconforming ministers implicitly claimed the right to preach according to the demands of conscience, some made their demands explicit. Thomas Cartwright, for example, argued in a tract printed secretly in 1572 that truth alone should set the standard for what was permissible to preach and to write. To objections that Puritan tracts were "too hotte for this time," he countered that the reformers had "uttered nothing but true, and necessary matter." Sedition or no, Cartwright and his supporters maintained, they would continue to voice their ideas.

As they saw it, God easily trumped the authority of king, queen, and Parliament.[98] By the late 1630s, numerous reformers were echoing Cartwright's demands for expressive liberties. Pamphleteers, including William Walwyn, Henry Robinson, John Lilburne, John Goodwin, and Richard Overton—a loose-knit band of Civil War–era "sectaries" and printers espousing widely divergent forms of Protestantism—called for broader freedoms of print, speech, and conscience.[99] Lilburne described his intention to "speake what I thinke": to "speake that which might be for [God's] glory and the good of his people," irrespective of the law's "Gag."[100] To remove such gags and "have a fair Hearing"—this was the expressed aim of the Puritan pamphleteers.[101] From their perspective, the Crown's actions "to suppresse or silence the publishing, practising, arguing, or debating" of religious "wayes [practices] or Doctrines" amounted to nothing less than a *"fight against God himself."*[102] It was a noisy battle, but it was one the reformers felt destined to win. "Where there is much desire to learn," wrote John Milton in the most enduring statement extolling liberty of expression produced in the seventeenth century, "there of necessity will be much arguing, much writing, many opinions. . . . many schisms and many dissections."[103] In arguments verging on the libertarian, some English reformers seemed to suggest that the best remedy for dangerous speech was, quite simply, *more* speech.

Unless, that is, the words in question offended God as the Puritans knew him. And therein lies the central ambiguity of the reformers' calls for loosening the fetters on public discourse. For while nonconforming preachers agitated vociferously for the right publicly to "speak what they thought," as Lilburne put it, they also pressed for new and tighter restrictions against such speech as they deemed reprehensible. As one historian has noted, Puritan critics of Elizabethan and Jacobean sedition laws were "not against the theory underlying the restrictions" so much as "the application of these restrictions" to their own statements of religious principle.[104] Other forms of talk deserved their censure and might even, they hoped, come under more rigid scrutiny than English civil and ecclesiastical courts typically applied.

Blasphemy, for one. Paradoxically, Puritan notions of expressive liberty vastly enlarged the kinds of utterances deemed blasphemous. Punishments for reviling the sacred dated to ancient Athens and had remained in force throughout centuries of Catholic rule. But while heresy frequently resulted in death, blasphemy—the *verbal* assault on the sacred—all but disappeared as a meaningful, separate category of offense in the early years of the Church. In England, blasphemy traditionally fell under the jurisdiction of the ecclesiastical courts, where it was frequently, if lightly, punished. In fact, in the decades immediately before the Reformation, blasphemy was so narrowly defined and so seldom prosecuted that, as Patrick Collinson has put it, "England lacked absolutely . . . any sense of what might be thought to constitute blasphemy"—at least by the Protestant definition of the offense.[105]

Reformers from Luther's day forward sought to remedy this situation, investing the notion of blasphemy with new meaning and seriousness. Calvin argued that speaking against God was the sole "unpardonable sin," one of the most serious offenses any human could commit. Stubborn, intentional blaspheming—"deliberately" to "reproach . . . the divine name"—betrayed the potential of the human voice. People who spoke against God sounded like "so many dogs . . . with their venomous bitings" and "barking."[106] Little wonder that many nonconformists argued for more stringent sanctions against blasphemers. Thomas Cartwright—the same pamphleteer who exhorted the Puritan faithful to "cry out and cease not"—also urged Elizabethan magistrates to enact the death penalty for blasphemy.[107]

Moreover, under this expanded Puritan definition, blasphemy encompassed much more than ravings against God. Images, ballads, rituals, dancing, cardplaying—all came to be seen as profanations of the holy Word.[108] Drama was especially suspect. As Phillip Stubbes wrote in his famous denunciation of the English theater, "the blessed word of GOD, is to be handled, reverently, gravely, and sagely, with veneration to the glorious Majestie of God." But even religious "stage-playes" treated Scripture "scoffingly, floutingly, & jibingly." There could be no dramatic performance of the Word—save, of course, sermons. The "word is God and God is the word," Stubbes cautioned. "[W]ho so ever abuseth this word on stages in playes and enterluds . . . maketh a mocking stock of him." For his sins, Stubbes argued, the blasphemous dramaturge "purchaseth to himselfe, eternal damnation." Parliament set a somewhat lower tariff. As of 1606, "jestingly or profanely" speaking God's name "in any stage-play, enterlude, shewe, may-game or pageant" would merit a substantial fine of £10.[109] The price for reviling or mocking God's name was high indeed.

In the public sphere—in the playhouse, in the pulpit, and in print—dissenting Protestants both extolled and feared the powers of an unfettered tongue. With unprecedented zeal, Puritan reformers fought for access to the ears of the public. If the tongue was created to proclaim God's majesty, they argued, why not shout his message from the rooftops, thunder it in the churches, and spread its glories through the presses? Why not, indeed?—provided, of course, that it was his message, *their* message. When it was not, reformers wondered why "whosoever wil set pen to paper now a dayes" was "permitted to goe forward," regardless of how "unseemly [to] christian eares his argument be." Might not "good lawes, wholsome sanctions, and Goldy [sic] statutes" stanch the flood of such abuses?[110]

In calling for expanded liberties for their own tracts and stiffer sanctions on words they deemed blasphemous, nonconformists wanted, in effect, to have it both ways: to promote speech and to preclude it at the same time. Even John Milton, who defined for a time the extreme radical edge of the multifaceted movement against the Church of England, believed that free speech was a good thing only up to a point. *Some* words, he cautioned, must always and necessarily "be extirpate." Truth was the principle, and some opinions could never ring true.[111] From a God's-eye view, the line separating the blasphemous from the sacred was clear enough. But down at ground level—in the courts and churches and taverns and theaters of early modern England—the line between the permissible and the rightfully "extirpate" seemed ever fainter. And the pressing question remained: who would decide how, where, and when to draw it?

Puritan ideals introduced similar confusion over the boundaries defining proper speech into the "little commonwealth": the godly household. In the family as in the public sphere, new ideas about religion sent mixed signals about who could speak, in what manner, and when. One set of messages elevated the role of women among reformed Protestants. A theology that emphasized the equality of all believers had profound implications for gender ideals both in church and at home. If there were truly, as Paul had written, "neither male nor female . . . in Christ Jesus"—if men and women stood equal before the Lord—then might each sex have a voice in spiritual matters?[112]

Some Puritans thought so. Among the most despised "popish" ceremonies were those that set female believers on a lower plane than their male counterparts. The ritual "churching of women" after childbirth, Field and Wilcox insisted, "smelleth of Jewishe purification" and had no place in reformed worship. Why should women be deemed shameful and unclean when husbands and wives alike belonged to the priesthood of all believers? Like men, women were called to account for their personal experiences of divine grace. There were even moments, some thought, when it could be appropriate for godly women to act or speak in the preacher's stead. In "time of necessitie," one pamphlet held, women could "minister the sacrament of baptisme . . . in a private house."[113] There might even be a "case extraordinary," John Robinson supposed, in which "a woman may reprove the church."[114] While some reformers went out of their way to extend the promise of individual redemption to female believers, anti-Puritan writers mocked the prominence of women among the nonconformists. The "shee-Puritan," scoffed John Earle, later bishop of Salisbury, "loves preaching better than praying," and "overflowes so with the Bible that she spills it upon every occasion." Although "Nothing angers her so much as that women must not preach" from the pulpit, she finds other outlets for her voice: "what she cannot [say] at the church she do[e]s at the Table: where shee prattles more than any." Women were said to be intoxicated with these dangerous freedoms; the Puritans' opponents frequently claimed that wives comprised a majority of nonconforming congregations—an accusation confirmed by parish records.[115]

Just as the dissenters granted women some increased latitude in matters of spirituality and church governance, so, too, did they seek to enhance the role of wives in family governance. Marriage, they insisted, was a positive good rather than a necessary evil; since Luther's day, mar-

ried preachers had served as exemplars of piety. Thus Puritan advice-
book writers, inheriting and expanding upon earlier Catholic humanist
precepts concerning marriage, thought it natural to place the "reciprocall
debt" between husbands and wives at the very center of the godly household. "[T]here is a mutuall bond of duty standing betwixt man and wife,"
proclaimed William Whatley in one of the era's most popular sermons
on marital duty. It was a bond based on love: a "very fervent and abun-
dant" affection that was, he wrote, "the life, the soule of marriage." Marriage was the "combination of two persons, into one home," a partnership in which the "good liking each of other" was essential. Since they
placed men and women upon such (relatively) equal footing, it is only
logical that Whatley, William Gouge, and others idealized a marital relationship in which women *spoke*. Men and women were to "unite their
endeavors for the common benefite." They would pray together, sing
psalms together, and "reade the Word of God together"; they would "often talke together, and be sorry together, and be merry together, and
communicate . . . each with other." A "continuall streame of familiar
conversation" would so "nourish love" that a husband's harsh chastise-
ment of his wife became unnecessary. For the "nuptiall love of yoke-
fellowes" was as "neare and close a fellowship" as was possible in a fallen
world.[116]

But this cozy, conversational marriage represents only one dimension
of the Puritan ideal. The reformers imagined the bond between husbands
and wives—like those linking the faithful to their ministers and subjects
to their rulers—to be egalitarian in some ways, authoritarian in others.
Their notions of proper female speech brought this dual-edged quality to
the fore.

Reformed ministers simultaneously lionized and demonized women's
speech. This particular ambiguity can be laid at the feet of Saint Paul,
whose writings were both deeply influential in reformed Protestant
thought and deeply conflicted about women. On the one hand, Pauline
precepts held that male and female were "all one" in the Lord, and that
husbands should love their wives "as their own bodies." Yet Paul also
noted repeatedly that women were "not permitted . . . to speak" publicly, but rather were "commanded to be under obedience." "Let your
women keep silence in the churches," the apostle declared. For a woman
to teach, or even to speak in public, was "to usurp authority over the
man." Such usurping, Paul made clear, profoundly violated the right order of the world—and the Church. Wives should "submit" to their "husbands, as unto the Lord."[117] For according to Paul, the submission of
wife to husband mirrored that of the believer to God. Puritan authorities
took the Pauline notion that the "husband is the head of the wife . . .
as Christ is the head of the Church" very seriously indeed. The Protestant man was not only "King in his family"; he was also, and more important, "God's immediat officer." His wife was "the Deputie subordinate,
and affectionate to him, but not altogether equall." Thus if Protestant

thought elevated the wife's moral—and verbal—authority, it raised her husband's still higher.[118]

By casting the husband as both king and preacher to the godly household, Puritan writings on marriage made female misspeaking a more serious crime than it was among the general population. If ordinary English folk knew scolding as a kind of petty treason, the Puritans heard it as virtual blasphemy. "The Lord in his word cals [the husband] the head," Whatley reminded his readers. The man who allowed his wife to rule over him created a "deformed family" that "inverted" the "order of nature." Women's words all too often gave birth to such deformities. All "wise-men" knew of the "talakativenes [sic] of women": their "readines to speake, and multitude of words." But feminine weakness was no excuse. To Puritan moralists, women who "scold with their husbands, and raile upon them, and revile them" were not comic figures, but "monsters in natures, botches of humane society . . . next to harlots, if not the same with them." They deserved, Whatley argued, the harshest of punishments. "Let such words leave a blister behinde them, and let the canker eate out these tongues."[119] Perhaps shrew taming was not so far removed from the Puritan sensibility after all. Like Paul himself, Puritan authorities knew two faces of marriage: one rooted in the spiritual equality of all believers, the other in the worldly subjection of wives. The first tenet raised women's voices at home and in church. The second tightened the scold's bridle.

WHAT, THEN, WAS THE "Puritan" contribution to the notions of right speaking that English migrants brought with them to New England beginning in 1620? It may seem that there was not *one* Puritan view of governing the tongue, but many. This is not quite right. Nonconformists did not advance a plurality of opinions about speech. They outlined a single philosophy that was riven with internal contradictions: a chiaroscuro of freedom and restraint, fellowship and hierarchy, volubility and silence. The English legacy, broadly speaking, imparted an acute awareness of the power of words and an equally acute anxiety about their perils. To that cultural baggage, the Puritan worldview added a new degree of openness and a new degree of tension, for a heady dose of confusion. Where speech was concerned, Protestant reformers were decidedly undecided.[120]

This was problematic enough in pre–Civil War England, where the reformers had little opportunity to translate their ideals of verbal governance into a program to govern the realm. Still, the hot rhetoric of religious dissent threatened to set the English social order on fire. By the second quarter of the seventeenth century, there was good reason for both the Crown *and the reformers themselves* to fear the discontented murmurings spilling forth from conventicles filled with "masterless men" and prophesying women. The radical freedoms of speech advanced during the interregnum by sectarians, including the Ranters, the Levellers, and especially the Quakers, revealed just how precarious the Puritan notion of right speaking really was. Protestant theology had broadened the definition of what it was possible and pious to say: of who could speak to whom, in what manner, and when. It did not take long for the most radical interpreters of such doctrine to "shak[e] off that timorousnesse and awe" with which they had addressed authorities and imagine that they had the "faculties and abilities . . . to try all things," think all things, dare all things, *say* all things. "Let every one speak what he knowes," proclaimed the Digger mystic Gerrard Winstanley. In the face of prophecy, such radicals said, all the book learning and all the worldly authority of all the ministers and magistrates in all of England came to nothing. There could be no voice of authority—no ruling father—in a political family governed solely by the unbridled tongues of the faithful.[121]

Imagine the power and danger of these beliefs in England's with its tiers of judges and clergy, with its powerful Parliament and throngs of courtly minions, with its ample and long-established mechanisms for holding words in check. Now transplant these forceful ideals to a radically different context: one where the (English) body social had yet to take shape. Where the political family would be comprised of people "removing further and further" from home, breaking away from the safety and authority of "father and mother" to "cleave each to other" a world away. Where new and hitherto unheard-of tongues, governed by new rules, would hold forth. And where nonconforming Protestantism would be not just a language of dissent, but the lingua franca. Possessed of the "gift of tongues," intent upon "publishing" God's "name where it is not knowne," godly migrants would work to convert the "barbarous Nations" of the so-called New World and inspire the fallen hordes of their own land.[122] In New England, prospective migrants learned, it would be *imperative* to speak out—loudly, publicly, and often.

But who would draw the line between the possible and the permissible? Could people living at the far western edge of the known world be counted upon, as Thomas Adams urged the faithful in London, to "[r]emember the bounds" between godly and "unsavoury speeches"?[123] Who would ensure that the subtle mastery of ministers over the prayers of their reformed flocks, of magistrates over the pleas of their godly subjects, of husbands over the tongues of their loving wives, was protected?

It was a difficult task under the best of circumstances, much more so in the colonial world. For the "first fashioning of a politicke body," as one minister cautioned, was an infinitely "harder taske then the ordering of that which is already framed." Even "suche a Companye of faithfull people" as the group that set its sights upon Massachusetts was vulnerable to the imprecations of the discontented—people like the "multitude of Rude and misgoverned persons[,] the verye scomme of the land," who had hindered the erection of "a right forme of Government" in earlier English "plantations." Could New England endure any better the "scandalous reports" that such "malicious spirits can devise and utter"?[124]

During the perilous winter of 1630–1631, the first that John Winthrop spent in New England, a London-based member of the Massachusetts Bay Company made a gift to the struggling settlement of a small parcel of "new bookes that are lately come out." Among the several volumes was an enormously popular tract by English Puritan Jeremy Dyke entitled *The Mischiefe and Miserie of Scandalls Both Taken, and Given*. The book, which was first printed that year and would see eight editions before the decade was out, included a lengthy and vivid description of the "bleeding wounds" caused by scandalous words, and a set of directions for avoiding, or at least minimizing, the hurt. It would prove to be, in some ways, a redundant message. For who could know better than these new New Englanders the harm that arose when scandals "open[ed] the mouthes of many"?[125]

Several years later, John Harvard included a copy of Dyke's *Scandalls* in the library he bequeathed to the college that bears his name. An identical volume remains today in Harvard's rare-book library, where a modern reader can peruse the instructions for governing the tongue that found their way across the Atlantic to John Winthrop more than three and one-half centuries ago. The tract was a long one for its day, tipping the scales at nearly 250 thick linen pages. Yet cradled in the Lucite protector that cannot possibly keep its faded leather binding from crumbling to dust, it seems a rather paltry thing.[126] Bound together with another of Dyke's works in cramped octavo format, it is slight in every sense. How frail and impotent a weapon it must have been in the colony's fight to promote godly speech and drown out those whom Dyke called "evill speakers." How little Dyke knew—could have known—of their lives.[127] Who in England could imagine how loudly the spoken word would resonate in the eerie quiet of that "howling" wilderness? Both Puritans and their detractors would soon find out.

A MOST UNQUIET
HIDING PLACE

What if New England was no different? The question has dogged me since I undertook this project. It is easy enough to demonstrate that early New Englanders came to cherish their rules for right speaking, and that they imposed penalties upon those who breached them. But were theirs different rules, different penalties, different *mentalités* from those of other early modern peoples? Isn't anxiety over loose words and concern with reputation endemic to face-to-face societies, a seeming universal of village life? Does the vaunted exceptionalism of England's northern colonies—which, in any case, is very much in doubt these days—extend to the Puritan understanding of speech? What, in short, is the exclusive New England "angle" to my story?

Only close, comparative study will yield a fully satisfying answer to this question. I hope others are curious enough to pore through local court records, church archives, and personal papers to discover how (and whether) the meaning of speech in Massachusetts differed from that in Maryland, or the Carolinas, or England and Scotland, or even Connecticut and Rhode Island.[1] But I want to pose a different question, one that treats speaking as a cultural practice as much as a social one. Rather than asking whether the verbal culture of colonial New England was indeed exceptional, my task is to explore why Puritan migrants themselves worried so much about the novelty of their ways of ordering language. At its very core, the New England experiment was *about* trying to be different from what had existed before: different both from England and from Europe's other overseas ventures. Spoken words played a vital role in this vision of difference. Speech was to be the central marker of what many dared to hope would be not just New England's distinctiveness, but its superiority.

What if New England were no better? The thought gnawed at many of those who journeyed to the infant colonies of New Plymouth and Massachusetts Bay during the 1620s and 1630s. Throughout every day they spent in the strange new world of North America, behind every action they performed, beneath every word they uttered, was this fear: what if New England were just the same—the same as England or, worse still, as other colonial ventures? What if the Puritan "errand" decayed before it had even a chance to thrive? Where speech was concerned, the stakes were high, perhaps impossibly so. In New England, it was hoped, a godly man could give voice to beliefs that would have been suppressed in England, while still decrying wrongful words. From New England, it was promised, good news would overspread the globe, while malicious rumors would stop dead. In New England, in short, words would function as they had done no place else on earth. The tongue would simultaneously proclaim the ecstasies of belief and articulate a civil social order.

Such a paradoxical vision would appear almost impossible to realize. Yet in one respect, at least, the fondest wishes of New England's founding generation seemed entirely justified. How could New England fail to outshine the dim light of contemporary England? From the relative quietude of the Elizabethan settlement, the country had descended by the second decade of the seventeenth century into open conflict on matters religious. As dissenters saw it, leaders of the Church of England conspired to "stop the mouths of the more godly" by slandering and silencing nonconforming ministers.[2] While God's Word was stifled, the hot rhetoric of factional strife broke out everywhere. Many dissenters had reason to believe that they were living through what John Winthrop labeled "evill and declininge tymes" that could only "growe worse and worse."[3]

Searching for what minister John Davenport called "a safe and quiett abode" in which to live according to the dictates of Scripture, some had already fled to Holland. For many others, New England promised what one prospective émigré referred to as a more "comfortable . . . refuge": a place where preaching and hearing God's Word would form the basis of a new civil order.[4] "When the people say to them that prophecie, *Prophecie not,*" John Cotton exhorted, it was time for people of conscience to *"Arise"* and come away: to "plant a Colony" where no obstacle would impede *"the liberty of the Ordinances."* Such a place would ring with pious words and yet, somehow, remain "peaceable and quiet." No "quarrel, or contention" would follow them across the Atlantic. Instead, New England's migrants would find the solace of a "peaceable roome"—or, in Winthrop's words, "a shelter and a hidinge place for us and ours."[5] With the Word as its guide, how could New England *help* but fare better than England in its doleful, fallen state?

And how could it but fare better than other colonial outposts? New England would not, *could* not, suffer the fate of Virginia or the sugar islands. Virtually everyone alive in England would have been aware, as the founders of the Massachusetts Bay Company noted with characteristic understatement in 1629, that some of "those plantations, which have been formerly made, succeeded ill." There had been, they knew all too well, "great and fundamental errors in the other" English ventures overseas.[6] Jamestown's "errors," in particular, were known to include examples of nearly every type of barbarism, from Indian massacres, to famine-induced cannibalism, to political anarchy. Even so fervent a booster as John Smith had to admit that, to its English-born inhabitants, Jamestown had been "a miserie, a ruine, a death, a hell." Surely no godly migrants wanted to follow the example of a colony whose exigencies were such that Englishmen had devised a recipe for "roasted, boyled or . . . powdered [salted] wife"![7] Little wonder the leaders of Plymouth and Massachusetts Bay spent so much time pondering the causes of such costly mistakes and plotting how they were "like to be avoyded" in New England.[8]

One of the lessons New England planters learned from the trials of Virginia was to beware of the dangers of speech. To be sure, Jamestown settlers had had plenty of other worries. But John Smith himself conceded that one of the chief instruments of that colony's misery was the spoken word. In many instances, Smith believed, Virginia had fallen victim to word of mouth. The settlement, peopled as it was with many a "craftie knave" and "ancient maligner," was awash in angry rumors from the start. Indeed, those who made it out of Jamestown alive spent their time "so railing and exclaiming against Captaine Smith" and the colony's other leaders that newcomers "hated him ere ever they see his face." By 1631, when Smith summarized his hard-earned experience in a pamphlet offering advice for migrants to New England, Virginia had weathered "many a stormy blast" of invective from its "ignorant contradictors" and "calumniating detracters." Its example made clear that any plantation so "scorned . . . spoken of but with much derision" faced formidable obstacles to its success.[9]

They were obstacles New England's planters strove mightily to transcend. Only rulers of "weake Judgement," they concluded, would allow themselves to be "contemned," or permit the "insolente cariadges" of the discontented to "touche the publicke." The leaders of Massachusetts and Plymouth would turn away the sorts of "unfitt instrumentes" who had made such a hash of things in the Chesapeake. And they would act decisively against any who "murmureth, mutineth, and secretly conspireth."[10] After all, New England's planters were not tobacco-farming, labor-craving profit seekers, but "voluntary Exiles for the Word of God."[11] The Word would be their guide, their mission, and their shield.

From the first, then, New England was primed for a contest over speech. People there would be called upon to speak more freely than ever before, and yet to practice a higher degree of self-control than in England. For in this new world, the Word of God (and the words of the godly) would have to cut through all the calumnies of all the naysayers on both sides of the Atlantic. Moreover, the transcendent authority of Scripture would have to penetrate the baffling tongues of those be-nighted "savages" who saw this "new" England as their ancient home. There was much for the English tongue to accomplish, and many dangers to be feared.

But surely God would not let them down. Wasn't it the case, as John White argued, that they could "depend upon Gods engagement in the worke" and "expect . . . successe from his hand"? Wasn't it logical that, while "perfection of thinges" is never "founde in the beginnynges"—grim beginnings such as those in the Chesapeake—New England might yet "proceede to those thinges which are perfectt"?[12] God would do his best to make it so. For in Scripture, New England believed it had a stalwart ally. Stronger than "Walls, and Bulwarkes, and Fortifications"—stronger, surely, than the heated words of potential detractors—the Word would keep them safe. "[L]et the Name of the Lord be your strong Tower; and the word of his Promise the Rock of your Refuge," John Cotton preached. *"His word that made Heaven and Earth will not fail."* [13]

But what if it *did* fail? Such soaring hopes all but ensured a debilitating fear of defeat. If, at some moments, it seemed clear that a society gov-erned by Christian-like conversation could not help but prosper, in other, darker times, the vision seemed elusive, even improbable. What if God's Word were simply no match for the kinds of words that a colonial setting would nurture? What if governing the tongue proved no easier in New England than it had proven in England—or, grimmer still, in Virginia? What if New England were no different? What if New England were no better? *What if, in fact, New England were worse?* It was unthinkable, unconscionable, yet not, somehow, unlikely.

YOU COULD HAVE heard a pin drop in seventeenth-century America. The relative absence of meaningful, human sound was one of the most noticeable features of colonial life. Rolling thunder, howling animals, pounding surf: these the colonists heard in abundance. But the noise of heartfelt human communication filled the air much less often and much less fully than in the longer settled, more densely populated villages of Europe. Indeed, in Puritan New England, where leaders strove diligently to erase any hint of popery, not even church bells broke the deafening silence. In this respect, New England had much in common with all of Europe's overseas plantations. If early modern people in general suffered from what they saw as a shortage of vital information, people in the colonial world felt their isolation from the traffic of news and stories far more acutely. For the first generations of New England planters, the sense of being cut off from the conversations they had left back home weighed heavily upon them. The "mighty ocean" they had traversed lay, Nathaniel Morton wrote, as a "bar and gulf to separate them from all the civil parts of the world." As Edward Johnson would recall in the 1650s, many felt that "the Ditch betweene England and their now place of abode was so wide, that they could not leap over [it] with a lope-staffe."[14]

Faced with so widespread and enduring a shortage of communal story-wealth, the inhabitants of early New England greedily hoarded whatever stray words happened their way. In this atmosphere of homesickness and silence, letters from home became what David Cressy has called "an emotional lifeline, a cord of communication, that stretched across the wide ocean."[15] More than a written text intended for private consumption, a letter was a recorded speech act, often apprehended aurally rather than visually. In those first years, a missive from home might be, as Joshua Scottow recollected, "carried many Miles, where diverse *came to hear it*."[16] It was this opportunity for resuming, in writing, half-finished conversations with absent loved ones that drove men, women, and children to the docks to welcome arriving vessels from overseas or from elsewhere in the colonial world. Even during the initial "starving times," news-hungry colonists in Plymouth and Massachusetts Bay seem to have awaited ships' landings as much for their cargo of words as for their supply of badly needed provisions. When the *Lyon* arrived from England in 1631, John Winthrop noted that "divers of the assistants and most of the people, of the near plantations" turned out to greet it. Ships, it was said, "brought news," arguably the most precious kind of commercial freight.[17] Indeed, well into the second half of the seventeenth century—long after local printing presses became established and a burgeoning colonial economy guaranteed a frequent traffic of goods and letters—people from every station of New England society still found themselves, as John Pynchon put it in 1669, constantly "longing for news."[18]

This sense of shared hunger for any and all loose words had dramatic consequences for the cultural construction of speech in the colonies. Following the as-yet-unwritten economic law of supply and demand, scarce words became inordinately precious words. We today are so used to groaning under the information overload that characterizes life in the late twentieth century that it is hard for us to imagine the ways in which speech resonated in a climate of profound information scarcity. With few words to choose from, people tended to hang on every one. The court records of early New England are filled with examples of preternaturally careful listening: a witness recalling a neighbor's exact words decades after the fact, a mother taking pains to "overhear" the most intimate conversations of her daughter and son-in-law, groups of men gathering local intelligence at a court day or militia muster. It is no exaggeration to say that the greater part of the New England town's celebrated "watchfulness" was, at its core, a posture of deliberate *"hearfulness."*[19] The colonial world was a milieu in which, as Richard Brown has pointed out, "great attention was paid to who-said-what-to-whom, the precise words, the tone of voice and inflection."[20] In sum, the colonies' atmosphere of scarcity virtually ensured that talk became a primary focus of talk.

The heightened value that New Englanders, as colonials, placed on speech had two seemingly contradictory effects. On the one hand, it meant that good words in, from, and of New England were treasured. Joshua Scottow memorialized the earliest years of English settlement in Massachusetts as a time when "good News from this far Country . . . was as Cold Waters to a thirsty Soul." Likewise, the receipt of good news from England prompted the celebration of many a day of thanksgiving in early Massachusetts.[21] But hearfulness had a negative side as well as a positive one. The same dearth of information that enhanced the value of good news made ill words extraordinarily *costly* in the colonies. It soon became clear that a land where speech could accomplish great wonders was also one where words could do grave damage. "[A]nie may have eare to doe us hurt," warned John Humphrey before he became deputy governor of Massachusetts. And, as William Wood cautioned, those who "are nimble-eared to hear faults" were often "ready-tongued to publish them." True, the colony had vociferous boosters—those Wood deemed "well-willers"—who did their best to spread the good news "by word of mouth." But somehow, the "ill-willers" seemed always to get the jump on them. Good news traveled so slowly, while the "dampe of ill report" quickly drowned its victims in gossip. With thousands of miles and several months separating false reports from any attempt at correction, ripples of discontent could become waves of scandal before anyone had a chance to air the truth.[22] How could godly migrants avoid learning John Smith's lesson all over again?

Just as New Englanders agonized over the consequences of a profound absence of conversation with like-minded English folks, they also wrestled with the disquieting *presence* of ways of speaking wholly unfamiliar to them: those of the region's "Indians." Indeed, throughout the colonies, the speech of the native inhabitants of the Americas formed an ever-present backdrop to the construction of English settlements. As white immigrants struggled to come to grips with the sheer novelty and baffling diversity of native languages, they were forced to reexamine their own understandings of "civility" and, especially, of the relationship between speech and social order. If, as Karen Kupperman has recently argued, the experience of migration prompted colonists to reinvent their identities—to define "what made English society English"—then describing, classifying, and apprehending Indian speech was central to this work of "self-fashioning."[23] The need to come to terms with the radical "otherness" of the languages and peoples of the Americas made speech matter as never before.

Language, in the early modern worldview, was a moral and cultural arbiter, one of the primary attributes that distinguished "civilized" peoples from "barbarians." Indeed, the word "barbarian," derived from a Greek root meaning "foreign-speaking," had acquired a primarily linguistic meaning by the sixteenth century. Thinkers such as Spanish reformer Bartholomé de Las Casas argued that a shared language was the building block of civil society.[24] Yet the peoples of the Americas had no common tongue. In fact, many European chroniclers argued, linguistic differences were the chief, if not the sole, dividing lines between various native groups. Indeed, some of those who had heard the Babel of tongues in the so-called New World made Indian speech the central symbol of Indian savagery. The sheer number of native languages constituted a kind of linguistic anarchy, which was thought to be directly responsible for what European observers saw as social anarchy: the apparent absence of large-scale societies among the natives of the eastern seaboard. To writers such as Johannes de Laet, a director of the Dutch West India Company, it seemed only logical that nations divided by many languages would have "no sense of religion. . . . no form of political government."[25] From the European point of view, to sound like a barbarian was to be a barbarian, and to sound civilized was to be civilized. There was, in the early years at least, little room for a cultural "middle ground."[26]

This was so, in large measure, because of the limitations of the Europeans' own conceptual vocabularies. English, Spanish, Dutch, and French colonists from the fifteenth through seventeenth centuries had essentially two ways of explaining the enormous differences they heard between their own speech and that of Native Americans. Confronted with words and gestures utterly incomprehensible to them, white colonists tended, as Stephen Greenblatt has written, either to "imagine the Indians as virtual blanks—wild, unformed creatures," or, conversely, to "imagine the Indians as virtual doubles, fully conversant with the language and culture of the Europeans." It was a dizzying sleight of hand practiced with no apparent discomfort by early modern ethnographers. Sometimes natives were said to lack language altogether, like those whom Columbus planned to "bring . . . back to their Majesties, *so that they can learn to speak*." Alternatively, they might, as Thomas Morton later said of the natives of New Plymouth, be thought to speak in perfect classical forms, using "very many wordes both of Greeke and Latine, to the same signification that the Latins and Greekes have done." At one moment, Greenblatt writes, the natives were believed to have no language and, hence, "no culture; the next moment they have ours."[27]

Both of these contradictory understandings of native speech show how unsettling the experience of genuine linguistic difference could be for European colonists. This was especially so for the biblically minded voyagers to Plymouth and Massachusetts Bay. After all, as John Eliot knew, Scripture held out a promise to one who "walketh righteously, and speaketh uprightly": "Thou shalt not see a fierce people, a people of a deeper speech than thou canst perceive, of a stammering tongue, that thou canst not understand." But here dwelled such people; here resonated such a tongue—indeed, *many* such tongues. The Bible described the new Jerusalem as "a quiet habitation." But here a cacophony of "savage" voices interrupted that promised repose.[28] Indian languages, in short, exploded all the Europeans' existing categories, stymied all their Old World expectations. Here was linguistic difference on a scale previously unimagined—indeed, unimaginable. And, perhaps, unwelcomed: for if New Englanders sometimes emphasized how their own understanding of words and Word departed from that which prevailed in England, they surely did not wish to sound like savages. Yes, they had wanted to reinvent their language. But how completely? What, they often wondered, did the stark contrast between the linguistic environment of their new home and that of the world they had left behind mean for them? How would hearing—and speaking in—Indian tongues change white New Englanders' understandings of their own voices?

One way of bridging the gap between Old World and New World speech was to try to understand native languages by learning their vocabularies, their rules of pronunciation, their internal grammars, and their subtle inflections. This was particularly important to reformed Protestant colonists, for whom intimacy with God's Word was the sine qua non of genuine faith. Spreading the gospel required, John White argued, that "we may be more perfectly acquainted with their language, and they with ours." The limited degree of mutual comprehension that had allowed previous generations of explorers and natives "to trade one with another" and to understand the "outward sense" of each other's cultures was painfully inadequate to this higher purpose. White wondered how one could "expresse unto them things meerely spirituall, which have no affinity with sense, unlesse wee were throughly [sic] acquainted with their language, and they with ours?"[29] For such colonists as White, transcending the otherness of New World languages was not just desirable, but essential.

Writing was one way to do so. An important part of the European effort to come to terms with American languages was the attempt to "reduce" native speech to the printed page. Beginning soon after Columbus and continuing through the nineteenth century, a sustained campaign for Indian literacy took a twofold approach, striving both to create Roman alphabetic versions of Indian speech, and, simultaneously, to instruct natives in reading and writing European vernaculars. In both instances, this drive away from the act of speaking and toward the quieter disciplines of reading and writing must be understood as an effort to confine and routinize Indian languages: to bring the mediation inherent in script to the unpredictable medium of native speech. As the sixteenth-century grammarian Richard Mulcaster put it, the "stranger denisons" of the Americas would benefit from being made to "bond to the rules of our writing."[30] From the perspective of America's native peoples, the consequences of this literate "bond" to European culture appear to have been mixed at best. If the ability to read and write brought the experience of God's grace nearer to some Indians in New England, it may, as one historian has recently argued, quite literally have brought death to others.[31] From the European vantage point, however, the payoff was clear. Literacy meant civility, while pure orality sounded "Brutish, Savage, Barbarous"—capturing only the poisonous side of the tongue's Janus-faced nature.[32] Writing in 1674, nearly a century after Mulcaster, Daniel Gookin maintained that "to teach" local natives "to speak, read, write, and understand the English tongue" went a long way toward "civiliz[ing] the barbarous Indians."[33]

That Gookin was still wrestling with the dislocating effect of native languages more than fifty years after the beginning of white settlement in New England shows how pernicious a barrier to the godly society colonists believed Indian speech to be. Indeed, from the first years of colonization, Europeans had mused about how difficult a task it would be to catalog, classify, translate, transcribe, and otherwise pin down native tongues. One Dutch observer of the Mohawks, for example, thought their language "very difficult" and noted that "it costs me great pains to learn it." In fact, he reported, "the fundamentals of the language" spoken by the Mohawks were so baffling to Western ears that it seemed as if "they changed their language every two or three years"—just often enough to keep their European trading partners guessing![34] Other settlers claimed that the natives they encountered in North America spoke "an easy language, which is soon learned." Yet even observers who thought Algonquian words "made-up" and "childish" found them difficult to imitate. "It also seems to us," one Dutch minister in New Netherland wrote, "that they rather design to conceal their language from us than to properly communicate it."[35] John Eliot, the Puritan minister and gifted linguist whose translation of Scripture into the Massachusett tongue was the first complete Bible printed in the Americas, felt sure that God, at least, understood what the Indians said. Since "Jesus Christ and God by him made all things, and makes all men," white and "Indian" alike, Eliot explained, "hee knowes all *Indian* prayers also." But even as late as 1647, when Eliot published his report on the progress of the gospel among the Massachusett, few Englishmen and Englishwomen could claim as much.[36]

But if most New England colonists remained unable to comprehend fully what local natives actually said—either to their white "saviors" or to one another—this lack of understanding did not stop European listeners from using native speech patterns to distinguish a "good" Indian from a "bad" one. Good Indians were good speakers, cherishing rules for right speaking similar to those the English prized. Pliant, generous, polite, respectful—some Indians spoke in ways that confirmed their "civility." William Wood suggested that, just as "a tree may be judged by his fruit, and dispositions calculated by exterior actions," so, too, "the Aberginians" manifested their "well-disposed natures" through their speech. Like the English, they knew the value of quietness. "[H]e that speaks seldom and opportunely . . . is the only man they love," Wood explained, while "Garrulity is much condemned of them." Indian women were expected to be especially decorous, Wood argued, never breaking into "cross words or reviling speeches." In fact, he noted, he had once heard a native censure an Englishwoman for railing at her husband.[37] Similarly, Roger Williams, one of the most sympathetic ethnographers of the seventeenth century, praised the habits of speech he observed among the Narragansetts of Rhode Island. Their "courteous *Salutations*" to one another, he argued, lent "a savour of *civility* and *courtesie* even amongst these wild *Americans*." Gathered in a circle, each with "his pipe of their *Tobacco*," the natives listened in "deepe silence" and gave rapt "attention . . . to him that speaketh." The hearts of Puritan preachers must have leapt at the thought of such respectful listeners.[38]

Whether or not they grasped the sense of what natives were saying, then, English observers thought they understood the social hierarchies Indian speech expressed, and made much of the fact that some natives conceived of speech much as English folk did. Indians demanded words of respect from their inferiors. They prized rhetorical dexterity in their political and religious leaders and insisted upon silence in their women. They avoided quarrels and guarded their reputations against the loose words of others—all just as Englishmen ideally did.[39] In short, Indians seemed to appreciate the conceptual link that the English believed so essential: the link between speech and civility. Perhaps the linguistic differences between the settlers and the natives weren't so intractable after all. Maybe there was even reason to hope that the colonial world might soon attain linguistic "quietness."

But other signs hinted that quietness would not be so easily achieved. If, at one moment, native speech seemed tractable, respectful, rule bound, it seemed at others to articulate the very essence of savagery. For every native who "desired to learne and speake our language," there were many "*wicked* Indians" whose only tongue consisted of "scoffes and scornes."[40] For every "Aberginian" wont to "speak seldom and then with such gravity as is pleasing to the ear," there were "insolent" Abenaki prone to "lashing out into excessive abuse," and Mohawks "fiercely calling out '*Hadree Hadree succomee succomee*,'" which one English listener rendered as, "we come, we come to suck your blood." For every controlled display of political oratory, there were terrifying "imprecations and invocations" and "many a hideous bellowing and groaning."[41] For every native "*Articulation* in Speech," there was much "*Ululation, Howling, [and] Yelling.*"[42] Indeed, Indian words sometimes struck English ears as less than human. Powwows—native shamans often reputed to have diabolic powers—were heard on occasion "roaring like a bear, other times groaning like a dying horse."[43] After two generations of continual contact and conversation with New England natives, Mary Rowlandson would compare the Narragansetts' "roaring, singing, ranting, and insulting" to the braying of "Wolves," "hell-hounds," and "ravenous

Bears."[44] From the English perspective, even in the late seventeenth century, cross-cultural communication sometimes seemed like cross-species conversation.

How much more significant, then, were the chances of serious miscommunication during the first years of settlement? And how much more serious the consequences? The records of New Plymouth and Massachusetts Bay give ample support to Greenblatt's claim that the "early discourse of the New World" was "full of questions that cannot be asked or answers that cannot be understood."[45] Even the services of such legendary interpreters as Samoset and Squanto (Tisquantum)—natives who, in William Bradford's words, "spoke to them in broken English, which they could well understand but marveled at"—could not fully bridge the tremendous gaps between English and native speech ways.[46]

Sometimes, the slippage that occurred between what the Indians meant and what the English heard could be comic. Plymouth captain Miles Standish and his men, for example, found they "could scarce forbear to break out in open laughter" when greeted by a repentant sachem in Nauset (Eastham) one morning in January 1623. The previous night, local natives had apparently stolen "beads, scissors, and other trifles" from the visiting Plymouth company, and Standish had demanded the return of his goods lest "he would revenge it on them" that had committed the theft. The chief appeared before him the next day with the goods in tow and offered a strange apology: a form of speech without words perhaps intended to substitute for mutually unintelligible tongues. Approaching Standish "in a stately manner," the sachem "thrust out his tongue, that one might see the root thereof, and therewith licked his hand from the wrist to the finger's end, withal bowing [to] the knee." Edward Winslow, in his narrative of the encounter, surmises that the native leader was "striving to imitate the English gesture"—of bowing? of hand kissing?—having been "instructed therein formerly by Tisquantum." But the mimicry, if that's what it was, was executed too crudely to move its intended audience. Standish found the apology, performed "in so rude and savage a manner," to be utterly sidesplitting.[47]

More often, however, the miscommunication that was part and parcel of the New World's Babel was downright perilous for speakers on both sides of the cultural divide. The Plymouth planters repeatedly caught wind of "many secret passages" among local native groups. There were, in those first years, reports of "continual rumours" circulating among the Indians. Some English observers overheard "horrid" cursing and "devilish . . . conjurations . . . in a dark and dismal swamp." Even the beloved and much-needed Squanto was suspected of "private whisperings" with "other Indians."[48] Exactly what was so threatening about these sotto voce exchanges? Surely it was the simple fact that the English understood not one word. There were many "long," threatening, "audacious," and *important* pronouncements of which even Standish, whom Winslow deemed "the best linguist among us, could not gather anything."[49]

Thus when a Narragansett messenger named Tokamahamon arrived in Plymouth in November 1621, wearing a smile and bearing "a bundle of new arrows, lapped in a rattlesnake's skin," the Plymouth elders had no way of telling whether he was "a friendly Indian" or an enemy advance man. Based on "the common talk of our neighbour Indians" (talk that, no doubt, the English only half comprehended) about a Narragansett conspiracy against the planters, Standish held the man for questioning. But it was not until Squanto returned days later that the "manner of the messenger's carriage" could at last be decoded. With one look at the parcel, Squanto knew it to be a threat rather than a greeting. He told Bradford flatly "that to send the rattlesnake's skin in that manner imported enmity, . . . a challenge." Squanto may also have helped the governor prepare the colony's response: the return of the skin "stuffed . . . with powder and shot." It proved to be a timely and forceful rebuttal: a "message" that induced "no small terror" in the "savage king."[50] But it was also one the colonists could not possibly have uttered without considerable help. The Plymouth fathers knew that their "high words and lofty looks" ultimately provided little defense against hostile neighbors with whom they could barely communicate. It was no exaggeration when one early chronicler reported that "if [Tisquantum] were dead, *the English had lost their tongue.*"[51]

To be left speechless in "a vast and emptie *Chaos.*" To be surrounded by strange men chanting words that sounded like *"Woath woach ha ha hach woach"* and meant . . . God only knew what.[52] To be deprived of the solace of nourishing conversation with kith and kin, yet made newly vulnerable to the heated words of one's enemies. This was the very essence of linguistic colonialism: the confusion of tongues visited upon all early settlers, and all native inhabitants, in Europe's New World. It must have been a truly terrifying prospect, for colonists and colonized alike.

The leaders of the English migration to New England tried mightily to hold this fear at bay. They would not succumb to the disordering impact of American babble. Loudly, they discounted the impact of the natives and their strange tongues. If Indians did not speak real languages, New England planters reasoned, neither could they be counted "civil inhabitants." As such, they posed no real obstacle to the planters' grand design for the creation of a new speech order driven by God's Word. Unlike previous colonial ventures, New England, its promoters said, would be a place where the pious could "displaie" the power of the gospel through "zealous preaching" and godly "professing." It would be a place where "the bitter contention" of English religious discourse would be drowned out by rhetoric more godly but no less hot: by the noise of the faithful "disputing, and inveighing earnestly one against another" in the "heat of . . . zeale" for the Word.[53] It was a confident vision indeed.

Yet like all utopian dreams, the migrants' plan to create a hiding place that would be both "quiet" and filled with godly noise would prove difficult to achieve. And Indian voices were hardly the only obstacles to its realization. By 1622, the same year Winslow and Bradford published their paean to the superhuman fortitude and mellifluous tongues of Plymouth's zealous professors, other causes for doubt had surfaced. The realities of the colonial world—the lessons of John Smith—had already begun to intrude upon the reformers' imagined quietness. Set against the silence of a "hideous and desolate wilderness," the Word sounded all too puny and the words of "ill-willers" all too shrill. In the background, the din of "wild beasts and wild men" was ceaseless.[54] With all of these dissonances ringing in their ears, could they still hope to fashion a political family in which faithful brethren would intone God's Word more freely and purely than their English counterparts? If they could not rest secure that New England would be, in this sense, better—that this foreign, rocky soil would yield sweeter fruits than had their native ground—they knew one thing for certain: *Here, little would be the same.*

DECEMBER 1620. PLYMOUTH HARBOR. The deck of the *Mayflower*. A "vast ocean" lies behind them and a "whole country" stretches out ahead. But what sort of country? The landscape is cloaked in deep winter, the weather "sharp and violent." The denuded "woods and thickets" visible from the ship are deserted by all but the "savage barbarians" who, doubtless, are ready to "fill their sides full of arrows." The sense of emptiness is palpable.[55] They know they're not in England anymore. Nathaniel Morton, who will not arrive in Plymouth until these first straggling Pilgrims have suffered through three long years, could only imagine the barrenness of that first vista. There are "no friends to welcome them, no inns to entertain or refresh them, no houses, much less towns, to repair unto to seek for succour." In short, they see: *nothing.* Nothing but a void entirely too large, and too profoundly silent, for a company of 102 scared, shivering migrants even to begin to fill.

This is emptiness of the deepest sort. But it is not the kind of emptiness that frightens John Robinson. Robinson, the beloved spiritual leader of the English Pilgrims at Leyden, will never make it to New England. But his sense of the challenges the place would hold, spelled out in a farewell letter to the faithful written in July 1620, will prove truly prescient. The void that Robinson frets over is not the likely dearth of food, nor the certain shortage of housing, nor even the longing for distant loved ones (including himself). Although he knows that all of these absences will be devastating, what worries him more is the utter lack of a social order to contain the migrants. And not only that. It is the absence of the architecture of society, combined with the *presence* of a certain disquieting ethos—a habit of the migrants themselves—that makes him especially anxious. Robinson fears that their "intended course of civil community" will, in and of itself, prove to be "a continual occasion of offense."[56]

Precisely what about these self-proclaimed "Pilgrims" and their "intended course" does Robinson suspect will "fuel . . . that fire" of civil unrest? He does not say. It is clearly not their "divers motives" for migration, nor even the fact that many of them are "strangers . . . one of another," for he addresses these difficulties separately. Indeed, it is not the planters' disparity so much as their *fraternity* that unsettles Robinson. Their mission to erect a pure church, to sow the gospel in the wilderness, will force them to fashion an orderly, "civil government" while trying to deal with each other as brothers. The English "body politic" of which they declared themselves the saving remnant had been composed of unequals: husbands and wives, fathers and sons, superiors and inferiors. But as Robinson notes, the Leyden émigrés "are not furnished with any persons of special eminency above the rest." Thus by dint of necessity as well as by the lights of their theology, the migrants will have to set up a different kind of authority. In northern Virginia (their intended destination), there will be, at long last, no priestly trappings and no reprobate gentlemen: no "gay coat" to stand for leadership. But this lack of counterfeit rulers, while celebrated, also means that the migrants will have to exercise great "care and conscience." To base not just a church but a whole society upon fraternal bonds will require greater than usual measures of "brotherly forbearance" and devotion to the "common good." Voluntary bonds are, Robinson knows, necessarily fragile ones. A polity "knit" together by allegiance to the Word is easily undermined by words. He warns them of the dangers of heated speech, telling them that the "taking of offense causelessly" or the giving of it carelessly will shake their little "house of God" to its foundation.[57]

Long before the *Mayflower* took Cape Cod in her sights, the leaders of the Leyden migration must have realized the need to heed Robinson's warnings. They had just put to sea when vicious words broke out. Bradford later recalled the fate of one of the crew, a "proud and very profane young man," who passed the early days of the voyage "contemning" other passengers for their "seasickness" and "cursing them daily with grievous execrations." Fittingly, Bradford thought, the offender was stricken with "a grievous disease" of which he died midvoyage in a suitably "desperate manner." But if God had intervened to still one calumniating tongue, it soon became obvious that not every misspeaker would, by dint of divine will, take sick and die. Other remedies were needed.[58]

In November 1620, "occasioned partly," as Bradford wrote, by a stream of "discontented and mutinous speeches" that some of the "strangers" had vented while the party was still at sea, the faithful men in the company quickly sought to express their allegiances to one another in a more official and enduring form. The famed Mayflower Compact, in which some forty-one men of Plymouth pledged to "Covenant and Combine" themselves into a "Civil Body Politic," can thus be seen as a response to the dissensions given voice through heated speech. The colony's detractors had proclaimed that "when they came ashore they would use their own liberty, for none had the power to command them." The compact answered their threat by articulating that power to command (a program of "Laws, Ordinances, Acts, Constitutions, and Offices") and spelling out the need for the "due submission and obedience" of the tiny English populace. But this formalization of a new authority was not enough. Throughout that first troubled winter, during which roughly half of the settlers died, the air was filled with "discontents and murmurings . . . mutinous speeches and carriages." As prolonged suffering took its toll, civil conversation failed. Before the end of the winter, Bradford reported, men who had once "been boon companions in drinking and jollity" carped angrily over scarce provisions. "[I]f they died, let them die," one said of his spiritual brethren. Another was heard "cursing his wife, saying if it had not been for her he had never come [on] this unlucky voyage, and anon cursing his fellows." Like nearly everything else in Plymouth, the tongues of the desperate were rapidly proving ungovernable.[59]

Moreover, as John Smith might have predicted, the colonial milieu gave ill-willers' heated words extraordinary range. It did not take long for the murmurs of Plymouth's malcontents to reach across the Atlantic. When the *Mayflower* set sail for England in April 1621, her cargo consisted of what the historian Charles Adams evocatively called "nothing more substantial than tidings": letters as well as the scandalous reports of those who had seized the first opportunity to abandon the infant plantation.[60] And although the colony's London-based financial backers were quick to express their outrage that the planters had sent back "no lading in the ship," the *Mayflower*'s July landing did generate a thick, if not a profitable, traffic in rumors. Thomas Weston quickly decided that he had heard enough to form his own opinions of the causes of the colony's troubles. In a letter addressed to Plymouth's first governor, John Carver (who, unbeknownst to Weston, was then already dead), Weston blamed words for the settlement's problems, suggesting that if the colonists had devoted but a "quarter of the time" they "spent in discoursing, arguing and consulting" to money-making ventures, they would long since have made the Adventurers rich. When the letter reached Plymouth in November, William Bradford, Carver's successor as governor, penned an angry reply urging Weston to ignore the slanders of those who "wounded others" in order to "salve their own sores." "[T]heir hearts can tell their tongues they lie," he argued. But Bradford's words were faint, faraway, and long in coming—not reaching London until April 1622. In the meantime, Weston knew only what he heard. All of it was negative. The planters should not underestimate the importance of generating "good news," he insisted. Instead, Plymouth's only exports seemed to be "treacherous" reports that, as Weston put it, tended to "set us together by the ears, to the destruction of us all."[61]

In the ensuing years, it became clear to the Plymouth elders that Weston was more often the source of these ill reports than their recipient. When he arrived in the colony in 1623, rude speech traveled with him; he and his followers had scarcely set foot in the place before they

unleashed a torrent of "reproaches and evil words." As Weston continued, in Bradford's words, to "quib behind their backs" and assault other
planters with "provoking and cutting speeches," his "private whispering"
began to "nourish a faction" among the "weaker sort." Ultimately, Bradford quelled these rumors by allowing Weston's corrupt limb to depart
from the "General Body" and carry on as independent settlers, or "Particulars."[62] But even as the specific wound healed, the general malaise deepened. Talk of even the most trivial of the colony's shortcomings—the
quality of the water, the presence of "mosquitoes," the freshness of the
local fish—found eager audiences in London.[63] So it was that by 1624,
leaders of the settlement found themselves in a most ironic position. The
very same people who had journeyed to the edge of the known world
because the Jacobean clergy had dared to "stop the mouths of the more
godly" were now looking for ways to stanch a veritable flood of too-free
expression. The conversation of godly brethren was proving to be no less
problematic than the more authoritarian rhetoric of fathers and sons.

Yet however much the thick cloud of malign words that surrounded
their venture frustrated the Plymouth fathers, it was not their most urgent priority where language was concerned. More worrisome still was
the continued absence of the very kind of speech that had driven many
of the Leyden congregation across the Atlantic in the first place: godly
preaching. Perhaps the most fitting symbol of the Old Colony's linguistic
predicament was the curious fact that a pure church gathered out of the
world failed to attract even a competent minister for nearly a decade.
John Robinson, who promised in one of his farewell letters that he would
soon "speak [rather] than write to them," delayed his departure from
Leyden year upon year. While the faithful awaited the voice of their
revered minister, ruling elder William Brewster sermonized and lay members of the tiny congregation "prophesied" on disputed points of Scripture.[64] But of the kind of preaching William Perkins had described—the
deep, searching, and inspiring interpretations of God's Word that formed
the very marrow of nonconformist theology—of this, there was none.

Thomas Morton, surely the cleverest of the plantation's many detractors, played up the irony of this situation for high comic effect. How
had it come to pass, he mused, that "no man amongst" such a godly
company "had the guift, to be in Jonas steade"? Plenty among them could
read "the Bible and the word of God, and useth the booke of common
prayer." But this form of worship, sufficient for millions of pious Angli-
cans, was enough to send the Pilgrims "headlonge to perdition." No, they
insisted on a more authentic "meanes" to grace. What a "poore thinge is
that, for a man to reade in a booke," lamented Morton's mock separatists.
"[G]ive me a man hath the guiftes of the spirit, not a booke in hand."
The primacy they placed upon godly speech—on the spontaneous, spoken interpretation of the Word—made theirs, Morton later joked, a
"path so hard to keepe."[65]

It was a difficult path indeed. For not only did the Plymouth faithful endure a lack of godly preaching. They were also visited, in those crucial early years, by a number of would-be ministers whose voices made a mockery of Perkins's prophetic arts. John Lyford, an ordained Anglican who was the first who tried to fill Robinson's considerable shoes, was one of the most ill-spoken sort imaginable, guilty (as the Pilgrim elders saw it) both of vacuous preaching and of treasonous words against the colony's government. Lyford played the part well enough when he arrived in Plymouth in March 1624. Bradford recalled that Lyford had addressed them with such "reverence and humility as is seldom to be seen": bowing, cringing, weeping, flattering, and praising the planters' accomplishments. But despite his earnest profession of faith and loyalty, Lyford quickly allied himself with John Oldham, one of the chief murmurers in Weston's "faction," and began to display "a spirit of great malignancy." First in "private meetings and whisperings" and later more openly, Lyford and Oldham spurred their "vile or profane" followers to "speak against the church here." When a suspicious William Bradford intercepted a packet of letters to England in which the pair vented their "slanders and false accusations" against the plantation, Lyford was fittingly "struck mute." But his repentance—including a tearful and lengthy apology for speaking "slanderously" of the congregation—was short-lived. Within "a month or two," he proceeded again to "justify what he had done" in another series of letters to the Adventurers. Although Lyford never matched Oldham for sheer venom and "choler," his words could hardly have sounded less like Robinson's cherished voice.[66]

Why had such a trial been visited upon them? Where was the electrifying preaching they craved so hungrily—the sermons of men whose skill with the spoken word would, they had hoped, make the tiny settlement famous the world over? Where were those giants like John Robinson, John Cotton, and Thomas Hooker: men whom Plymouth planters would later refer to as "Mighty in word and prayer"? By midcentury, Massachusetts would already have mourned the deaths of more and better preachers than had ever uttered a word in the pulpit at Plymouth. Why could they, too, not snare

> A man of might at heavenly eloquence,
> To fix the ear and charm the conscience;
> As if Apollo[']s were revived in him,
> Or he had learned of a Seraphim.
> Spake many tongues in one: one voice and sense
> Wrought joy and sorrow, fear and confidence[?][67]

Instead, they were treated in 1628 to the pulpit stylings of a "young man" whom Bradford names only as "Mr. Rogers"—a preacher later found to be so "crazed in his brain" that they sent him packing the very next year. Even Ralph Smith, the colony's first permanent minister, who arrived via

Salem in 1629, hardly broke the losing streak. Damned with faint praise from the first (Bradford labels him "a grave man" but no more), he left the Plymouth church only partly of his own volition some eight years later.[68]

To Thomas Morton, so vocally at odds with the Pilgrim authorities, the whole situation was laughable: a real-life incarnation of the topsy-turvy world that was a stock image in Renaissance comedy.[69] In Plymouth, he told the readers of his popular tract, "harmeles Salvages" spoke "sentences, of unexpected divinity," while counterfeit divines like the fictitious "Master Bubble" practiced "blinde oratory" so stultifying that it soon "luld his auditory fast a sleepe." (Even Bubble's grace "at dinner" was so long and drawn out, Morton quipped, that often "the meate was cold" by the time he was through.) In Plymouth, everyone was permitted to be a "publike" preacher. Why, even the "Cow keeper" was urged "to exercise his guifts, in the publik assembly on the Lords day"—so long as "hee doe not make use of any notes." In Plymouth, Morton alleged, any-one whose "tongue outrunne his wit" had all the qualifications necessary to become a separatist divine. Yet though all the colony's "worthies" prophesied without restraint, none evinced truly "speciall gifts." In short, Plymouth was a place overwhelmed with concern for the weightiness of words, and blessed with not one soul whose voice carried any weight at all. As far as Morton was concerned, the role of New World Jonas re-mained available in 1637; he proposed to claim it for himself.[70]

To my mind, Morton's is some of the most canny English comedy of the seventeenth century. From the perspective of the Plymouth elders, however, there was nothing funny about Morton's words. His lively bur-lesque was but one more example of the linguistic chaos that had taken root in the first years of the plantation. Lackluster preaching and damag-ing, far-reaching rumors—these, if nothing else, Plymouth had in abun-dance. And the consequences, Bradford and others knew, could be dire. Given the ever-shaky support of the colony's financial backers, ill words—be they Lyford's, Oldham's, Morton's, or those of more ordinary malcontents—carried more than their usual potential for harm. "[S]lan-ders and false accusations," one early chronicler feared, would resound "not only to their prejudice," but to the plantation's "ruin and utter sub-version." Who knew, Bradford wondered, "what hurt these things might do"? It is no exaggeration to suggest that at many junctures during Plym-outh's first decade, the fledgling colony's very survival hinged upon the ability of Bradford and others to control the production and the recep-tion of heated words.[71]

The year 1623. London. The stately countinghouse of one of the "general"—the group of metropolitan Adventurers supporting the colony in Plymouth. Three years have passed since the *Mayflower*'s landfall in the New World. Troubles still abound. Talk of the planters' struggles—reports of the obstacles God has placed in the Pilgrims' path, and of the afflictions they visit upon one another—flies thick and fast on the docks of the Thames. It is a time for reassurance: a time for thirteen worried investors to try to bolster the spirits of their friends (their *human capital*) across the ocean. This is the message they wish to convey: *Don't panic. Persevere.* No matter how low the venture's reputation has sunk by the ripe old age of three, things are sure to turn around. In time, the Adventurers promise, rumors of another sort will replace the morass of nasty gossip that threatens to bury the plantation. All will celebrate the "joyful news" of the planters' untoward achievements. In time, "all men shall know you are neither fugitives nor discontents." In time, reports of their triumphs will make these pilgrims justly famous—"honourable amongst men." In time, perhaps, but not quite yet. The ship containing the letter conveying the Adventurers' "hearty affection" is met by a band of settlers so pitiful, so obviously malnourished, and so distressed that, Bradford writes, "all were full of sadness." "[R]agged in apparel and some little better than half naked," the would-be Pilgrims hardly seemed destined to be known by "all men" for anything but their failures.[72]

The year 1630. Plymouth. William Bradford's tiny study. Against all odds, Bradford—the self-designated voice of the colony's Old Comers— proclaims the Adventurers' hopeful prophecy fulfilled. "Thus out of small beginnings," he writes, "greater things have been produced by His hand that made all things of nothing." God has stepped in, and word of New England's success is spreading. "[A]s one small candle may light a thousand, so the light here kindled hath shone unto many, yea in some sort to our whole nation," Bradford exalts. The "joyful news" predicted back in 1623 has at last become a reality; a beacon of truth casts a blinding light over dark clouds of gossip and doubt.[73]

It is a sunny view, to be sure. It is also a *retrospective* view, bathed in the rosy glow of nostalgia.[74] Reality circa 1630 was somewhat more ambiguous. True, the Old Colony had grown, but not exponentially so; its original flock of one hundred souls had been augmented by births and by a decade's worth of new arrivals, till it reached just over three hundred. The Plymouth pulpit could at last claim its first settled preacher, though his anemic sermonizing did not come close to replacing the glorious voice that had fallen silent in 1626, when John Robinson died having never left Europe. In short, although there were, by 1630, reasons for guarded hopefulness, there was not yet cause for celebration.[75]

Moreover, it is difficult to determine whether this mood of cautious optimism did anything to stem the flow of heated speech to and from Plymouth. "Joyful news" both in and of Plymouth remained, I would venture to guess, in short supply in the early 1630s. Indeed, there is evidence to suggest that the kinds of rumors leaking out of Plymouth gave those contemplating the move to the more rapidly growing settlements of Massachusetts Bay reasons for doubt. Promoters of New England strove to answer in their tracts a question that must have been frequently asked: did pious brethren tend to become unauthoritative authorities and unsubject subjects? Did the nonconformist impulse toward freer (religious) speech impede the growth of civil conversation? There was reason to suppose, by 1630, that zealous brethren, too-free speakers, made second-rate planters.

John Smith certainly thought so. Was it any wonder, he asked, that the sins of "pride, and singularity, and contempt of authority" had so often surfaced in Plymouth? Surely such failings were endemic to a colony founded by "discontented Brownists, Anabaptists, Papists, Puritans, Separatists, and such factious Humorists." Did it not seem to follow naturally that among such an "absolute crue" comprised "only of the Elect," *"few could command and fewer obey"*?[76] Others more sympathetic to the Puritan cause seemed to agree. It was the experience of Plymouth that caused the leaders of the new plantation at Salem to wonder, in 1629, whether "this wilderness might be looked upon as a place of liberty, and therefore might in time be troubled with erroneous spirits." And it seemed only logical that those who arrived in New England "expecting all libertie in an unsetled body" became, when confronted with newly formed "Authority," too "ready to blemish the Government with such scandalous reports as their malicious spirits can . . . utter."[77]

The challenge, in 1630 as in 1620, was to find a way to allow godly conversation to flower in the colonial world without permitting those of "ill affected mindes" to "make that place a nursery of faction and rebellion."[78] Plymouth was, in this sense, an antimodel. For all their heartfelt attempts to spread the good news of the gospel throughout the English-speaking world, the planters at Plymouth had had little success when it came to liberating the spoken word and regulating it at the same time. They had prophesied earnestly and yearned after good preaching. They had banished devisers of rumor and condemners of authority. They had passed laws forbidding freemen to "speake or doe, devise or advise any thing or things . . . directly or indirectly by land or water, that doth shall or may tend to the destruction or overthrow of this present plantations."[79] But in so many forms, from petty neighborhood slanders to transatlantic treason, harsh words had kept right on coming.[80]

Despite the profound differences between Cape Cod and Jamestown, the experience of Plymouth only confirmed, in this sense, the "one principall" John Smith had drawn from his experiences in Virginia. To those who would begin again in Massachusetts, he spelled out his veteran's wisdom. "In this your infancy," he counseled them, "imagine you have many eyes attending your actions, some for one end, and some onely to finde fault." In fact, it was really the *ears* of the world that were poised to "find fault." Successful planters would "neglect therefore no opportunity, to informe" all hearers of their "orderly proceedings . . . : contrary to the common rumour here in *England*." In short, Smith exhorted them: *Spread joyful news and control damaging gossip. Get the good Word out and keep the bad words in.* Precious advice, he was certain. So good, in fact, that he believed any who found a way to follow it would doubtless become "the most admired people of all our plantations for your time in the world."[81] Plymouth had not done so—at least not yet. Would Massachusetts Bay?

ACT AS IF THERE were many eyes, many ears upon them. John Winthrop, for one, took this counsel of his colonial forebears to heart. The fate of Virginia had proved it. The fate of the English Puritans had proved it. And perhaps most pointedly, the fate of Plymouth had proved it: Massachusetts faced a difficult road. Erecting a European society at the edge of the world had never been easy. But erecting a *godly* society would prove especially rough. Like the settlements of the "Apostles times," Winthrop said, New England would be both a "community of perills" and a "Community in [pursuit of] some speciall service for the Churche." It would thus be a place to which special rules would apply, as well as a community uniquely subject to the judgments and murmurings of others.[82]

How might the passengers aboard the *Arabella* create a society so exemplary that the very fact of its existence would stifle rumors and inspire praise? This is a central theme of Winthrop's "A Modell of Christian Charity," a lay sermon written (and presumably delivered) while he was en route to New England in 1630. In what is almost certainly the most enduring example of seventeenth-century American oratory, Winthrop inspired his fellow passengers to meet their formidable task. Their enterprise, he warned, contained a paradox at its very core. The "Bond of brotherly affecion" that was to be the foundation of their new polity coexisted uneasily with the hierarchical "Condicion of mankinde": God's disposition that "in all times some must be rich some poore, some highe and eminent in power and dignitie; others meane and in subjeccion." The Puritan "errand" into New England would thus, of necessity, entail a delicate balancing act between the twin goals of mutuality and hierarchy. Like parts of a corporeal body, like members of a godly household writ large, Massachusetts settlers would have to seek a mean between the competing imperatives of zealous freedom ("liberallity") and decorous restraint.[83]

Their success in this difficult mission would, Winthrop knew, be measured largely in words: by the quality of their "conversacion one towardes another," and by the way others spoke about them. For their plantation lay exposed as a "Citty upon a Hill": visible to "the eies of all people," audible to the cocked ears of all people, vulnerable to the *mouths* of all people. What would people hear of Massachusetts, and what would they report? Would "men . . . say of succeeding plantacions: [']the lord make it like that of New England[']"? Or would the colony "be made a story and a by-word through the world"—the "prayers" of well-wishers "turned into Cursses upon us"? Plymouth had shown that a community intent upon being lauded as a "prayse and glory" could easily become an excuse to "open the mouthes of enemies to speake evill of the wayes of god and all professours for Gods sake."[84] What kind of light would Winthrop's "city upon a hill" send out to future dreamers of new worlds: a welcoming beacon, or a warning sign? There were no ready answers. But one thing was certain: speaking freely with restraint would prove *at least* as difficult in Massachusetts as it had proven in England, just as it had proven in Plymouth.

As in Plymouth, the special dangers that unfettered tongues posed to a plantation in its infancy became apparent almost immediately—in fact, before the *Arabella* even pulled out of port in Falmouth in April 1630. Although Winthrop and other leaders of the Massachusetts Bay Company made the promotion of godly speech a priority on the voyage, their efforts to supply the passengers with a nourishing diet of sermons failed to prevent heated words from erupting. As a punishment for "using contemptuous speeches in our presence," one young man found himself "laid in bolts" on the deck "till he submitted."[85] That anonymous offender may have been chastened, but many more misspeakers followed suit; the familiar litany of transatlantic complaints broke out soon after the group's arrival. By November of that year, a Puritan preacher in Essex, England, had already received dire news about the settlement—a report that it "cutts me to the hart to heare." By December, John Humphrey, a company man still in London, feared that the colony was beginning to "bring upon ourselves that contempt and reproach of the foolish builder." Making the settlement a gift of Jeremy Dyke's recently published treatise on slanders, *The Mischiefe and Miserie of Scandalls*, was, it seems, Humphrey's less-than-subtle way to drive home the point: "rumour" and "ill report" were everywhere. By 1632, even the colony's staunchest supporters had to marvel at "what discoragements the divell putts in most mens mouths against your plantations." It had not taken long for the "false accusations," "mutteringe," and "railing speeches" of "ill willer[s] to our government" to reach the ears of court and Crown back home.[86]

Indeed, Massachusetts rapidly came to know the same kind of linguistic topsy-turvy so often heard in early Plymouth. Native groups addressed the planters in a dizzying variety of unknown languages. Servants turned their tongues against even the most pious of masters. Barely a year had passed in Boston before Phillip Ratliffe and Thomas Fox, two servants of the colony's first governor, were heard "uttering mallitious & scandilous speeches" about their master and against "our churches and government" more broadly. Despite the severe punishment visited upon the two—both were whipped and Ratliffe lost his ears, though not his tongue—others quickly took up their example. That same summer, a youth in nearby Watertown was convicted of "ill speeches . . . towards his maister."[87] And, some months later, the servant of "one Moodye, of Roxbury" was heard to proclaim that "if hell were ten times hotter, he had rather be there than he would serve his master."[88] Massachusetts was fast becoming the sort of place where common sailors could be heard cursing, threatening, and reviling the government.[89]

Yet this was not the most damaging kind of speech heard in the early years of white settlement in New England. Ill-spoken servants and foul-mouthed sailors were hardly unique to the colonial milieu, let alone the exclusive progeny of the Bible commonwealth. Their surly language, however lamentable, impinged upon only half of Winthrop's social vision: hierarchy. Their words showed that some would always need to obey (even if they had to be compelled to do so) the commands of others.

Much more disquieting than the contemptuous expressions of servants and seamen were outbursts which threatened not just hierarchy, but *fraternity*. Loose words were not encouraged, but that heated speech did erupt among the better sort of men within this godly brotherhood merited real concern. For if brothers could not respectfully dispute their equals—if they could not divulge themselves freely, fully, decorously, and quietly—then surely the whole Puritan impulse toward open communication was in danger. But this was precisely what seemed to be happening. Winthrop had imagined a polity that would "entertaine each other in brotherly Affeccion" and "rejoyce together, mourne together, labour, and suffer together" as "members of the same body."[90] Instead, brethren in Massachusetts could be heard too often to strive together, contend together, contradict one another, and deny each other like members of so many disparate, competing bodies. Challenges to Winthrop's imagined fraternity of speakers seemed to spring up everywhere. It was "straunge" indeed, John Humphrey reported, "to see how little brotherly love" was in evidence "in brethren."[91]

Could one man, be he preacher or magistrate, articulate an image that conveyed both fraternity *and* authority? Where brothers ruled each with the other, disputing points of divinity and knitting themselves into one body, who was the head of the political family? These were the questions posed both explicitly and implicitly by many of those who spoke against the leaders of church and state during the first years of English settlement in Massachusetts.[92] There were plenty of righteous brothers, misspeakers insisted, but too few fathers. The "best of them" in the colony's nascent ruling stratum was, Thomas Dexter quipped, "but an atturney." Speaking in an "insolent" manner, standing defiantly "with his armes on kembow," Dexter was the worst nightmare of such men as Simon Bradstreet, John Endecott, and John Winthrop—all of whom were targets of his words. He was a "goodman," one of respectable rank and station, who failed to defer to the voice of authority and asserted his own voice instead.[93]

And he was not alone. Indeed, better men than Dexter—men who should have known how to speak like English gentlemen, like *Puritan* gentlemen—fell into worse expressions. Captain John Stone clearly delighted in his verbal "outrage" against assistant Roger Ludlow, who, he punned publicly, was more of a "just as[s]" than a justice.[94] Ensign William Jennison, a deputy to the General Court, was more direct. "I pray

God deliver mee from this Court," he announced, complaining of some "injustice" the magistrates had done him.[95] From all corners of the colony—from gentlemen and yeomen, from sailors and ships' captains—the verdict was the same: the leaders of the Bay Colony were not godly rulers, but "rebells & traytors." Their churches were not a mirror of heaven so much as "a humane invention" in which "the ministers did dethrone Christ, & set up themselves." *Their authority was all pretended:* the governor "but a law[y]er's clerk," the court a deviser of "lawes to picke mens purses," the faithful "a stinking carryon." "[W]hat understanding hadd [the governor] more then himselfe"? John Lee wondered. What kind of authority was this, indeed?[96]

It is easy to see why both the substance of these expressions of contempt and the mere fact of their utterance would have confirmed the darkest forebodings of Bay Colony leaders. Such words were evidence not only that New England was subject to the dangers of the spoken word, but that it was, somehow, especially so. Was it a coincidence that Massachusetts, a place where preachers "commended" to their congregations "the exercise of prophecy," was also a place where people had a tendency to speak out of turn? Could such a man as Thomas Dudley, certainly one of the better sort, find a way to follow the dictates of his faith and "discharge his conscience in speaking freely" without offending the "public peace"?[97]

The leaders of Massachusetts tried mightily to erect such a speech order. Despite their willingness to impose tough penalties on condemners of the commonweal (fines, whippings, public penances, bodily mutilation, even banishment), they maintained in the colony's first years a hard-fought allegiance to the verbal openness evoked by Calvin. Slander, insolence, contempt: these were rooted out and punished without remorse. But discussing, disputing, searching, questioning: these verbal postures were permitted, even encouraged. Provided that the tone and, as we shall see in the next chapter, the *players* involved were carefully chosen, the dialogic spirit of the English Puritan conventicle remained very much alive in New England—at least for a time.

Where else, for example, would a high government official, his deputy, several local ministers, and an entire congregation come together to resolve disputed points of theology through open, public debate? This was precisely the tack that Winthrop used to lay open the doctrinal errors of one Richard Brown, an elder in the Watertown church. On the one hand, the colony's actions against Brown could be interpreted as evidence of a stringent policy where dissident utterances were concerned. Brown had verbally "published" the dangerous opinion that "the churches of Rome were true churches," and the colony's self-appointed word police sought to silence him. But the *way* they did so is equally important. "The matter was debated before many of both congregations," Winthrop recalled, and Brown's opinion "concluded [to be] an error" by majority vote. Ultimately, the elder was relieved of his office for his "unfitness in regard of his passion and distemper in speech." But that resolution came only after repeated attempts at communication, conversation, disputation.[98] In England, this sort of congregational discipline had often pitted nonconformist ministers against the law. In New England, the process of dissecting, disputing, and explaining dissenting opinions *was* the law.

When this interrogative style succeeded, it did so splendidly. Where both a misspeaker and his target really were brethren—high-status men who thought and spoke of each other with mutual respect—the so-called rule of the Apostle, which urged neighbors to discuss one another's faults openly, directly, was all the law that was needed. Through heartfelt conversation, the parties on both sides would come truly to "hear" one another, as Scripture promised.[99] The one whose words had given offense could be persuaded, as Thomas Dudley was in 1632, "to be silent in them." Expressions of "protestation" might then be delivered and received "in love . . . and not by way of accusation." And even when the parties spoke to each other in "great fury and passion" and "grew very hot" in their speech, they might both soon be "pacified." So it was with Winthrop and Dudley, who, despite months of heated contention, were able to talk their way back to a state of brotherhood: a relation based on "love and friendship" in which they might address each other "without any appearance of any breach or discontent."[100] In the early years of Massachusetts, leading men often evaluated each other's verbal demeanor with this kind of elasticity. Words harmed, words healed. Brothers knew how to talk things through.

But it did not always turn out this way, even among metaphorical siblings. The problem with resolving disputes through dialogue was that conversation was notoriously open-ended. Those who "dealt" with a misspeaker could not always bring "him to acknowledge his error." An offender whose words had provided neighborhood malcontents with an "occasion to murmur against" the government might not be prevailed upon to "heal" the breach "by some public explanation of his meaning."[101] In some cases, the Puritan penchant for open dispute backfired, providing a bully pulpit for a dissenter's voice rather than an occasion to publish testimonials to communal harmony. When this kind of turnabout occurred, Massachusetts authorities found themselves, as John Smith had quipped, "beaten with their owne rod."[102]

Roger Williams, a Cambridge-trained preacher whose beliefs leaned toward separatism, was the first to teach the colony's leaders this difficult lesson. Soon after his arrival in Massachusetts during the winter of 1631–1632, Williams began loudly and publicly to "declare his opinion" on matters of doctrine. In itself, this implied no breach of the rules of right speaking; as a minister, Williams was expected (even *paid*) to unfold his opinions. The problem was that in many important specifics—including the status of the Church of England, the place of "unregenerates" in independent churches, and the role of magistrates in punishing ecclesiastical offenses—his beliefs were at odds with those of the nascent Massachusetts orthodoxy. Such differences had broken out before. So there was, at first, no reason for Winthrop and other members of the court to doubt that Williams's declared "brotherly affections" toward them would provide the necessary context for an open yet respectful debate on the issues. And this is precisely what took place in the fall of 1633, when Williams first "convented" with the governor and his assistants to discuss his "errors." Confronted with the assembly's "arguments to confute the said errors," Williams did as he was expected: he "returned a very modest and discreet answer" and "appeared penitently" before the next court. By the close of 1633, Williams had managed to give the company "satisfaction of his intention and loyalty." He had spoken like a brother, and would be treated like a brother once again.[103]

But Williams's tongue would not stay still. Moving first from Boston to Salem, from there to Plymouth, and then back to Salem again, Williams restlessly sought a congregation receptive to his views. By the spring of 1635, his earlier "modesty and discretion" had again given way to forwardness and assertiveness. And also to *persuasiveness*: many of Salem's faithful were beginning to agree with him. In April, the General Court charged him with a dual violation of the colony's speech order: first, of having "publicly" advanced notions that a majority of the ministers had declared to be errors; and second, of having accused those selfsame ministers of "tak[in]g the name of God in vain." When Williams appeared before the court in July, little trace of his earlier brotherly tone remained. Once again, "Much debate was [had] about these things." Once again, his "opinions" were found "to be erroneous, and very dangerous." But this time, there was no peaceful resolution—no fraternal conversation. This time, there was only a promise from the magistrates: "expect the sentence" that "he who should obstinately maintain such opinions . . . were to be removed."[104]

The warning was clear enough, but Williams held fast to his convictions and to his claims to expressive liberty. When the Assistants reconvened in September, he "maintained" and "justified" his beliefs. Given the option to reflect soberly and take up the matter at some later date, Williams chose to "dispute presently" before the court. This, the court declared, was no conversation, for none of his brethren could "reduce him from any of his errors." No, this was sedition. Brother or not, Williams had to pay the price. For having "broached & dyvulged dyvers newe & dangerous opinions, against the aucthoritie of magistrates . . . & churches here," and for having "*mainetaineth the same without retraction*," he was ordered to depart from the colony "within six weeks . . . not to returne any more without licence from the Court." With winter fast approaching, Williams received an extension of the date for his banishment until the following spring—with one proviso. He was again warned to mind his tongue: "not to go about to draw others to his opinions." But the "infection" of his words continued to "spread." When he left the colony for Narragansett Bay in January, he had "drawn above twenty persons" from the Salem congregation to go with him.[105]

Williams's noisy departure was a wake-up call to the leaders of Massachusetts. Although they had succeeded in rooting out the source of erroneous opinions and, in time, in excising their cause, their preferred method of discipline had clearly come up short. Godly conversation—even among self-proclaimed brethren—had failed to effect the necessary melting of hearts. The voice of authority had prevailed in the end, but only by the slimmest of margins. It must have been with this in mind that most of the colony's civil and clerical authorities (then-governor John Haynes, along with Winthrop, Dudley, John Cotton, Thomas Hooker, John Wilson, and Henry Vane) came together soon after Williams's departure to consider how to deal with any future "jar or difference" among the faithful. It was their first sustained, self-conscious effort to construct a posture of authority. And that posture, in large measure, consisted of a new and careful formulation of a ruling voice.[106]

What should magistrates *sound* like? How could godly brothers continue to "deal freely and openly . . . each with other" while still projecting the kind of paternal mastery that was especially important during "the infancy of plantation"? These were the issues debated by this assembly of worthies throughout the morning and afternoon of 18 January 1636. Taking that evening as a time for sober reflection on the many exchanges of the day, the group came together the next morning to share their deliberations. The result was a set of fifteen "articles," which Winthrop copied into his journal. Their written form is richly appropriate; for the most part, these precepts focused on ways to forge the natural hotness of speech into the stronger, more lasting medium of authority. The group agreed, for example, that "the magistrates should (as far as might be) ripen their consultations beforehand, that their vote in public might" resound *"as the voice of God."* In private, the magistrates would strive to "be more familiar and open each to other, and more frequent in visitations" during which they might "in tenderness and love, admonish one another." But their public face—their public *voice*—would be slightly different. They would "appear more solemnly in public, with attendance, apparel, and open notice of their entrance into the court." They would postpone the discussion of contested issues until they were alone, or find ways to express any differences among them with new "modesty and due respect." They would "specially" note and punish "All contempts against the court, or any of the magistrates." And if disagreement among them was inevitable, they would stifle themselves, revealing their "distaste" for each others' opinions neither in word nor gesture. In short, they would learn to speak as fathers among brothers.[107]

The men assembled in Boston on that winter day had ample reason to hope that such carefully crafted voices of authority might indeed prevail with their equals; men such as Roger Williams would be more firmly and satisfyingly "dealt with" in the future. But what about the other members of the godly household? What about wives? For the most part, they had not raised their voices against the newborn polity. Few women had come before the General Court at all; virtually none had done so for crimes of the tongue.[108] There was as yet little reason to worry about an outbreak of scolding on the shores of Massachusetts. Indeed, there was every reason to suspect that Puritan women were content to occupy their rather ambiguous place: speaking to God, silent before men. John Cotton's wife was one such exemplar. Admitted as a covenanted member of Boston's First Church based on her own unique experience of divine grace, she nonetheless declined to "make open confession" of her conversion. This, her husband said, "was against the apostle's rule, and not fit for women's modesty." And so, as John Cotton had requested, the elders "examine[d] her in private," where she was "asked, if she did consent in the confession of faith made by her husband." A husband's "modest testimony of her," a goodwife's consenting nod: these were the only official words required of a female church member.[109] Her silence reminded those around her that submission to authority and awareness of hierarchy were cornerstones of the godly society.

But there were also competing imperatives in Puritan thought, and other ways that the combined experience of New World Babel and religious nonconformity might free the tongues of the faithful, including the female faithful. So, at least, Thomas Morton believed. When he wrote, in 1637, that the people in New England "are all publike preachers," he was referring not just to godly brethren. It appalled him to report that women, too, were included in the ranks of the professing faithful. With all the bathos of a modern-day tabloid journalist, he related the greatest scandal of all. "There is amongst these people a Deakonesse made of the sisters," he alleged, "that uses her guifts at home in an assembly of her sexe, by way of repetition, or exhortation: such is their practise."[110] It was indeed their practice at the beginning of 1637. But as the magistrates turned their ears away from disputes among the brethren and attended the words of wayward wives, the practice would not survive long.

THE MISGOVERNMENT
OF WOMAN'S TONGUE

Perhaps the cold came as a relief. The "extremity of weather" that marked the winter of 1637–1638—cold so deep that "the bay was all frozen up, save a little channel"—cost some in Massachusetts their fingers and toes, others their cattle, and still others their lives. Yet metaphorically, at least, the chill in the air must have offered a welcome antidote to the heated rhetoric that had engulfed Boston and surrounding villages during the preceding months: an epidemic of "foul errors," bred "secretly," that had "tainted" the colony's public discourse.[1] The austerity of a New England winter certainly provided the appropriate backdrop to the scene that unfolded in Boston's First Church that March, when the congregation's elders came together to freeze Anne Hutchinson out of their circle of godly fellowship. If Hutchinson could be driven beyond the Massachusetts pale, they reasoned, spring might indeed mark a rebirth for the colony, the inauguration of a new order embodied by new languages of deference and authority.

When Thomas Morton published his biting *New English Canaan* the year before, he had lampooned the clerics who presided over the spiritual life of Massachusetts Bay for tolerating the presence of "a Deakonesse" prone to unfettered "exhortation."[2] Now those same ministers could assure the anxious faithful—the godly multitude whose ears daily awaited good news from the Puritans' "city upon a hill"—that they did so no longer. After months of shouting matches with Hutchinson and like-minded dissenters, the elders had at last found the voice in which to deliver their censure. The assembly that gathered for the March 1638 hearings included such oratorical luminaries as John Cotton and Thomas Shepard, but it was Salem minister Hugh Peter who best articulated the essence of Hutchinson's sins. "You have stept out of your place," he told her, *"you have rather bine a Husband than a Wife and a preacher than a Hearer; and a Magistrate than a Subject."* The price of such breaches of social and verbal order, Pastor John Wilson went on to make clear, was excommunication, the spiritual analogue to the General Court's earlier verdict of banishment.[3]

To step out of one's place; the charge sounded clear enough and, by early modern standards, quite ominous. But what did it mean? As the verbal contests between godly "fathers" and their dissenting "brethren" that punctuated public life during the first years of the New England colonies remind us, the realities of constructing a new polity wreaked havoc with the very notion of people's rightful places. The expressive impulses of Puritan thought complicated matters still further. Who should speak, and who should listen? What did the voice of authority sound like? If the leaders of the nascent Bay Colony imagined hierarchy to be divinely ordained and hence immutable, the contours of this vaunted orderliness had remained, at least for a time, ill defined. Yet sometime between the arrival of the *Arabella* in the summer of 1630 and Anne Hutchinson's melodramatic downfall nearly eight years later, an act of translation occurred. Winthrop's blurry vision of order—his image of a body politic in which the "highe and eminent" presided over the "meane" and subject through a language of fraternal indulgence—acquired sharper focus.[4] "High" had been defined as a male ("husband"), public ("magistrate") speaker ("preacher"). And the godly woman— "wife," "subject," and "hearer"—had become the very symbol of what it meant to remain quietly below.

How had it turned out this way? How did lay silence, and especially female silence, become a cornerstone of social order in Massachusetts? John Wilson placed the blame squarely upon Hutchinson herself—more particularly, upon her speech. The "Misgovernment of this Woman's Tounge," he explained, "hath bine a greate Cause of this Disorder" and, he implied, of the new definitions of order articulated in response.[5] Although Wilson, one of Hutchinson's chief detractors, was hardly a sympathetic observer, his diagnosis rings true. Until Hutchinson's oratory began to captivate scores of listeners, the issue of female speech had attracted scant notice from the leaders of New England. None of the condemners brought before the colony's General Court in the early 1630s had been female, nor did preachers seem to feel a need to inveigh against women's fabled loquaciousness. Those few mentions of woman's words that do survive from New England's first years suggest that "the apostle's rule . . . for women's modesty" remained unchallenged in the public arena, while godly men conversed freely with their wives at home.[6] Then Hutchinson opened her mouth. Her words convulsed the whole of Boston, overspread much of the surrounding commonwealth, and eventually drew comment from dissenters in Old England as well as New.[7] Suddenly, it seemed, the Old World scold had gained a toehold across the Atlantic, right in the middle of an experiment in godly living that placed words and the Word at its very marrow.

Finding a way to govern Hutchinson's famously misgoverned tongue would prove, in the end, both a challenge and an opportunity for New England's leaders. The challenge was philosophical as well as practical, for it required outspoken dissenters to find a voice with which to quash spoken dissent. And therein lay the opportunity. Silencing Hutchinson offered New England's leaders a chance to define their own voices as the speech of authority by classifying the words of disorderly women as an archetype of social danger. In so doing, they reasserted the connection between ungoverned speech and unbridled women, a link that had seemed obvious in much early modern popular literature but had not figured prominently in English Puritan writings. The consequences, for female speech and for lay speech alike, would prove deep and enduring, as Ann Hibbens and other women who faced the colony's clerical and civil authorities in the early 1640s could have attested. Indeed, one could argue that the problem of female speech, made so spectacularly manifest by Anne Hutchinson, would never quite recede from the consciousness of New Englanders.

SOME PURITAN CHRONICLERS of the so-called Antinomian controversy would have us believe that dark clouds full of ominous foreboding announced Hutchinson's entrance upon the New World stage. One of Boston's faithful remembered hearing Hutchinson "slight the ministers of the word of God" even before she came out of England.[8] Others played up their recollections that she had "spake rashly" during the Atlantic crossing or, at the very least, had done so "at her landing" in Boston. And had not Hutchinson's loudly professed opinions on matters theological resulted in what Winthrop later called "some delay of her admission, when shee first desired fellowship with the Church of Boston"?[9] Possessed of the clairvoyance born of hindsight, Winthrop and others claimed that they had sensed danger from the very moment the Griffin discharged Hutchinson onto New England's shores, if not before.

However prescient the ministers wished to appear in retrospect, the record suggests a decidedly more ordinary opening act for Hutchinson's life in New England.[10] In his journal, Winthrop failed even to mention her presence among the two hundred souls who landed in Boston on 18 September 1634. Her shipboard murmuring, if he heard of it at all, failed to distract him from the other worries of the day: news that the Church of England intended to "regulate all plantations" overseas, and rumors of "threatening speeches" against the colony by sailors "aboard the bark of Maryland."[11] If what one preacher would later call the "corruptness and narrowness of [Hutchinson's] opinions" initially raised some hackles among the town's religious elite, the preachers' qualms were hardly insurmountable. On the first Sunday in November, just weeks after she had first glimpsed the "meanness" of New England, Hutchinson "gave full satisfaction" of her conversion to John Wilson and John Cotton and became a covenanted member of Boston's First Church, as her husband had done the week before.[12]

Church membership marked only one dimension of Hutchinson's "elect" status. Socially as well as spiritually, "Mister" and "Mistress" Hutchinson cut large figures in the tiny, rough-hewn village of Boston. William, whose success as a merchant made him virtual gentry by Massachusetts standards, quickly assumed a prominent role in local affairs. His various offices, including deputy to the General Court, magistrate for small causes, town selectman, and deacon of the First Church, were both measures and instruments of civic leadership. As befitted such an "honest and peaceable man of good estate," William Hutchinson rapidly assumed a public voice: voting, judging, allotting, praying.[13] Just as William (landowner, officeholder) exemplified the community's standards of maleness, Anne Hutchinson at first appeared to embody the best of Puritan womanhood. John Cotton remembered that "[a]t her first comming she was well respected and esteemed," by him and by others. "I heard," he recalled, that "shee did much good in our Town, in womans meeting [and] at Childbirth-Travells," where she was both "skilfull and helpfull."[14]

Ironically, Hutchinson's eloquent speech—the very fluency that would later occasion her downfall—initially endeared her to many, including Boston's leading men. When she began to hold prayer gatherings in her home during the week, Cotton praised her "good discourse with the women about their spiritual estates." So long as her guidance served only to clarify and amplify the doctrine preached by rightful ministers, the clergy welcomed her aid. Her *private* conferences," Cotton recalled, fit comfortably with woman's role as spiritual nurturer: her charge "to water the seeds *publikely* sowen." Hutchinson's work cultivating the faithful was helping the delicate plant of piety bear fruit in Massachusetts. Through her verbal persuasion, Cotton noted, "many of the women (and by them their husbands)" were "shaken and humbled," drawn into the fold. "All this was well," he said, "and suited . . . the publike Ministery."[15]

In short, although Hutchinson would come to sound extraordinarily unquiet—a woman possessed of what Winthrop termed "a very voluble tongue, more bold then a man"—she did not seem so at first.[16] To be sure, she voiced strong religious opinions, even assuming on occasion a prophetic tone, as she had done when she proclaimed that "she had . . . a sure word that England should be destroyed" for its popish corruptions.[17] But such modes of expression were very much in keeping with the tenor of the times. Lay "prophesying"—including, on occasion, *female* prophesying—had been fashionable among English nonconformists since Elizabeth's day.[18] By the mid-1630s, the well-known heat of Puritan rhet-

oric had grown hotter still, particularly in New England. Just a year before Hutchinson's arrival, Cotton himself had presided over Boston's first
revival, urging sinners to testify publicly to the work of grace upon them,
and indulging in what Winthrop praised as an edifying "exercise of
prophecy."[19] In this hothouse spiritual atmosphere, magistrates believed
that private exhortations—including those of Anne Hutchinson—could
only help to bring about the melting of hearts that was necessary to
God's work.

But by the spring of 1636, Hutchinson's role in the colony's public
discourse had begun to sound unseemly. Had the prophetess changed her
message or her tone? Had her audience grown too large? Had the boundaries of acceptable feminine speech contracted without her notice? The
ex post facto nature of the surviving evidence makes the roots of the
shift impossible to disentangle. What remains clear is that Hutchinson's
voice became intolerable, even to the ears of such early supporters as
John Cotton. As the balance of power between the prophetess's private
musings and the ministers' official homilies shifted, the clergy decried
what they perceived as the increasingly public nature of Hutchinson's
oratory. They also feared that Hutchinson's message dangerously suited
her medium, for the fact of her speaking combined with the content of
her utterances to particularly dangerous effect. Prizing the inner workings
of divine grace over adherence to religious or social covenants, Hutchinson and other "Antinomians" used their own public voices to urge the
godly to stop their ears against legitimate ministers. Nursed on a steady
diet of such heresies, the body social, a fragile organism in its vulnerable
infancy, had become critically ill. As Thomas Shepard put it, the "Flewentness of [Hutchinson's] Tonge and her Willingness to open herselfe
and to divulge her Opinions" had resulted in "the infection of many" in
Massachusetts.[20]

What was the chief symptom of this festering disease? How did this
plague make itself manifest? Many believed that disorderly speech was at
once cause and symptom of the colony's sickness. Even during the first
year of the controversy, before Hutchinson herself took center stage in
the drama, the turmoil in Boston's churches centered on words: questions, pronouncements, and prophecies that openly countered the minister's voice. The context of the dissenters' words—"at our publike Lectures," "in the open Assembly"—made it impossible to turn a deaf ear to
their slanders. Moreover, the opinionists' tone seemed calculated to sting.
"[W]e must kill them with the word of the Lord," Hutchinson's brother-
in-law, John Wheelwright, preached in January 1637. The impact of such
rhetoric upon the ministers and magistrates who were its targets was almost palpable. Thomas Weld likened the violent style of the "objections
made . . . against our doctrine delivered" to hearing "halfe a dozen Pis-
tols discharged at the face of the Preacher."[21] The dissenters' ungoverned
speech overwhelmed "the pure and perfect truths of Christ (delivered by
the mouth of his Ministers)," much as "the jarring sound of ratling

Drums" would drown out the "silver Trumpets" of "the Angels."[22] Such outbursts reminded the clergy that when their tone and content were sharp enough, mere words could rend the social fabric. What was called for in response was a forum in which to articulate anew the voice of ministerial control. When private persuasion through a series of letters and earnest conferences failed to silence the dissidents, the ministers convened a synod at Cambridge in August 1637.[23]

Assembled in council, the clergymen at last had a chance to reconstitute the language of uninterrupted authority. To counter the spontaneous cacophony of the Antinomians, the synod relied on what Thomas Weld called "plaine Syllogisticall dispute": a purposeful exchange of questions and responses based on the decorous forms of classical rhetoric. Having settled on "nine of the chiefest points," the ministers "disputed of them all *in order*, pro and con." Arguments were "framed" and rehearsed "[i]n the forenoones," "in the afternoones produced . . . in publick," and not followed until the next day by the written "answers" of "the Adversary."[24] The convulsive pistol shots of Antinomian discourse were pitted against the ritualized duel of a formal debate.

The synod's dialogues—elaborate set pieces performed before the lay public—had a practiced, incantatory, and, above all, controlled quality. Where dissenters "refused to forbear speech unseasonably," the ministers demonstrated the virtues of civil conversation among godly men. As if following a script, the pastors first listed the eighty-odd "erroneous opinions, which were spread in the country . . . next the unwholesome expressions; then the scriptures abused." After the inventory of opinions (variously classified as "blasphemous," "erroneous," or simply "unsafe") was read aloud and "condemned by the whole assembly," the ministers "subscribed their names" to a petition denouncing the heresies. Then, as was so often the case among Cambridge-trained clergy, "open dispute" unfolded among the brethren. But the tenor of their disagreement was so controlled and respectful that "the questions were soon determined," and "they came to understand each other better."[25]

Having "debated and resolved" each point of contention, the assembly issued a series of pronouncements: rules that would match the powerful extemporaneous shouting of the dissenters with the ministers' own verbal mastery. To protect the voice of clerical authority, they distinguished acceptable female speech—the kind heard in conventicles in which "women might meet (some few together) to pray and edify one another"—from the unacceptable practice of convening a larger "set assembly," conducted in "a prophetical way." The synod also articulated the distinction between the verbal prerogatives of preachers and those of their lay hearers. To the dissenters who had been known to "make much disturbance by public questions" after lectures, they proclaimed that a "private member might ask a question publicly, after sermon, for information" only if it were "very wisely and sparingly done, and that with leave of the elders."[26] As the assembly drew to a close in September, the clergy must have hoped that such rules would allow them to meet the dissenters on firmer ground, shielded behind a newly unified voice of religious orthodoxy. But although the synod succeeded in defining the kind of speech with which the colony's authorities would proceed against their enemies, it failed to silence the "opinionists."[27] The symptoms of the colony's ills persisted into the fall of 1637, when, at last, the court was ready to take on the woman whom Winthrop later called "the head of all this faction."[28] It is at this point that Hutchinson herself becomes prominent in the records.

The magistrates and ministers found a most felicitous target in Anne Hutchinson. Before she took center stage in the drama, the colony's enemies had been hard to pigeonhole. Of varying wealth, age, sex, and social status, the Antinomians were difficult to classify and, therefore, tough to shout down. But Hutchinson was different from a John Wheelwright or a Henry Vane. Rather than an intellectual and religious equal guilty of speaking out of turn, she was a woman completely "out of her place." Hutchinson thus presented the colony's leaders with an easy personification of evil: female evil. The dissenters' clamorous voices, filtered through Hutchinson's persona, could be reduced to the disorderly chatter of women and "tamed" accordingly.

By focusing on Hutchinson's role in the controversy, the authorities were able to insist that a dramatic breach of gender roles—especially of their verbal component—lay at the root of the Antinomian heresies. Hutchinson, it seemed to her judges, inverted every principle of Puritan womanhood. The "Vertuous" woman described by preacher Benjamin Wadsworth spoke "in a courteous, obliging, respectful manner. In her tongue was the law of kindness."[29] But Hutchinson's speech more closely resembled that of Eve than it did that of the silver-tongued matron from Proverbs. As Cotton Mather later noted, her capacity to "seduce women into [her] notions, and by these women . . . the husbands also" resembled the treacherous verbal skill of humanity's "first mother."[30] Like a serpent "sliding in the darke," Hutchinson used "cunning art"—in the form of her "bewitching" tongue—to "insinuate" her opinions into the Puritan Eden.[31] Thus instead of being the pious mother of a godly family, she became "the breeder and nourisher" of the errors identified by the Cambridge synod. The infectious opinions overrunning New England's churches were the living offspring of Hutchinson's "nimble wit and active spirit," sprung full-grown from her "very voluble tongue."[32]

Indeed, Hutchinson's "haughty and fierce" verbal style made her more than a depraved nurturer. She was "more bold then a man," father (as well as mother) to a corrupt family of deluded believers.[33] In a bizarre inversion of the generative act, Hutchinson had used "the Flewentness of her Tonge," Thomas Shepard believed, "to sowe her seed in us." Her verbal openness suggested, by analogy, sexual licentiousness. In light of her propensity for overly free speech, John Cotton noted, it would hardly have been surprising to find Hutchinson practicing free love: the "pro-

miscuus and filthie cominge togeather of men and Woemen without Distinction or Relation of Marriage."[34] William Hutchinson—already symbolically unmanned by his wife's overbearing speech—would have been
in no position to reject a more literal cuckolding. Anne Hutchinson's
outspokenness had rendered him virtually impotent, "a man of a very
mild temper and weak parts . . . wholly guided by his wife."[35] Viewed
through early modern gender categories, Anne Hutchinson was indeed
what Hugh Peter had claimed: more "a Husband than a Wife."

At its most elemental level, then, Hutchinson's transgression of New
England's gender-speech order was an assault on family hierarchy. But, as
the family analogy for social relations predicted, her offense did not stop
there. Hutchinson's voice reached beyond her household into the collective life of the community. John Cotton reminded her that God had
intended her rhetorical "gifts" to be used solely "to instruct [her] Children and Servants and to be helpfull to [her] husband in the Government of the famely."[36] But Hutchinson apparently found this stage too
small for her talents. Unwilling simply to play husband to her inverted
household, she had cast herself as a preacher to the wayward churches of
New England. In scale and in spirit, her prayer meetings—biweekly ses-
sions that had come to include scores of listeners of both sexes—vied
against the formal services held in the colony's meetinghouses for the
attention of the faithful. "[Y]our Ministry is publicke," Winthrop commented derisively.[37]

Indeed, Hutchinson's entire discursive posture had come to resemble
that of the Puritan minister. As a laywoman, her part should have been
limited to "search[ing] the Scriptures" for evidence "confirming . . . the
truths delivered" in lectures. Instead, Hutchinson authored her own
truths. Not content merely to echo the texts of male authority (either
Scripture or the ministers' sermons), "shee would comment upon the
Doctrines, and interpret all passages at her pleasure, and expound dark
places of Scripture," twisting "whatsoever the Letter held forth . . . to
make it serve her turn."[38] Opening, declaring, correcting; commenting,
interpreting, expounding—she aped the accomplished oratory of the
learned man in "a posture of Preaching to a multitude." Her followers
praised her "able Tongue," and hailed her as a "Woman that Preaches
better Gospell then any of your black-coates that have been at the Nin-
neversity." But such interpretive authority voiced by a woman, as Winthrop and others knew, could only "weaken the Word of the Lord in the
mouth of his Ministers."[39] The mere fact of her "teaching" placed her
decidedly outside the boundaries of feminine piety.

The substance of these unwomanly lectures, Hutchinson's doctrine,
amplified her challenge to the minister's exclusive right to interpret
Scripture. In her trials, Hutchinson made clear that the only voice to
which she conceded mastery was the direct Word of God—a "voyce unto
the Soule, meerely immediate." No minister, nor even Scripture, could
come between the mouth of God and the ears of the faithful. The clergy's

weekly attempts to intercede between believers and the Word, Hutchinson convinced her followers, smacked of despised "legalism." She contended (so her judges said) that "the Law, and the Preaching of it is of no use at all, to drive a man to Christ." In fact, she argued, "[a]ll verball Covenants, or Covenants expressed in words, as Church Covenants, vowes, &c. are Covenants of workes."[40] Like a magistrate, Hutchinson passed sentence on the preachers whom she dismissed as legalists, effectively claiming that only she (or God himself) could pronounce the Word her followers should live by. "[S]urely had this Sect gone on awhile," one skeptic mused, "they would have made a new Bible."[41] Indeed, both the role of the Bible as the governing narrative of New England and the part played by Puritan ministers as its authorized "translators" seemed in jeopardy when Hutchinson appeared before the General Court in November 1637.

Instead of composing a new gospel, however, Hutchinson authored her own downfall. To silence this "misgoverned" female tongue, the authorities needed Hutchinson's cooperation. In order for "her owne mouth" to "deliver her into the power of the Court," it was essential that she speak during her trials in the commanding public style that her judges claimed she used so freely in her daily life. Hutchinson obliged the judges with a verbal display that uncovered the full extent of the threat her voice posed to New England's social order. In their subsequent accounts of the proceedings, the presiding magistrates and ministers underscored a particular facet of her speech during the trials: the prophetic tone in which she asserted that God spoke directly to and, more dangerous, through her. The judges and subsequent chroniclers alike have construed Hutchinson's admission that she had experienced "immediate revelation . . . the voice of [God's] own spirit to my soul," as the fatal flaw in her testimony. Certainly her claim to converse directly with God was unseemly, granting her the power to "distinguish between the voice" of a godly minister and "the voice of antichrist," and thus placing her among the ranks of Abraham, Daniel, and Paul. Winthrop argued that the followers of such a mystic would "look for revelations" and, therefore, would not consider themselves "bound to the ministry of the word" or be "subject to controll." It was Hutchinson's direct line to God, he claimed, that forced the court to cast her out.[42]

Perhaps Hutchinson was, in fact, the visionary that Winthrop and others made her out to be. Listening to God's voice, she may indeed have "walked by such a rule as cannot stand with the peace of any State." But there can be little doubt that classifying her verbal style as "prophetic" offered the judges a simple way out of a knotty problem, a convenient category through which to define and thus to silence Hutchinson's restless tongue. By representing Hutchinson's speech as ranting "above reason," the authorities mustered "proofe sufficient to proceed against her" without having to acknowledge the dark underside of her verbal threat: the way in which her words exposed the potential for disorder inherent in the Puritans' logocentric universe.[43] For did not all Puritans prize the Word above its preachers and thus, to some degree, elevate grace over laws? Casting Hutchinson as an unbridled prophetess rather than as a godly nonconformist, the magistrates confined her within a long (and firmly defunct) tradition of extemporaneous lay preaching in which inspiration counted more than intellect. Interpreted as prophetic, Hutchinson's voice could be tailored to popular notions of feminine passivity, irrationality, and emotional excess.[44]

But did Hutchinson fit the bill? The records of her trials suggest that Hutchinson's judges may have inflated the prophetic aspect of her self-presentation. Had she truly appropriated the Old Testament voice of Joel, justifying her ministry by telling the magistrates, "It is said, [']I will poure my Spirit upon your Daughters, and they shall prophesie, &c.['] If God give mee a gift of Prophecy, I may use it"? Winthrop recalled—or reconstructed—the exchange in his published post mortem of the Antinomians' "ruine." Yet the ostensible transcript of Hutchinson's civil trial omits the episode.[45] Did this prophetic voice issue from Hutchinson's "owne mouth"? Or did it derive instead from popular notions of women's speech, stereotypes that conveniently allowed Hutchinson's judges to focus on female failings and thus to ignore the obvious connection between too-free speaking and Puritan thought?

The modern reader of the trial proceedings finds other facets of Hutchinson's ungoverned speech that may have been more threatening to the state's vaunted peace than were her "bottomlesse revelations." Though they may have heard outbursts of visionary "railing," the magistrates and church elders confronted, for the most part, a woman whose verbal style closely resembled their own "syllogisticall" approach.[46] With wit and rhetorical flourish, she matched her judges verse for biblical verse, rule for rule, law for law. "I hear no things laid to my charge. . . . Name one Sir," she challenged. "What law have I broken?" she demanded, and "In what particular?" Told that her sympathy for the dissenters transgressed the "Law of God and of the State," Hutchinson responded by asking, "What breach of law is that Sir?" And then, confronted by Thomas Dudley's recollections of her "strange opinions," she countered, "I pray Sir prove it that I said [the ministers] preached nothing but a covenant of works. . . . Prove this then Sir that you say I said."[47] Such obvious skill in the men's game of verbal thrust-and-parry was arguably more damning than Hutchinson's sometime prophetic mode.

Hutchinson pressed on, lawyer-like, leaving her examiners on the ropes. An exasperated Winthrop countered with his famous retort: "We do not mean to discourse with those of your sex." Yet as he must have known, Hutchinson was beating them at their own game, using a male discursive style, not a female one. She had forced the magistrates to engage her as if the proceedings were a dialogue between equals. "Do you think it not lawful for me to teach women"? she taunted. Then "why do you call me to teach the court?" Winthrop blustered defensively in response: "I have brought more arguments than you have." Yet even he had to acknowledge her skill with words. "It is well discerned to the court," he quipped, "that Mrs. Hutchinson can tell when to speak and when to hold her tongue." Coming as it did after a lengthy display of what Cotton referred to as her gift for "ready utterance," Hutchinson's heretical claim of immediate revelation was a godsend to her judges. With their heads held high, they could dismiss this deft rhetorician as a babbling woman.[48]

The "law" Hutchinson had broken, Winthrop noted, was "the fifth commandment," the sacred text ordaining the submission of all members of the civil and religious polity to their rightful "parents." By speaking against her metaphorical "fathers" in the church, she had "stirred up [her] hearers to take up arms against" their rulers.[49] The price for this verbal rebellion against family, church, and commonwealth was nothing short of expulsion from the colony. Having infected the godly with her persuasive speech, she was commanded by the pastor *as a Leper to withdraw . . . out of the Congregation.*"[50] Although banishment was the court's sentence, enforced silence was the metamessage of the judgment. "*Say no more,*" Winthrop ordered her, confident at last that his decree might bridle her tongue.[51]

ANN HIBBENS AND her husband, William, like Anne and William Hutchinson, had been inspired by John Cotton's preaching in Lincolnshire. They joined their minister in Boston, Massachusetts, late in 1638. The town that greeted the Hibbenses that winter was, in many respects, a different place from the hamlet Anne Hutchinson had shaken to its foundations. As a physical entity, Boston no longer seemed quite so rickety; its population, of nearly fourteen hundred English inhabitants, had more than tripled since Hutchinson's arrival.[52] In social terms, too, the town had undergone a period of painful growth. The Antinomian challenge had schooled the ruling elite in the importance—and the fragility—of hierarchy, exposing the menace of heterodox opinions, particularly when espoused by those who made words into weapons. After 1638, it was inevitable that the speech of rebellious citizens, especially of disorderly women, would be interpreted in light of Anne Hutchinson.

Had Ann Hibbens ever heard Hutchinson prophesy? Perhaps the two had been acquainted in Boston, England. Although the sparse records of Hibbens's life in Massachusetts never mention the Antinomian episode, it is impossible that she did not know of the rebellion. Hibbens and her husband arrived in New England just months after Hutchinson left for Rhode Island, as details of the controversy were engrossing audiences on both sides of the Atlantic.[53] Aftershocks of the Antinomian turmoil continued to rattle Boston, where outbursts from a few intractable "opinionists" occasionally jolted both church and commonwealth. In September 1639, less than a month before the Hibbenses joined the First

Church, the congregation excommunicated a widow for "speaking evill of Authority" by defending Hutchinson "in open Court." Despite efforts to quash debate on the subject, the topic of whether or not Hutchinson had "deserved the Censure which was putt upon her" had yet to recede from public consciousness.[54] Dwelling in a town of fewer than fifteen hundred English folk and belonging to a church that covenanted under four hundred saints, Ann Hibbens must have heard talk of the stain Hutchinson's words and actions had left on Puritan womanhood. And, if the local rumor mill failed to disclose any details of the case, Hibbens's husband could have filled in the gaps, sharing his firsthand impressions of the infamous Jezebel after visiting the exiles as an emissary of the church in 1640.[55] By reputation if not by sight and sound, Ann Hibbens knew Anne Hutchinson well.

Hibbens's own "common fame" would grow similarly in the small world of mid-seventeenth-century Boston. But in comparison with Hutchinson's ordeal, her story leaves a faint impression on the historical record. In fact, only the merest outlines of her life and death in Massachusetts would survive but for the assiduous note-taking of Robert Keayne, whose journal of proceedings at the First Church captures both Hibbens's voice and the words the elders used to censure her.[56] Where Hutchinson's case spawned a veritable publishing industry, few scholars have rushed to follow the colony's authorities in judging and interpreting Hibbens's challenge.[57] Read against the backdrop of Hutchinson's spectacular misdeeds, Hibbens's tale appears ordinary: a commonplace story spun out in rich detail because of the historical accident of Keayne's surviving minutes. Ann Hibbens's was, quite simply, an unquiet female voice heard in Hutchinson's wake, interpreted by the colony's authorities after the conceptual links between gender, speech, and social order had been defined in reaction to the leader of the Antinomians.

Ann Hibbens's story shared with Anne Hutchinson's an optimistic beginning. The early days of the Hibbenses' lives in the New World seemed fraught with promise. Their wealth placed the family, much like the Hutchinsons, among Boston's elite. William Hibbens quickly assembled the kind of public profile appropriate to his social station. Described as a "gentleman" upon his admission to the First Church, he soon became a magistrate and an elder of the congregation. Indeed, despite the fate of his wife, the community's respect for William Hibbens seems only to have increased over the course of his life. He was called upon frequently to serve as an assistant on court days, and to represent the church or colony on important missions at home and overseas.[58] For William Hibbens, one of the town's ruling men, notoriety meant acclaim; his voice was meant to be heard. His word—in court, in the church, presumably in everyday encounters—became increasingly valuable in Boston. What is less clear is the extent to which Hibbens's speech counted in that most elemental locus of society: his own household.

During those first years, Ann Hibbens also came to be known for the power of her speech. But as Hutchinson had made only too clear, for a woman such prominence often meant infamy rather than esteem. Ann Hibbens lived (and spoke) under a different set of expectations from those that governed her husband's tongue. She occupied a liminal position in the community's speech-status hierarchy, expected to articulate both the social elevation of her wealth and the "natural" submission of her gender. Such women were, as one widely read authority on the family instructed, "superiors to some" but "inferiours to others." The Puritan gentlewoman would do well to keep in mind the mantra William Gouge had commended to all godly folk: *"I have under me, and am under authority."* [59] Ann Hibbens did not. Her insistent verbalizing blurred these overlapping lines of mastery and deference until the boundaries between them were all but erased. Her appearances before the First Church in the fall and winter of 1640–1641 were the culmination of months of bickering in which she had pitted her word against the reputation of several men in the congregation—men who, she mistakenly thought, were "under" her.

At the beginning of this lengthy dispute, Hibbens may well have been speaking in a way that befitted her gender role. Many Puritan commentators saw marriage as a true, if unequal, partnership in which both husband and wife had speaking parts to play.[60] Perhaps it was a belief in the shared burdens of the marital estate that inspired William Hibbens to "give [his] wife Leave" to engage some carpenters (or "joiners") to work on the Hibbens home. It fell within her purview, he said, "to agre with the Joyner, & to order the bussines with him as she thought good." Acting within the verbal compass of the "deputy husband," Ann Hibbens contracted with Goodman Crabtree and his men. Soon after, however, the household's peace was shaken when some "difference did arise about the worke."[61] And, although her presence in discussions about contracts and household affairs was, in itself, unexceptional, Ann Hibbens's combative verbal style in resolving these points of "difference" transgressed the boundaries of proper female speech and, eventually, landed her before the elders.

The problem began when Crabtree and his crew concluded that "the worke was to[o] much for the price." Acting every inch the boss, Ann Hibbens refused to accept this assessment and accused Crabtree of "breach of his promis, and neglectinge his worke," and called for other bids. Restlessly, the elders said, she had "sent from workman to workman & from one to another to vew the worke & to [a]prayse" the cost. Arbitrators had tried to resolve the matter in what Brother Davis estimated to have been "at least 20 or 40 severall meetinges." When these efforts, too, came to naught, Ann Hibbens raised the stakes, charging that the various joiners had colluded in "a Confederacy" to command a higher price than the job merited. She spread the allegation far and wide, "publishinge it all abroad to ministers, magistrats, Naighbors & others," eventually drawing such lofty men as John Winthrop into the fray. Like the gadding woman condemned in Scripture, Hibbens had "gone from person to person, from House to House, & from place to place" to vent her "slanders & evell Reports." Certainly, William Hibbens had "given leave" for his wife to "agree" with the joiners. But Ann Hibbens had burst the limits of this verbal license with her public and confrontational—indeed, *masculine*—style of talking. She had not merely agreed, but had fiercely negotiated: insisting that it was necessary to "recken" and "Bargayne" with the men, impatiently "publishing" her own viewpoint. The church elders termed her manner "unquiet," referring to both her troubled spirit and her unbridled tongue. Was it any wonder that they felt "much unsatisfied with [her] discourse"?[62]

Hibbens's verbal style indeed appears to have been somewhat highhanded. Frequently changing her mind about the details of the job, she addressed the workmen in a manner the elders deemed "Impertinent," "unprofitable," and "suspitious"; "proud & Contemptius & unreverent." In short, John Wilson noted, Hibbens had failed to follow the rule of Christian charity in her speech: she had "used such speeches to . . . Brother Davis & other workmen, whan *thay would not Speake as you doe.*"[63] Wilson must have found it ironic: she—a woman!—had spoken to these godly men in a manner they would hesitate to use with her. She spoke (to use Gouge's language) as if they fell "under" her authority, failing to recognize that she—by virtue of gender, despite her lofty social status—belonged under theirs. Instead, she had passed sentence on them, warning that the very "timber of the Ro[o]me would Crye out for Judgment agaynst" their sins.[64] But, as the magistrates had been forced to remind Anne Hutchinson, they were her judges, not she theirs. Thus she was brought before the elders to "give Satisfaction" to those her words had offended and to the community whose peace she had disrupted. To ensure that she would "stir no more in it," indeed, that she would *"speake no mor,"* was the elders' expressed goal.[65]

Hibbens's appearance before the congregation on the afternoon of 13 September 1640 found her uncharacteristically reticent. It could not have escaped her notice that the men authorized to judge her mortal soul included many of those who had condemned Anne Hutchinson little more than two years before. So, too, Wilson, Cotton, Winthrop, Weld, and Shepard could hardly have helped recalling their experience with Hutchinson's "misgoverned" tongue as they evaluated Hibbens's sins. Was it out of respect for the clergy's increasingly well defined notion of proper feminine speech that Hibbens answered the charges against her with stony silence? The elders thought not. Brothers Penn and Button heard her stillness as a mute expression of "Contempt" and "disrespect," while John Wilson wondered if "some bodely infirmetie is upon her." One man in the congregation suggested, more generously, that Hibbens might not be "resolved yet that it is Lawfull for her to speke in the church." But others deemed this improbable; her sudden "scruple" about "the Lawfullnes of a womans Spekinge in the church" appeared ironic at the very least. Was she too decorous to speak, or merely too shrewd—concerned that it might "be a snare to her to be put to give a presant Answr"? Did a hint of sarcasm color John Cotton's voice when he assured her that it was fully permissible for her to speak when spoken to? Unmoved by her feminine reticence, the elders asked her to "give answr to the church" in tones of "reverence and submission."[66] In short, Hibbens was commanded (as Hutchinson had been) to speak like a penitent Christian, a pose defined by the kindly tongue of the virtuous woman.

Ann Hibbens might more closely have approximated the obligatory tone of reverence and submission had she been allowed to "expresse [her]selfe in wrightinge," as she requested. Placing distance between her thoughts and her words, the act of writing her responses might have saved her from costly mistakes. Perhaps it was for this reason that Cotton proclaimed the "practice of wrightinge" to be "uncouth in the church": at odds with the spontaneous verbal impulses of Puritanism.[67] Speech—less fettered, less mediated than writing—was a truer window into one's conscience. Certainly it seemed to be so in Hibbens's case. For no sooner had she opened her mouth than she damned herself with the same disputatious style Anne Hutchinson had earlier used. Her efforts at confession, the elders argued, were "Constrayned & not free." Indeed, Hibbens's attempt at an apology sounds more like the doublespeak of a modern-day politician than the "ingenious" admission of shame the congregation had hoped for. She would concede only that "thear was sinne one both p[ar]ts," hers and the joiners'. Though she "desier[ed] to be humbled" for the "mistake" of her carriage, Hibbens emphasized that "thear was no sinn intended," only "such an apearance of Evell as might give offence to others." Thus she was "hartely sorrow"—for the false impressions others had drawn from her tone rather than for any "Evell" she saw in herself. "I cannot accuse my selfe of any Lye," she demurred, "whan I did speake it, I did thinke it to be soe as than I spake."[68]

The elders were quick to point out that there was a paradigm of penitent discourse in their midst, one Ann Hibbens would do well to imitate. Why, they wondered, did she fail to follow the lead of her husband, whose "meeknes of spirit in humblinge him selfe" served as a veritable model of the voice of Christian charity? Almost cringingly, William Hibbens apologized at length for "Callinge one of my Bretheren Sir insteed of Brother," an offense even the pastor considered "soe small a matter" that "fewe or none in the Congregation" had even noticed it. Throughout the proceedings against his wife, Hibbens spoke rarely and, when he did, always respectfully. Where his wife interjected brazenly, William Hibbens quietly begged indulgence: "I desier to speake one thinge"; "I humbly crave Leave to speake a word." Although fearful for his wife, he placed the community's need to expiate sin above his personal happiness. When he testified, he promised to "Lay asside the other relation" of husband to wife "and speake as a Brother." Indeed, so eager was Hibbens "not to hinder the church in thear proseedinges" against his spouse that he appeared almost "sorry" to "have any ocasion to speake" on her be-half.[69] William Hibbens knew that even among "brothers," a command-ing tongue governed best when shrouded in the veil of Christian mod-esty.

Yet the congregation may have wondered whether William Hibbens's speech was not, in fact, too timorous, for he was clearly "overmatched" by his wife's emphatic words. Did this display of role inversion before the elders also speak volumes about the Hibbenses' life at home? As Ann Hibbens continued to split hairs about the nature of her sin, the elders began to articulate the gendered character of her offense. The minutiae of her dispute with the carpenters receded to the background as the pro-ceedings came to focus upon her unwomanly demeanor: her fault in "Transgressinge the Rule of the Apostell in usurpinge Authoritie over him whom god hath made her Head and Husband."[70] She led where she should have followed, "takeinge the power & Authoriti wch god hath given to him out of his handes," comporting herself "as if she wear able to manage it better." The elders of the First Church treated the verbal authority Ann Hibbens claimed within her marriage as "a playne breach" of Pauline prescription. By "exaltinge [her] Selfe agaynst [her] guide & Head" when she "should have submitted" to his word, they said, she "doth . . . make a wispe" of William Hibbens. His weakness was her fault, the result of her total disregard for the community's emerging no-tions of social and linguistic order. On 20 September, the pastor admon-ished her for ignoring his counsel in church as she had rejected her husband's at home.[71] When he pronounced the sentence of admonition, Wilson offered Hibbens a simple choice: either she could "be quiet" (in her marriage as in the commonwealth) or, should she "refuse soe to doe," she could endure the "further destruction" of her "unmortified flesh" and the "p[er]dition of [her] soule."[72]

By the time the elders reopened the matter in March 1641, Ann Hib-bens had been given nearly five months to ponder the alternatives and accept the wisdom of the pastor's words. In the first moments of this second hearing, the period of contemplation seemed to have served its purpose. Hibbens held her tongue in check, asking that her husband be permitted to speak for her because, she suggested, "he will be better herd" (which seems likely) and "Cane better Expresse my thoughts" (which is doubtful). William's calm voice helped the assembly to arrive quickly at some resolution of the dispute with the joiners. But, Cotton noted, "an-other poynt" remained troubling: the "subjection" Ann Hibbens owed her husband, a duty she had cast aside "as if [she] had more witt & Care" than he.[73]

As if these renewed allegations of unfeminine deportment triggered a relapse, Ann Hibbens responded defiantly, reasserting her claims against the joiners and her right to level such charges. Stating that her husband "did give [her] Leave" to pursue the matter, she harped on the fine points of the dispute rather than addressing the broader issue of her shameless and unwomanly intransigence. Cotton challenged her to "speke playnly to the poynt . . . that you wear uncharitable *in thinkinge & speakinge.*" Instead, Hibbens dared the elders to recall her exact words. "I doe not remember that I did use any such wordes," she demurred. "I am willinge to suspect my owne selfe," but "I doe not remember that I spake the wordes." Ignoring repeated attempts to steer her toward appropriate responses—the "signe[s] of sorrow & brokenes of spirit" that would restore the subordination of hearer to preacher, subject to magistrate, and wife to husband—she continued to haggle over the phrasing of past arguments.[74]

Her audience found the tone of her replies "straynge & intollerable," "very Leane, & thin, & poore, & sparinge." Her voluble insistence upon her own version of events over the objections of such exalted authorities as "our Honored Magistrate mr winthrop" appeared nothing short of "I[n]corigable." Hibbens's "many hard expressions" reminded the elders that the heart of the matter remained "her want of wivelike subjection." And, it seemed, she was proud to admit as much. Drawing a rule from God's words to Abraham, she asserted that "a man should harken to the Counsell of his wife." The elders saw this misguided belief that woman's voice should prevail in marriage—that "the Husband must harken to his wife . . . not the wife to the Husband"—as the wellspring of all of Hibbens's sins. Her "counsel" had made "a cipher of her Husba[n]d & his Authoritie," they noted. The ministers did not need to point out that their authority, too, was threatened by her willful demeanor.[75]

"I desier to be sorrowfull," Hibbens told the congregation. But, to the end, she failed to muster the submissive tone of remorse. "Repentance," Brother Penn noted, "is not the intent of her speech." Her atonement was expressed in the subjunctive: "if I should doe soe, it wear a greate sine." Charged with lying to the church, she took a guarded, "syllogisticall" tack: "I doe not remember that I speake as thay accuse me or with that meaninge as thay gather, but if thay say soe, I must Submitt to it, becaus I Canot disprove them." Reminded that she had "transgresse[d] the will of her Husband," she countered again: "My Husband did give me Leave."[76]

But the elders knew differently. There could be no "leave," no permission that would entitle a woman to speak as Ann Hibbens had spoken. She had "usurped" when "she should have obayed." Through the power of her unruly tongue, she had made herself "Eminent." She had "exalted her owne witt & will & way above" her husband's, even above the word of the ministers and magistrates. Indeed, she had "thrust [her]selfe into gods Throne & seate," presuming to judge "the harts of men." This, Cotton maintained, was "gods peculiar Prerogative." Yet the prerogative was not God's alone; ruling men (including Cotton himself) were empowered to speak with analogous authority. It was just such a voice that the elders used to "Cast [Hibbens] out from that societie" whose rules she had shown "soe slight an Esteme of."[77]

As had been the case with Anne Hutchinson, John Wilson authored the end of Ann Hibbens's tale. The congregation would once again be made aware of the terror that awaited a woman who, "agaynst Natuer," followed "the evell example of diverse other wifes" (perhaps Hutchinson herself?) instead of "the Rule of the Apostle." Such unruly women, the elders remembered from 1638, occasioned "unquietnes [in] the famely" and, by analogy, brought disorder to the church and commonwealth. Conscious of the "daynger" that "many hath [already] bine infected" by her noxious speech, the elders were eager to excise the "Leprosie" in their midst. Thus Wilson excommunicated Hibbens for her "want of subjection to soe wise & discrete a Hed . . . wch god hath set to be your guide, whose Counsell you should have followed." He denounced a marriage turned upside down, a perverted union in which the wife dared to speak as if her husband were "a Nobody, as if his wisdom wear not to be compared to" hers.[78] Because she "continued Impenitent and obstinate . . . not hearkning to her husband at home; nor to the brethren and sisters in private, noe nor yet to the whole Church in Publique," the pastor delivered her soul to Satan.[79]

BOTH ANNE HUTCHINSON and Ann Hibbens were thus cast out, sentenced in effect (as Winthrop had ordered) to "say no more." Their silence was designed to serve as a model, an object lesson for all women who might step—or speak—out of their places in the nascent Puritan society. But in the near term, at least, the colony's leaders had trouble making their verdicts stick. Although both women eventually died for their transgressions, each remained, in her own way, gallingly "unquiet."

Anne Hutchinson lived in exile, first in Rhode Island and then in present-day Westchester County, New York, until she was killed in an Indian attack in 1643. Although the authorities drove her far from the fellowship of the First Church, Hutchinson continued to rankle like a thorn in the side of the godly. The Boston elders who solicited news of their "wandringe sheepe" in 1640 dared to hope she had at last accepted "submission or subjection to the church." But Hutchinson told the church's emissaries (whose number included William Hibbens) that she "knew no church" in Boston. The elders sought evidence that she and her followers "were in Covenant with us as a wife to the Husband." But here, too, their hopes were frustrated. Asked if he were "tide to [the church] by our covenant," William Hutchinson replied that he was "more nearly tied to his wife than to the church." Like a wife subject to the will of her husband, William Hutchinson followed Anne's lead.[80] Given the inverted loyalties of the Hutchinson household, was it any wonder, as Winthrop wrote, that Anne Hutchinson's persuasive voice "continued to breed disturbance," even at great remove? To him, it seemed unsurprising—even divinely just—when the perverted mother of such misplaced loyalties "was delivered of a monstrous birth." News of this malformed fetus, along with rumors of the "great admiration" Hutchinson's preaching continued to inspire, prompted what Winthrop referred to as strong "suspicion of witchcraft." Her role as false prophet, pretended magistrate, and ersatz husband had transformed Hutchinson into that ultimate symbol of female power and perversity: the witch.[81]

For Ann Hibbens, too, the years following her excommunication were anything but quiet. Like Anne Hutchinson, Hibbens continued to stand out in her community because of her ungoverned speech. But where Hutchinson inspired acolytes, Hibbens found only enemies. Known as a "discontented" woman "of hard favour and turbulent passion," she apparently continued to flout the community's demand that women bridle their tongues in public, choosing instead to vent her "natural crabbedness." While he lived, William Hibbens's acknowledged eminence protected his wife. But almost immediately after his death in 1654, Ann Hibbens was presented to the Court of Assistants on suspicion of witchcraft. This time, it was ordinary men and women rather than the colony's ruling elite who decried her "quarrelsome" tongue. First Church minister John Norton, who opposed the proceedings against Hibbens, was mortified that such a gentlewoman would be "hanged for a witch, only for having more wit than her neighbours." But although the authorities tried to prevent her execution, their efforts in Hibbens's and Hutchinson's earlier trials to define woman's "wit"—to articulate the boundaries of proper female speech—can only have helped to transform Hibbens from scold to witch. In May 1656, the General Court was forced to accept the jury's second guilty verdict and convict Hibbens of witchcraft, condemning her "to hang till she was dead" on 19 June.[82]

The deaths of Hibbens and Hutchinson stilled their tongues but failed to end their stories. For the unbridled words of these two "verye dayngerous" women continued to reverberate, echoing beyond the narrow confines of their individual histories. Together, they bequeathed an important legacy to the white inhabitants of Massachusetts Bay: a tangle of messages about the links between gender, speech, and authority that New Englanders would spend years trying to unravel. What had it all meant?

In many respects, the stories of Ann Hibbens and Anne Hutchinson shared a moral. Both were elite women who could boast far greater than average status, wealth, and learning.[83] Both translated their fluency with the spoken and written word into a defiant verbal posture that represented, as Hugh Peter had said, a stepping out of place. As New England struggled to define the kinds of authority appropriate to a community of saints, it came to seem vitally important that such elevated matrons comport themselves as gentlewomen: "mistresses" of a circumscribed domain who remained subject to their husbands and their metaphorical "fathers" in church and commonwealth. Instead, Hutchinson and Hibbens spoke as if the prerogatives of status were genderless.

And so, despite the unrelated issues under scrutiny in each case, such breaches of gender norms became central to both trials. Certainly Hutchinson's judges were eager to ferret out the doctrinal "errors" circulating in their midst. When many of the same men were called to act as arbiters of Hibbens's fate, they were deeply concerned with just prices and fair dealing. But almost in spite of themselves, the authorities came to focus on expectations of feminine demeanor as much as upon heresy or haggling.[84] To dispute with Hutchinson was to be forced to "discourse with those of her sex." To wrangle with Hibbens was to withstand the "hard expressions" of a woman who had made herself wrongfully "eminent." To "reduce" these offenders was to articulate a voice of magisterial and ministerial authority against feminine silence. For the havoc these voluble women had wrought made clear that a godly society hinged on maintaining both gender order *and* linguistic order. Both of them had been accused of unmanning their mates in the same very particular fashion: not (as women were fabled to do) by taking up lovers, liquor, or rolling pins, but by speaking commandingly. *Words* were the weapons that had turned the Hibbens and Hutchinson marriages upside down, reducing once-powerful husbands to "wisps," "ciphers"—to men of "weak parts." In Hibbens's as in Hutchinson's case, the ability of heated language to alter the balance of power between husband and wife (and thus between preacher and hearer, magistrate and subject) was made plain to all hearers.

Yet for all the elements common to their cases, Hutchinson and Hibbens had each posed a unique threat to her community. If the likeness of the two cases demonstrated to the leaders of Massachusetts that spelling out the relationship between gender, language, and authority was vital to the colony's survival, the singularity of each trial revealed that speech was capable of attacking the social order on more than one front. Both cases probed the relationship between women's voices and their ordained subjection and thus forced civil and clerical authorities to articulate the limits governing public discourse. But Hutchinson and Hibbens advanced different—and, in some ways, competing—definitions of what constituted overly free public speech.

Hutchinson's words created the discord of an old voice in a new world.[85] Despite her sometime mastery of the techniques of "syllogisticall" debate, what the authorities heard from her was an archaic version of feminine religious discourse: the irrational power of prophecy. Hutchinson's claim to speak to and through God forced the colony's leaders to reconsider the tradition of worship in "conventicles"—the private prayer groups used, at least since Elizabethan times, to fortify the Word dispensed from the pulpit. In dissident English churches, lay prophecy and ministers' sermons had coexisted symbiotically, even harmoniously. But as Hutchinson's insistent voice made clear, amateur preaching could sound positively cacophonous in New England, where the Puritan sermon was the language of state power rather than an oppositional discourse. Hutchinson's "lectures" rivaled the ministers' attempts to style themselves as the only group fluent in this language.[86] Projected against the linguistic priorities of the "New England Way," her speech sounded more diabolical than divinely inspired. In England, Hutchinson's claim that "the mouth of the Lord hath spoken it" might have seemed plausible, even stirring. In New England, it began to sound like the devil's own voice.[87]

Of course, extemporaneous prophecy had never been the exclusive province of women. Certainly, the clergy's reactions to Hutchinson had far-reaching implications for would-be lay "preachers" of either sex. But the combination of gender and prophetic speech placed Hutchinson and other women like her beyond the pale, while men who committed similar transgressions could return to the fold. Consider, for example, the case of John Wheelwright, Hutchinson's brother-in-law and chief supporter. Though he was banished in 1637 for challenging the colony's ministers in his famous fast-day sermon, many avenues of expression—official as well as private—remained open to him. An epistolary dialogue with John Cotton was one such channel. In a series of letters exchanged in 1640, Cotton and Wheelwright debated lingering points of contention as adult men on a relatively equal footing with one another. To a peer, such as Wheelwright, Cotton felt free to concede mistakes in his own handling of the controversy. Though he chastised his wayward brother, Cotton did so as one preacher to another, gently denouncing Wheelwright as an overzealous but legitimate minister. Since his goal was the rehabilitation of his former colleague, the tone Cotton adopted was one more suited to "coaching" than to punishing.[88] And with Cotton's help, Wheelwright did recover his commanding public voice. He managed almost simultaneously to maintain his righteousness in a published tract and to demonstrate adequate penitence to the community of saints in Massachusetts. By 1671, his preaching was deemed sufficiently godly for the Harvard College pulpit.[89]

Even the unabashed Roger Williams continued from his exile in Rhode Island to participate in the discourse of government with the ruling elite of Massachusetts. Where Winthrop had told Hutchinson to "say no more," he entreated dialogue from Williams, debating contested issues in tones of "Wisedome and Gentlenes." Closer by virtue of gender alone to Winthrop than to Hutchinson, Williams even traded gossip about "Mrs. Hutchinson" and her "monster" with the Massachusetts governor.[90] John Cotton, too, appeared compassionate and altogether respectful toward his lapsed brother in Rhode Island. Striving to convince Williams of the "sandinesse" of his reasoning, Cotton addressed him as a fellow believer: "beseech[ing]" Williams's indulgence, soliciting his "affection," relying on his good "judgement."[91] Never in his efforts to redeem Williams did Cotton take up the imperious tone with which he had commanded Hutchinson and Hibbens to desist from their errors in thinking and speaking.[92] Toward an intractable man, reasoned dialogue—with *two* speaking parts—was the appropriate form. With the cooperation of such leading men as Cotton and Winthrop, Williams continued to possess an authoritative voice, one that he "published" from the pulpit as well as in letters, official pronouncements, and printed tracts.

Such was the experience of elite male challengers to ministerial authority in the early days of Massachusetts. Like Wheelwright, they might rise from the shame of banishment to preach at Harvard. Like Williams, they continued to be treated as gender and status peers, conversants-in-exile. They remained, in short, godly brethren: fallible and temporarily fallen, to be sure, but members of an enduring discursive fraternity nonetheless. It was their membership in this fraternity that allowed them to revisit, rethink, and restate what they had said amiss. Hutchinson's words, in contrast, could not be retracted or reframed. Her prophecy would have no other public outlet in the New England establishment: not from the pulpit, not in an exchange of letters, not through the London press. Her sentence of silence was irrevocable, her exile absolute.

Ann Hibbens raised her voice in a very different sort of public speech: the discourse of trade and commerce. The issues she disputed were not prophetic, but economic. Hibbens spoke as a woman trying to participate in a rational society with a developing economy; prices, value, and collusion, not inspiration and revelation, were her province. Although it often fell within the compass of Puritan matrons to speak to their husbands' business affairs, Hibbens's restless tongue quickly defined the boundaries of this license.[93] The medium, not the message, was the central problem in Hibbens's case. But for the speaker's sex and tone, the authorities might have nodded in happy agreement with the version of commerce Hibbens articulated: a notion of trade in which concern for the common good outweighed desire for personal gain. What the authorities questioned was Hibbens's right, as a woman, volubly to demand *anything*. When they determined her fate, the elders of the First Church decided that their congregation's public dialogue on earthly affairs would be as riven by gender as its discourse of learned religion.

Admittedly, men as well as women tested the boundaries of the commercial sphere in early New England. But as the records of other disciplinary proceedings before the First Church make clear, for a man the kind of offense Hibbens committed could be venial. Hibbens herself must have known the mixed fortunes of fellow communicant Robert Keayne, whose meticulous note-taking brings her case to life. Keayne faced the elders during the winter of 1639 on charges of usury and remained a contentious figure throughout his life in Boston. But unlike Hibbens, he managed to satisfy the congregation with a "penetentiall acknowledgment" that purchased his readmission to the church and allowed him to resume a public voice in the colony's affairs.[94] Even Richard Wayte, one of Hutchinson's supporters, who was disarmed by the court for his link to the Antinomians in 1637, and excommunicated by the First Church as a common thief in 1640, could rise from ignominy to become sheriff of the Bay Colony by 1654.[95]

Neither Keayne nor Wayte, neither Wheelwright nor Williams, had fallen as far from the path of righteousness as Hibbens and Hutchinson had. These men were sinners, surely, but they remained godly men none-theless—temporarily debased brothers rather than women whose habits of speech and conduct placed them outside the social order altogether. It was easier, therefore, for a male offender to restore himself to a position of respect. Should he adequately repent of his theft, his heresy, or his un-Christian usury, he could promptly reclaim the voice of a man. No such option existed for Hibbens or Hutchinson. To give "satisfaction" to the elders and magistrates, they were asked to reframe—that is, to rephrase—their entire identities. They needed to find within themselves a woman's tongue, a way of speaking they had virtually defined in the negative. The judgments against them made clear that neither the public discourse of religion nor the arena of commerce would tolerate their aggressive partic-ipation. Through the trials of Hutchinson and Hibbens, both the van-ishing art of prophecy and the emerging discourse of commercial negotia-tion were deemed unsuited to women's tongues.

The colony's authorities pronounced this gendered linguistic order most directly in their verdicts condemning Hutchinson and Hibbens. But in the ensuing years, the censures of these unquiet women would con-tinue to reverberate in other, less immediate ways as the civil and clerical leaders of Massachusetts wove the outlines of a new economy of speaking into the very fabric of governance. In the broadest sense, the colony's emerging elite met the challenge of Hutchinson's and Hibbens's speech by defining a new orthodoxy and by spelling out the voice in which it would be pronounced.

In the churches, this emerging orthodoxy elevated the minister's voice while curbing the speech of laypeople. No longer, new rules announced, would the meetinghouse degenerate into what Harry Stout has called "a Babel of competing voices all claiming to speak in the name and place of God."[96] The protocol outlined in the 1648 Cambridge Platform di-rected trusted elders to safeguard the preacher's verbal prerogatives by permitting the faithful to "speak in the church" only with "leave from the elders: nor continue so doing, when [the elders] require silence." As John Cotton noted, the elders would thus act as gatekeepers for the con-gregation's tongues, deciding when to "open the door of speech and silence in the assembly."[97] Protected against spontaneous interruptions from the floor, the minister could address his flock with confidence, speaking as if with the voice of God.

Although these new rules fortified the ministry against verbal assaults by men and women alike, the doors of the church were closed to female voices with particular force. In 1650, John Cotton published a tract to help clarify the thorny question of when women were "permitted to speak in the Church." He must have had Hutchinson in mind when he warned that the woman who spoke during meetings "under pretence of questioning for learning sake" might "so propound her question as to teach her teachers." Cotton knew from hard experience that such a woman "might soon prove a seducer" to many. The godly wife with earnest queries on points of doctrine should, as Scripture directed, "ask her husband at home," lest she "exceed the bounds of womanly modesty." Perhaps recalling Hibbens, Cotton reminded his female parishioners that they might open their mouths only under exceptional circumstances, such as being asked to speak in a "way of subjection" in order to "give account of [an] offence."[98]

Indeed, by the 1640s, most New England congregations had decided that even women's conversion narratives were best related in private. Writing in 1650, Edward Johnson felt compelled to account for the fact that, while the typical godly man "publikely . . . declares the manner of his conversion . . . some men cannot speak publikely" of their experiences of grace. The desire of the occasional New England man to make a private confession, Johnson explained, likely stemmed from his "bashfulness." In contrast, women's silence in church required no such rationale. Johnson added flatly, as if it were a matter of common sense: "women speak not publikely at all."[99] Common sense, in this instance, was surely defined by the echoes of Hutchinson's overly public voice. If the communicative economy in New England's churches in the mid–seventeenth century was best imagined, as Cotton Mather later wrote, as "a speaking *Aristocracy*" presiding over "a silent *Democracy*," Hutchinson had ensured that women would never figure among the former, and would be counted only partly among the latter.[100]

In civic life as in the meetinghouse, authorities rushed to codify the links between gender order, decorous speech, and social peace that Hibbens and Hutchinson had made so dramatically evident. Symbolically, at least, the magistrates delivered their response in the form of the *Body of Liberties*, which, along with the expanded *Book of General Lawes and Libertyes* (1648), made up the first comprehensive code of written law in the Anglo-Atlantic world. Deputies to the General Court had agitated for explicit, universal laws as early as 1634. But if the drive for a body of positive law came initially from common men who wanted to curb the discretionary powers of magistrates, Hibbens's and Hutchinson's cases showed the colony's leaders that they, too, would benefit from standardized procedures that could help govern the tongues of quarrelsome defendants.[101] A fixed legal code would spell out the contrast between the way a Hibbens or a Hutchinson understood her own voice and how the authorities heard it: between (as Hutchinson herself had written) preaching the "Truth of God" and "Railing or Reviling."[102] Without expressed definitions of "unlawful dissent," Winthrop lamented in 1637, "a wife, a childe, a servant may doe any thinge . . . though the husband, father, or maister deny their consent." Functioning much like the ruling elders whose duties were described in the Cambridge Platform, the *Body of Liberties* would serve as a gatekeeper for public speech, a bulwark between order and "anarchie." [103]

Was the emblematic disorder of Hutchinson's speech ringing in their ears when the magistrates wrote the infallibility of orderly, authoritative discourse into law? In 1637, with the Antinomians in full voice, the General Court assailed "the contempts which have of late bene put upon the civill authority" and agreed on new rules against defaming the magistracy. Anyone who dared to "openly or willingly defame any court of justice, or the sentences or proceedings" of the court, "or any of the magistrats" faced fine, imprisonment, disenfranchisement, and possibly banishment.[104] Speech against the colony's newly established religious orthodoxy was similarly proscribed. Thenceforth, even "private meetings for edification in religion" had to respect the magistrates' notions of appropriate "number, time, place, and other circumstances" so as to avoid giving "just offence." [105]

In effect, then, the *Body of Liberties* defined the outer limits of New Englanders' access to Word and words, making "free" speech conditional. As the court had explained to Wheelwright's supporter John Coggeshall in 1637, "we doe not challenge power over mens consciences, but *when seditious speeches and practises discover such a corrupt conscience, it is our duty to use authority to reforme both.*"[106] The *Body of Liberties* and subsequent editions of the colony's laws refined that authority, making clear, for example, that a male property holder's "liberty" to speak in the civic arena hinged upon his decorousness. In public settings, such as the town meeting, all expression was to be couched in a "respective" and "orderly" manner, phrased "inofensively" and "Christianlie." [107] Speech to one's superiors was far from the only aspect of verbal demeanor bounded by law. Myriad varieties of wrongful speech were accounted crimes of varying degrees of seriousness. Indeed, several of the colony's biblically derived capital laws focused explicitly or implicitly on verbal transgressions, including legislation against blasphemy that transformed the scriptural precept that "by a mans words he may loose [sic] his life" into civil law.[108] Other statutes reproved such speech offenses as lying, swearing, and heresy with punishments ranging from a half hour in the stocks to outright banishment.[109] To be sure, such laws policed the borders of proper speech for men and women alike; in theory, at least, these rules were genderless. But if men were told to raise their voices cautiously before authorities, Puritan women must have known that the public arenas in which their speech might be considered "orderly" or "inoffensive" were few indeed.

In addition to defining the kinds of verbal freedoms inhabitants could take for granted, the *Body of Liberties* ensured that written documents— particularly the law itself—would be the fundamental basis of power in Massachusetts. The magistrates explained that the very "Countenance of Authoritie" rested upon the "expresse law of the Country . . . established by a generall Court." With this in mind, the entire legal code was to be "Audably read and deliberately weighed at every Generall Court." Those called before the bar would receive a "transcript or exemplification" of relevant sections of the court's "Rooles, Records, [and] Regesters."[110] Such procedures ensured that subjects would encounter their political "fathers" through orderly written records, and that the voice of authority articulated by the magistrates would live on in print.

The *Body of Liberties* buttressed "well-ordered conversation" by constructing a framework of laws, transcripts, and procedures—procedures designed to rationalize the public discourse of all the colony's white inhabitants, regardless of gender. But men and women would not have experienced these new limits equally.[111] True, the legal subordination of disorderly speech closed off an important avenue for male dissent. But as the experiences of John Wheelwright, Roger Williams, Richard Wayte, and Robert Keayne demonstrated, office holding, publishing, and legitimate preaching remained within reach, even for outspoken men. For most women, though, a turbulent voice was often the only possible vehicle for public expression. The majority of women were less fully a part of the written world than were men; even such well-schooled women as Hutchinson and Hibbens typically lacked access to nonverbal sorts of "publishing." Formal "roles, records, and registers," like learned tracts and treatises, had no place in most women's lives. Of course, inferring behavior from law is a knotty problem at best. But what seems certain is that the men and women who lived in New England after Hibbens and Hutchinson lived with new norms, new rules. And these rules governing speech, in their conception and likely in their effect, were in large measure rules about gender.

Yet the Cambridge Platform and the *Body of Liberties* represent only one side of Hutchinson's and Hibbens's legacy: the ending the Massachusetts authorities wrote for the story. In a sense, this ending held: Hutchinson and Hibbens died, and laws were constructed to counter the type of challenge they had voiced. But to what extent did the articulation of this newly established language of authority transform society in early New England? Certainly ungoverned speech persisted in the wake of Hibbens and Hutchinson—perhaps especially so. Did others consciously tread in what Nathaniel Hawthorne sentimentally referred to as "the footsteps of the sainted Ann Hutchinson"?[112]

It would exaggerate the impact of Hutchinson and Hibbens to claim that their unquiet examples spurred an explosion of "protofeminist" speech. But the records make clear that their challenges continued to reverberate, shaping the meaning of spoken words in the protean world of early New England.[113] Could the elders of the First Church help but hear echoes of Hutchinson in 1642, when they excommunicated Anne Hett for "open blasphemus speeches of hatred against God . . . and likewise for her stubborne unrulinesse toward her husband"? Or again, in 1647, when they accused Mrs. Sarah Keayne of inverting the relationship between preacher and hearer by "Irregular prophesying in mixt Assemblies and . . . Refusing ordinarily to heare in the Churches of Christ"?[114] Did John Winthrop think of Hutchinson when Lady Deborah Moody, hitherto known as "a wise and anciently religious woman," began to profess the heresy of anabaptism in the Salem church in 1643? The subsequent mention in his journal of Moody's exile cheek by jowl with a description of Hutchinson's death in Westchester suggests that he did.[115] Indeed, it may have seemed as if Hutchinson's barbed tongue had inspired women as far away as New Haven, where Mrs. Anne Eaton, wife of that colony's governor, was censured in 1644 for offenses to the body politic that began with "suspicious" and "unpeac[e]able words" and grew to include crimes as grave as heresy and breaches of the fifth commandment. And, like Hutchinson and Hibbens, Eaton answered the authorities not with expressions that bespoke a melting heart, but rather with "an ostentation of empty words" that "added unto the former offenses new offenses."[116] Was this yet another example of Hutchinson's success in "framing a new way of conversation"?[117] Indirectly, at least, Hutchinson had indeed bequeathed a legacy to future generations of turbulent speakers and their appalled hearers. Subsequent articulations of religious dissent were interpreted by the colony's leaders through the lens of "Hutchinsonianism." Traces of her ideas, along with similarly unquiet modes of verbal expression, turned up in the Gortonists' and Quakers' "heresies," while the virtual publishing industry assessing Hutchinson's ordeal made her voice a lasting literary emblem well into the nineteenth century.[118]

Hibbens, too, became part of her community's common fame. Her story entered the stock of local lore that helped New Englanders to define themselves and to understand the relationship between gender and order in their daily lives. Although she was officially silenced in 1656, rumors of her diabolic power long outlived her. In 1684, Nathaniel Mather queried his brother Increase about why he had failed to include "the story of Mrs. Hibbins's witchcrafts" in his anthology of the colony's "remarkable providences."[119] As far away as London, nearly three decades after her execution, the tale of Hibbens's untamed tongue continued to find an audience.

Yet however widely such ripples of feminine dissent continued to spread, we should not suppose that the unruly tongues of Hutchinson, Hibbens, and their linguistic "kin" represented the only type of public speech possible for women in New England after 1640. If, on one level, these women's stories illustrate the limits governing female tongues in the courts and churches of early Massachusetts, their tales also hint at a contrary message. The trials of Hutchinson and Hibbens remind us not simply of the fetters New England's leaders imposed upon women's words, but also, indirectly, of the *prominence* Puritan ideals would grant to some female voices in some public settings at some moments during the seventeenth century. It is significant that Hibbens and Hutchinson—no less than male offenders—were asked to account publicly for the errors of their words and ways. Among the first women to suffer the consequences of speaking their minds too loudly, too openly in early New England, Hibbens and Hutchinson were hardly the last to answer for themselves—both for good and for ill—in Puritan courts. As criminals and as civil defendants, as plaintiffs and as witnesses, New England "goodwives" continued to come before the bar. Whether they were called there to defend their names or to have their say against an errant neighbor, they spoke in the service of God's higher truth. And importantly, they did so with magistrates' encouragement.[120] For the voices of female witnesses and litigants, just as much as for the contentious words of an Anne Eaton or a Deborah Moody, Hibbens and Hutchinson had provided important models.

First and foremost, though, Anne Hutchinson and Ann Hibbens established with certainty that ungoverned speech posed a particular threat in the Puritans' New World, and that the "misgovernment" of women's tongues might be especially damaging to the common peace. Women's words, their trials had shown, could "frett like a Gangrene and spread like a Leprosie, and infect farr and near," corroding "the very Bowells of Religion" and society. "God knowes," John Cotton lamented, "whan thay will be cured." Rules had been put in place to contain the plague of disorderly speech. But when such an epidemic would next "infect" the body politic, and whether the lessons the authorities had learned from Hibbens and Hutchinson would point to effective remedies, was, in the late 1640s, anybody's guess. "I have many things to say but you cannot bear them now," Hutchinson had proclaimed upon her arrival in Boston in 1634.[121] Would New England's ears be ready the next time?

"PUBLICK FATHERS" AND CURSING SONS

In a sense, preaching caused the death of John Cotton. Late in 1652, as he journeyed across the Charles River "to preach a sermon at Cambridge," Cotton "took wet in his passage over the ferry." When it came time to deliver the homily, he noticed "a failing of his *voice* . . . which ever until *now* had been a clear, neat, audible voice, and easily heard in the most capacious auditory." He would never recover; from his throat to his lungs, the affliction proceeded apace. Soon, those who longed to hear the "gracious words that proceeded out of" the "mouth" of this *publick father*" would have to content themselves with whispers from his death-bed. At the end, he met his ultimate voicelessness peacefully, "lying *speechless* a few hours" before breathing "his blessed soul into the hands of his heavenly Lord."[1] But if Cotton embraced the final stilling of his voice, others in Massachusetts bemoaned it. "To suppress an instrument of so much good with silence," John Norton eulogized, would prove "an injury to the generation present, and to many an one that is to come."[2]

By 1652, the grave nature of this sort of "injury" had become clear enough. Cotton's was not the first "heavenly eloquence" to pass from New England's midst, and it was certainly not the last. Hartford pastor Thomas Hooker, likewise known for his "dexterity in preaching," had died in 1647. John Winthrop, who strove so mightily to define the voice of the godly magistrate, spoke his last in 1649; Thomas Shepard followed within six months. After Cotton uttered his final words, the curtain of silence descended thick and fast. Thomas Dudley, Winthrop's sometime successor, died in 1653; Plymouth's William Bradford succumbed in 1657. Even the saving words of John Norton, a man said to be "singularly endowed with the tongue of the learned" and just in his late forties when he replaced Cotton in the pulpit of Boston's First Church, would endure only briefly; by 1663, he too, unexpectedly, had perished. Edward Winslow, Theophilus Eaton, John Dunster, Ezekiel Rogers, John Endecott: from the pulpit and from the bench, each of these "publick fathers" had said his last by 1665. By the time John Wilson departed this world in 1667, none of the oratorical luminaries of the first generation was left to eulogize him.[3]

Looking back in 1669 on the trials and triumphs of New England's first half century, Nathaniel Morton compared this momentous generational passing to a slowly descending darkness. Like the comet that streaked across the region's skies while Cotton lay dying, he wrote, these earthly luminaries had shimmered brightly and then "waxed dimmer and dimmer" until they "became quite extinct." When their "burning and . . . shining light" at last "went out," the erstwhile city on a hill was plunged into shadow. "In Boston once how much shin'd of our glory," John Norton had mused upon Cotton's death, barely a decade before his own. Now, with such "lights extinct, dark is our hemisphere."[4]

A stirring image, to be sure. Yet in some ways, the extinction of Cotton's celestial glow was a symbol poorly matched to the changes overtaking New England in the mid–seventeenth century.[5] At its core, the void left by the deaths of the "greatest stars" of Cotton's generation was due more to a muffling than to an eclipse: to the quieting of a generation's spoken authority. The trials of Anne Hutchinson and Ann Hibbens had cemented the principle that fathers, "publick" or otherwise, would set the standards for godly speech. Now, starting barely a decade later, those same fathers were succumbing to the silence of the tomb. It was all well and good to maintain, as John Norton did, that the prayers of the faithful could keep alive the voices of their departed leaders, just as Paul's writings had ensured that "Abel being dead many thousand years since, yet speaketh."[6] But typological metaphor could go only so far against biological fact. And the biological fact was that many, too many, of New England's first fathers never again would say a word.

Yet however deafening, the perpetual silence of such men as Cotton and Winthrop was not the gravest linguistic challenge New England faced in the 1650s and 1660s. For as the authoritative voices of a generation of ruling fathers faded, the unquiet rumblings of their sons and daughters seemed to crescendo to fill the void. Governing the speech of New England's "children" (broadly construed) was one of the central issues of the mid–seventeenth century. If the voices of disorderly wives were a principal threat to the stability of Massachusetts in the 1630s and early 1640s, the colony's interpretation of the fifth commandment took on a slightly different cast in ensuing years. As New Englanders struggled to make sense of the passing of their fictive fathers and the rising of a new generation of would-be patriarchs (including, after 1660, the restored Charles II) to succeed them, the behavior—and particularly the *speech*—of "children" to their "parents" became an issue of paramount importance. Quite suddenly, it seemed, undutiful children were everywhere: in the family, in the churches, in the commonwealth at large.

Was it not ever so? The answer, I would suggest, must be yes *and* no; concern over the relationship between words and filial devotion was both enduring and novel. Writers on family duty had long extolled the importance of verbal politeness within the household, and would continue to do so when even the faintest echoes of the words of New England's first fathers had passed from public memory. In a world in which the family was imagined as a model for the state, children (especially sons) learned that respect for their parents (especially fathers) had wide-ranging social consequences.[7] Moreover, authorities had long tended to agree about what, precisely, constituted respect. New England's civil and clerical leaders were neither the first nor the last to maintain that childlike reverence meant, first and foremost, deferential speech. Children's words "both *to* and *of* their parents," William Gouge explained, "must savour of reverence." "Silence" and "patience" were a child's best maxims; "*swift to heare*" and "*slow to speake*" compliments of the highest order. A submissive voice, Cotton Mather advised, would literally "*Speak the Reverence*" that godly sons and daughters owed godly fathers and mothers.[8]

While young men and women alike learned to defer to their parents, gender complicated their speaking parts. For in reverentially calling his erstwhile ruler "father"—which, as Gouge pointed out, was "a title of great dignity"—the boy used a moniker he would inherit.[9] Dutiful "*Daughters,*" as Mather noted, shone "as *Corner Stones polished after the fashion of a Palace.*" A vital part of the social edifice—the very "corner stones" upon which it was built—girls remained metaphorically fixed; their voices as wives and mothers would closely resemble their demeanor as girls. Sons, in contrast, were "*Young Plants.*" Like their sisters, they were tender, fragile, dependent—but also moving, restless, striving: in Mather's words, "*growing up.*"[10] Even while deferring to the voices of their parents, boys thus prepared themselves for "greater matters": replacing their fathers as ministers, magistrates, householders, freemen; as fathers in their turn—and, of course, as public speakers.[11] Which meant that sons were always and everywhere liminal creatures. As "young plants," they represented the promise and the uncertainty of future harvests. In their sons, fathers hoped, the lessons of family duty would blossom. But fathers also feared: might these seedlings mature only to bear the bitter fruits of impiety and disorder? The destiny of the whole New England "errand" hinged, it seemed, upon the ability of its sons to master the family-school's most difficult lesson: the precarious balancing of deference and mastery.

And therein lay the urgent timeliness of this issue in the middle of the seventeenth century. The verbal contest between parents and children, archetypal in many respects, took on heightened intensity as the first generation of New England's public fathers spoke their last. Did the maturing of New England's first homegrown generation in fact provoke an epidemic of misspeaking, an increase in either the quantity or the rancorousness of invective hurled against the colonies' natural and metaphorical parents? The kinds of data left to us—records that allow us to hear criminal speech vividly, but ordinary utterances only rarely—makes such a question impossible to answer. What is clear enough, however, is that public *concern* with the rhetoric of filial duty (or its absence) reached something of a fever pitch in New England's third decade.

It did so, for one, in the churches. In congregations across Massachusetts, Plymouth, Connecticut, and New Haven, battles raged about the relationship of children and grandchildren to the faith of their forebears. Many of the great theological struggles of the mid–seventeenth century—including the famed debates over the Halfway Covenant and infant baptism—were rife with expressions of generational tension.[12] So, too, were ministers' reactions to what they considered the most pernicious new sect invading New England at midcentury: the Quakers. Born amid the cultural upheaval of the English interregnum, Quakerism was an ecstatic brand of Protestantism, a religion that promised both a new form of piety and a new language in which to express it. To orthodox ears, the disorderly speech of the Quakers was part and parcel of their challenge to Puritan preachers. Was it mere happenstance, Increase Mather wondered, that "*Quakerisme* . . . began to infest the World" almost at the moment John Cotton fell silent?[13] The bloody conflict between Puritan preachers and Quaker missionaries in the 1650s and 1660s was, in large measure, a generational battle over speech: a struggle between waning Puritan fathers, waxing Quaker prophets, and confused, vulnerable lay "children."

Clergymen were not the only ones to be alarmed by the seeming plague of disrespectful words; New England's courts also evinced concern. Beginning in the late 1640s, legislatures throughout the Puritan colonies enacted laws making actions *or speech* against one's parents a capital offense. In Massachusetts, for example, any "stubborne or rebellious sonne, of sufficient yeares & understanding, viz., 16" who refused to hearken to "the voyce of his Father, or the voyce of his Mother" faced the gallows. In like manner, children over sixteen years who transgressed the fifth commandment with either their words or their deeds—those known to "curse or smite their natural father or mother"—could be hanged.[14] Words of contempt for one's metaphorical parents (the clergy and judiciary), while not capital in nature, could result in the civil deaths of banishment and disenfranchisement.

Such punishments, however harsh, merely fulfilled the promise of Scripture, which "expresly condemned" both the "mocking and cursing" and the physical disregard of parents, "the reward whereof is by Gods law death."[15] In New England, bench and pulpit colluded on the point. Thus every father and mother, every son and daughter, knew the fate of those who breached that vital commandment. They also knew precisely how to recognize such a grievous transgressor: not only his actions but his every utterance would speak contempt. What a powerful object lesson, then, must every parent and child have drawn from the fate of Salem's John Porter.

THERE WERE TWO John Porters in early Salem—senior and junior, father and son. Although an unusually large corpus of evidence documents the rift between them, perhaps none of it speaks so eloquently as the mute objects each left behind at the end of his life. When John Porter Sr. died in 1676 at the age of eighty-one, he was Salem's largest landowner, a wealthy man by the standards of his day. He left an estate worthy of his status: goods and property valued at almost £3,000, including more than fourteen hundred acres of farmland; scores of livestock; a large "mansion" house crowded with the trappings of a life of plenty (numerous chairs and tables, six elaborate bedsteads, sets of fine "holland sheets," even the proverbial "silver spoones"); and five servants.[16] How striking, in the context of such abundance, is the condition in which death found Porter's eldest son only eight years later. In the spring of 1684, John Porter Jr. followed his father to the grave, leaving little to mark his passing. Fifty-some years old when he died, the younger Porter had neither wife nor "issue."[17] He had lived out his mean and relatively short life in what must be considered extreme poverty even by the lights of the seventeenth century, owning no home or property, surrounded by only a few head of livestock, a "sadle & bridle," a poor set of "wearing Aparel," a chest filled with "trifells," a single bed, a "Ruge & blankets," and some farming tools. Taken together, all his belongings would have fetched no higher a price than the hay stored in the elder Porter's barn.[18] John junior had failed, in the fullest sense of the word, to inherit. In a half century, he had never earned his rightful patrimony: his father's land, his father's trade, his father's name, his father's voice.

In a community that placed great stock in the orderly transmission of property and status from one generation of males to the next, the disparity between the two Porters' estates hints at a grievous and lasting breach in family government, a breach with profound implications for both parent and child. In fact, the relationship between the younger and the elder John Porter was so troubled, so tortured, so disorderly, that the evidence from their probates barely scratches the surface. Although neighbors may have bemoaned the Porters' fate, none would have found it shocking that words had hewn this deep chasm between John Porter and his namesake. At the root of their battles lay an endless string of nasty remarks—invective John junior hurled at his father, year-in, year-out, for much of his adult life, a litany of heated words that had prompted a wealthy and otherwise generous man to abandon his firstborn to utter penury. And significantly, John junior's speech rankled his fictive "parents" as well as his natural father. His "unheard of expressions" were not only deeply felt within his family, but also officially debated at the highest levels of the Massachusetts judiciary. Porter's sharp tongue made him a bad son to his parents, a bad brother to his brothers, and a bad master to his servants. More dramatically, his words reached outward and upward to make him a bad citizen of Massachusetts and a bad subject of the king. From the small theater of seventeenth-century Salem, Porter's words rang with such power that they reached the ears of Charles II across the Atlantic. Thus the drama of the Porters presents the spectacle of speech forceful enough to rend father from son, subject from magistrate, colony from metropolis.

How did John Porter's words assume such monumental—and malign—proportions? Surely no one could have predicted that misspeaking would become his "trade." Expectations for any child born to such a pillar of the community as John Porter Sr. would undoubtedly have been high. Elected as a deputy to the General Court of Massachusetts during his early years in Hingham, the elder Porter brought with him to Salem a reputation befitting a man of his wealth and piety. There, townspeople confirmed the high regard in which they held him by placing their trust in his word for more than three decades, calling upon him frequently as an overseer of wills, a juryman, and an arbitrator of local disputes, depended upon to evaluate the words of others.[19] But perhaps the most telling indicator of the community's faith in Porter's good judgment was his acknowledged expertise as a surveyor. He was frequently sought after to draw, to reinforce, and to remember human boundaries on the landscape.[20] How ironic it must have seemed, then, that Porter's signal failure in a long and otherwise exemplary life was a manifest inability to draw and maintain the lines of authority within his own family. Like his Boston contemporaries William Hibbens and William Hutchinson, Porter's public mastery appears not to have held sway in private. But unlike Hutchinson and Hibbens, it was not Porter's wife but his firstborn son whose unruly tongue exposed this inability to govern at home.

Writing from a distance of more than three hundred years, it is difficult to determine exactly when or why the lines of respect and submission in the Porter household became blurred. One thing seems certain: the breach between father and son did not stem from paternal neglect. The elder Porter made every effort to impress a sense of familial authority upon his eldest son. Admitted to Salem's First Church shortly after his arrival in town, John senior appears to have taken pains to share his faith with his children, each of whom was baptized in turn.[21] Sometime after he had begun his long fall from grace, John Porter Jr. reflected wistfully on his father's efforts to bestow "the litle light of the word of God" upon the household by seeing to the family's regular attendance to "the publick ministry" and leading daily devotions at home.[22] Outwardly at least, John Porter Sr. was a model Puritan father who should, by rights, have been blessed with a model son.

It must soon have become clear to the elder Porter that his namesake would prove no such blessing. Though the adolescent Porter appeared fleetingly on the right side of the speech barrier when his testimony before the county court helped to convict a slanderer in 1648, he soon ran afoul of his society's expectations for young men.[23] Sometime during the 1650s, John senior dispatched his son on a trading venture, advancing him a fortune of "about fower hundred pounds of money & goods . . . for his improovement in two voyages to the Berbadoes, & . . . England."[24] The surviving evidence discloses nothing of the purpose of the journey. Did the elder Porter involve his son in his mercantile dealings because John junior, then aged twenty to twenty-five, had shown an aptitude for commerce? Perhaps (this version of the story might run) the substantial sum Porter's father "committed" to him attested to bonds of trust and confidence between father and son. The subsequent history of the Porters suggests darker possibilities. By the time he went abroad, young John was approaching the age at which men in his society first married. Yet he was then, and would remain, steadfastly single. Were there already signs that his path through life would be a lonely and erratic one? Did John senior have some reason to fear that his intended heir would fail to secure his rank and estate through marriage? Porter's fourth son, Benjamin, likewise never took a wife. And John senior himself was nearly forty years old when his first child was born. Did prolonged boyhood and delayed manhood run in the family?[25] Was this a source of worry for the elder Porter? Did John senior send his son abroad to shape him up, so to speak? Perhaps the voyage was intended to purchase his son's good name rather than to enhance an already existing fame.

Whatever motivated the expedition, it soon became clear that the younger Porter's foray into the world of trade was ill-fated. For John junior "did not only prodigally wast & riotuously expend" the £400 that his father had fronted him but, once in England, "ran himself further into debt" and "was there imprisoned." Despite the shame he must have felt upon receiving word of his son's detention, the elder Porter worked to secure the boy's release, discharging his debt with the "charritable asistance of some freinds." Drawing on the Bible's lessons of forgiveness, John and Mary Porter then welcomed home their prodigal "wth love & tendernes as their eldest sonne, & provided for him."[26]

Publicly, John Porter Sr. followed a righteous path, embracing his lost sheep. But the exploits of the younger Porter had sorely tested his father's capacity for Christian forgiveness. It seems likely, in fact, that the home to which the wayward son returned was marked by an atmosphere far more highly charged than the climate of unconditional "love and tenderness" later described by the court. Though the daily life of the Porter household remains largely obscure, the records hint at lingering bitterness on the part of the elder Porter. Talking with friends during "a fit of sickness" that overcame him in 1657, he requested that, should his illness prove fatal, John junior be granted only £5, a horse, and half an acre of land. Neighbors counseled him that "he had done wrong in giving his son so little." But "Farmer John" remained unmoved, convinced that his son had already run through "his portion" on the disastrous trip abroad.[27] The wound John junior had inflicted upon his father was deep and, no doubt, infected their day-to-day relations. But just as deep was the elder Porter's hostility: his inability either to quiet or to turn a deaf ear to the rantings of his disorderly son.

In time, stirred by some combination of his father's grudging acceptance and his own inner demons, the younger John Porter cast off the prodigal's mantle of renewed submission and reverence. As the months the not-so-young John remained in his father's household wore into years, his speech to his parents became increasingly "profane, unnatural and abusive." In November 1661, he testified in the county court against his father, who stood accused of improperly detaining a neighbor's cow. That same fall, his brother Joseph and a family servant reported that they often heard John mock his father, saying sarcastically: "thou Robin Hood; thou Hipocrite; thou art a good [church] member thou art a Fit grand jury man." His tirades against his mother were both more frequent and more base. She was "a gamar [grandma] pisse house" or a "gamar Shite house" whose tongue ran on like a common "pearemonger."[28] The parents to whom Porter owed his very liberty as well as the allegiance and love prescribed by the fifth commandment had become, in his words, lowly objects of contempt.

In another time and place, such insults, although clear breaches of both filial duty and simple good manners, might have been counted personal rather than public tragedies. Not so in the New England of the 1660s, where godly speech and paternal authority had assumed acute social significance. The Porters tried to resolve the matter among themselves, placing what John junior termed a "strange Distance" between himself and the rest of the family through an agreement under which he was not "suffered to visitt [his] fathers house."[29] But this, the elder Porter and the courts came to agree, was a partial solution at best, offering the son insufficient correction, granting the parents inadequate protection, and leaving the state exposed to an incorrigible verbal menace. Thus it must have seemed only natural when the dispute overspread the family circle. Having tried to still John junior's tongue "privately," his father realized his duty to do so "more publickly" and at last "sought releife from authority," compelling his son to answer for his words in court.[30]

If the elder Porter made the opening bid in this court battle, young John soon raised the ante. Not content to stop at his father and mother, he turned his sharp tongue outward, unleashing his verbal poison against local officials. Served with a warrant to appear in court, young John responded first with symbolic communication, as "he tooke the warrant and broke it to pieces." In case the gesture remained unclear, Porter translated his body language into "words in contempt of authority." A "turd for Hathorne & his Comission," he cried, denouncing court officers William Hathorne and Edmund Batter as "a coople of logreded poopes [low-graded popes]." "I will not goe beffore them," he proclaimed. "I will goe before Better men then they be."[31]

When he came before Hathorne, Batter, and the court the following month, "young" John Porter (then about thirty years old) appeared broken in spirit and in speech. His demeanor at the bar publicly demonstrated the kind of modest language that might have kept him out of trouble in the first place. The time he had spent awaiting trial had convinced him, he claimed, of the need "to make [his] peace" with family and community alike. To his parents, he spoke of a renewed commitment to "humble and childe like duty" and "unfeigned submission." Lamenting a life filled with "many Sad Disasters," he hoped that his father might prove as willing to "forgive & forgett" as he himself was to "acknowledge Conffesse & for sake yea to Deteste & :abhor" his numerous "miscarriages." Toward the magistrates, too, he professed uncharacteristic humility. Admitting that he had "shamefully abused" his parents and "the Commissioners," he promised to "behave himselfe rispectfully, to all authority, and with all humble dutye unto my parents, and so to all other relations." He pledged, in short, to become (however belatedly) a "true Childe" and a "Dutyfull Sonn" to both his "natural" and fictive fathers. His contrite tone seems to have persuaded the court. After letting him languish in the county jail for several months, the magistrates bound John junior to good behavior and released him, once again, into the custody of his father and mother.[32]

If young John's verbal humility was as "reall" and "unfeigned" as he claimed in November 1661, his ability "to be soe happy" in the home of his parents was short-lived. Neither the court's leniency nor divine grace helped him to control his tongue in the following years. For despite (or perhaps because of) his father's apparent willingness to forgive him, John junior resumed and even intensified "his former wicked course."[33] Though declared to be "of sufficient capacity to understand his duty," Porter's invective began to take on a frenzied, even lunatic air. Driven by what appears to have been a combination of drink and mounting despair to abandon his erstwhile tone of filial submission, Porter attacked the members of his household and the local authorities with renewed virulence.[34] Words continued to serve as his weapons of choice. His growing catalog of verbal misdeeds included repeat performances of earlier scatological and slighting insults, as well as increasingly angry threats of violence against people and property. He called his mother "the rankest sow in the towne" and condemned his father as "a thiefe" who "had stollen 14 barrills of the governours sider." He threatened to "cutt down his fathers house and Barn," to "shoot with Bulletts all his fathers horses & cattle," and to beat servant Morgan Jones. And once again,

Porter did not confine his harsh words to the household. He impugned Hathorne and Batter as "base corrupt fellow[s]" and called them "a company of lye[r]s" for their efforts against him. When he said that he "did not care a turd for hawthorne & his father," we can assume that Porter was expressing his disdain for all of his would-be parents.[35]

By 1663, it had become clear that no accommodation between John Porter Jr. and New England's ideal of community-as-family was possible. As his words insistently demonstrated, Porter was an insufferable anomaly in the "little commonwealth": neither a godly father nor a submissive son. His "Abhorred & unheard of Rebellious opprobrious vilifying & threatning speeches . . . agt his naturall parents" and his continued "Contempt of Authority in high & reproachfull speeches" could no longer be "passed by." Finding himself "over pressed" by his son's words, the elder John Porter again appealed to the Salem court to stem the tide of "his sonnes wickedness & incorrigiblenes." The magistrates declared John junior's bond for good behavior forfeited and, deciding his transgressions were "of a high nature," committed him to prison in Boston to await trial.[36]

The scene that unfolded before the Assistants in Boston the following March was far less harmonious than Porter's earlier appearance in Salem. This time, virtually the entire household—with the notable exception of the offender's mother, Mary—attested to the corrupt words of the accused. Publicly owning what Cotton Mather called the "continual *Agony*" that befell the parents of "miserable Children," John Porter Sr. effectively admitted his own failure as head of his family and "openly complained of the stubbornes & rebellion of . . . his sonne."[37] John junior's brothers Israel, Benjamin, and Joseph described for the court a litany of speech crimes before which his prior verbal assaults paled. The testimony of three servants completed the picture of a household kept in continual turmoil by the abuse that rained from young John's mouth.[38]

For his part, John junior showed none of the willingness to eat his words that had marked his previous court appearance. Granted "liberty to answer for himselfe," he spoke as if determined to prove the charges against him, as he "impudently denied some things," justified others "by vaine pretences," and "gave no signe of true repentance." Absent any effort by Porter to temper his harsh tone, the Assistants showed little leniency. Prevented only by the "tender & motherly affections" of Mary Porter from treating her eldest son as a capital offender, the magistrates sentenced him to symbolic execution. The following Sunday, he would be "Carried . . . Imediately after the lecture to the Gallowes" and "made to stand on ye ladder by the executioner wth a Roape about his necke for one hower & then . . . tied to the great Gunne & whipt severely wth thirty nine stripes."[39] Thereafter, he was ordered "comitted to the house of Correction" and "not thence releast" until the colony's high courts saw fit. And fearing that his wicked words had not sufficiently hardened his parents against him, the Assistants further specified that

"the keeper or m[aste]r of the house of Correction suffer neither his father or mother or any other person whatsoever to releave him wth any
other diet than [that] the . . . house provides."[40] Because the younger
Porter had so clearly outstripped his father's ability to govern his son's
tongue, the court assigned him another "keeper and master."

In the end, the jailer would prove no more capable of containing the
young man's rage than the prisoner's father had been. John Porter Jr. had
once vowed prophetically that "in case he would keepe him in prison, if
ever he gott out againe, he would vex & trouble" his father till the end
of his life.[41] When John junior escaped his cell in the spring of 1665, he
set out to make good his threat. It was, perhaps, the only time his word
could be trusted, for he succeeded on a grand scale, "vexing and troubling" the colony's highest authorities as well as his "natural" family.
Porter fled to Rhode Island and brought his case before a more elevated
panel of "fathers": royal commissioners Richard Nichols, Robert Carr,
George Cartwright, and Samuel Maverick, who were then sitting in War-
wick.[42] His alleged crimes against his parents, Porter told them, were
nothing but "rebellion pretended"; Massachusetts, not himself, was the
true undutiful child. For despite his frequent pleadings, no justice "colde
be attained" there, "by no meanes." Jailed at the "pleasure" of corrupt
men like Hathorne—who was his chief "abusser," the "attorney against
him," his "Judge," and (as the father of his brother's wife) an interested
"party in the case"—Porter found himself "conssigned where there should
be noe redress." What choice did a loyal English subject have but to
elude his self-interested, provincial captors and seek "a full hearing of
the whole matter" before a higher authority?[43] The commissioners agreed
to hear the case. Adopting Porter as one of their own, they returned
him to Boston under the paternal embrace of "his majesties protection,"
safeguarded by their assurance that he would remain free of "all molesta-
tion or restraint."[44]

The General Court contested the "adoption," and the arena of contest
quickly shifted from the topsy-turvy Porter household to the political
family of colony and king. Believing their "patent" to be "greatly in-
fringed" by the commissioners' intervention in the government of Porter's tongue, the court attempted in vain to regain custody of their wayward "son." By reasserting control over his speech, the court hoped, they
could begin to recover their power as his "fathers."[45] Thus they explained that the commissioners had deprived Massachusetts of its "full &
absolute power & authority for the government of [the] subjects of this
colony" by acting to protect Porter, who the General Court denounced
as "the vilest of malefactors." For years, John Porter Jr. had dared to
presume verbal parity with his father and local magistrates. Now, by en-
dorsing the claims of this undutiful man-child, the commissioners had
forced the colony's best men to "stand equall" with Porter "at the barr
of another tribunall." For the commissioners to sanction such a grave
transgression of authority, first of a father over his son, and now of magis-

trates over their subject, was to open a "breach . . . in the wall of our government" that would prove "an inlett of much trouble." Verbal deference was the mortar that held together the "wall of government." Without this social glue, the court feared, the whole edifice of the Bible commonwealth might crumble. If "such malefactors" were permitted "to passe unpunished," they implored, there would be no "colony of people here, at least [not one] such as now, through the goodness of God," Massachusetts had been "encreased unto."[46]

However heartfelt, these arguments left the commissioners unmoved. Having failed to prevail on legal principle, the court brought out the heavy artillery: a verbatim "narrative" of Porter's evil speech. Porter's words, they must have thought, would speak for themselves; the commissioners would recognize the atrocity of such "unheard of & unparrelled outrages" and deny the appeal. Whether the royal commissioners concurred that Porter was a "notorious offender" must remain in doubt, for their papers on the case were destroyed when the Dutch captured one of their number during his return to England.[47] It seems likely, however, that the litany of insults that the General Court accounted "horrid evills" would have sounded quite dim from the vantage point of Restoration London. Would it have seemed quaint, if not faintly fanatical, that the "vilest malefactor" in all Massachusetts was an ill-mannered overgrown boy, "a vile, prophane, & common swearer" who called his father "shittabed"? Yet the colony's authorities never doubted the significance of the case. Enforcing a subject's "duty unto his superiors, according to the fifth comandment," meant regulating the speech of every citizen.[48] Family government and provincial government alike required the government of the tongue.

Although the battle between the court and the commissioners was cut short, the local struggle over Porter's speech continued. But neither his natural nor his metaphorical "parents" would again muster the tone of righteous outrage that had marked their actions against their wayward son before 1665. Cowed by the Crown's protection of Porter, the colony's magistrates allowed him to remain at large. Acting out of misplaced optimism or simple battle weariness, Mary and John Porter Sr., too, showed unwarranted mercy, permitting their son to "come home to his father." But if family and community were prepared once more to "pass by" his insufferable behavior, John junior himself proved characteristically relentless. By the summer of 1668, his "rayling, slanderous reproachfull words" had again reached such a fever pitch that there was "little rest or quiett" for anyone in the household. This time it was a servant, John Barnes, who begged the county court for help. Porter's "almost dayly . . . miscalling" and "threatening," Barnes explained, caused him to "goe in feare of [his] life." John senior did not testify in support of Barnes's claims. Was the elder Porter, then seventy-three, at last resigned, defeated by the daily barrage of verbal abuse from his now forty-year-old son? My "master would relieve me *if he knew how*," Barnes told the magistrates. But apparently John senior did not know how. Indeed, the magistrates could hardly help but notice how thoroughly John junior's harsh words had eroded the elder Porter's authority, overturning his household to the point where a servant had to plead his master's case against the patriarch's own son. Faced with such overwhelming evidence of paternal impotence, the court agreed to act in loco parentis, committing young John to prison indefinitely.[49]

And still the two John Porters fought on. In 1670, the aging younger John made good his threats to destroy his father's property and felled twenty or thirty of his trees.[50] Nearing eighty, the elder John Porter brought his evil-tongued son to court several times more but seemed ready to concede what had become a lifelong fight.[51] Preparing to depart this world, John Porter Sr. described his "great greife" over the "Rebellious & wicked practises" of his son.[52] This exhausted father must have both dreaded and delighted in the fate that awaited the unrepentant prodigal: the Bible's promise of *"Death; Yea, an Early Death, and a Woful Death."*[53] Neighbors, servants, and surviving members of the Porter family would have sensed divine justice when at last, in 1684, John junior died the squalid and lonely death of the undutiful child.

But those who had lived through the saga of the Porters would have known that the story could not have so neat an ending. Long after the younger John Porter had felt the sting of God's curse against disobedient children, it would have been clear to people in Salem that he had not borne his punishment alone. For both father and son were deeply implicated in the drama and its outcome. Such sons, Cotton Mather later reminded the parents of New England's *"ungodly children,"* were intended by God to "serve as *Glasses"* in which mothers and fathers might "Behold" the terrible truth of their own *"Sinfulness."*[54] What sort of mirror did the incorrigible words of John Porter Jr. hold up to his "parents," at home and in the community at large? If his insistent, ungoverned speech prompted his metaphorical fathers to look within themselves, how much verbal mastery—and what sort of masculinity—did they find there? Porter's short but noisy life had illustrated the importance of the verbal component of filial duty. But so, too, must his tale have dramatized the need to buttress the voices of paternal control. Surely New Englanders knew what Elisha had prophesied: that when *"Children Learnt their wicked Language from their Parents, . . . God punished both of them together."*[55]

WE HAVE ALL KNOWN the likes of John Porter. Alcoholic, melancholic, or just plain eccentric, such characters shout their way into our lives more often than we might hope. But the sanctions we apply to our cursing sons and daughters are typically informal; their misgoverned tongues are considered private rather than official dilemmas. Which means, for the most part, that we imagine such foulmouthed men and women as singular beings. They are not cultural types, let alone biblical antitypes.

Theirs, we suppose, are personal shortcomings; their heated words say something about their own emotional health rather than about our collective well-being.

Could the same have been said of Salem's John Porter Jr.? Was he, too, considered simply as a pathological individual, thus rendering his significance more personal (or at most, familial) than cultural? In some respects, he was unique indeed. Despite the existence throughout New England of capital laws against filial rebellion, Porter was the only child to face the gallows for such crimes.[56] Yet the unusual extent of Porter's prosecution under the law underlines rather than undermines his importance. After all, his were hardly private failings. To the contrary, his nonpublic speech attracted widespread and enduring public attention. In fact, Porter's behavior seems less striking on balance than the community's reaction to it. The salient question then is not, why did Porter speak as he did? but rather, why did so many people at such high levels of colonial officialdom devote so much energy and time to the doubtful task of shutting him up? They did so, I would argue, precisely because John Porter was *not* alone. If his words sounded "unnatural," "unsufferable," even "unparalleled" to the ears of New England's leaders, such expressions were hardly (as the court once put it) "unheard of."[57] Censuring him was worthwhile—indeed, was *essential*—not because of the irrepressible nature of his irreducible self, but because of the threat posed by the several cultural types that he so vocally embodied.

Most immediately, Porter called to mind the speech of other undutiful children, figures whose presence in New England households seemed increasingly audible as parents of the founding generation aged. In nearly every corner of the region, Porter might have found allies in his war of words against his father. For much to the dismay of magistrates and ministers, after about 1650 a handful of prodigal sons and at least a couple of thankless daughters could be heard shrilly shredding the fifth commandment. In New Haven, the daughter of parents as eminent and righteous as Captain Daniel Howe and his wife stunned the court by cursing her mother within earshot of several neighbors.[58] Closer to home, Porter might have followed the example of Mary Rowden, who, in addition to cursing her neighbors, was heard to "call her father rogue, whelp and toad."[59] And just months after they jailed John Porter for his words, the Massachusetts Assistants had to contend with the "desperate & diabollicall speeches" of the inaptly named Belief Gridley, who came to court accused of "unnaturally reproching his father by Calling of him lyer and drunkerd and drunken sot" and of threatening "to burne his fathers house about his ears." Gridley's words, too, the magistrates labeled "Unherd of wickednesses."[60] But it must have been abundantly clear—indeed, ever more so—that to label such words "unheard of" was to subscribe to a legal fiction. Such a godly gentleman as Newbury's Joseph Hill could remind a local "rebellious son" of the Bible's threat that "the Ravens of the vally would put out his eyes" if he did not stop railing against his father.[61] But increasingly, as John Porter made so very audible, the sons and daughters of New England proved unable, and perhaps unwilling, to heed such dire predictions.

Just as the familial model for the early modern state predicted, those who loosed their tongues against one set of parents were apt to speak against them all. John Porter certainly did not stop with his father; his insults sought ever higher, more important targets. Directed first against his "natural" parents, next at town officials, then at more eminent magistrates, and finally against the entire corporate enterprise of Massachusetts Bay, his words rippled outward across the concentric circles according to which New Englanders conceptualized authority. In this respect, too, Porter had plenty of company. Much like Porter, Elizabeth Perkins of Ipswich began her career as a misspeaker by reviling her mother. From there it did not take long, the county court argued, before this "virulent, reproachful and wicked-tongued woman" had "spocken aganst" all those whom she "ought to Reverans and oner": her in-laws, her husband, even the local minister. Similarly, servant Hugh Hancock's "railing & threatening speeches" against a fictive father—his Salem master—were only a prelude to his "railing words against the contry."[62] What mattered in such cases was not only, as one yeoman said of his foul-tongued apprentice, that an inferior's "speakeing slitely & Contemptuously" was "intolerable to be borne in a family."[63] At issue, as Hancock, Perkins, and Porter himself reminded the magistrates, was how quickly speech against authority could metastasize, spreading from localized reviling of a particular individual to a broad-based rejection of the whole notion of a patriarchal verbal order.[64]

It was in this context of a "child's" speech against his *political* "fathers" that Porter's remarks resonated most widely. While the group of sons prosecuted for verbally assaulting their natural parents remained small (and that of daughters accused of doing so, smaller still), the number of those charged with hurling invective at the public fathers of New England was considerable.[65] Porter's trials are but three of more than two hundred cases heard between 1630 and 1692 by the Essex County courts and the higher courts of Massachusetts in which remarks against the colony's "parents"—leaders in the family, court, church, or town—landed the speaker before the magistrates. Indeed, censuring words against authority constituted the largest single item of business in an already busy docket of litigation over speech.[66]

The problem was an old one by Porter's day. From the very beginning of white settlement in the region, the difficult task of calibrating the balance between free Puritan consciences and governed English tongues had plagued the leaders of Massachusetts, Plymouth, and New Haven. Fashioning a voice with which to compel expressions of deference from a band of godly brethren had been one of the great challenges of New England's first years. Negotiating the boundaries between soul liberty and paternal authority over uttered thoughts had been particularly tricky when it came to the words of high-status men, those members of the godly commonwealth for whom a public voice was a defining personal prerogative.[67] It was for this reason that, despite the very real threat posed by such female misspeakers as Anne Hutchinson and Ann Hibbens, condemning authority had emerged in the early years of Massachusetts Bay as chiefly a man's failing. We cannot assume, of course, that only men actually derided those in power. But we do know that, like Porter, the great majority of those prosecuted for raising their voices against the civil and ecclesiastical authorities of the colony were male.[68] Moreover, speech against authority quickly came to be seen as a privilege—or a pitfall—of men of a certain social status. By definition, the *targets* of verbal contempt were public fathers. More striking is the degree to which the *perpetrators* also possessed significant standing in their communities, as was the case when sons bad-mouthed their fathers.[69] In this sense, speech against authority was a crime of social proximity, an abuse of the generous parameters within which relative equals discussed affairs.[70] When high-status men denounced their leaders, they spoke against would-be "fathers" who in other contexts were brothers, status peers. Verbally blurring the lines of mastery and deference, such misspeakers as Porter called attention both to the power of words and to the tenuousness of colonial authority.

If using one's words to confuse the prerogatives of gender and status with those of public office was always a dangerous proposition, it became especially so at moments when the voice of authority was itself most tentative. Of course, court records do not disclose the actual volume of speech against those in power; they testify instead to the dedication of civil leaders to "catching" heated words. The distribution of presentments for contemptuous words over the seventeenth century makes clear that such dedication experienced marked ebbs and flows, increasing dramatically at times of political and social strain. Thus during the first decade of settlement, when New England's public fathers were young and their ruling voices newly formed, the courts were especially sensitive to the danger posed by derisive words. They became so again in the late 1650s and early 1660s, when the rousing oratory of New England's founding generation was fading, the clamorous voices of various sorts of rebellious children were rising, and the pronouncements of Charles II were threatening to drown out homegrown authority altogether. Just over a decade later, the bloody conflict the colonists dubbed King Phillip's War again made magistrates' ears especially alert to contemptuous remarks. As the court explained when it rebuked George Corwin for his "great contempt of authority" in 1676, "clamors against the goverment" represented an especially "ill example in . . . times of danger."[71] In part, then, John Porter's words resonated so widely because he spoke out in dangerous times.

If the degree of attention paid to contemptuous words tells us much about Puritan leaders' sense of their own vulnerability at different points in time, the substantive content of such remarks discloses the ingredients of power in early Massachusetts. Those who, like John Porter, denounced their public fathers forcefully enough to wind up in court had, in effect, articulated the components of a good name in the breach. Their words, therefore, function as a kind of distorting mirror, offering misshapen reflections of the countenance of authority at moments in which the image of respectability was most mutable.[72] By examining the insults New England leaders deemed to be the most hideous "blemishes" upon their common fames, we can discern otherwise hidden features of the public faces they strove to put forward.[73] Here again, Porter stands as a kind of antimodel. His retort to the Salem commissioners—that he would "goe before Better men then they be"—captured the greatest anxiety of Puritan authorities. Particularly during those times when, as Ipswich condemner Joseph Medcalfe proclaimed, "Newengland" was "allredy . . . in a sade case," clerical and civil leaders were acutely sensitive to remarks that cast doubts on their fitness for office, their competence to lead.[74]

Where civil authority was concerned, competence meant wisdom, fairness, and at least a hint of above-the-fray imperiousness. Magistrates were supposed to be, as Porter himself had put it, "better men." Instead, condemners of authority told all who would listen, the reverse was true. The colony's laws were capricious, its officials corrupt, and their authority makeshift. Some condemners decried a legal system that, they argued, imposed draconian penalties for petty crimes. The "Coartes at Ipswich," Thomas Wells proclaimed, were "all one [with] the Inquishon howse in spayen: when a man is onse brought into Coarte . . . he had as good be hanged."[75] The colony's statutes, these offenders reminded their neighbors, were human inventions, not "Gods law."[76] And what fallible humans lawmakers were. Justice depended upon the whims of magistrates who, as minister Edward Norris was alleged to have remarked, were apt to "change their judgment for a dish of meat." "[W]hat became of all the fines?" another man wondered aloud. The answer was written on the bodies of the judges: they used their ill-gotten wages to "b[u]y sack" and "feast ther fat gotes."[77] Those who spoke against the courts let it be known that while New England's erstwhile better men claimed the natural authority of parents, they actually exercised "an arbitrary power."[78] The danger of such a statement would not have been lost on the court—not during the interregnum, at any rate. For what were Puritans renowned, if not for the casting off of arbitrary power? Might not those who voiced such sentiments convince their less vocal neighbors that the leaders of this new England had no more legitimacy than the Old World's "low-graded popes"?

If civil authorities were "low-grade" imitation popes, condemners accused religious leaders of being the real thing. They pointed out that New England's churches, much like her courts, were but "a humane invention," gaudily painted like "a whoare" or "a strumpet" to cover an inner barrenness.[79] If churches were strumpets, ministers were no better than whoremasters: men of pretended piety whom John Leigh dismissed as "Roges that weare cloaks."[80] And if God's messengers were lesser men, what hope was there for the doctrine they delivered? Since a minister's voice was his stock-in-trade, the most damaging invective against the colony's religious leaders asserted that their preaching itself was inadequate. How damning, for example, was the comment Mistress Holgrave of Gloucester let fall while chatting with a neighbor: the "teacher was soe dead," she mused, that "if it were not For the law, shee would never com to the meetinge." Such a poor speaker was unmanly as well as ungodly: "fitter to bee a Ladies Chambermad then a Preacher." Salem's Andrew Moss apparently agreed, explaining to a neighbor collecting funds for the preacher's upkeep that he had "heard the minister preach but once" because "he had a book, which would do him more good."[81] Indeed, some mis-speakers implied, what passed for preaching in New England was little more than noisy caterwauling. Thus Henry Walton claimed that "he had as Leeve to hear a Dogg Barke as to heare mr Cobbett Preach."[82] And it was said that John Higginson, far from speaking like an angel, "bawled like a bear."[83] For a New England audience, to be a dog or a trained bear was to lack precisely those qualities that defined ruling men—intellect, autonomy, piety, and especially speech.[84]

Regardless of the specific words they used, the underlying message promoted by such misspeakers was remarkably consistent. Authority, they said, was less immutable than it seemed. Power could be thwarted, and "natural" hierarchies could be socially—verbally—overturned. "Slighting," a term used frequently to describe such diminishing insults, nicely sums up this dimension of speech against authority: these words made big men small. When slighters spoke, the arbiters of justice became the most fundamentally unjust of men, while ministers were transformed into lackluster orators. The most godly were reincarnated as the most "dogly," and those who most deserved to be brought low claimed to stand equal (as the court had said of Porter) to the most high. When slighters spoke, in short, the fathers of a community were made sons while their undutiful children usurped their voices.

These slighters were John Porter's fictive siblings. His family tree included not only those who cursed their parents at home, but also the much larger group of malcontents (like him, mostly elite and mostly male) who used words to undermine the well-ordered family that New England aspired to be. Their utterances, designed to spotlight the least flattering features of the region's civil and clerical leaders, created a hideous family word-portrait: a distorted and destructive image that those in power had every reason to detest. But why did they *fear* such words so? We may still wonder, as perhaps the royal commissioners did when they heard the colony's complaints against Porter, precisely what accounted for the degree of sheer horror with which New England's leaders reacted to such insults. To understand why the General Court thought that John

Porter and his ilk "justly rancked among the vilest malefactors" in Massachusetts, it is necessary to explore not only the substance of his remarks, but also their medium.[85] Why, we must ask, were spoken words such devastating weapons in this particular place and time? One answer to this question lies with yet another group of John Porter's rhetorical kin.

THE ELDER JOHN PORTER probably spent 21 September 1657 much as he did any other Sabbath: praying, singing psalms, and listening to edifying sermons. Unless he was ill or traveling abroad on some mercantile venture, that morning would have found him in his customary seat in the Salem meetinghouse, directly behind "that wch is Called the magistrate seate" and among the most prominent men in the town.[86] And maybe, given his express hopes that the "publick ministry" would shower his children with the "litle light of the word of God," Porter brought his eldest son to church with him that day.[87] If so, the two were well-positioned to witness the spectacle that unfolded. No sooner than minister Edward Norris "had done" with the service, one Christopher Holder—a Quaker evangelist who had landed in New England the previous year—began "speaking a few words." A few too many, apparently, for town commissioner Edmund Batter, who would have been seated alongside Salem's most eminent, just in front of the elder Porter. Batter sprang to where Holder stood, yanked him "back by the hair of his head," and "violently stopped" the errant speaker's mouth "with a glove and handkerchief, thrust therein with much fury." If Samuel Shattock, one of Porter's fellow townsmen who had recently evinced Quaker tendencies, had not forcibly "pulled away the hand of the said" Batter from Holder's mouth, the would-be professor of God's Inner Light might literally have "choked" on his own words.[88]

Just what had Holder said to provoke such dramatic censure? There is no way of knowing; fittingly, only the act of stifling his words survives in the records. Perhaps he delivered the kind of dire prophecy that Thomas Harris uttered in Boston the following year, when he told the faithful assembled at the First Church that the "Dreadful terrible day of the Lord God of heaven and earth is coming upon the inhabitants of this Town and Country." Harris suffered a fate almost identical to Holder's, as two church members dragged him from the meetinghouse, a third "took me by the hair of my head," and a fourth "put his hand upon my mouth that I should not speak."[89] From the Puritan perspective, such efforts to silence Quakers, however "barbarous" (as one Quaker polemicist labeled them), were both necessary and appropriate.[90] For if the sect's turbulent rhetoric had already become something of a lingua franca among religious radicals in interregnum England, its likes had never before been heard in Massachusetts. Anne Hutchinson in full voice could scarcely compare with it. As John Wilson warned his Boston congregation, Quaker prophets spouted poisonous rhetorical novelties: "things spoken which they never heard of before . . . things as came not out of the mouth of God."[91] Cramming a glove into Holder's mouth was merely a crude, overly literal attempt to forestall the introduction of yet another strain of malignant words into the well-ordered community of speakers and listeners that—at least in the ideal—comprised the Bible common-wealth.

Indeed, it is scarcely an exaggeration to say that the decades-long battle between orthodox New Englanders and Quaker "invaders"—a bat-tle that saw its bloodiest skirmishes between 1657 and 1661, and one fought particularly fiercely in the Porters' own town of Salem—was at bottom a struggle over the cultural meanings of speech. Packed into the ritual gagging of Holder and others like him was a world of sociolinguis-tic questions. Who could speak to whom? When? Where? In what man-ner? And most important, who was to decide? True, these were not new questions for New England. But Quakers—those who assailed New En-gland from without as well as those whose voices sprung up in the re-gion's midst—forced the issue in novel ways.

They did so because they believed language in general and speech in particular to be matters of tremendous import. Speech was, as ethnogra-pher Richard Bauman has explained at length, a primary "cultural focus" for seventeenth-century Quakers, and a paradoxical one at that. Quakers decried ordinary or "carnal talk," words that they believed articulated the fleshly corruptness of humanity. In many situations, therefore, they re-garded silence as a triumph over base, worldly speech. At the same time, however, they glorified other modes of speaking, particularly when the utterance passed directly from God via the mouth of a devout witness.[92] The Quakers' attempts to refashion the world thus hinged on their efforts to reinvent words. Their understandings of language reappraised the cur-rency of speech, debasing the value of some utterances and inflating the worth of others.

Whichever the direction the revaluation took, many Puritan listeners were horrified.[93] They were horrified, not least, by the "enthusiasts' " atti-tudes toward Scripture, which Quakers considered to be words of God rather than *the* Word of God.[94] Inverting arguments that Puritans them-selves had once used against Anglican "legalists," Quaker pamphleteers said New England's spiritual leaders were worse than Catholics: that they were, as Francis Howgill wrote of Boston's John Norton, "*Egyptian[s]* who would limit" the voice of God "to Paper and Ink, to words and Syllables sounded and written in diverse Tongues, Languages, and Caracters." While their detractors "set the dead letter before the living Spirit," Quakers hearkened after the sound of God's voice, which, they pro-claimed, "will not be limitted or confined to this or that form of words."[95] Puritan listeners, of course, put a different spin on the issue. To them, invoking the possibility of a return to the practices of the early Church, an era when "word of mouth" had pronounced the "Rule of life," was blasphemous.[96] Quakers, Salem's Francis Higginson proclaimed, "hold their own speakings are a declaration of the word (Christ) in them, thereby making them . . . to be of equal authority with the holy scriptures." In addition to being sacrilege of the worst sort, this was, Higginson implied, the height of irony, since Quakers were "as horrible railers as ever any age brought forth, a generation whose mouths are full of bitterness, whose throats are open sepulchers."[97]

Perhaps even more menacing to the ears of New England's leaders were those "mouths full of bitterness" denouncing the voices of established ministers and magistrates as well as the authority of Scripture. Thus Humphrey Norton condemned the denizen of Boston's loftiest pulpit as a "babling Pharisee." John Norton's audience, his Quaker nemesis reported, seemed not to notice the preacher's "lifeless expressions" and "feigned words." Passively, they "gaped on him, as if they expected honey should have dropped from his lips." But, the Quaker insisted, "little but Gall and Vinegar fell from him while I was there." Not only vinegar but also venom flowed when Puritan ministers preached; the "Doctor of Divinity" might sound "as smooth as oil," but "under his tongue" lurked "the poison [of] Aspes." Civil leaders, too, were said to speak with pretended righteousness. Quaker John Rous challenged the General Court: "If you be magistrates of God, speake in the Majesty of God." "We do I hope," Governor Endecott replied. Rous disagreed, telling his erstwhile judge that "More gravity would become you."[98] Quakers were neither the first nor the only constituency to denigrate New England's leaders. But they were surely among the most vitriolic in their attacks. And, more important, they were the first to insist that the core values that undergirded New England's economy of speaking were, in and of themselves, horribly flawed.

What was amiss, Quaker witnesses proclaimed repeatedly, was easy enough to hear: like so many established authorities before them, New England's Puritan leaders mistook orderly speech for righteous speech. Their university days had so steeped them in "the Art of *speaking by rote, and trading in words*," that their authority had come to depend upon verbal "cunning"—on the scholastic's facility for "handling [one's] tongue deceitfully."[99] Like "a Phylosopher, a Star-gazer, an Astrologian or a Stage-player," New England leaders trafficked in "black dark sentences which are like Enchantments."[100] Their learned disquisitions failed to state even the most humble truths, for their words were not laws so much as spells. Genuine godly speech, Quakers asserted, was not contingent on status, education, age, or gender. A farmer, a vagabond, a child, even a woman: God might speak through each and any of them, in any place, at any moment. The words of the meanest layman were thus as worthy as a "legitimate" preacher's, and equally deserving of an audience. Titles, doffed hats, lowered eyes, muted voices: these expressions of deference belonged to the world, not to the Lord, who alone should determine the rightful boundaries of speech and silence.[101] Puritan listeners might react with horror to forms of worship in which "girls are vocal . . . while leading men are silent." But as Higginson himself recognized, Quakers "have only their own mode of speaking," a mode that rendered words at once too lofty to admit human impediments, and too base to merit them.[102] They asked only that "all may freely come, and all have liberty to speak (unto whom the Word is revealed) one by one."[103] What could be simpler, or more radical?

Yet however denuded of the empty trappings of respect, Quaker speech was not merely elemental. It was also, after its own fashion, deliberately *ornamental*. Despite (or because of) their distrust of worldly words, Quaker missionaries and their converts often turned speech into spectacle. Going run-of-the-mill slighters one better, they were dramatists who thought carefully about the staging and scripting of their pronouncements. Claiming perfect liberty for their divinely propelled tongues, Quakers substituted their own brand of theater for the Puritan oratory they despised.

They manifested an excellent sense, for example, of the role physical setting played in determining the impact of their testimonials to the Inner Light. Speaking, they knew, was a form of "publishing"—indeed, the most effective medium through which to disseminate any message within the face-to-face world of seventeenth-century Massachusetts. And Quaker witnesses were determined not merely to proclaim their beliefs, but to see that they were "preached and published upon the house top."[104] Thus Quaker misspeakers, more consistently than any others, displayed an uncanny knack for delivering their messages in contexts that took maximum advantage of the power of speech. Playing to audiences gathered to share the collective moments of life in early New England—those assembled "in open Court" or "in the meeting house"— Quaker condemners turned ceremonial occasions upside down.[105] Intended to showcase the masterful voices of public fathers, such scenes became, instead, theatrical vehicles for rebellious sons and daughters. It is fitting, therefore, that Quakers typically stood accused not of stealthy backbiting or of gossiping, but of "affronting" Puritan authority. Their sense of truth (and their penchant for drama) admitted no secrecy; they delivered their pronouncements "in the face of the country."[106] Little wonder that the word "open" or "openly" so often amplified accounts of Quakers' words against New England.[107]

Not only the stages from which Quakers issued their pronouncements but also the whole somatic presentation of their words was ritualized, set apart from the everyday. And while Quakers themselves believed that their timbre, affect, and gestures bespoke piety, Puritan listeners found them ungodly in the extreme. Magistrates detested the Quakers' "bold," "Rayling," "impudent & insolent" tones of voice. The language of their bodies likewise seemed to express disdain for Puritan manners. Much as John Porter amplified his scornful words to the Salem commissioners by tearing up their warrant, many Quakers tended to "shew contempt" through "theire gestures & behavior" as well as through their speech.[108] Imagine, for example, the scene Zacheus Gould created when he strode into the Ipswich meetinghouse and "sate him downe upon the end of the Table (about wch the minister & cheife of the people sit) with his hatt fully on his head, & his back toward all the rest of them." Peering into the face of authority while turning his back on his neighbors, Gould spoke symbolically without saying a word.[109] Other Quakers were known for their unflinching stares. When a neighbor asked him "why the Quakers gazed or stared so in the faces of men & women," Arthur Smith of New Haven Colony made the disconcerting reply that "by looking on men," he "could tell whether they had the marke of the beast upon them."[110] Several New England Quaker women used a more dramatic brand of body language when they appeared naked in public, one striding "through the Towne" of Salem and another walking boldly "into Newbury meeting house." As Bauman and others have argued, such sign-performances said many things.[111] But among their various meanings they offered one vital cue to their audiences: mark carefully what I am about to say.

Listeners who did so could not have been disappointed. The soliloquies Quakers delivered contained a startling blend of the poetic, the prophetic, and the profane. Some drew heavily on the slighter's debasing invective, dismissing preachers or magistrates as "a company of wild Beares," or branding them "proud, problematical, base, beggarly, pickthank[?] fellow[s]."[112] Others, like Goody Crab of New Haven, employed an Old Testament idiom, shouting down those whom they labeled "Baalls preists" as "shedders of bloud," and calling directly upon God to "power out thy vengance upon" the Quakers' enemies.[113] More appalling still must have been outbursts that foretold the future—a most unwholesome future at that. The men who had cut off the ears of Quaker witnesses would find themselves, Humphrey Norton warned, "bound in that Lake of oblivion for a thousand years."[114] Striking a similar note, Marmaduke Stephenson cried out from the gallows that the leaders of New England "shall be cursed for evermore," adding that "the mouth of the Lord of Hosts hath spoken it." "This is your hour and the power of darkness," pronounced William Robinson, also sentenced to die. Quickly, "the drummer beat up his drum" to drown out the words of the condemned, while presiding minister John Wilson commanded Robinson to "Hold thy tongue! be silent!" But the assembled townsfolk had already gotten an earful of words they would not quickly forget.[115]

And therein lay one of the particular dangers posed by Quaker speech. Messages delivered in such a dramatic, almost incantatory style were sure to be inordinately *memorable*, enduring in rumor and taking on mythic lives of their own. What small tragedy would fail to bring to mind Christopher Holder's promise that "woe & misery will come upon you: in the day that you thinke not of it: even as a theife in the night"?[116] Such curses—vivid, specific, yet somehow capacious—spoke to a multitude of future ills. Perhaps this is why, some four decades later, Cotton Mather was able to recall precisely how it felt "to be assaulted with such language" as Quakers had used in the late 1650s.[117] As Mather's use of the word "assault" suggests, such invective was almost tangible. In foretelling the demise of their persecutors, witnessing Friends embraced the ability of speech to *do*. Drawing on a long tradition that imbued words with quasi-magical power, Quaker prophecies did not merely sound, but resounded—both while they were spoken and afterward, in memory, as experience tested them, replayed them, and sometimes proved them true.[118]

Using words to wound was effective, to be sure. Indeed, it was a familiar gambit in the English-speaking world of the seventeenth century. Thus however arresting, such prophetic language may ultimately have held less terror than another feature of Quaker rhetoric—one virtually unique to the sect's adherents. If, at some moments, Quaker prophets spoke as if words were things, they claimed at others that the act of speaking possessed no gravity at all. Truth, not words, had power. Which meant that speech, in and of itself, could neither heal nor harm. The medium didn't matter, so long as the message was God's and not the devil's.

This premise, which flew in the face of New England's folkways as well as its laws, meant that the communication between Puritan leaders and Quaker speakers was cross-cultural, a veritable recipe for linguistic confusion.[119] Quaker prisoners pressed their judges: were "we . . . not called hither to speak, as well as to be spoken to?" To which the governor responded, "Yes, when we give you leave." Yes, that is, but no. Yes—but *to speak* means something very different to us than it does to you.[120] Such mutual incomprehension also marks an exchange between William Leddra and the magistrates who would soon decide to execute him. After enduring a public tongue-lashing from Leddra, the court exclaimed, "How dare you . . . Revile Magistrates and Ministers." Leddra's response reveals an understanding of language—indeed, a whole worldview—totally at odds with that of his interrogators. "[I]t is not Reviling," he countered, "to Speak the Truth." And more: that *"he knew no [more] hurt in Speaking English [than] in wearing Cloath[es]."*[121] It was, to Puritan ears, a shocking statement. Yet it was one with which many Quakers vocally concurred. Zacheus Gould of Ipswich, for example, told the court there that "they had nothing to doe [i.e., no right] to injoyne him silence." Salem's John Burton argued that he had more claim to speak than the county magistrates when, "upon being commanded silence, he commanded them silence and continued speaking."[122] And when Endecott promised Katherine Scott that he would "witness against your railing spirit," she replied, "I deny all railing, and have spoken nothing but the Words of Truth." In the topsy-turvy language of the Quakers, preachers were liars, railing was truth, and speech itself was nothing and everything at once. Was it any wonder, as Endecott told Scott, that Quakers seemed to have entirely "too much tongue"?[123]

Doubtless he would have said the same of John Porter Jr. Much like the Quakers who so vocally "obtruded" themselves into his own neighborhood, Porter rejected the very notion of governed speech. Of course, proclaiming that he "did not care a turd for" authority, prophesying that he would live to "vex and trouble" his father, and denouncing the Bay Colony before the king did not make Porter a Quaker.[124] No witness for the Inner Light, Salem's most famous rebellious son surfaces in none of the records that document the loose-knit community of Friends in seventeenth-century New England. Indeed, despite their own penchant for heated talk, I doubt that the Quakers would have been proud to count Porter in their number. But maybe the mere presence of the Quakers and the linguistic foment they introduced helped to train—or, rather, to *untrain*—Porter's tongue. And possibly, enduring the ranting of Christopher Holder and his ilk in the late 1650s taught Salem commissioner Edmund Batter to be ever-vigilant against loose words, even when it came to the point of prosecuting a neighbor's foul-tongued son. And perhaps it was no accident that a young man who witnessed the gagging of Holder so angrily refused the stifling of his own voice nearly a decade later.[125] The Quakers neither created nor formally recognized John Porter Jr. But the habits of speaking they brought to New England helped shape the ways in which his words, and those of other undutiful children, were understood and punished.

ONCE "AFFRONTED" BY the newly violent rhetoric of the 1650s and 1660s, what was a magistrate or minister to do? Impose silence, the easy answer beckoned. And, for a moment in September 1657, Edmund Batter was able to do just that. With a handkerchief, a glove, and a newly enacted law at his disposal, he managed to stifle Christopher Holder—at least for a time.[126] But in the long run, the battle against such men as Holder, and their efforts to reinvent the notion of governed speech, would not be so easily won. Although they might on occasion dismiss Quaker rhetoric as "a mixed bundle of words and [a] heap of nonsense," Puritan authorities realized in more sober moments that the Quakers' way with words made them a truly formidable enemy.[127]

In their attempts to vanquish that enemy, New Englanders drew on every weapon in their legal and rhetorical arsenals. Labeling Quaker opinions "contagious, noysome, & mortall diseases," the General Court invoked its duty as "the father in the commonwealth" to use all available means to protect the civic "household" from pestilence.[128] Recognizing that this particular "infection" was spread from mouth to ear, they passed laws to prevent Quaker words from contaminating the godly. Quaker preachers were denied entrance into colonial harbors or, failing that, banished (along with their opinions) beyond New England's pale. Their books were confiscated and destroyed, while the hands of repeat offenders were burnt to keep them from further "publishing" their heresies in writing.[129] In addition, the General Court ordered that "none [be] suffered to converse or speak with" the Quakers who languished in prison, and even specified that "a sufficient fence" be built about the jail yard to "debarre persons from conversing" with such contagious offenders. Likewise, a person heard "speaking in [Quaker] meetings" received a fine far higher than one who came solely to listen.[130] And those who refused to heed such restrictions on their speech, returning to the places from which they had been driven and again preaching their message, would first "have one of [their] eares cutt off," then the "other eare," and finally "have theire toungues bored through with a hot iron."[131] Thus the ears that had failed to hearken to authorities would be severed, and the tongues that had refused all government would be permanently stilled. Surely there could be no more fitting deterrents to such "presumptuous & incorrigible contempt of authority."[132]

Yet even still, even in spite of magistrates' willingness to impose draconian penalties (including the ultimate silence of the noose) upon Quaker misspeakers, the "daingerous, impetuous, & desparat" words kept right on coming.[133] They tumbled from the lips of professed Friends and their sympathizers: from the likes of Salem's Joseph Gatchell, who freely and publicly told one of Salem's magistrates to "Kisse my asse"; and from such women as Gloucester widow Mary Hammond, who proclaimed that "to goe to here your parson or preest or what you will call him is the way to hell."[134] But significantly, in the 1670s and 1680s, such words were uttered by non-Quakers as well. Thomas Baker, for example, used a Quaker-style idiom and body language when, presented with a warrant for his "unseemly carriage and laughing in time of public worship," he replied that "he did not care a turd for all the Law in the Country," further said that the authorities were "whores birds & shold kiss his Arse," and then "held up his backside & bid them kiss It."[135] And could the Ipswich magistrates help but detect echoes of William Leddra in the words of Hannah Downing, who, when reminded by a neighbor to "have A ceare what you say," countered that *shee did not ceare what shee said*?[136] Would a godly New Englander have thought such a thing before hearing the Quakers? Perhaps. But would she have *said* such a thing? Not as a matter of record, at any rate. Many historians have noted that Quakerism ultimately won few followers in New England. But if Friends listened closely, they might have counted any number of converts to their habits of speaking, if not to their beliefs. Or so, at least, it seemed to New England authorities.

Little wonder, then, that the much ballyhooed decline of Puritan piety in the late seventeenth century was so often imagined as a debasement of the currency of speech. The death of a generation of commanding orators had left in its wake, William Stoughton preached in 1668, an ill-mannered cohort of "Sermon-proof" listeners and ungodly speakers. All at once, it seemed, the air was filled with "Oaths & false Swearings," "Slanderings and Backbitings," "Contentions and Disorders," "Rudeness and Incivility."[137] "*Cursing* and *Swearing* begin to grow common" in New England, Joshua Moodey lamented. "It was not so in our *first* Dayes," he remembered. "I lived near twenty years in this Country before I heard an Oath or a Curse." But by 1686, the "Evils of an unruly tongue" regularly overwhelmed the godly "as [they] pass along in the Streets." Chief among the unruly tongue's evils, of course, was "contempt of authority, civil, ecclesiasticall, and domesticall." "[W]ofull *breaches of the fifth Commandment*" had become, Increase Mather reported in 1675, "a prevailing evil," one that threatened "the ruine of this Land."[138] Indeed, words against superiors, Puritan leaders believed, represented nothing less than the mechanism of New England's "declension": an audible sign that a shared understanding of the natural power of fathers was unraveling. The subsequent history of the colonies would, in effect, prove them right. The demands of future generations of rebellious sons and daughters for the prerogatives of their elders would belie any notion that patriarchy—verbal and otherwise—was either inborn or immutable.

In the meantime, civil and religious leaders applied themselves to the formidable task of cleaning up the mess contemptuous speech left in its wake. From the Restoration forward, however, they did so with help from an ever-diminishing array of tools. For after a band of gossiping Quakers proceeded to "fill the royall eares of our soveraigne lord the king with complaints against" Massachusetts, the remedies available to curtail the expressions John Norton labeled "*Heresy Turbulent*" were themselves severely curtailed. Crown officials, taking their cues from the common law rather than from the law of God, decreed in effect that even the vilest of misspeakers, be he a Quaker or a rebellious son, could not be put to death—not even in New England.[139] Confronted with such reinvigorated royal authority, the aging patriarchs of Massachusetts had to reinvent themselves as dutiful children: as "sonnes," hitherto "fatherlesse," now striving desperately to "growe up as a revived infant under its nursing father" in London. Had a colonial governor ever felt his own "impotency of speaking" so acutely?[140]

How could a paternal voice that was itself so tentative, so (in Endecott's words) impotent, hope to silence those who used speech differently, dissidently? The question arose repeatedly in late-seventeenth-century New England, never with more force than at a meeting of New Haven's magistrates on the afternoon of 11 March 1658. Called together to pronounce sentence upon Humphrey Norton, the judges were treated to a ferocious display of Quaker invective. Norton, they reported, "was so unruly with his tongue"—using a "boisterous, bold manner of speakeing" and uttering "such abominable, erronious, reproachfull, wicked speeches"—that "it was not fitt he should be suffered." Some of the "Elders present," deciding that he must be "wholey put to silenc[e]," took matters into their own hands. According to Norton's own report, several in the audience seized him and "caused a great Iron Key to be tyed cross his mouth" to prevent him from saying anything further.[141] To a seventeenth-century audience, the symbolism would have been rich. The tongue, as Puritan thinkers including Thomas Adams had written, was at its best when confined behind a door, a "wicket" through which "unsavoury speeches" could not pass. God had provided humans with a "double fence . . . to confine it, the lips and the teeth," and respectful men and women would do well to "Remember the bounds."[142] But like Norton, they often failed to do so. Which was why, as John Cotton had noted back in 1644, orderly speech required gatekeepers, minders of the keys of power and knowledge who knew when and how to *open the door of speech and silence,*" and when and how to close it.[143] With the aid of a "great iron key," this metaphorical door was firmly shut upon Humphrey Norton's words—for the moment, anyway.

But how effective were such censures in the end? As the ultimate political victory of the Quakers proved, not every misspeaker could be literally gagged into submission or hanged to the point of perpetual silence. The colony also needed ways to reclaim its John Porters: to welcome home its prodigal sons as speaking members of their communities. What such offenders had said needed, in effect, to be *un*said, lest the power of the fathers come *un*done. It should not be surprising that for many speech offenders, words proved an important part of the remedy.

SAYING AND UNSAYING

Nathan Webster's neighbors had little respect for his authority and still less regard for his word. Webster was a liar, and worse: a man who spoke in an imperious, domineering manner, using the verbal prerogatives of his office as constable of Bradford, Massachusetts, as a pretext for berating the town's inhabitants. As he himself put it, he often "fell to wording of it." By 1681 (and doubtless long before), many in Bradford had grown weary of the constable's verbal pyrotechnics. Coming together in groups of two, three, or more, standing in the fields or sitting by their hearth fires, they considered how best to salve the wounds Webster's words had inflicted upon "so many honist men." During one such discussion, Webster's sister-in-law assured a neighbor, John Tenney, that her kinsman was "sory" for his conduct—implying, Tenney supposed, that regret alone could undo the damage Webster had done to the common peace. Tenney disagreed. Webster, he argued, had "disgrast" his neighbors "openly in the face of the cuntry." His angry words were the cause of torments that, Tenney said, "we canot beare." Sorrow expressed in the confines of Webster's family could scarcely heal the hurt. To serve as an effective remedy for his wrongs, Webster's remorse would have to manifest itself openly, publicly. Tenney explained: *"exept the plaister be as bigg as the sore it will not doo."* [1]

Tenney's proverbial wisdom, pithy and vivid, resonates beyond the tiny circle of Bradford's small politics, beyond the struggle between Nathan Webster and his neighbors.[2] Indeed, the records of early New England confirm that Tenney's understanding of the damage caused by harsh words found nearly universal agreement among civil and religious leaders as well as among his neighbors. Few doubted that rude speech could rankle like a "big sore" on the body social. As anyone who had witnessed the trial of Anne Hutchinson, or Ann Hibbens, or John Porter, or any of the hundreds of other misspeakers presented by local magistrates or named in civil actions by their neighbors could attest, speech had fundamentally public, if not overtly political, consequences. Words exchanged in private seldom remained private. The mutable nature of speech itself, along with the habits of people living in this face-to-face world, meant that insults traded among neighbors tended to escalate quickly, often becoming (in Tenney's phrase) blots upon "the face of the country."

How could a face—a reputation—thus blemished be wiped clean of the aspersions that had marred it? As their victims knew only too well, wrongful words leaked a particular sort of poison and demanded a particular sort of antidote. The most important element of the cure, as Tenney implied, was that it be administered *publicly*. For virtually by definition, damaging words were public property, held in common by all who heard them (whether they did so firsthand, secondhand, or thirdhand). And when a bit of invective or a nasty rumor entered a community's repertoire of taunts and tales, it was difficult to dislodge. Libelous writings could be held in check through controls on printing technology, and offensive texts that slipped through the net might be disposed of with relative ease, as Quaker tracts were during the 1650s and 1660s, for example.[3] Spoken words were different. Since verbal attacks lived on in the memories (and conversations) of those who witnessed (and repeated) them, their "texts" could not be purged by fire; once heard, offending words could not be unheard. They could, however, be eaten, recanted—in period vernacular, *unsaid*.[4] Provided that the time, place, and manner of the "unsaying" were painstakingly scripted, such offenders as Webster could harness the power of words in the service of their victims, effectively undoing ungoverned speech by applying its opposite. Which is to say: words (public, penitent, and cautious) were widely considered the best remedy for words (public, arrogant, and reckless).

The consensus on this point, among common people and public officials alike, was simply overwhelming. In civil suits before the Essex County courts during the fifty years from 1636 to 1686, victims of slander demanded a misspeaker's apology more often than any other form of recompense—more often than they sought fines alone, bonds for good behavior, court-administered admonitions, other types of public shaming, or recourse to arbitration, combined.[5] Magistrates followed a similar pattern in punishing criminal speech offenders, particularly slighters of civil, religious, or familial authority.[6] Although apology was not invoked in every incident of wrongful speech, heated words were the occasion for virtually every compulsory public apology mandated by several early Massachusetts courts. Nearly 95 percent of all acknowledgments ordered by the Essex County magistrates, and over 90 percent of those compelled by the Court of Assistants or the General Court, were assigned to cure verbal injuries.[7] Clearly, then, people in John Tenney's world believed that an apology, properly performed, *worked.* A potent cure as well as a popular one, public apology was deemed effective even against especially virulent words. Such dangerous misspeakers as Anne Hutchinson, Ann Hibbens, and John Porter Jr., for example, were offered several chances to end their ordeals by publicly retracting what they had said amiss. So, too, numerous Quaker offenders learned that, despite the existence during the 1650s of laws making the expression of Quaker opinions a capital crime, they might still "give satisfaction for what [they] hath spoken" against the country through a "publicke acknowledgmt."[8] The courts further demonstrated the value they placed on apologies by setting public acknowledgments equal to fines as high as £200.[9] In early New England, a ceremonial unsaying was as good as gold—indeed, better.

But why? From a late-twentieth-century perspective, the effectiveness of public apology seems strange, for at least two reasons. First, the value John Tenney's neighbors placed on spoken retraction wreaks havoc with our own ideas about the currency of compensation. Given a choice between "only words" and some more tangible form of restitution for a slight upon our good names, most of us would tend to take the money and run. Understanding the high price early New Englanders were willing to pay for public unsayings of wrongful words, then, means coming to terms with the ways in which speech *was* tangible in their world. More puzzling still, from a modern vantage point, is another aspect of public apology: the wholehearted faith the ritual invested in the words of speech offenders, people whose voices had already been proven untrustworthy. It seems ironic, at the very least, that convicted speech abusers would be punished by being set upon a platform and invited (once again) to unleash their tongues. In our own, more cynical age, the penalty smacks of sentencing the proverbial fox to guard the henhouse.

Clearly this was not the case in seventeenth-century New England, for a host of reasons that demand explication. To uncover the way in which public apology accomplished its work—how it compensated the victims of heated speech and, at the same time, chastened and reclaimed its perpetrators—is to go to the heart of the meaning of the spoken word in that place and time. To do so, we need to ask several questions about the cure John Tenney sought to impose on his acid-tongued neighbor. First, we might ask Tenney about the genesis of his ideas on the subject. Where did he learn how best to ease the pain words so readily inflicted? Did the ritual of public apology belong to Puritan thought, to English law, to folk wisdom—or to some convoluted mix of all three? In addition, it is necessary to analyze what might be called the sociology of the punishment. For which misspeakers was Tenney's protocol prescribed, and for which offenders was it proscribed? Were some words deemed more "unsayable" than others, or was the unsayer's identity the crucial factor? Of course, we also need to explore in greater detail the ingredients of the "plaster" itself. What kinds of preparation led to a successful public apology? And which dramatic elements—settings, gestures, and especially *words*—added up to a satisfactory performance? Finally, it is important to look at those instances in which Tenney's protocol went awry—in which the cure seemed to be worse than the disease. Governed speech was a potent medicine. But what happened when unsayers substituted prescriptions of their own?

IN MANY WAYS, apology is universal. Much like the ability to talk, there is something essentially human about admitting fault, owning up. At its most generic, saying "sorry" is a kind of everyday magic, a social lubricant capable of smoothing out the tiniest but most ubiquitous of interpersonal frictions.[10] But if apology, in this informal sense, is omnipresent, the kind of ceremonial acknowledgment that John Tenney expected of Nathan Webster has a particular history. To be sure, the healing power New Englanders attributed to a public retraction of wrongful words would likely find analogues in many face-to-face societies: communities in which individual reputations claimed overarching importance, communities whose basic currency, in a sense, consisted of retold stories (whether flattering or belittling) about its members. Yet the ritual had more specific contexts as well. The unsayings of wrongful words that were a regular feature of civil justice in early Massachusetts drew from several wellsprings of New England's culture. Whether John Tenney knew it or not, the remedy he prescribed for his neighbors' ills had roots deep in medieval Catholicism as well as in reformed Protestantism, in law as well as in religion, and in England as well as in New England.

Though Puritan theologians may have been loath to admit it, central elements of the penitential practices of early New England—in both sacred and secular contexts—recalled the "Romish" faith. From the era of the early Church, acts of penance had claimed social as well as spiritual significance. Throughout medieval Europe, too, the formula for atoning for one's sins prescribed one part private contrition and several parts public display. Indeed, until at least the late sixteenth century, religious confessions were communal affairs; parishioners acknowledged their sins openly, before an audience that typically included their neighbors as well as a local priest.[11] To many early Protestant reformers, such ceremonies of atonement resembled nothing so much as a latter-day trade in indulgences, the sale of redemption for a price. Exalting the inner experience of repentance over its outward trappings, Luther, Calvin, Zwingli, and others took issue with Catholic rites of penance that seemed to substitute form for substance. Yet Protestants were not immune to the power of performance. They, too, looked to public confessions to counter those transgressions (including theft, usury, and, significantly, slander) that scandalized a community in addition to endangering individual souls.[12] In early modern England, then, repentance remained an external as well as an internal affair. The figure of the penitent, clothed in sackcloth or wound in a white sheet and professing remorse to the congregation gathered for morning prayer, would have been familiar to English-born folk from a variety of religious backgrounds. Redemption, any churchgoer could have attested, required words as well as thought. Even among Puritans, the message of penance was proclaimed not only by the heart, but also by the tongue.[13]

Or perhaps, I should say, *especially* among Puritans. For the custom of public confession was not only retained in early New England; it was also perfected there. As David Hall has argued, ceremonies of repentance took on heightened significance in settlements where other kinds of rituals were condemned as popish relics. Without competition from the pageantry of street theater or the visual splendor of religious iconography, absent the reassuring rhythms of saints' days, stripped even of the physical grounding of sacred space, people looked to the "great cycle of sinning and repentance" to make sense of their lives. The meetinghouse lay at the heart of this culture of confession. In regular biweekly worship, and on special fast days devoted to the shared expiation of shared sins, godly men and women came together to reenact the "moral allegory of repentance and renewal."[14] Becoming a full member of a New England church was itself an act of public confession; prospective (male) communicants narrated their spiritual failings and their experiences of divine deliverance to the waiting ears of the congregation.[15] And on many a Sunday, church members sat riveted during another kind of ceremonial apology, as the voices of sinners bemoaning their breaches of God's laws filled the hours after services. Not all transgressions required such open displays of repentance. So-called private offenses—those that involved only the sinner and her conscience, or unfolded before at most a few witnesses—were best dealt with in a dialogue between the sinner and the preacher. But public offenses required public retractions. And sins of the tongue, while not the only transgressions acknowledged in New England churches, were the most quintessentially public of sins, virtually defined by the presence of an audience.[16]

New England's churches did not shoulder alone the burden of rooting out sin. In the early modern world, trespasses against God were often identical to breaches of law. Particularly in New England, where civil courts dealt with moral offenses that would have fallen to ecclesiastical tribunals in England, crime was sinful and sin was criminal. This legal culture shared with Puritan religious culture an intense focus on securing a wrongdoer's admission of guilt. Prizing righteousness over rights, trials centered on discovering and condemning sin rather than on protecting a neutral standard of due process.[17] And how better to convey righteousness than through public punishments? Punishing crime, like atoning for sin, was a social drama as well as a personal one—a chance to redeem offenders, to chasten observers, and to reassert the structures of authority. Enacted in public, penalties such as time in the stocks, bodily mutilation, execution, and apology were forms of spectacle: elaborately staged affairs in which the power of the state, the guilt of the offender, and a warning to the audience were all on display.[18]

If the broad outlines of shaming punishments were something of a constant in the seventeenth century, their details—the crimes they condemned, their various incarnations—varied.[19] Compulsory public apology was not a generic form of humiliation, but a particular sort of legal theater that showcased a particular type of offense: wrongful speech. Throughout its history in England, court-mandated apology had been strongly connected to injurious remarks, a link that authorities maintained throughout British America.[20] This nexus of speech crime and speech punishment reflects the faith early modern jurists placed in "proportionate justice," ceremonies in which right and wrong switched places. There was a decidedly Old Testament cast to sentences that matched eye for eye, tooth for tooth, word for word. One of the virtues of public apology, then, was that it created a perfect equilibrium between punishment and crime.[21] Though he did not elaborate this ideal in all its theoretical complexity, Bradford's John Tenney certainly understood the allure of proportionate justice—the satisfying symmetry, in his words, of a "plaster" molded to fit a given "sore." Speech offenders had diminished their neighbors or their betters with contemptuous words uttered in front of too many people. Their public statements of sorrow were designed not only to compensate their victims, but also literally to reverse the crime.

Of course, not every sin or crime committed in early New England was met with a formal, public apology. Indeed, had this been the case, people would have had time for little else but listening to their neighbors' professions of remorse. If Puritans believed they were sinners all, who among them was so benighted (or, as they might have had it, so blessed) as to pronounce their shortcomings for the world to hear? The answer would appear to be simple: it might seem that any and all whose sins (or crimes) were of a sufficiently public nature could be counted on to deliver a public message of repentance. The reality is somewhat more complex. In theory, Puritans believed that men and women, gentlepeople and commonfolk, children and adults, Christians and heathens were all equally prone to sin. But in practice, all ranks and sorts of people were not equally likely to expound upon their failings in public.

First, and least surprising, an offender's age shaped conventions of public apology. The degree of self-consciousness (and, perhaps, the level of public sinfulness) required for such an open profession of one's guilt meant that children virtually never repented, either in church or in court. John Porter Jr. was the exception that proved the rule. Under normal circumstances, a child's profession of sorrow remained a family affair.[22] In addition to an offender's maturity, his or her social status was a consideration. Despite preachers' laments about the growing plague of insolent servants in New England, the records reveal few examples of laborers called to own their words against their masters or their betters.[23] And it goes almost without saying that an apology, a ceremony that hinged upon the ability of offender and judge to speak the same language (in a cultural as well as a semantic sense), was an English person's privilege or peril. I have found not a single example of a slave, a free African, a Native American, or even a white ethnic called to account in this manner during the entire seventeenth century. In all of these ways—in terms of age, status, and what we today would call race—apology spoke to the perverse equality between the targets of offending words and their speakers.

The rough parity between unsayers and their victims was reflected in the sex of the players as well. To a significant degree, the medicine of public apology was applied along gendered lines. During any given court day, or on any given Sabbath, one would have been more likely to hear a man make his repentance known than to hear a woman do so. It was not, to be sure, *unheard* of for a "daughter of Zion" to apologize openly for her failings, particularly in the context of church discipline. It was, however, quite unusual. Between 1632 and 1692, the members of Boston's First Church had a chance to hear male communicants make "acknowledgment in the publique face of the Congregation" a total of thirty-three times, while throughout that same period they witnessed only three women doing the same.[24] In fact, during those years, more than four times as many women (a total of thirteen) audibly *refused* the church's call for them to acknowledge their sins openly. Anne Hutchinson and Ann Hibbens had plenty of company in this regard.[25]

All of which means that pious matrons received decidedly mixed messages about women's proper voices from the apologies of their fellow churchgoers. Imagine yourself a female member of the First Church, casting about you for examples of how best to control your own tongue—a task that, you have been warned, women must approach with special diligence. Over the course of several Sundays, you notice the following: Most of the men called to profess their faith or to lament their sins do so, publicly, openly, and without incident. Hannah Bourne, on the other hand, displays feminine modesty by remaining silent while the elders repeat the narrative of her conversion to the congregation. Anne Hett interprets womanly quietude somewhat differently: she *speaks* her submission when she implores the entire congregation to accept "hir publike penitentiall acknowledgement" for her "open blasphemus speeches of hatred against God," and other sins. And Ann Burden, for her part, (scoffingly?) blends Goody Hett's and Goody Bourne's approaches, refusing the church's call to apologize by explaining that "shee was Commanded silence from the lord."[26] Perhaps still more women make themselves heard on the other side of disciplinary proceedings, speaking or nodding their assent (or disdain) for the acknowledgments of their fellow sinners.[27] Exposed to such a diverse array of female voices, you might well conclude that women's tongues are indeed particularly difficult to govern, oscillating (as they seem to do in the First Church) between silence and scolding, their modesty either unimpeachable or irredeemable.

In court, too, the discourse of apology was thoroughly, if subtly, gendered. Tied more closely to episodes of slighting speech than their church-centered counterparts, court-ordered acknowledgments were meant to compensate respectable men for the damage that words had inflicted upon their public "faces." Like those whose names they sought to restore, apologizers tended to be men of a certain status: people credited with public voices, people with access to the discourse of governance.[28] This is not to say, of course, that female misspeakers failed to express remorse. In many ways, the reverse is true. Despite their near inaudibility in the theater of public apology, women were a model, if not *the* model, of verbal deference in the early modern period. Regularly reminded of their duty to remain chaste and silent, New England's goodwives were well-versed in the language of submission. Self-shaming appears to have come easily to them—more readily, perhaps, than it did to their husbands, sons, and brothers.[29] In Massachusetts, women comprised nearly half of those who confessed privately and voluntarily, a proportion that far exceeded their share of those accused of most crimes. Quietly beseeching the court's compassion as "a poore weak woman," the female penitent would have been a familiar, even an emblematic, figure.[30] Indeed, one of the reasons that New England magistrates called so few women to account publicly for their wicked speech may reside in the willingness of female misspeakers to eat their words quickly and privately, before the wounds they caused had a chance to deepen into official, legal injuries.

Yet as Hutchinson and Hibbens demonstrated, not every woman wore the mantle of verbal deference so lightly. It is in the cases of those who did not—women who misspoke in confrontational (male) styles, and who failed (immediately, privately) to mend the rifts their words had caused—that the gendered meaning of public apology emerges most fully. The punishments assigned even to those female misspeakers whose words and styles most closely resembled men's reveal a tension between the association of women with submission, and their presumed unfitness for its expression in public speech. For many female slighters, performances of regoverned speech consisted, ironically, of remaining silent in the face of onlookers. Like Ipswich's Elizabeth Perkins, the woman who failed to control her tongue might more readily be exhibited under a sign that described her offense than asked to proclaim it herself. Convicted of uttering a litany of insults against her family and local authorities, Perkins was sentenced to display herself with a paper "pinned on her head . . . written in capital letters, 'FOR REPROACHING MINISTERS, PARENTS AND RELATIONS.' " The magistrates designed the penalty, they noted, so that *"due testimony might be borne against* such a virulent, re-proachful, and wicked-tongued woman."[31] The wicked-tongued man, in contrast, bore testimony against himself. Thus John Allen began his pub-lic apology for "notorious and barbarous speeches against authority" with words that neatly captured his gendered relationship to the ritual: *"I owne."* As a man entitled to "own" his voice, he owned his verbal mis-deeds, too. Called before the court, he asserted right order by speaking with a tamed tongue, not by displaying a silent one. "Take my word," he urged the sentencing magistrates. And, accustomed to crediting male speech, they did.[32]

HOW DID ALLEN REACH that point? What enabled him to "own" his foul words, successfully and publicly? It goes almost without saying: the Salem magistrates did not agree to "take his word" simply because he was male. What he unsaid, and where and how he unsaid it, were just as essential to the success of his performance as was the ritual's gendered sociology. But even before unsayers could make use of the dramaturgical and linguistic conventions that would help them to reclaim their rightful voices and disavow their wrongful words, they had to attain the proper frame of mind. In the ideal, at least, much of the ritual's work occurred before an offender ever opened his mouth to apologize.

Despite John Tenney's disdain for his neighbor's private feelings of sorrow, successful public apologies began at home, as monologues within the offender's heart and head. As preacher Joshua Moodey explained, the "harsh and severe" work of repentance called for unflinching meditation upon one's sins. The "Wound" had to be "opened and search'd before the Plaister be laid on."[33] Following the "rule of the apostle," concerned neighbors, kin, or fellow church members might give a nudge to this intrapsychic struggle, taking pains to make wrongdoers aware of the evil in their words. For in the best Puritan tradition, impassioned dialogue often melted hearts. As John Winthrop noted on one such occasion, it was "upon conference" with several of his eminent brethren that a mis-speaker had come "to acknowledge his error."[34] If solitary reflection and neighborly counsel failed to prompt an offender to make an earnest ac-knowledgment, harsher measures might be called for. As the elders who strove to extract an apology from Ann Hibbens explained, "some sharper Corsive had need be aplied to Serch in to the bottome of the Sore."[35] This searching, the elders surely knew, took time. While the courts could insist that an apology be performed quickly, churches (as befitted their focus on the hereafter) were more patient, often waiting months, and sometimes years, for tiny pangs of guilt to ripen into large words of re-morse.[36] In the end, it hardly mattered whether the "corsive" was applied by a misspeaker's conscience, a minister's pleading, or a magistrate's compulsion, for the result was much the same. "Satisfactory" apologies were born when offenders came to know the depths of their own sin-fulness.

However hard-won, such feelings of sorrow were not enough. Inward contrition was but a first step on the path to restitution, an initial negotiation between the deliberateness of thinking and the capriciousness of saying. True healing began only when offenders made the stirrings of their consciences audible.[37] Those who were capable of recognizing the gravity of their transgressions also realized the need to bring their penances to a more public stage. A godly misspeaker might strive "to pacify his conscience by secret confessions to God, etc." But he also knew he would "have no peace" until he could "bring his heart to . . . make public acknowledgment."[38] The victims of harsh words, too, knew the importance of "publishing" their reparations, often explaining that the setting in which an insult had been uttered gave the remark its power to wound. Thus William Knowlton argued that the couple who had slandered his wife deserved a shaming sentence because of "ye greatness of ye slander being . . . in so publig a manner before many people."[39] The misspeaker who confined his "scandalizing" remarks to paper, or delivered them "in private to the persons" (nick)named, might get away with a private declaration of remorse.[40] But those who "did publikly reporte" their slights forfeited the chance to apologize informally. It fell to them, as neighbors and magistrates alike demanded, to "audibly publish" their heartfelt regret.[41]

Not just any public forum would do. True to the notion of proportionate justice, magistrates ordered misspeakers to perform their penances in settings that mirrored the scenes of their crimes, before audiences who might well have heard the original invective. Misspeakers who openly denigrated religion thus professed their sorrow in the meetinghouse, preferably "in a full meeting," in order to ensure the largest number of godly hearers.[42] Offenders who violated the civil order by slandering a magistrate or a neighbor were typically asked to recant "unto the Court," or "in some publik meeting" in town.[43] Likewise, men who denounced their military leaders were compelled to apologize "at the head of the Troop" on a "day of exercise," so that "Souldiers may hereafter learne, what obedience thay owe unto their Comanders."[44] And those who had verbally assaulted their victims in multiple locales might be ordered to retrace the route their words had followed. Edmund Marshall, who said while in a shop that served as a nodal point for regional gossip that four local women were witches, had to perform a stations-of-the-cross-style penance, "publishing" his apology "in the meeting houses in Salem, Ipswich and Gloster."[45] And he had to do so post haste. Magistrates tended to insist that an apology be delivered as soon as (publicly) possible: on "the next day of exercise," during "the next Lord's day," or even "before the breaking up" of the present court session. Harsh words had a lengthy half-life, enduring for years in collective memory. The period during which they might be taken back was brief indeed. Victims needed to know that the wounds they had endured would be salved when their neighbors next came together as a community.[46]

Once the stage had been set, the real drama of ritual unsaying began. Holding forth in settings designed to give their messages added resonance, offenders employed a vocabulary that was part personal narrative and part habitual incantation, a recitation that merged the reformed Protestant's belief in inner grace with the Catholic's emphasis on outward performance. For centuries, penitents before the Church had relied on rhymes and other tricks of memory to goad them toward confessions that were "simple, humble, pure, faithful, And frequent, unadorned, discreet, willing, ashamed, Whole, . . . tearful, prompt, Strong, and reproachful, and showing readiness to obey."[47] New England speech offenders, too, knew the power of formula. Their symbol-laden discourse of repentance included sights as well as sounds: conventions of dress, posture, and affect that served as visual cues to a penitent's true remorse.[48] When John Underhill, a hero of the Pequot War esteemed for his "bravery and neatness," entered Boston's First Church "in his worst clothes . . . a foul linen cap pulled close to his eyes," he wore his "melting heart" on his sleeve. His abject appearance, along with his piteous "blubbering," "deep sighs and [an] abundance of tears," added weight to the confession, helping to convince the congregation that his apology was genuine.[49]

Ultimately, though, an offender's "blubbering" was only a backdrop. Tears, after all, could be counterfeit. As one listener in Boston's First Church put it, "thear maybe trew Repentance with out teares," and "teares with out repentance."[50] What really counted was that a penitent "spake well"—testifying "earnestly and humbly," as Underhill finally had done.[51] For at its core, apology was a manner of speaking: a ritualized expression about expression, representing order and disorder as a spoken "script." To be sure, we rarely know whose script an apology represents; in most cases it is impossible to determine whether the offender, the court, or a private complainant composed a given acknowledgment.[52] The historian, remote from the scene, is at a loss to discover whether the apologizer's humiliation was state-imposed or self-imposed, or indeed whether the offender felt any genuine remorse at all. But if the records of public unsayings tell us little about how sorry people were, they offer rich evidence of strategies for appearing sorry, for getting oneself off the hook. Whoever authored them, the surviving texts of these acknowledgments do reveal self-consciousness—the victim's, if not the unsayer's.[53] Much as the slighting words for which people sought redress disclose the components of a good man's good name in the breach, the motifs of apology contain the words that best repaired one's common fame.

Reparation began in earnest with the unsayer's opening words. Apologizers typically prefaced their recantations by disparaging the words they had used to disparage others. By denouncing the act of denouncing, misspeakers simultaneously affirmed their own guilt and validated the community's definition of "good" speech.[54] Thus Simon Tuttle told the Ipswich magistrates that "what I spake was pverse and sinfull, and of a

very haynous nature," while others condemned their words as "false &
rep[roa]chfull," "passionate, and unadvised," "hasty and proud"—even
"unseemely, and ungodly, and as they say divelish language."[55] The message of reversal was clear from the start: the language of apology (pre-
meditated and humble) was the very antithesis of heated words.

Having embraced the difference between righteous and sinful ways of
speaking, offenders next faced the task of explaining their lapses. Ac-
counting for one's descent into ungoverned speech was a delicate matter,
for the unsayer had to be watchful that explanation didn't become ratio-
nalization—what one Wenham elder decried as "self condoning."[56] For
if victims craved some pretext for the wrongs they had suffered, they also
needed assurance that harsh words were inexcusable. Most misspeakers
blamed their verbal failings on the grievous sin of pride. One defamer
admitted that he had acted "out of the pride of my harte" in making
"turbulent and factious" allegations against the church of Wenham. Another added that his own proud nature, bolstered by "the suggestion of
satan," had led him to voice his "equivocal delusions."[57] Others were
more prosaic. By maligning their neighbors or the state, they explained,
they had allowed their tongues to be governed by selfish passion rather
than by reasoned deliberation. William Horsham conceded simply that
he was not "In my Right Minde" when he spoke "In Soe Groose a Manner." A tendency to be what another offender called "to[o] free in . . .
mirth and drinke" was said to have loosened many a tongue.[58] Whatever
the immediate cause of his errors, the unsayer's account was much the
same: "I was so weake," indeed, sinful, to speak in such a manner. "I was
verry much out of the way at that time." And, most important: "I doe
condemn myself for it."[59]

Self-condemnation paved the way for the next element of the discourse of public apology. To underscore that they did "not justify . . .
but acknowledg[ed]" the evil of their words, misspeakers applauded the
penalties leveled against them.[60] Like Wenham's John Shipley, unsayers
understood that their duties included "justifying God and the church and
condemning" themselves "as worthy of the censure," if not of "hell itself."[61] In the language of acknowledgment, censure was always "justly
deserved" and "judicially passed," while mis-speakers were "justly suspected" and "Justly sentenced."[62] In short, such offenders proclaimed,
the court was right to convict them, the church was righteous in disciplining them, and their neighbors had every reason to sue them. They
maintained, moreover, that their disavowals of erstwhile sinfulness and
assertions of the court's justice were products of free will, voluntary af-
firmations of the rules of right speaking. Even the slighter who, like
Thomas Miller, recited an apology written for him by the court was likely
to emphasize that his was a "free & ingenious [ingenuous] recantation."[63]

Miller's rather tortured construction of the "freedom" with which he
made his apology actually represented his situation perfectly. Penitent
misspeakers had been made aware of the "enormities" of their transgres-

sions from within and from without, and had to attest to both influences. John Porter Jr. emphasized the former when he told his father that he was not "Constreyned to humble my selfe" by "Suits or Law." Instead, he insisted, his repentance came "from my Soule"; it was his "reall Sence of my Dutye & hearty Sorrow for all my Slightings" that made him "begg [his parents'] pardon." Joseph Rowlandson struck a more delicate balance, explaining that an "inward cognisance" of his wrongdoing had combined with the "external call . . . of Lawful Authority" to produce a genuine, public expression of sorrow.[64] Such offenders knew that owning verbal wrongdoing had two sides; they had to show they were convinced of their own guilt in order to be appropriately mindful of the court's conviction.

After unsayers demonstrated that they despised their own words, valued the word of the magistrates, and accepted their twin "convictions" from within and without, they proceeded to the heart of the ceremony of public apology: a verbatim recitation of what they had said amiss. The pivotal scene in almost every unsaying was a word-for-word restatement of the insult that constituted the offense, and victims and authorities alike placed great emphasis on its precision. Apologizers were loath to make their retractions "too short" or "too general." When an offender such as Wenham's George Norton claimed that he could not "remember the words" of which he stood accused, his unsaying was deemed a failure. If, as the prophet Ezekiel had warned, "not remembering of one's own evil ways . . . does argue a neglect of the spiritual watch," the reverse also seemed true. It was "out of the abundance of the heart" that the penitent's "mouth speaketh," and "a broken heart could not contain itself in a few expressions." In other words, less was emphatically *not* more where apology was concerned. To the contrary: as one Wenham elder put it, the "more particularized" the acknowledgment, the better.[65]

This faith in the value of the specific over the general—in the almost magical properties of what Robert St. George has called the "said" of heated speech—meant that the ceremonial venues of New England often rang with the sound of convicted speech offenders restating their worst.[66] Examples of insults resaid as they were unsaid are positively legion: In an effort to "wipe of[f]" the "aspersion" he had leveled against a neighbor, Walter Lewis expressed remorse for having "declared that Hannah the wife of John Keene of Boston Inkeeper, hath had the french pox."[67] Marblehead's Richard Glass could not fully apologize without reminding the assembly that his sins "Agst God" consisted of calling "Erasmus James cheating rogue, one-eyed rogue, one-eyed dog."[68] Having been "wronged" by the rumormongering of one Hugh Glanfield, Mrs. Elizabeth Hamons insisted that her detractor make a full "acknowledgment & confession." Glanfield obliged, spelling out "all and every perticular"; organized under three separate headings, the recitation of his "fals[e]hoods & untr[u]ths" would have lasted two full minutes.[69] Indeed, in a number of cases, the text of an acknowledgment comprises the sole remaining record of a long-faded slight. Through her apology alone we discover, for example, that Elizabeth Legg's "sin of slighting and reproaching Mr. Walton" consisted of "Saying I Could have a boy from the Colledg that would preach better . . . for half ye wages." Or, we learn, Robert Swan's "seditious manner" involved proclaiming that "men were led about by ye Lawes like a Company of Puppy-dogs."[70] The audiences gathered to witness such unsayings would likewise have been reminded of two things: first, of the depth of the offender's repentance; and second, of the very words of the transgression.

This makes the seeming effectiveness and certain desirability of such verbatim retractions all the more arresting. If we "hear" some slanders for the first time during the course of an offender's apology, might not some seventeenth-century listeners have experienced the same shock, or even delight, of discovery? What kept the act of ritual unsaying from becoming an occasion to publish malign words? To modern ears, the notion of retraction-through-restatement is perhaps the strangest aspect of public apology. We are familiar with the concept of published "corrections" (printed rather than spoken in our text-centered society) accepting blame for information stated in error. But the corrections regularly offered by our own periodicals almost never repeat a mistake, preferring instead quietly to substitute the "right" fact for the wrong one. Indeed, a retraction offered in seventeenth-century style might strike us as downright odd, as one recently did the editors of the *New Yorker* who reprinted the following "Correction of the Week": "In the City Beat section of Friday's paper, firefighter Dwight Anderson was misidentified. His nickname . . . is 'Dewey.' Another firefighter is nicknamed 'Weirdo.' "[71] We all get the joke, which serves to remind us that today, most people slighted by misprints feel their interests to be better served by getting the true story out than by repeating an embarrassing misstatement.

Not so in early New England, where civil plaintiffs and the state alike drew comfort from a controlled restatement of the words against them. And this fact—that *resaying* was the core of *unsaying*—provides an important clue about what public apologies were designed to do and how they did it. Acknowledgment was a ritual that righted a speech community that had been turned upside down. By framing abusive words within a context expressly designed to negate their power, the ceremony gave listeners a chance to correct any errors that had poisoned their memories of past conversations. One unsayer used medical imagery to explain this aspect of his apology. "When it is knowne what the disease is," he told the court, "it is halfe cured."[72] Like a vaccine administered after the fact, the "cure" for wrongful speech entailed a controlled reenactment of the disease. By inoculating listeners with a weakened dose of his offending words, the unsayer helped to put rumors to rest.

From this central, literal "restatement," the ritual proceeded to a broader message of reinversion: an endorsement of right order through a display of right speaking. Images of eminence and lowliness dominated this phase, in which apologizers emphasized their own vulnerability and exalted their victims' restored power. Thus John Putney referred to the Salem magistrates as "the Athorety set up by God," while styling himself "a pore man" pleading "humbly" before them. Having uttered "unsutabel expressions . . . that were *to[o] high for mee*," John Hoare sought to reduce himself to a more appropriate station: "humbly *to Cast my selfe down* to your honors feet . . . in all humility."[73] The impact of such statements, with their promise that "high" and "low" might once again change places, must have been palpable. Where slighting speech had collapsed or reversed social distinctions, public apology reiterated the distance between fictive parents and their errant children, affirming that "the eminent sarvants of Christ" (who surely resembled "the kings of Israell of ancient time") deserved the reverence of the "poor sinfull pashonate Creature" before them.[74] With such vivid language, these "poor creatures" reminded their audiences that the gap between the masterful voices of public fathers and the deferential tones of their dutiful sons was great indeed.

The unsayer's closing remarks cemented the renewed distance between the victorious target of malign words and their wretched speaker. Offenders typically ended their recantations by pronouncing themselves undeserving and placing their fates in the hands of their victims-turned-vanquishers. "I Ly att your marcy," Nathaniel Hadlock conceded to the Salem magistrates. "I cannot exspect any favor." Only "fatherly compassion" might restore such a fallen son to his place in the community.[75] Please, just "this once," Simon Tuttle entreated the court, "pitty me." Or, as John Smith asked the target of his words, Salem's William Browne, "passe it by, and forgett it."[76] Whether penitents sought absolution from the state, an individual, or, ultimately, from God, they struck the same chord. Forgiveness, they said, was a matter of mercy, of pardon, of a victim's willingness to "pass it by." The offender was entitled to nothing. Only by symbolically renouncing the prerogative of public speech—a masculine privilege that, presumptuously, they had advanced as a right—could slighters resume speaking parts.[77]

This is precisely what they planned to do. Deflated by the ritual but buoyed by their neighbors' forgiveness, mis-speakers concluded by envisioning themselves as participants in the community's ensuing dialogues. My "wicked miscarige shall caus me to morne all my days," Nathaniel Hadlock lamented, "and [I] shall by the help of god be so warned by this" that "I shall never be so carles in my words any more." Arthur Mason, too, hoped "to manifest [his] sincere repentance" for speaking against the colony's Assistants "by a more inoffencive conversation towards all."[78] John Davis could promise only that he would "endeaver to be more watchfull over my tongue for the future."[79] If the written records offer any indication, he stood a good chance of keeping his word. From that day forward, he, like all unspeakers, could rely not only on his own renewed capacity for self-government but also upon the community's watchfulness (more properly, *hearfulness*) to keep him in line. Moreover, as Salem's Elizabeth Goodall put it, the apology would continue to serve as "a warning *to mee & to us all* never more to jest or speake foolishly vainly or slitely."[80] Long after the ceremony ended, neighbors would continue the work of unsaying, their ears ever-alert to the dangers of heated speech.

And in this sense, despite its heavy overlay of disgrace, the ritual of public apology was an optimistic one for unsayers and their victims alike. Addressing the future as much as restating the past, the ceremony was a model of what today's criminologists call "reintegrative shaming": a punishment designed to turn dangerous wrongdoers into solid citizens.[81] As such, acknowledgment was a "plaster" charged with two kinds of healing: a cure both for those whom speech had wounded and for those who had used speech to inflict pain. Apology gave linguistic deviants considerable agency to effect this twofold remedy. At the same moment that they were compelled to speak themselves small—to represent the principle of submission verbally—unsayers were given a voice in the community's public discourse. Their shaming sentence was thus, ironically, a vote of confidence in their speaking futures, an affirmation of their ability to renounce ungodly words and restore themselves to moderate speech.

NOT ALL UNSAYERS deserved such a vote of confidence. This composite sketch of the features that made up a "satisfying" acknowledgment only shows the ritual working smoothly, an ideal that was not always fulfilled. For in the end, ceremonies of unsaying reflected the intentions of authors, actors, and audience in roughly equal measure. Despite the attempts of victims and the state to script their detractors' apologies, these performances were, like speech itself, notoriously fluid. As soon as a misspeaker took center stage, the content of the narrative—not to mention the meaning listeners assigned to it—was up for grabs. To be sure, this was always the case when discipline was conducted as spectacle. But during public executions, at least, magistrates could count on having the last "word." In the case of apology the opposite was true; the transgressor was entrusted literally to pronounce the goals of authority. Either the performer or the audience might easily alter the script, as indeed they did on occasion. At every point in the ceremony, apologizers added their own nuances to the state's design. Which meant that leading men sometimes had reason to fear, as Thomas Dudley said during Anne Hutchinson's trial, that an offender's "Repentance will be worse than her Errors."[82]

The tension between the authoritarian intentions of public apology and a more anarchic reality could surface even during the punishment's most "private" phase. Neighbors and church elders hoping, through informal dialogue, to stir a sinner's conscience sometimes met with proud and lasting resistance. The leaders of Massachusetts learned this lesson early at the hands of Anne Hutchinson, who thwarted the shaming message of apology as thoroughly and openly as she had disregarded notions of proper feminine speech. Boston's elders reported that they "took much paines" with her, "labouring to convince her" of the need to recant. At various points in the process, they "conceived hope of her repentance" and even imagined that Hutchinson would eventually come to "acknowledge her errour." But far from readying herself to unsay her dangerous words, she continued to "gain-say" the church.[83] Though her words reached farther than most, Hutchinson was hardly alone in her obstinacy. The workmen seeking an apology from Ann Hibbens for her slights of their good names met with similar intransigence. "Insteed of" speaking to his "satisfaction," Brother Davis told the First Church, "she did more unsatisfie me."[84] Wenham's George Norton likewise "stiffly stood unto" a defense of his words throughout the "divers hours" invested by the "brethren" who "visited him and labored much with him." After months of coaching on the finer points of repentance, Norton remained, they said, "in a kind of sullen frame," cool to the notion "that the church would force him to confess"—hardly the frame of mind, they didn't need to add, likely to produce a "satisfactory" acknowledgment.[85]

Indeed, the apologies delivered by such impenitent unsayers miscarried in any number of ways. They might, for example, literally fall "short of expectations," encompassing less than the sheer mass of words necessary to ease the community's pain. George Norton's several apologies failed on this score, being judged, as one of the Wenham brethren said, "bare and scanty. . . . so scant he could not have said less."[86] Ann Hibbens's attempt at a public acknowledgment, too, struck those who heard it as a paltry thing: "very Leane, & thin, & poore, & sparinge." Such an abbreviated expression of remorse, the very opposite of "freely & openly & readely" confessing one's sins, was simply no match for the expansiveness of wrongful speech.[87]

Being stingy with words was not the worst an unsayer could do. Stinting on remorse was surely preferable to denying it outright, as some of those required to apologize did all too readily. Framing the requisite account of one's words as an excuse was one way of mitigating the punishment's shaming message. Thus Topsfield minister Thomas Gilbert, accused of maligning his congregation as "ye basest, & unworthiest people that ever hee Came amongst," blamed his words on "ye weather—its unseasonablenesse & to 4 distempers wch ye weeke before had dogd him."[88] Though John Sandy of Ipswich admitted reporting that Martha Lampson "did steal a fann from us," he excused the slander as a product of "ye mis information of others."[89] Some misspeakers went so far as to couch their entire statements in the subjunctive. In fluent doublespeak, Edmund Bridges told the Essex County magistrates: "[I] do accknilege that it is [a] mattar of blame unto me in . . . so far as i do and shall acknowledg" it to be, or so far "as is or shall be legeoly proved against me."[90] Wenham's elders dismissed such carefully crafted displays of "non-

remembering" as "strange" and "disdainful." Far from owning his wrongful words, the misspeaker who took up this "manner of confessing"
sounded as if he were "telling . . . a tale in [the] third person."[91]

But despite such injunctions from authorities, unsayers were forever
splitting hairs. Anne Hutchinson elevated equivocation to an art when
she attempted to clarify a knotty theological tenet by proclaiming, "I doe
not acknowledge it to be an Error but a Mistake."[92] George Norton, too,
played the thesaurus with the Wenham elders, infuriating them by referring to "that which was a lie" as "an untruth." These razor-thin semantic
distinctions, the church made clear, had no place in the theater of acknowledgment. Rather than counteracting the slipperiness of speech, a
tendency to "mince and extenuate" one's words only enhanced it. Instead
of retracting his words, an apologizer such as Norton recanted his recantation, appearing "in the same breath" to "unsay what he seemed to say
before."[93]

Reversals piled upon reversals: relying as they did upon speech for
their very foundation, public apologies were particularly vulnerable to
this sort of about-face. John Cotton must have thought that he had prepared for such an eventuality when he took it upon himself to paraphrase, for the benefit of "the Congregation which heard not," the words
of remorse Anne Hutchinson had allegedly offered church leaders. "The
Sume of what she sayd is this," Cotton told the assembly:

> she doth utterly disalow herselfe and condemne herselfe . . . and she con-
> fesseth the Roote of all was the hight and Pride of her Spirit. Soe for her
> slighting the Ministers she is hartely sorry for it. For her particular Rela-
> tion in her Spech to the Disgrace of him [them?] She is sorry for it and
> desiers all that she hath offended to pray to God for her to give her a hart
> to be more truly humbled.[94]

So far, so good; Cotton had crafted a wholly suitable acknowledgment
that stuck closely to the formula. Moreover, the blend of vocal repentance on Hutchinson's behalf and womanly silence on her part must
have seemed appropriately feminine—indeed, considering her reputation
for wanton public speech, miraculously so. But Cotton's secondhand
apology could not drown out Hutchinson's own famously "misgoverned"
tongue. It soon became clear that the remorsefulness Cotton ascribed to
her bore little relation to what she had actually (un)said. Where Cotton
described utter disavowal and hearty sorrow, Hutchinson herself spoke in
"circumlocutions, and seemed to lay all the faults [to] her expressions."
Instead of genuine regret, she offered "a slye Interpritation," attempting
to excuse "groce Errors" with "soe slight an Answer." No wonder Thomas
Shepard found her performance wanting. "I should be glad to see any
Repentance in her: that might give me Satisfaction," he told his fellow
ministers. Such a slippery apology, particularly from a female offender,
allowed for scant optimism about the chances for an eventual cure.[95]
Quite the contrary: such performances as Hutchinson's made clear that

where speech was the medium, it was all too easy for an offender to "repent of his repentance."[96]

And indeed, some unsayers did so openly. Not content to rely on evasions and half-truths, a handful of those called upon to apologize appear deliberately to have flouted the conventions of penitential discourse. Several misspeakers, for example, took pains to make clear that their convictions were imposed strictly from without, "drawn and extorted" rather than "free" and "full."[97] Thus in his apology for denouncing the "coruptions" of "our court . . . in Newengland," Joseph Medcalfe insisted that he did "not remember that I soe sayd." Yet since "it is testified by three wittnesses," he continued, "I doe confesse and acknowledge these words to be causles & scandalous," and "*if I did speake them* [I] have cause to be ashamed and crave pardon."[98] What exactly had Medcalfe confessed? Richard Leader was even more pointed. Condemned by the General Court for having "in a high degree reproached & slaundred, the Courts, magistrats, & goverment of this common weale" and the "towne & church of Lin," Leader barely concealed his disdain for authority during his acknowledgment. In the end, he said, he would be exonerated by "the righteous Judge of heaven & earth, which in his due time will manyfest the truth, & acquite the innocent, & reward the guilty according [to] theire deserts." But in the here and now, "the thinges beinge testifyed by two wittnesses," he grudgingly conceded that "the Court had cause to proceed agaynst me."[99] After pointing out that the Ipswich magistrates had "injoyned" that "as part of ye sentence I . . . make my confession & acknowledgment" for having defamed the church, Rowley's Henry Sewall proclaimed: "I doe now in the prsence of god & of this reverand assembly freely acknowledg my evell."[100] Just how freely, and how sincerely? those who heard him must have wondered.

Although they may have done so under duress, unsayers like Medcalfe, Leader, and Sewall preserved at least the semblance of penitential discourse, admitting that the words attributed to them were (in Sewall's phrase) "causeless and scandalous"—and presumably, deserving of censure. But there were those, however few, who refused to concede even that much. Newbury's John Atkinson Sr. was one offender who turned a sentence to profess his "sorrow" into a very different sort of public spectacle. After losing a long-standing dispute with his neighbor James Merrick, Atkinson was ordered to acknowledge his slanders at the gathering that would take place when John March "doth rayes his house." Standing before the crowd that July afternoon, with Merrick eagerly awaiting vindication, Atkinson pulled out a paper upon which his apology was written and began to speak. He started promisingly. Stating that he "had agreed to make acknowledgment for slander in saying that James Mirik had told a hundred lies," Atkinson "confessed that he was wrong." The error, Atkinson then explained, lay in "being so surten As to the number of lies[.] I know not how maney liges that he huf tould And I am sore [sorry] that I wais so positife in the serten number that I charget him with." The record discloses nothing of the crowd's reaction.[101] But surely none who witnessed the scene—not the arbitrators who had compelled the acknowledgment, not the men and women in the audience, and certainly not Merrick himself—escaped the sting of Atkinson's sarcasm. In this case, the plaster didn't fit the sore; it irritated and enlarged it. Such unsayings were resayings and worse—ceremonies of misrule in which verbal disorder masqueraded as verbal governance.

IT WOULD SEEM, on its surface, that these distorted acknowledgments must have undermined New England's notions of social (and, more pointedly, of verbal) order. Did the always-lurking possibility that an Anne Hutchinson, a George Norton, or a John Atkinson might abuse the bully pulpit of public apology compromise the remedy's potency? Did the presence of a small cohort of offenders intent upon undoing their unsayings really matter? In other words, it becomes necessary to ask: did John Tenney's medicine deserve the faith his neighbors placed in it?

The answer, I would argue, is a qualified yes; the remedy worked for certain people living in a certain place and time. Throughout the seventeenth century, unsayers who undid their unsayings accounted for only a tiny fraction of those who came forward without undue coercion (or, at least, without outward signs thereof) to eat their wrongful words. There are many reasons that this was the case, not least of which is that the ritual of unsaying had what amounted to a pre-screening process built into it. The private conversations that preceded public discipline—certainly in church and likely in court as well—offered authorities a chance to break the wills of reluctant confessors or, if need be, to postpone an offender's statement until the requisite melting of heart had (apparently) taken place. Recall, too, that not just anyone was called upon to retract heated words in such an open manner. The "men of parts" who dominated the ranks of New England's unsayers were, on the whole, socially redeemable. They were "fathers" or "sons" who had spoken out of turn rather than badwives who, like Anne Hutchinson, had "stept out" of their places altogether.[102] Especially in its civil incarnation, public apology was reserved for offenders who could be trusted with the power of public speech, a fact that kept satirical performances such as Atkinson's to a minimum.

Granted, some tricksters eluded detection and managed to take their places upon the soapbox of unsaying. Yet even they scarcely hampered the ritual's power. For like all moments of ritual inversion, upside-down unsayings both challenged and reified the hierarchies they mocked.[103] Nearly all of those who, however reluctantly and partially, apologized for their heated words—the spiteful and clever John Atkinson included—tacitly affirmed the ceremony's underlying message. They admitted that there were unacceptable words, wounding words; that neighbors and authorities could define those words; and that victims had a right to demand redress *in words*. Stubborn offenders might quibble with the particulars, questioning which words were theirs, hinting that the courts made them feign contrition, implying that they still despised the targets of their invective. But ultimately, the apologizer's intentions were all but incidental. Just as the misspeaker's state of mind (be it a furious "passion" or a drunken "distemper") could not take away the sting of angry words, neither could an unsayer's reticence wholly diminish the power of healing words. The effectiveness of apology-as-cure rested in the performance itself. Expressed shame was genuine shame.[104]

Reluctant to unsay words he denied having said in the first place, Major William Hathorne equivocated "in open Court." "[T]here are words charged on me . . . which words I never spake," he protested. Nonetheless, he continued, "I freely confesse, that I spake many [other] words rashly, foolishly, & unadvisedly, of wch I am ashamed, & repent me of them, & desire all that tooke offence to forgive me, as his majesties commissioners have freely done."[105] Despite his initial denial, Hathorne earned the court's forgiveness. If the magistrates felt threatened by his open disagreement with the official version of his word crimes, Hathorne's articulated commitment to the ideal of governed speech—his avowal of the danger of "rash," "foolish," and "unadvised" words—must have reassured them fully. Regardless of which words they were willing to "own," such offenders expressed a core truth of their society: the fundamental notion that speech mattered. Unsayers affirmed that misspeakers, their neighbors, their victims, and their betters spoke, in the richest sociolinguistic sense, a common tongue.

Still, there were signs that this shared language, like apology itself, was as much rhetorical fiction as lived reality. For even during the most thoroughly Puritan years of the Puritan colonies, some New Englanders denied the very notion of governed speech and, in this sense, spoke other languages. Asserting that "it is not Reviling to Speak the Truth," and that "he knew no [more] hurt in Speaking English [than] in wearing Cloath[es]," prophetic railers such as William Leddra treated speech as a lesser medium of exchange than did most New Englanders in his day.[106] John Farnham also debased the value of unsaying, jeering and laughing at the Charlestown elders who asked him to retract his professed support for local Baptists. Instead of penitently recanting his contemptuous words, Farnham strode out of the church "saying he cared not though [the] elders were offended," and assuring listeners that the day of his excommunication "was the best day that ever dawned upon him."[107] Religious radicals—Leddra was a Quaker and Farnham a Baptist—figured prominently among those who denied all fetters on public speech. But they were not alone. Godly men, too, sometimes refused to retract wrongful words on the grounds that speech was nothing to be sorry for— that, as Boston physician Isaac Waldron put it, "words spoke in his passion . . . was no such abominable action."[108]

Although he could not have known it at the time, the future belonged to people like Waldron, people to whom Puritan notions of expressive liberty—the "just freedom of speech" Wenham's elders granted George Norton, paradoxically, by compelling him to apologize—felt confining.[109] Just as the redemptive power of unsaying was restricted to "redeemable" offenders, so it was limited to a particular historical context: to communities that placed great stock in the power of saying. Isaac Waldron's world remained one in which reputation was a central form of wealth, in which speech had enormous power to make or unmake a good name, and in which spoken apologies were the preferred form of restitution when words wounded.

But over time, as we shall see, New England slowly ceased to be such a place. By the end of the seventeenth century, the conditions that had made towns like Salem, Ipswich, and even Boston so hospitable to the shaming work of unsaying had begun to change. As these still-young communities grew in size, economic complexity, cultural diversity, and geographic range, the currency of reputation (and with it, the value of the spoken word as coin of the realm) lost some of its purchase. Prosecutions for speech offenses declined as litigants concerned themselves increasingly with other brands of larceny, thefts of property rather than of esteem. No wonder those who still considered words worth suing over tended to demand different compensation: repayment in coin rather than in kind.[110] Perhaps Isaac Waldron anticipated all this as early as 1676. Talk, he seemed to sense, was becoming cheap—too slight to hurt, too scanty to heal. The good doctor seems to have doubted the efficacy of John Tenney's cure, perhaps suspecting that once words lost their malefic powers, apology would not make much of a palliative.

At the same time, however, Waldron would have known that some kinds of speech remained costly indeed, even in the rapidly changing world of Boston in the 1670s. Even one who believed that words uttered in passion constituted too slight an offense to merit much notice would also have heard, on occasion, words that were too momentous to be "unsaid": Words that could not be taken back. Words that were felt to be not only wounding, but lethal. Perhaps Waldron himself had heard tell of the sharp tongue of Connecticut's Katherine Harrison, who had been charged with witchcraft and heated speaking several times between 1668 and 1670, only a few years before he expressed his doubts about the power of speech.[111] During the fall of 1668, in an attempt to pacify her accusers, recover her reputation, and protect her estate, Harrison offered an apology to Michael Griswold and his wife, two neighbors whom the Hartford magistrates had convicted her of slandering. Harrison wanted, she told the Griswolds, to repair the damage she had inflicted upon them by "speakeing both rash & sinfull words in my heat & passion." To that end, she administered a dose of John Tenney's favorite medicine, promising "to make the playster as Broad as the sore & more," and offering to apologize "when & where & in what maner you shall appoynt me[,] in as Large & ample maner as either you & your wife or any of your freinds shall desier unto both yours & theirs full contentment."[112] The Griswolds refused her apology, making clear, in essence, that no words could be sufficiently "large & ample" to remove the sting left by Harrison's sharp tongue. For in addition to uttering garden-variety slanders, she had been heard cursing her neighbors and foretelling their futures—sometimes with uncanny accuracy.

Over this type of magical speech, heard in New England since Anne Hutchinson's day, the countermagic of apology held little power. The damage these sorts of words inflicted was too palpable, too permanent. In 1692, people in Salem would confront a veritable epidemic of such deadly words. What would John Tenney prescribe to heal them then?

THE TONGUE
IS A WITCH

The setting: Boston and its environs, the first stormy months of 1692. The temper of the times: confused, troubled, anxious in the extreme. And the level of noise: positively deafening. Cacophonous enough, in fact, that no less eminent a preacher than Cotton Mather feels compelled, for the first time (though hardly the last), to inveigh in print against loose words—in particular, against unfettered female speech. Instructing the pious matrons of New England on the "character and happiness of a virtuous woman," he recalls for them the psalmist's decree: "*I will take heed unto my ways that I sin not with my Tongue; I will keep my Mouth with a Bridle.*" Mindful of the "usual" charge that women's "*Tongues* are frequently not so Governed by the *Fear of God*, as they ought to be," he exhorts the "daughter of Zion" to cultivate a "silver tongue"—speech rare and pure, free of boastful "dross." Mather urges her, "Be careful that you don't *Speak too soon.* . . . And be careful that you don't *Speak too much.*" For " 'tis the *Whore*, that is *Clamorous*, and the *Fool*, that is *Full of words.*"[1]

First printed in March 1692, Mather's pocket-sized volume on female conduct must have found an eager audience.[2] No daughter of Zion could have failed to notice that there were clamors aplenty that spring—more hubbub, perhaps, than had ever before been heard in New England. From the north and west, where English settlers warred against the French and their Algonquian allies, came doleful tales of battle and Indian captivity.

From across the Atlantic, where representatives of colony and Crown argued over the fate of Massachusetts's founding charter, came disturbing political news.[3] But while echoes of these distant turmoils unsettled many in Boston, the loudest din was homegrown, a racket caused not (as Mather claimed) by clamorous whores or wordy fools, but by a veritable plague of suspected witches and demoniacs.[4] Through the voices of the bewitched and the possessed, God's displeasure with New England had suddenly become audible, emerging "with an unusual and amazing loudness" that, minister Deodat Lawson feared, would "make the ears of those that hear . . . to tingle." Lawson and Samuel Parris, his successor in the pulpit of beleaguered Salem Village, witnessed the pandemonium firsthand. The devil had burst forth upon Massachusetts like a "roaring lion," Lawson wrote. Parris added, "when he shall be silenced, the Lord only knows."[5]

However dire, the verbal disorders emanating from Salem that spring would have been familiar to New Englanders. The belief that the "unruly" tongue was formed in the very "image of the divell" was both older and more widely held than the narrow confines of Salem village life might suggest. Nearly a century earlier, English divine William Perkins, a theologian revered by New England's magistrates and clerics, had reminded his followers that "when thou speakest evill, thy tongue is kindled by the fire of hell and Satan comes from thence with a coale to touch thy lips." Anglican preacher George Webbe put it more succinctly. "The *tongue* is a *witch*," he proclaimed in 1619.[6] Not just any tongue, Webbe might have added, but the female tongue in particular. Just as those trying to make sense of what they heard in Salem knew that the devil often announced himself through disorderly speech, so they also considered *women's* verbal wrongs especially suspect.[7] Throughout the long history of witchcraft in the West, the feminine and the diabolic had been closely linked. Women comprised upward of 80 percent of those suspected of witchcraft, as well as the vast majority of those thought to be directly "possessed" by the devil.[8] What pulled women into Satan's orbit? In large measure, they were snared by their own words. The authors of the *Malleus Maleficarum*, a fifteenth-century treatise whose authority was felt in New England as well as in Europe, argued that women's "slippery tongues" made them the likelier servants of the devil. Kramer and Sprenger suggested, therefore, that witch-hunters look no further than the "wicked woman['s] . . . hot words," "evil blandishments and violent importations" for evidence of diabolic goings-on.[9] As the anonymous author of a pamphlet entitled *The Anatomy of Woman's Tongue* explained, "a Woman's Tongue . . . is the Devil's Seat."[10]

Early modern learned culture, then, had much to say about the links between words, witchcraft, and women. But for most people in New England, being able to hear a witch was a skill honed less through book learning than through hard experience. From the late 1630s, when the "bewitching tongue" of Anne Hutchinson had lured converts with almost preternatural ease, settlers there had been subject to a steady flow of diabolically powerful words—so much so, in fact, that one traveler who visited Boston in 1680 said that he had "never been in a place where more was said about witchcraft and witches."[11] The talk had started more than forty years before, when Jane Hawkins, one of Hutchinson's followers, was accused of having "converse[d] with the Devill," an allegiance she revealed through the oddities of her own speech.[12] Hawkins escaped the noose in 1638, but a decade later, Charlestown's Margaret Jones would not be so lucky. Rendered suspect, in part, by the consequences of "some angry words passing between her and her Neighbours," Jones bore out the accusations against her by the "very intemperate" way she spoke at her trial: "lying notoriously, and railing upon the jury and witnesses."[13] If New England's witches had distinctly unquiet voices, the *victims* of witching words could be louder still, the occasion (as Increase Mather wrote) of great "noise in the Countrey."[14] Possessed or bewitched girls were said to make "Railing and Slander" a "very Frequent Theam" of their discourse. Like Boston's Martha Godwin, whose symptoms first appeared after a suspected witch gave the girl "bad Language," the bewitched often evinced their diabolic torments by trading a feminine style of "obliging and vertuous Conversation" for one peppered with "multiplyed Impertinencies." "Shee'd Hector me . . . and threaten me," Cotton Mather wrote, recalling with horror the way the uneducated girl had verbally lampooned his published work.[15]

Bewitching, lying, railing, slandering, hectoring, threatening: how far removed was the witch's way of speaking from the judicious, infrequent, and sober conversation of the silver-tongued woman! Where Puritan matrons spoke softly with tongues of silver, witches, their victims, and the demonically possessed ranted with tongues of fire. Indeed, the witch was not merely a lapsed version of the Puritan matron but her inverse. In a world understood to be "composed of contraries" (God and Satan, order and misrule, head and heart, male and female), the witch defined the virtuous woman in the negative. But she also did more. Not content simply to hold a dark mirror to feminine quietude, the witch's words turned the right order of family, neighborhood, and state upside down. Such an overturning was not difficult to accomplish. For a world made up of contraries was also, as historian Stuart Clark has noted, "a reversible world," a fragile system whose stability hinged upon its members' willingness to hold fast to their allotted rungs on the ladder of creation.[16] The witch audibly refused this assignment, instead using her voice to stand a world of opposites upon its head. No wonder, then, that being able to identify a witch (and thus to label and to vanquish her) was a matter of such overriding importance to people in early New England. What hung in the balance was not just the orderly progress of day-to-day life, but also, more broadly, the success or failure of the entire Puritan "errand."

But how was one to recognize a witch? In New England as in other face-to-face societies, people searched for the demonic at the margins of their cultures. Scholars have long argued that colonial witch-hunting played a vital role in maintaining social boundaries of many kinds, including those separating deviant from normal behavior, premodern from capitalist *mentalités*, and male prerogative from female encroachment.[17] What has been less well understood is that through witch-hunting, New Englanders also policed the outer limits of language itself. Who could say what to whom, and what were the consequences of words gone wrong? Such questions about the relationship between language and power were often on the minds of early New Englanders, and the words of accused witches threw them into particularly sharp relief. For when witches spoke, the slender boundary between saying and doing—always permeable in the early modern world—seemed to vanish entirely. Witches' speech was a type of action. Perhaps it was with this in mind that Cotton Mather referred to himself and his fellow ministers as "Ear-witnesses" to witchcraft and possession.[18] The phrase is an evocative one, resonating throughout the records of witch-hunting in the American colonies. Like Mather, people in seventeenth-century New England believed they could hear the devil's presence in a neighbor's speech before their other senses confirmed the diagnosis.

What, then, did a witch *sound* like? The answer was multifold, hinging not least upon who the listener was. Witchcraft was an ambiguous or "multivalent" term in premodern culture, holding different (and overlapping, and competing) meanings for people from different segments of society. Ordinary men and women heard the witch as somebody whose occult powers could be blamed for the myriad sufferings of daily life. Protestant clerics and magistrates, in contrast, denounced her as an enemy of religion who "hast entertained familiarity with Satan."[19] Labeling these rival versions of witchcraft belief clerical and lay, elite and popular, or Puritan and traditional, scholars have long sought to measure the gulf separating the common person's dread of malefic "magic" from the theologian's fear of a diabolic "antireligion."[20] Common to all these interpretations is the suggestion that the witch sounded (subtly or greatly) different to the neighbors whom she harmed than she did to the ministers and magistrates who might formally call her to account. To be an ear-witness to witchcraft, then, was to listen not only for what Mather called the "stretched and raised Rhetorick" of the devil, but also for what ordinary folks knew as the "tatling & tale Bareing," the "muttering" and "threatning," and the "fauneing & flattering" that marked everyday exchanges with a witch.[21]

The timbre of witchspeak also varied in another important way: over time as well as from hearer to hearer. Throughout the seventeenth century, the level of satanically inflected speech rose and fell, at some moments remaining a low murmur and at others becoming a high-pitched roar. Without question, the cataclysmic trials in Salem, virtually the last official expressions of witch fear in the colonies, were also the loudest. In those first, dismal months of 1692, a steady drip of bewitching words grew into a torrent of public, verbal abuse. What did witches sound like in that tumult-filled year? In their neighborhoods, as we shall see, their voices were much what they had always been. But in meetinghouses and in magistrates' parlors, their words began to assume a new coloration—one that would eventually lead elite ear-witnesses to question the prosecutions in Salem and, indeed, the nature of witchcraft itself.

IF SPEECH WAS THE currency of New England towns in the seventeenth century, the witch's words had the highest value of any speaker's. Perhaps this central irony was one of the fearsome reversals enacted by the devil: witches, arguably the most despised and distrusted speakers in their communities, were at the same time the most literally credible. There was no escaping their pronouncements, for *what they said came true*. Carried on the witch's tongue, words broke free of their moorings in a system of signs and referents and became vessels of actual, palpable power.[22] The perverse truths articulated by the spiteful, muttering witch struck at the very foundation of local life: the dominion of men over their wives and farmers over their stock, the ability of parents to protect and nurture their children. Although the theater of her malice was small, the impact of her words in the community setting was enormous. Crops failed. Babies and animals died. Luck ran out. The witch's tongue, her neighbors believed, could author all this destruction—and more.

Where did the devastating power of the witch's voice originate? Her neighbors would have a ready answer. The witch, they might say, conversed with the dark powers that governed a magical world, forces whose malign potency then infected the witch's own speech. One accused of witchcraft would doubtless offer a different account. She would agree, no doubt, that words made witches. But she would likely place the blame less on her own scolding than upon the invective of others. From her perspective, the verbal wrongs that added up to witchcraft would consist chiefly of the abusive words uttered *against* suspects. As Elizabeth Sawyer, England's infamous Witch of Edmonton, proclaims in William Rowley's 1658 drama of that name, the witch was "a common sink / For all the filth and rubbish of men's tongues / To fall and run into." Known for her "curses, imprecations / Blasphemous speeches," and "detested oaths," Sawyer tells the audience that her "bad tongue" was by her neighbors' "bad usage made so." " 'Tis all one," she explains, "To be a witch as to be counted one."[23]

Sawyer's soliloquy is self-serving, to be sure. But there is something to her explanation. For if, as John Demos has argued, witch rumors beat "a thick trail of talk" across New England neighborhoods, it is often difficult to discern the trail's point of origin or, indeed, its initial direction. It is, as Rowley's title character herself suggests, a classic chicken/egg dilemma. We don't know which came first: the suspect's ill words, or the slanders used against her.[24] We do know that outside of the Salem trials, nearly one-third of those accused of witchcraft in New England filed suit against men and women who, they argued, had defamed them by calling them witches. In fact, a substantial number of "informal" witchcraft accusations (those that never resulted in an indictment or a trial) survive in the records *only* in the form of an alleged witch's attempt to defend herself against the words of others. And it is certain, moreover, that the records of slander litigation greatly underrepresent both the quantity and the pitch of verbal innuendo encircling reputed witches.[25] At the very least, the loose talk of neighbors was an essential step in making a witch's presence known to those around her. It seems likely, in addition, that such gossip played a vital role in her very creation.

Consider, for example, the rumors that swirled around Jane James throughout her life in Marblehead. Convicted of stealing by the county court in the summer of 1639, she acquired a "common fame" as a "theef" and a "falce forsworne woman."[26] By 1650, neighbors had begun to cast her in the role of witch. That year, a nearby farmer reported that his garden would not bear "frughtes [fruits] . . . so long as he lived near that woman." He also recalled having seen an apparition resembling James floating "in a boat at sea in the likeness of a cat." Others said they had glimpsed her "going in a boat on the water toward Boston, when she was in her yard at home." Thus neighbors' stories began to transform Jane James from a "common Lyer" into an "old witch." The county magistrates apparently thought such tales had a hollow ring, and consistently judged James to have been defamed by their tellers.[27] But if she was never formally presented as a witch, she was convicted daily in the court of reputation, where her neighbors continued to denounce her as an "old hag," a "Jesable and [a] devil."[28] In James's case and in many others, to cry witch was to create a witch—in local estimation if not in legal fact or in magical practice. When Salem's Anthony Ashby exclaimed that Edith Crawford "was A witch & If shee were nott a witch allreddy she would bee won," he did much to assure the truth of his prediction merely by stating it.[29] Such a "bad Report" about a suspected woman would spur ear-witnesses to "take speshall noates of her life & conversation" in the future. Those "special notes," in turn, would yield further bad reports.[30] In this way, a witch was made rather than born—crafted, in significant part, out of the malign words of her neighbors.

This was so because, once uttered, the label "witch" proved so very hard to shake. As minister Samuel Willard argued in a tract inveighing against the proceedings in Salem, a (false) accusation of witchcraft left a stain of "perpetual infamy" on the innocent suspect. Indeed, no other allegation was "with more difficulty wiped off."[31] Having lived in its shadow for nearly twenty years, Jane James would certainly have concurred. And hers was hardly the longest sentence. Several of those on trial for their lives in 1692 had been accused during the 1660s or 1670s; one, the wife of Gloucester's William Vinson, had first been publicly denounced as a witch all the way back in 1653, almost forty years before she pled with Salem's Court of Oyer and Terminer to release her from the jail where she had lain "many monthes . . . charged with witch-craft."[32] Separated in time, the charges that dogged such women as Vin-son were nonetheless related, part of a web of stories that entangled generations. As Beverly's minister John Hale said of the accused Salem witch Dorcas Hoar, "When discourses arose about witchcrafts at [Salem] village," those "discourses revived" dormant rumors of Hoar's strange be-havior, some of them dating from "twenty two yeares agoe."[33] In short, it was a terrible thing to be, as one Scottish victim put it, "Imprisoned under the Name of a Witch." With "no hope of ever being in Credit again," even an innocent woman so labeled might well choose "rather to Die than to Live."[34] Accusations of witchcraft, no less than a witch's own speech, were not mere words so much as devastating acts—what one historian has called "the seventeenth-century verbal equivalents of nuclear weapons."[35]

Yet we should not suppose that the witch herself was linguistically passive, remaining silent in the face of her neighbors' opprobrium. To the contrary, the heat of the witch's own words was the stuff of legend in the Anglo-American world. To many popular writers in early modern England, the witch was, quite simply, a particularly heinous variety of scold, a woman whose harsh words more than merited the verbal affronts she received. Playwright William Rowley framed the question poetically: "She on whose tongue a whirlwind sits . . . Is not that scold a witch?"[36] True-crime pamphlets echoed drama, titillating readers with tales of no-torious suspects whose "speech" was "fell [i.e., cruel] and envious," and who trafficked in "clamors and malicious information."[37] Indeed, even writers who doubted the very existence of witches portrayed the accused as "Scolds." Famed English skeptic Reginald Scott argued that some women, through "their Words uttered," made themselves "odious unto all their Neighbors" and thus unfairly became witches in the popular imagination.[38] Witches were deemed scolds (and vice versa) in life as in literature. It is important to remember that the witch's words were inter-preted by her neighbors as contentious without necessarily being so in any objective sense.[39] Still, the connection between being accused of witchcraft and having a reputation for verbal aggression appears strong. In New England, accused witches far exceeded the general population (and especially the population of women) in rates of "assaultive" speech, lying, and railing against authority.[40] Neighbors' depositions confirm that, in the ears of her accusers, a reputed witch's malicious acts were inseparable from her sinister words.

Just what was so threatening about the voices of the accused? Some-times, what was labeled diabolical speech amounted to little more than a forthright—in fact, *masculine*—style of talking. Eunice Cole of Hampton, accused of witchcraft numerous times between 1656 and 1680, was known for speaking out, particularly on her own behalf. One neighbor recalled "being at . . . a meeting with the selectmen" (a setting in which a godly woman was unlikely to be seen, let alone heard) when Cole burst in and "demand[ed]" their "help." Some years later, the town constable accused her of "often finding fault," and of "complaining" about the maintenance the town provided her. Among her neighbors, Cole spoke as brusquely and impudently as she did with local authorities. When Jonathan Thing asked her what she was doing near his cattle, she retorted angrily: "what is that to you, sawsbox"?[41] Abraham Perkins, who claimed to have overheard "a discoursing" between Cole and the devil, reported that the witch "seemed to rant" at her infernal master, sounding "displeased" and "finding fault" with him just as she did with her human auditors.[42] Demanding, complaining, and blaming, Cole spoke as if she were entitled to the kind of verbal authority that, in her world, accrued only to men.[43]

Where Cole seemed inclined to talk like a man, the voices of other accused witches fell short in prototypically feminine ways; they were said to be rumormongers and troublemakers rather than affronters and revilers. Goodwife Bayley, called before New Haven's magistrates in 1655, was the archetypal gossip-turned-witch, deemed "very suspitious in poynt of witchcraft" largely because she resorted to "impudent and notorious lying" in order to "make discord among neighbours."[44] Sarah Bibber, one of the core Salem accusers, whom some suspected of witchcraft in her own right, was said to be "much given to tatling & tale Bareing," "makeing mischeif amongst her neighbors" by "spekeking againts won and nother very obsanely and thos things that were very falls."[45] Likewise, neighbors reported that Sarah Good, one of the first to hang in 1692, had regularly spoken "very crossely & Mallitiously" to them, calling their children "vile Names" and "mutring & scolding extreamly." So disruptive was Good's manner of speaking that Samuel and Mary Abbey, in whose house the accused witch and her husband lodged during the late 1680s, told the court that they had been "forced *for Quiettness sake*" to evict their unquiet boarder.[46]

Any sort of "cross" or malicious words were manifestly ungodly and even more dramatically unfeminine. But to be heard railing against one's spouse was especially damaging. For "calling her husband many opprobrious names" (among them, "old rogue" and "old devil"), Bridget (Oliver) Bishop was ordered to stand for an hour "in the public market place," tied back-to-back with her mate, with a description of their troubles affixed to her forehead. This public infamy, endured back in 1677, doubtless contributed to the lasting reputation for "falling out," "muttering," and "threatning" that shortened her path to the scaffold in 1692.[47] Alice Parker's neighbors deposed that she "scolded att" her husband and "called [him] all to nought" in front of "severall others," while Sarah Bibber manifested her "turbulent unruly spirit" by "call[ing] her husband bad names." Their unwifely verbal demeanor, the very essence of scolding, embodied the inversion at which the devil was so very skilled. Such "unbeseeming" speech upset the natural order of things, unmanning the witch's husband and forcing neighbors to intervene in order to bolster his authority.[48] Like so many social and linguistic disorders, witchcraft began at home.

The gendered verbal order of the witch's household was equally disrupted when the suspect in question was male, as approximately one in five of those accused in New England was. No less than their wives (who, indeed, were typically the primary suspects in any given family), male witches spoke in ways that defied gendered norms.[49] If the ideal Puritan man used his forceful-but-governed tongue to control those beneath him, the male witch was often cowed by his wife's ill words. The case of Hugh Parsons, who came before the court in Springfield, Massachusetts, in 1651 and 1652, is instructive in this regard. With her long-standing reputation for scolding, Parsons's wife, Mary, was the first in the family to be accused. Then, like many female suspects, Mary Parsons raised her voice against her husband, telling neighbors that she "suspect[ed] him to be a witch."[50] When neighbors, crediting these accusations, made Hugh Parsons the primary object of their witch fears, they used Hugh's anemic reactions to Mary's scolding as evidence of his diabolism. One deponent made much of the fact that Mary Parsons "spake very harsh things" against her husband "before his face." If Hugh Parsons "had been innocent," the witness reasoned, "he would have blamed her for her speeches," and "reproved her" accordingly. But Parsons had done the opposite. Displaying a distinctly unmanly willingness to endure an unwomanly tongue, Hugh seemed almost to welcome Mary's domineering voice. Since "he had such speeches" from his wife "daily," he told the court, "he made the best of it," supposing that Mary was likely to "speak as ill and as much as anybody else." Too often, people noticed, Hugh Parsons remained "wholly silent" in situations where it was his right—his masculine duty—to speak out.[51]

Yet such untoward reticence was not the whole of Hugh Parsons's gendered linguistic failure. If wifely silence was his preferred language at home, Parsons used a different kind of feminized speech among his neighbors. There, scolding was his speech style of choice. As he himself admitted, "in his anger" he often became "impatient and doth speak what he should not." Almost everyone who transacted business with Parsons agreed, having heard him "mutter and mumble," or lash out with "threatening speeches" against those who disappointed him. Dismayed over a failed bargain with Rice Bedortha, for example, he cautioned Bedortha's wife that he would "remember" her when she did "little think on it." He menaced John Mathews with a variation on what neighbors called "his usual speech": maligning his honesty, and vowing to "be even with him."[52] To be sure, such words were forceful stuff, full of a kind of malign power. But not masculine power. For when he himself scolded, much as when he passively accepted his wife's heated words, Parsons failed to talk like a man. People must have wondered why, for example, he so often proved unable to transact business to his satisfaction. Such negotiations fell firmly within the compass of men's speaking roles. If he felt himself ill-used in commerce, why did Parsons not seek restitution in church or in court? Why, in short, did he fail to find appropriate ways to speak (forcefully, respectfully) on his own behalf in a culture that gave men so many opportunities to do so?

Instead, men such as Parsons spoke like women, and like discontented women at that. And, as the period's popular wisdom held, "it is a great discredit for a man to be accounted for a scolde, for scolding is the manner of Shrowes [shrews]." Threatening and scolding—the weapons of those from whom life demanded silence—were no substitutes for masculine, authoritative speech. A godly man, secure in the quiet power of his well-governed tongue, knew better than to "strive to win the Cucking-stoole from" noisy women.[53] He had other speaking parts to play, other ways to make his voice heard. The male witch, in contrast, personified the scolding man, who, as one contemporary proverb declared, "hath a woman's tongue in his head."[54] In this sense, all witchspeak was feminine, regardless of the sex of the speaker.

Of course, the vast majority of people with reputations for disorderly speech—including women and men formally charged with scolding, gossiping, railing against their mates, and even the combative, masculine speech crime of "slighting"—were never branded witches. Indeed, if prescriptive literature offers any sort of window onto lived reality, we might suppose that New England women were *expected* to misspeak in these various ways. Even Puritan authorities, whose position on the "woman question" was moderate by the standards of the day, claimed that the "weaker sex," as a whole, "hath the glibbest tongue." All women, popular literature quipped, tended to be "flibbergibbes," "tatlers," "talebearers," and "rumour raisers."[55] The words of witches, however, took the ills of feminine speech to another level entirely. If the trouble with women was that their speech consisted of idle chatter, the trouble with witches was that their speech was anything but. Witches were known not just for scolding and "falling out" (serious breaches of social and gender ideals in their own right), but more pointedly for their "Evill wishing[s]": prophetic warnings and occult forecasts made real by their utterance. This penchant for "wichshing very bad wichchis"—wishes that all too often came true—made the witch's words stand out from the contentious speech that was a constant presence in New England's face-to-face communities.[56] While the remarks of common slanderers and railers cut their targets to the quick, the witch's words had a more palpable sort of impact, a sort not common to women in other areas of colonial life. Her "cursing" or "foretelling" burst the bounds of language and assumed material form. Put simply, you could take witches at their word—or, at least, you could do so in hindsight.

Unlike the immediate, deflating impact of an insult, the full force of a curse ripened over time. The diabolic power of a witch's wishes was experienced ex post facto, a retrospective diagnosis applied to inexplicable harms. This "remembered" quality of curses followed their linguistic form: they were acts of "overpowering speech" delivered "in the future tense."[57] Indeed, their very futurity guaranteed the long life span of curses. The fears of a man who fancied himself the victim of "witches not far off" might draw fuel from a friend's question: "did [the suspect] give you any suspicious words"?[58] Almost inevitably, the answer would be yes. And as one man on the receiving end of a suspect's "discontented words" put it, such exchanges were the sorts of "things" that tended to "run in my mind." The words of accused witch Mary Parsons pricked at this particular deponent's psyche only overnight before their import became clear; his cows took sick the very next morning.[59] But the meaning of other pronouncements took longer to emerge—a fact some accused witches seemed deliberately to exploit by pledging that an affliction would befall the terrified listener at some precise moment in the future, if not "be fore the weak was out," then "afore Seven years Came to an Eand."[60] With such ominous promises lingering in the air, it is no wonder that the records of New England witch trials are filled with recollections of the exact words that suspects exchanged with their neighbors anywhere from the previous day to "about on[e] or t[w]o and thirty years" before formal charges were filed.[61] Like the label "witch" itself, a witch's curse put down deep roots in collective memory.

What kinds of malign promises possessed such longevity? While the semantic form of a witch's curse was generic, the forecasts themselves were almost endlessly diverse—and inventive. Some of the "evil wishes" that plagued New Englanders were quite specific: that "one; or two of the best Cowes" a farmer had would die, or that a child would be taken ill.[62] Thus when Allen Ball and his wife refused Elizabeth Godman's request to borrow some buttermilk, Godman answered ominously, "you will save it for your piggs, but it will doe them no good." Just as Godman said, Ball reported, "after this his piggs all but one dyed, one after another."[63] In a similarly direct vein, Katherine Harrison of Wethersfield menaced ministers Josiah Willard and Samuel Hale by reporting that she would "shortlye See them gone Bothe them & theires."[64] When John Kimball and his wife declared that they "needed to get a dog," and yet refused to purchase one of Susannah Martin's puppies, Martin hissed, "Ile give him pupeys enough." And so she did; "within a few days," Kimball found himself plagued by a throng of occult puppies who assaulted him until he "thought my lif was going out."[65]

But if some curses all but spelled out the time, place, and manner of their intended results, most bespoke a generic malice on the part of the witch—an inchoate ill will that took on explicit meaning only in the recollection. Sometimes a curse's turn of phrase was proverbial or metaphoric, as when Mercy Disborough jeered that she would make Thomas Bennett "as bare as A birds tale," or when Hugh Parsons warned the victor in a civil suit against him that the judgment would rankle "as wild fire in this house and as a moth in [his] garment."[66] Likewise Benjamin Abbot, whose conduct during a land transaction provoked the ire of Andover's Martha Carrier, did not know what to expect when Carrier vowed to "stick as Closs" to him "as the bark stooke to the Tree," and to "hold my noss so Closs to the grindstone as Ever it was held since my Name was Benjamin Abbutt." Only later, when he "was taken with a swelling in my foot" and "a payne in my side . . . wich bred to a sore," did Abbot begin to make sense of Carrier's threat.[67]

Lacking the poetic flair of a Mercy Disborough, a Hugh Parsons, or a Martha Carrier, most suspects issued curses that were the verbal equivalents of blank checks for bad news. Thus Sarah Good warned a neighbor simply that she would "give her something," while Katherine Harrison promised a victim that she "would be even with him," or make him "Rue it hereafter."[68] In time, such mundane forecasts became self-fulfilling prophecies. A seventeenth-century incarnation of the modern-day psychic, Ipswich's Goodwife Batchelor could rest assured that any outcome would make good the threat she leveled at a neighboring cattle farmer: that some of his cows "would dye," others "would hardly escape and some others would live." In such cases, the harsh realities of premodern life conspired to realize the witch's promise, making her the author of the future. It was, as Batchelor's neighbors implied, an almost scriptural power, for "as she sayde so it came to pass."[69]

A witch's cursing, then, is one of the few linguistic forms that achieved its greatest potency when it was least direct. Which is why, perhaps, even a suspect's empty pleasantries could sound diabolic. Jeremiah Neal was sure that Ann Pudeater had been "pretending kindnes" when she made a simple request to borrow a "morter" from Neal's wife; Pudeater's chatter revealed itself as cursing only later, when Goody Neal sickened. Other curses masqueraded as flattery. Only "a Short tyme after" Alice Parker "fauned upon" Samuel Shattock's family "w'th very Smooth words," his child became gravely ill.[70] East Hampton's Elizabeth Garlick was also heard oozing praise at her victims. "[H]ow pretty [your] child Doth looke," she gushed to Goody Davis. But virtually as "sone as she had spoken," Garlick reversed herself, remarking, "the child is not well." Sometimes, she "laughed and Jeered" at her enemies, while at others, she would "cum fauninge" to them—thus comporting herself, Garlick's neighbors said, like a "duble tounged woman."[71] A true daughter of Eve, such a woman would "flatter and speake faire" to obtain what she wanted, only to respond "scornfully" once her "desires" were "gained." Her words might be "sweete as honey." But "sweete words," no less than hot ones, could "overcome" guileless hearers.[72] Thus from a neighbor's perspective, ear-witnessing a witch required the utmost care. And from the witch's own point of view, a reputation for being "double tongued" meant that speech itself became a double bind: she was damned (and *damning*) if she railed, and damned if she flattered.[73] Proper feminine discourse occupied the narrow middle ground between these two diabolic extremes.

Those who spoke out on behalf of the accused faced the difficult task of situating their wives, mothers, sisters, and neighbors within this relatively small discursive space. Just as testimony against a witch emphasized her clamorousness, petitions in support of a suspect often pointed to her decorous speech (or, indeed, her silence) as proof of her innocence. "[A]t all Tims by hur discors," her neighbors explained, Elizabeth How had proved herself to be a "Neighbourly woman Conssiencious in her dealing[,] faithfull to her promises & Christian-like in her Conversation." Even when How spoke of those whose "falls acqusations" endangered her life, the rule of charity governed her tongue. In the decade they had known her, Simon and Mary Chapman had "never herd hur refil [revile] eny parson that heth a kusid hur with wichcraft." Instead, How "pittied" her tormentors, prayed for them, and even insisted that such "afliktions" were all for the better, "for it med hur exsamin hur oun hart."[74] Pleading for his wife of fifty-five years, Thomas Bradbury likewise emphasized that this good Christian woman was the verbal antithesis of the witch. Mary, he said, had long been "a loveing & faithfull wife," content "in her place." And knowing "her place" meant, as Bradbury explained, that Mary was "not . . . able to speake much for herselfe, not being so free of Speach as some others may bee." Still, her quiet "life and conversation . . . amongst her neighbours" might serve, her husband argued, as a most eloquent deposition, "a better & more reall Testimoney of her, then can bee exprest by [her own] words."[75] The goodwife, in other words, followed the rule of Christian modesty all the way to the gallows, if need be, refusing to speak forcefully even in her own defense.

The witch, of course, had no such scruples. Where the voice of the daughter of Zion was self-denying, that of the witch was self-enlarging. She used words to augment her place by diminishing the power of others. Whatever its precise form, the metamessage of the witch's curse was the same: "I hope I shall see the downfall of you."[76] Her tongue was the weapon (alternately a sharp sword and a velvet noose) that helped her to realize this evil wish. If the goodwife was, by definition, a follower— in deed and especially in word—the witch, through her cursing, became a leader. She pronounced the destiny of others and, more unbecoming still, decided her own fate in the bargain. *As she said, so it came to pass.* No wonder, as English dramatist Thomas Heywood reminded audiences, the witch's cursing left households "turn'd topsie turvy" and families "quite upside down."[77] Her voice called to those around her: "Lets have a turn heels over head."[78] And the world around her heeded the cry as words became acts, plenty turned to want, and domination ended in "downfall."

IT WAS THE JOB of New England's civil and religious authorities to translate inchoate rumors of witchcraft into the precise rhetoric of sin and redemption, indictment and sentencing. Yet throughout most of the seventeenth century, magistrates proved loath to do so. If the rate at which suspects were convicted and executed is any indication, leading men were skeptical of the way ordinary folks defined witches. Excluding the Salem trials, just over one-quarter of those whose malign words and deeds neighbors brought to a court's attention were convicted of the capital crime of witchcraft.[79] This was so, in large measure, because authorities regarded witching words—the curses and threats that took center stage in the dramas that neighbors performed for the court—as uncertain proofs. Following the lead of English writers including Richard Barnard, John Gaule, and especially William Perkins, New England courts treated the kinds of verbal symptoms that the witch's neighbors so feared as insufficient evidence of a capital crime. To be sure, Perkins conceded, a "common report" that a suspect "is a witch," or tales of the "present mischief" that followed her "cursing and banning," constituted "special presumptions" that "probably and conjecturally note one to be a witch." But "strong suspicions" did not make "just and sufficient proofs." In Protestant theology (and, hence, in Anglo-American law), only one speech act made a witch: a compact with Satan, the promise that bound a fallen human to a fallen angel. And just two other speech acts could reveal the witch to the court: her own confession, or the testimony of two or more "witnesses of good and honest report" describing the same, indisputably diabolic act.[80]

Despite their reluctance to convict cursing women and men of witchcraft, New England's leading men shared, albeit in subtly different form, many of the core beliefs of ordinary, neighborhood witch-hunters. First and foremost, elites continually avowed the existence of witches and devils, peppering their own copious writings on the subject with references to the "Histories of the Witchcrafts beyond-sea."[81] So, too, they agreed with their less educated neighbors that women were the most plausible suspects. Although Satan had been known to recruit "both sexes or kinds of persons, men and women, excluding neither," Perkins explained, "the devil hath more easily and oftener prevailed with women."[82] Thus in New England, accused men were considerably less likely than their female counterparts to satisfy the official definition of the witch; before Salem, only two of the fourteen cases in which men were tried for the crime ended in hanging.[83] In addition to agreeing that the devil most often took the shape of a woman, Protestant beliefs overlapped with traditional ones in casting witchcraft as chiefly a crime of inversion—of (in Perkins's words) "rebellion and disobedience." But elites concerned themselves less with the everyday reversals pronounced by the witch than with a far more encompassing sort of overturning: the betrayal of God's order for Satan's. The witch, Puritan writers argued, was a heretic allied with the devil in his drive to create an antisociety: a dark mirror of a godly community, a world governed by inverted institutions, rulers, and doctrines.[84]

It seemed only fitting that this diabolic antisociety possessed its own native tongue, a nefarious language perfectly suited to the witch's avowed mission of destruction. And thus a final point of congruence between learned and popular understandings of witchcraft: their shared focus on speech. Though they concerned themselves with different aspects of her language, elites, too, made the witch's own voice central to her crime. Words inaugurated the witch's entry into the devil's antisociety, as she pledged herself in "league or covenant" to Satan and "renounced God . . . king and governor."[85] Having "verbally promised to covenant with him"—a pact she typically sealed with a signature or fingerprint rendered in blood—the witch became a full participant in the devil's world of misrule: attending his antimasses, partaking of his antisacraments, intoning his anti-Scriptures.[86] In short, the witch spoke the devil's antilanguage, an upside-down tongue in which "Railing" equalled "Blessing" and vice versa.[87] Or rather, Puritan writers often said, the devil spoke through *her*. Like all sinners, witches were (un)governed by Satan rather than governed by God. Which meant, as Thomas Hooker put it, that "the devill rules in them; *he speaks by their tongues*."[88] For elites, then, earwitnessing witchcraft held special horrors—and, perhaps, terrifying delights. From their perspective, the voice of the witch sounded quite different from the abrasive yet ultimately mundane tone that marked her presence in the neighborhood. For ministers and magistrates, listening to the witch meant engaging in a dangerous sort of eavesdropping: beholding (if not partaking of) the "Communion [i.e., communication] with Devils" that God had "interdicted," pressing an ear to the gates of hell and hearing, if only for a moment, the voice of the "Father of lies."[89]

If a magistrate were lucky, a suspected witch would use the devil's voice to damn herself, confessing with such force and detail as to be effectively "condemned out of her own mouth." As English jurist John Gaule explained, a witch's "owne mouth can speake her owne guilt best."[90] The Protestant focus on sin and redemption meant that confession was important in all matters of discipline, in court as well as in church. It was especially so where witchcraft was concerned. By admitting her devotion to the devil, the confessing witch simultaneously brought a clandestine sin into the open and gave voice to the authorities' definition of witchcraft.[91] Thus it must have been particularly satisfying to the magistrates when a suspect such as Boston's Goody Glover volubly confessed her allegiance to Satan in words "too blasphemous and horrible for any Pen . . . to mention."[92] Hartford's Rebecca Greensmith likewise admitted "in open court" that she "hast entertained familiarity with Satan." Hearing the witch repeat what Satan had "told her"—that "at *Christmas* they would have a merry Meeting" where "the Covenant between them should be subscribed"—was a close substitute for hearing the devil speak.[93]

Yet the most terrifying speakers of Satan's antilanguage were not witches per se, but rather those poor, tormented souls—almost exclusively young women—who were believed to have been enchanted by a witch or corporeally invaded by the devil himself.[94] Fasting and praying at the bedsides of such victims, New England ministers became privy to speech they deemed "amaz[ing]," even "marvellous to Hear."[95] Part of their astonishment stemmed from the very timbre and pitch of the diabolically influenced voice, which cast off every convention of verbal modesty. When taken with her fits, Elizabeth Knapp, a servant in the Groton, Massachusetts, household of Samuel Willard, "cried out" in a "violent" manner, alternating between "sudden shrieks" and "immoderate and extravagant laughter." At times, the "roarings and screamings" of the possessed were more than unfeminine: they were barely recognizable as human speech. Knapp "barked like a dog and bleated like a calf," while the Godwin children signalled the most acute phases of their bewitchment when they began to "bark at one another like Dogs, and . . . purr like so many Cats."[96] To say that such utterances were at odds with the verbal postures that young people—especially young women—were urged to assume before their elders and their betters is greatly to understate the case. The modes of speaking employed by girls like Knapp, as Samuel Willard noted, represented nothing less than "a dark resemblance of hellish torments."[97]

Equally unsettling were the implacable silences to which possessed and bewitched girls fell prey. Part of the power of their erstwhile muteness came from its signal unpredictability, as the possessed lurched between extravagant noisiness and complete, unalterable quiet. But more threatening still was what might be called the content of their silence. Diabolic language was defined, in significant part, by the words it purposefully excluded. Mercy Short, for example, appeared dumbstruck—"her Mouth" utterly "stop'd"—when "anything of Religeon" was discussed. Asked by Cotton Mather to pronounce "the Name of God and Christ," Martha Godwin replied, "I must not speak it," and fell silent. Elizabeth Knapp was literally gagged by the devil, so that whenever "she strove to speak," she felt "as if a string was tied about the roots of her tongue and reached down into her vitals and pulled her tongue down." Not only pious speech but edifying *hearing* was often beyond the reach of the possessed, whose ears "would immediately bee stop'd," as Mather wrote, if the ministers gathered around them "spoke any good Thing."[98] By refusing to hear and say what she ought, as much as by roaring and screaming when she should have remained silent, the possessed victim divulged the antigrammar that governed the devil's antilanguage. In so doing, she claimed for herself what the authors of the *Malleus* called the "power of silence." To her stunned audience, the demoniac's inability to speak (and to listen) must have sounded like a spiteful joke, a satiric twist on the notion that women should hold their tongues in public.[99]

If her unfeminine (indeed, inhuman) tone of voice and her pointed refusals to speak or to hear pious words parodied womanly quietness, *what* the possessed girl said further transformed the godly speech of Zion's daughters into the hellish ranting of the devil. Often, the first thing elite ear-witnesses noticed about the speech of the possessed was its skill-fulness. The goodwife discoursed comfortably in the cadence of the ver-nacular Bible, but the bewitched spoke in tongues, shocking hearers with an exact imitation of "the *Dutch-tone* in the pronunciation of *English*," a flawless recitation of Latin prayers, or an unexpected capacity to under-stand "the Greek New-Testament, and the Hebrew Old Testament."[100] And her linguistic gifts were not limited to philology. The virtuous woman knew Scripture, but the demoniac could cite chapter and verse with dizzying speed. Thus Mercy Short uttered "innumerable Things . . . which would have been more Agreeable to One of a greater Elevation in Christianity," garnering scriptural support for her arguments at a pace "no man living ever" could have matched. Margaret Rule, too, used "strains of Expression and Argument" that "a person . . . of the best Education and Experience and of Attainments much beyond hers could not have exceeded." Such "discourses," ministers knew, were "incredibly beyond what might have been expected" from speakers of such "small Education"—young women trained to speak seldom in their native En-glish tongue, and not at all in Latin, Greek, or Hebrew. In short, the demoniac "transcended her ordinary capacity," displaying fluency that greatly outstripped that of the virtuous woman.[101]

But even that was not the worst of it. For the speech of the bewitched was not merely prodigious; it was strangely authoritative. One of the signal features of the devil's antilanguage was the degree of interpretive choice claimed by its speakers. "[E]xcessively Witty" and "Insolent and Abusive" by turns, possessed girls "took an extraordinary Liberty" in their speech. Thus Martha Godwin, Mather recalled, recited from "a Jest-book . . . without any Disturbance," and "A popish Book also she could en-dure very well." But, Mather lamented (and here we glimpse her author-ity clashing openly with his): "it would kill her" to read aloud from "any Book, that (in my Opinion) . . . might have bin profitable and edifying for her."[102] Elizabeth Knapp was more pointed, telling Samuel Willard that he was "a great black rogue" who preached "nothing but a parcel of lies." In a perfect emblem of the carnivalesque speech order proclaimed by the demoniac, Knapp commanded the minister: "Hold your tongue, hold your tongue."[103] Like the spectral *"Robbers"* whom Cotton Mather accused of having *"stolen"* some "Discourses" that he intended *"to preach* . . . and hereafter to *print,"* the possessed girl absconded with the preacher's rightful voice.[104] She insisted that he hold his tongue when, as centuries of Christian tradition made clear, his speech should have compelled her silence. The positions of preacher and hearer reversed as clerical ear-witnesses became mere "standers-by," silently attending the "Speeches that fell from" the demoniac's mouth.[105]

Seated at the bedsides of the possessed or bewitched, ministers, physicians, magistrates, and other authorities became "Ear-witnesses to Disputacions that amazed us": conversations they variously described as marvelous and horrible, shocking and wondrous—indeed, as "some of the most Surprising Things imaginable." Surely there was a voyeuristic thrill in hearing words that divulged at least a few of the "Mysteries of Darkness," a secret language that ordinarily remained beyond the ears of mere mortals. No wonder New England clerics rushed to attend the possessed in the throes of their fits and felt compelled to describe, often in print, what they saw and heard during the course of those electrifying encounters.[106] But just as surely, they did so with enormous caution—caution in the hearing *and in the retelling*. For if, as Samuel Willard noted in the case of Elizabeth Knapp, there was "little good to be done by discourse" with the devil, still less good was likely to come from broadcasting such conversations indiscriminately. All listeners would do well to remember that the "things discovered from the Mouths of Damsels possest" might turn out to be "wonderful snares laid for Curious People," ministers among them.[107] The demonic verbal prowess of the possessed and the bewitched was thus something of a paradox, both a marvel that cried out for publication and a weapon that demanded the most conscientious handling.

And so, for most of the seventeenth century, New England elites interposed themselves between the voices of the bewitched or possessed and the ears of the lay public. They did so, first, by turning a suspicious ear toward the demoniac, testing her claims of possession or bewitchment against other possible explanations. No sooner had he heard Elizabeth Knapp's ravings than Samuel Willard summoned a local "physician" in hopes of discovering whether Knapp's "distemper" was "natural or diabolical." Knowing that "counterfeit" demoniacs had hoodwinked English authorities, those called to ear-witness a possession also had to consider the possibility of fraud.[108]

Even after a bewitched or possessed girl convinced hearers that her affliction was neither organic nor pretended, caution remained the rule. News of the demoniac's claims had to be filtered, if not "studiously suppressed." A cautious minister would strive both to "forbid" the afflicted "from *accusing* any of her neighbors" and to prevent "others from *enquiring* any thing of her."[109] For if her words were allowed to circulate casually—if "Reports" of her rantings were "carried from one place to another"—she might "wound a great part of the credit" of innocent people, herself included.[110] Which is why the first line of defense against demonic invasions was "Prayer and Fasting" in the victim's "haunted house," rather than at the local meetinghouse. Which is why Samuel Willard advised a girl suffering Satan's torments to "relate any weighty and serious case of conscience"—be it a confession of her own compact with the devil, or the accusation of a witch/tormentor—still "more privately": to one sympathetic minister, and to him alone.[111] If, as John

Demos argues, possessed girls indulged narcissistic urges by convening an assembly of prominent men to hear their voices, the attending ministers were not entirely complicit in their own seduction.[112] Despite their astonishment at witnessing "those Hellish and Diabolicall Cruelties, those strange Gestures, those dreadful Voices," preachers guarded their own tongues.[113] Approaching their role as interpreters of the devil's utterances tentatively, carefully, they reminded themselves of the prophet's dictum: sometimes, *"the Priest's Lips should keep Knowledge"* rather than spread it abroad.[114]

In addition to mediating between the voice of the bewitched and the eager ears of her neighbors, elite audiences engaged, perhaps unconsciously, in another sort of intervention: they distanced the utterances of possessed girls from their speakers. Simply put, the possessed and the bewitched were not believed—indeed, were not permitted—to speak for themselves. Instead of denouncing them as blasphemers against God and slighters of leading men, ministers treated demoniacs as silent vessels, passive *ventriloquae* channeling the devil's own voice.[115] In their published and private writings on the subject, preachers made clear that the "horrid and nefandous Blasphemies" that seemed to issue from the mouths of the possessed actually "belched forth" from the mouth of hell. Thus when Elizabeth Knapp spoke her worst, Samuel Willard noted that he "could not perceive any organ, any instrument of speech"—neither her lips nor her tongue—"to have any motion at all."[116] Digesting Willard's account in his *Remarkable Providences*, Increase Mather was more direct. The *"voice was not her own,"* he explained. The "Railings and Revilings" that appeared to be Knapp's were, in fact, "uttered by the Devil." With its "grum, low," and "hollow" tone, the demoniac's ranting was literally disembodied—or, at least, devocalized: sounding "as if it issued out of her throat" or had bubbled up from the depths of a "Belly swelled like a Drum." Ear-witnesses to such words heard not the possessed girl's speech acts, but those of the devil himself. *"He* railed," *"he* answered," *"he* rejoined," *"he* cried out"; *"he* spoke in her," while *she* "continued speechless."[117] Her words were not—could not be—her words.

This meant, in the end, that the demoniac did not have to live with the consequences of what she said. If the possessed were not thought to speak for themselves, neither did they bear ultimate responsibility for the wounds their words caused. Indeed, when understood as diabolic ventriloquy, the utterances of the possessed became perverse proofs of their innocence. Elizabeth Knapp's "distemper" could not be "counterfeit," Samuel Willard reasoned, precisely because "the reviling terms" uttered during her fits "were such as she never used before nor since." Because she "hath been always observed to speak respectfully concerning" Willard when she was well, it could only have been the devil who told him to hold his tongue. And thus, once the demon who had "entered in . . . at her mouth" could be persuaded to leave, the possessed girl's "speech" could be "restored to her." Resuming a normal voice, she could begin once again to live a normal—even godly—life. Which is precisely what Elizabeth Knapp, Martha Godwin, Ann Cole, and numerous other bewitched victims and demoniacs went on to do.[118]

And what of the "witches" whom accusers such as Knapp named and blamed? Unless they pronounced their own guilt by confessing (as Rebecca Greensmith and Goody Glover were said to have done), they too might be saved by the notion of demonic ventriloquy. In theory, at least, a belief system that projected the words of the possessed into the mouth of the devil promoted generosity toward the targets of satanic slanders as well as toward the ventriloquist herself. For the demoniac was the very embodiment of a liar. If the word of the witch among her neighbors was too trustworthy, too likely to come true, the word of the devil was, by definition, false. John Cotta, an English physician and authority on witchcraft whose findings were invoked by the likes of Increase Mather, reminded readers that to trust the accusations of the bewitched or the possessed was to "credit the Devil's mouth." And since the devil was, after all, "the Father of Lyes," he was "never to be believed."[119] Although they might flock to hear Satan's grum, low, hollow voice rumble from the viscera of a possessed girl, elite ear-witnesses knew better than to take what (s)he said at face value. Tempting as it must have been to hang on the devil's every syllable, Protestant ministers (and New England magistrates) knew better than to credit the word of the father of lies.

Or rather, they knew better until 1692. And then, without warning, long-established patterns of witch-hunting in New England crumbled under the weight of a torrent of accusations and prosecutions, a panic of witch fears on a scale never before seen in the colonies. The behavior of ordinary accusers may have shifted subtly in the 1690s, as discontented neighbors asked magistrates to intervene in disputes that, in less confusing times, might have been resolved outside the courts.[120] But the conduct of elites—of the ministers who preached about the wit and wiles and ways of Satan, and especially of the magistrates who presided over witchcraft prosecutions—changed far more dramatically. The trials in Salem, Bernard Rosenthal writes, marked both "the first and last time in the colonies" in which "authorities actively supported the accusers rather than seeking to suppress them."[121] It was in Salem, and only there, that elite ear-witnesses rewrote the rules governing witchspeak, disregarding in the process everything they had learned about the dangers of listening to the devil. Taking his word (via the mouths of "afflicted" accusers) for the guilt of scores of ordinary New Englanders, magistrates helped the trials in Salem to grow from their "very small" beginnings in the household of minister Samuel Parris to their infamous conclusion in a score of executions. It was, as minister John Hale (an early supporter of the trials who became, over time, one of their fiercest critics) later noted, a truly "Tragical End"; more alleged witches died at Salem in a few short months than had been hanged in the entire previous history of New England.[122]

For centuries, observers have argued about the reasons for the cataclysm, blaming factors as disparate as Indian attacks, mass psychosis, political instability, collective fraud, ergot poisoning, encroaching capitalism, genetic abnormalities, rampant misogyny, and, of course, the malice of the devil himself. The bulk of these explanations—at least those that remain viable in a secular age—point from one direction and another to the enormous cultural stress under which New England Puritans operated at the close of the seventeenth century. Theirs were not quiet times. In fact, the early 1690s was an era of crippling anxiety on the part of many elites: Anxiety about the vulnerability of a godly society in an ungodly world, and about the ability of tentative sons to fill the void left by the passing of their heroic fathers. Anxiety, not least, about the rightful voices of godly ministers and magistrates in a world of increasing pluralism—indeed, of enforced pluralism, if the Crown were to succeed in determining the religious politics of New England. Anxiety, in sum, about what Puritan moralists cast as religious, social, economic, *and linguistic* "declension": about what New England had become. By 1692, these concerns, first voiced half a century before, were familiar ones. Yet never had they been so acute, so consuming. And so, desperate for answers— as eager for news of their futures as were the fortune-telling "girls" who gathered by Parris's hearth—elites set aside their reticence about the trustworthiness of diabolical speech. As their desire to hear an explanation for their ills overwhelmed their ability to articulate social and verbal order, members of the Court of Oyer and Terminer (convened by the governor to preside over the trials of those accused in Salem) took the devil's word for what had gone wrong with Massachusetts.

The result was an escalating series of reversals: inversions of the sort that witchcraft so often caused, but on a grander scale than New England had ever witnessed. Instead of muffling the accusations uttered by the afflicted—who might, after all, prove to be mouthpieces for the father of lies—the court positively broadcast them. Instead of curbing women's public speech, magistrates encouraged it. The voices of Salem Village women had been approached with caution as recently as December 1689, when parish elders voted that only "persons . . . of the male kind" should profess the "repentance wrought in their souls, *with their own tongues and mouths.*"[123] But in 1692, other fears loomed larger, and women's speech was blazed abroad by ministers and magistrates who hung on every word. Having thus been invited to assume a public voice of unprecedented reach, the afflicted authored further reversals, as their accusations advanced from the few to the many, from the lowly to the eminent, and from women to men. Long a quasi-private affair, bewitchment became public theater in Salem.

Encouraged to perform as public orators, the afflicted spoke out brilliantly. Like the Quakers who, a generation before, had turned verbal assaults upon the colony into high drama, the coterie of Salem accusers had a knack for spectacular settings and gestures. As earlier demoniacs had, they received the prayers of family members, ministers, and other onlookers at their own bedsides. But unlike most of those afflicted earlier in the century, the symptoms of the Salem bewitched peaked in public, ceremonial settings: during "Publick Worship," "in open court," or during "a Publick Fast." When Deodat Lawson arrived to preach in his former pulpit in Salem Village in March 1692, he encountered "such an hideous scrietch and noise . . . as did amaze me," as "sundry of the afflicted Persons"—women ranging in age from preadolescence through midlife—fell into "Sore Fits" in the middle of his "First Prayer." Abigail Williams, among the youngest of the group, turned the rhythms of Puritan worship upside down when she, a mere girl, openly challenged the preacher's right to speak, demanding that Lawson "stand up, and Name your Text." He managed to finish the psalm, but Williams persisted, offering a snide critical appraisal: "It is a long Text." Claiming the floor again that afternoon, she questioned Lawson's interpretive powers as well as his taste in Scripture. "I know no Doctrine you had," she mocked. "If you did name one, I have forgot it." Mrs. Bathshua Pope, an afflicted matron whose honorific title indicates her high social status, went further still, shouting down Lawson at "the beginning of Sermon" by proclaiming, "Now there is enough of that."[124] Given the accusers' penchant for drama, it is no surprise that "a throng of Spectators" crowded into the meetinghouse the following day, eager "to see the Novelty" when some of the first suspects were "call'd . . . to answer" for their alleged crimes.[125]

Such audiences could not have been disappointed. For the hearings at Salem amounted to nothing less than a living display of the devil's topsy-turvy world. Inverting the grammar of a ritual that was designed to show-case the voice of civil authority, magistrates became bit players who ceded center stage to groups of laywomen: first to the afflicted accusers, and then to the confessing witches themselves. The judges might defend, at brief intervals, their hard-won role as the guardians of what John Cotton had called *"the door of speech and silence"* in such proceedings, telling one suspect that "they did not come to hear her . . . but to examine her," or scolding another for addressing the court "in a very wicked, spit-full manner reflecting and retorting aganst the authority with base and abusive words."[126] But for the most part, the magistrates confined themselves to an editorial role, as they allowed—indeed, *urged*—the bewitched and the exploding number of confessors-turned-accusers to weave ever more extravagant, detailed, and frightening narratives. Refusing to credit suspects' suggestions that the afflicted were either "distracted" or dissembling, the court treated Salem's accusers as trusted interpreters of the world beyond, calling upon them to act out agonies their audience could not feel (bites, pinches, pinpricks); to describe apparitions the judges could not see (a "black man," a "blew bird," a suckling cat); and to translate words the court could not hear (threats, mutterings, diabolic pacts).[127] Scholars have made much of the verbal cunning of the trial judges, noting how skillfully they turned a suspect's own words against her. ("How can you know, you are no Witch," one magistrate asked Bridget Bishop, and "yet not know what a Witch is"?) [128] Yet they have failed to note the extent to which these elite interlocutors remained captive listeners, their every word dictated by the bewitched.

And what tall tales the accusers told as the hearings wore on! Encouraged to describe their torments, the afflicted crafted stories of supernatural suffering beside which Elizabeth Knapp's possession paled. As the voices of those who admitted complicity with the devil swelled the chorus of accusers, the court heard ever more ornate narratives: tales of satanic masses and infernal baptisms, stories of witches riding through the air on poles, meticulous descriptions of the devil's attire, finely limned word-portraits of the very face of evil. As the plots of their stories became more detailed, the number of suspects rose in kind: from the "4 women and one man" named in the first confession-accusation (uttered by Samuel Parris's slave Tituba on 1 March) to the "500 witches in the country" whom Susannah Post mentioned late that August. [129] And as the sheer number of witches inched higher, the status of the accused rose as well. Early allegations against three marginal women from Salem Village (Sarah Good, a beggar; Tituba, a slave; and Sarah Osborne, long a target of her neighbors' hostility) metastasized into later claims against women *and men* from all across the region, and from a range of social strata. Eventually, accusations reached into the ranks of colonial officialdom to include clergymen, prominent merchants, and even the wife of the governor himself. [130]

The increasingly upside-down rhetoric of the Salem trials was never more apparent than during the examination of Captain John Alden: a wealthy trader and sometime soldier, the son of now-mythic Plymouth settlers John Alden and Priscilla (Mullins) Alden, a hoary-headed ancient who had seen his biblical threescore and ten—in short, as one account puts it, "one of the best-known men in New England." [131] Charged with witchcraft in May 1692, Alden might have anticipated a fair hearing. After all, his was exactly the sort of voice that had long possessed great authority in Massachusetts, and he was used to having his word count. But when he appeared before the Salem magistrates, he stumbled into a scene in which every speaker's role was precisely the opposite of what would have been expected. Instead of having a chance to affirm his own innocence, Alden stood silent as the court invited a "company of poor . . . Creatures" (whom Alden deemed "distracted," "possessed," or possibly "Witches") to elaborate upon their "Accusation" against him. Instead of asking Alden to speak for himself, the magistrates "several times" queried the afflicted girls, all but goading the "wenches" to captivate the audience with their "jugling tricks, falling down," and "crying out" against the suspect. The accusers were then allowed to redirect the scene, moving the entire assembly from the magistrates' parlor "down into the Street, where a Ring was made [around the accused?]," and thence to the meetinghouse, where Alden was ordered "to stand upon a Chair, to the open view of all the People." Thus displayed in the face of the crowd, Alden remained mute while one of his young female accusers cried out, "there stands Aldin, a bold fellow with his Hat on before the Judges, he sells Powder and Shot to the Indians and French, and lies with the Indian Squaes, and has Indian Papooses."[132]

Allegations of treason, miscegenation, adultery, bastardy, and, not least, witchcraft: these, of course, were the vilest of heated words, the most heinous of slanders. Compounding their effect was the fact that they were uttered not in the heat of an argument among fictive brethren, but by a group of young, low-status women against a mature, high-status man. Yet instead of commanding these slighters to be silent, the magistrates seemed to condone the girls' verbal assaults against the court's gender-status peer. When Alden at last "began to speak," wondering aloud at the "Providence of God in suffering these Creatures to accuse him" and insisting that "there was a lying Spirit in them," one of the ministers present "stopt Aldin's mouth" from further denouncing the proceedings. The court would take the accusers' word over his, as magistrate Bartholomew Gidney explained when he told the assembly that, although "he had known Aldin many Years, and had been at Sea with him, and always look'd upon him to be an honest Man . . . now he did see cause to alter his judgment." Upon the statements of the afflicted and nothing else, Alden's longtime friend abandoned him. Upon their word alone, he was delivered to prison in Boston, where he lay nearly four months before escaping with his life.[133]

Were it a singular story, Alden's experience might be accounted a personal rather than a collective tragedy. But in 1692, such about-faces were anything but unique; to the contrary, they were the very essence of what went on during those topsy-turvy months at Salem, that strange interval in which elite listeners credited the word of ungoverned young women over that of their targets, regardless of the gender, rank, or "common fame" of the latter. Acting on what Samuel Willard later denounced as the "bare say so" of the afflicted and of confessed witches, the magistrates sent nineteen people to the gallows.[134] Reversal heaped upon reversal, as witches who admitted their guilt thereby freed themselves from the consequences of the law, while those who proclaimed their innocence courted execution. Confession, hitherto the core truth of New England's covenant communities, became at Salem a lie, an empty utterance without legal or religious repercussions for its speaker. And the fantastical tales told by the accusers became, in turn, the only truth, the sole arbiter of life and death.[135]

Yet the heated rhetoric of the afflicted, the confessors, the magistrates, and some ministers was not the only language spoken in Salem. There existed another model, a godly and sober mode of discourse that might, in another moment, have served as the exemplar according to which others should govern their tongues. It is one of the bitterest ironies of the Salem trials that the most moderate utterances came from those who refused the familiar penitential script and maintained their innocence. In a stunning rejection of the trope of the sinner's last dying words, every one of the nineteen witches hanged in 1692 "denied the Crime to the Death," often in words of breathtaking constancy and piety.[136] George Burroughs, "carried in a Cart . . . through the streets of Salem to [his] Execution" on August 19, "made a Speech for the clearing of his Innocency," a statement comprised of such "Solemn and Serious Expressions . . . so well worded, and uttered with such composedness, and . . . fervency of Spirit, as was very affecting, and drew Tears from many" in the crowd. Ascending the gallows only three days after her husband had been pressed to death with heavy stones, Martha Corey, too, "concluded her Life with an Eminent Prayer upon the Ladder." Mary Easty likewise died "knowing my own Innocencye . . . and seeing plainly the Wiles and Subtility of my accusers," speaking words of farewell that her listeners deemed "Serious, Religious, Distinct, and Affectionate."[137] Surely, one observer noted, the voices of the confessor-accusers would not prove so unwavering; would they, too, "stand to their Self-condemning confessions, when they came to dye"?[138]

Of course, not all of Salem's victims met their fates so placidly. Sarah Good responded to her judges with words that ring across the centuries, linking the rhetoric of early Protestant martyrs with that of latter-day civil libertarians. Exhorted on the gallows by minister Nicholas Noyes to "Confess . . . she was a Witch," Good refused any pretense of feminine modesty. "[Y]ou are a lyer," she rejoined. "I am no more a Witch than you are a Wizard, and if you take away my Life, God will give you Blood to drink."[139] That Good's voice was powerful there can be no question. Her words echoed beyond the grave (if we are to believe Cotton Mather) to torment Mercy Short. And in due time, her final curse came to pass (as neighbors might have said), when Nicholas Noyes died "choaked with blood" in 1717.[140] But where it counted, on Salem's gallows, her voice wasn't loud enough. Seduced by the newly credible words of the afflicted, the listeners who mattered—those whose job it was to distinguish the voice of the witch from that of the demoniac, and from that of the Christian martyr—could not hear her. For several more months, the direct and sober words of people like George Burroughs, Martha Corey, Mary Easty, Sarah Good, and many others went unheard as the riveting stories spun by their accusers claimed the public's ear.

THE SETTING: Salem Village, the troubled November of 1694. The temper of the times: still confused and anxious—but also, in the aftermath of the witch-hunt that has finally slowed to a halt during the winter of 1692–1693, the mood is solemn, contrite, even embarrassed. The pitch of public discourse, too, has changed since 1692. Now it is the low murmur of rumor rather than the rhetorical violence of the witch's cursing that sets the people of New England together by the ears. Tales of the "Tragedies" of Salem have spread "Plague-like" across the colonies and beyond, "giving a brand of Infamy to this whole Country, throughout the World." The stories are so damaging, Joshua Scottow fears, that "*New England* will be called, new Witch-land."[141] Once again, more than sixty years after John Winthrop laid out his vision of New England, colonists confront their extraordinary vulnerability to malicious gossip. How exposed to the eyes and ears of the world their "Citty upon a Hill" remains! How readily their failures are "made a story and a by-word through the world"![142]

This, then, is the tense backdrop against which a penitent moves to the front of the Salem Village church to profess "openly before the whole congregation" his remorse for having "unadvisedly expressed myself." "I do humbly own this day before the Lord and his people," he tells his hearers,

> that God has been righteously spitting in my face. . . . And I desire to lie low under all this reproach, and to lay my hand upon my mouth. . . . I do most heartily, fervently, and humbly beseech pardon of the merciful God through the blood of Christ, of all my mistakes and trespasses in so weighty a matter; and also all your forgiveness of every offense in this or other affairs, wherein you see or conceive I have erred and offended; professing, in the presence of the Almighty God that what I have done has been, for substance, as I apprehended was duty,—however through weakness, ignorance, &c., I may have been mistaken.[143]

In many ways, the scene would have been familiar to white New Englanders living at the close of the seventeenth century. Though they didn't hear it as often these days as they once had heard it, the rhetoric of unsaying—with its images of high brought low, and of speech ("unadvised expressions") made silence ("my hand upon my mouth") made speech again (the apology itself)—had been a potent social medicine in their communities for decades. Though it had been briefly sundered during the Salem trials, the grand cycle of repentance followed by redemption was also familiar—indeed, it had long been the organizing principle for their earthly lives. In this sense, the apology recited that Sunday late in 1694 was but one more performance, if not an especially fine one, of a widely accepted script.

Yet however well-worn the outward trappings of the scene, those who heard this particular apology could not have helped noticing that much had changed. The sin in question, for one thing, was unprecedented; the "weighty . . . matter" for which the unspeaker begged God's and the church's forgiveness was nothing less than the Salem cataclysm itself. More novel still was the identity of the speaker. For the man who pledged that day to lay his hand upon his mouth and speak no more divisive words was none other than the church's pastor, none other than Samuel Parris himself.

Chalk it up, perhaps, to witchcraft: here was the grandest reversal of all. In the Salem Village church, preacher and penitent had switched places. Instead of silencing the layfolk who, since 1692, had persisted in "loudly and fiercely . . . clamoring against" him, Parris was effectively disciplined by them. Instead of putting a stop to the "confused calumnies" of his detractors, he was forced to endure *their* denunciations of *his* unquietness: Their claim that he "preached . . . scandalous immoralities." That he had allowed the peace of his church to be destroyed by the "distracting and disturbing tumults" of recent years. That, by permitting the "noises made by the persons under diabolical power and delusions" to thwart the "hearing and understanding and profiting of the word preached," he had forced many in the congregation to flee in search of a place "where we might hear the word in quiet." Indeed, his erstwhile auditors wondered aloud in 1694, *"who was the church's mouth"?* Certainly not its minister, they argued. Parris had listened imperfectly, "believing the Devil's accusations" instead of the protestations of the innocent. And he had spoken improperly, "swear[ing] positively against the lives" of people whose guilt he should have questioned, even committing "perjury" on behalf of the afflicted.[144] In so doing, he had fatally undermined the authority of his own voice, and thus had forfeited any claim to the pulpit from which his lay detractors and many of his ministerial colleagues would shortly conspire to eject him.[145]

However painful his reversals of fortune in the 1690s, Samuel Parris was not alone. In the wake of the Salem trials, numerous men with voices of authority were forced, as Samuel Willard had prophesied, to "eat their words": to admit that they had listened to the wrong speakers and, in the process, had become the authors of a tragedy.[146] By the mid-1690s, the shift in elite opinion that had begun during the trials was nearly complete. Some openly denounced the proceedings as displays of "superstitious" countermagic that "the reasonable part of the world" had been right to "laugh at."[147] Others who, like John Hale and Increase Mather, had cautiously supported the trials at the outset, found themselves lamenting that "a great deal of innocent blood" had been spilled in the end.[148] Even Cotton Mather, who passed into popular mythology as one of the chief instigators of the witch-hunt, was hard-pressed to reconcile his continuing belief in witches with the grim realities of 1692.[149] The consensus among the magistrates and clergy was overwhelming. What had happened in Salem, they acknowledged (some angrily, some sadly, some only by indirection), was not "reall witchcraft," but rather some dark semblance thereof: a collective delusion in the throes of which "many considerable persons of unblameable life and conversation were cried out upon" and legally murdered.[150] The only question, it seemed, was what had caused "so many in so small a compass of Land" to "leap into the Devils lap at once."[151]

To accept that the devil had toppled the workings of justice in Massachusetts was, Cotton Mather feared, to call into question "all the Rules of Understanding Humane Affairs."[152] But if this ex post facto reassessment of the trials was thoroughgoing, it focused with special vehemence on the power of speech, particularly on the words of Salem's accusers. Their voices, which had seemed so extremely credible during the trials themselves, were carefully revalued—and utterly *de*valued—in the aftermath. Once venerated as the sole translators of things unseen and words unheard, the afflicted were reimagined as the ultimate speakers of untruth. Those who would treat them "charitably" saw them as "possessed" or "distracted" sufferers who had unknowingly voiced diabolic or insane fantasies. Others were less generous. A "common vogue," Samuel Willard noted, held that "our Afflicted" were "scandalous persons, liars, and loose in their Conversation"—in short, not to be trusted. Robert Calef, the bitterest critic of the witnesses, whose fits he called "pretended," denounced them as "lying," "rank Wenches" who deluded onlookers with "hocus" and "easy trick[s]."[153] At best, then, the afflicted had been demonic ventriloquists, speechless speakers whose "Tongues" were "improved" by the "Father of Lies." At worst, they were cunning impostors, whose "foolish, ridiculous Speeches" might have been dismissed as "Romantick or Ridiculous stories," had only the consequences of their "merry talking Fit[s]" been less dire.[154] Whether they were deceitful or demented, the implication was the same: the word of the afflicted should not have been credited. Indeed, Salem's harshest critics proclaimed, the court would have done better to listen to such witches as Martha Corey, who, well before the first hangings, had warned her interrogators: "We must not beleive all that these distracted children say."[155]

If the credibility of the afflicted was demolished in the post mortem reassessment of Salem, the words of confessing witches fared little better. Indeed, in some ways, theirs was a more clear-cut case. By owning a connection with Satan, those who confessed had admitted their allegiance to the greatest liar of all. Thomas Brattle reckoned it this way: If those who confessed had truly been "under the influence of some evill spirit," their words were "unfitt to be evidences either against themselves, or any one else." If, on the other hand, their compact with the devil was a fiction (one perhaps born of coercion), the would-be witches were "flat lye[r]s." In either case, the magistrates should have "frowned upon the said confessours, discarded them, and not minded one tittle of any thing that they said." Surely no "man of sense," Brattle argued, could "regard the confessions, or any of the words, of these confessours."[156]

But that is precisely what the Salem magistrates had done. In 1692, the colony's leading men had listened to the wrong witnesses, and then had unleashed the power of their own voices against such sober, chaste speakers as Mary Easty and Captain John Alden. In so doing, those in charge of the trials called into question their own capacity for careful ear-witnessing and authoritative speech. Did the magistrates speak like pious men, cautious men—like (in Brattle's phrase) "men of sense"? After Salem, such questions could be posed with new directness. For how could any one set of voices—even those of the ministers who spoke for God— claim to speak with perfect authority once it was obvious that, when it counted, words had failed them? Thus while he condemned those who used Salem as an excuse to "despise dominions, and speak evil of Dignities," Brattle insisted that it had become necessary "with dutifullness and subjection . . . with modesty and due reverence to debate the premised failings" of men "in public place." "I never thought Judges infallible," he explained. Those who spoke with authority, no less than ordinary folks, had to be told when they fell short.[157] This meant, in effect, that New England's children might sometimes advance a righteous claim to speak against their erstwhile parents. John Hale, a preacher who, in 1692, had used the authority of his voice to testify against several women whom he now believed to have been innocent, spoke in part to his own failures of speech and hearing when he noted, "our Fathers were imperfect men."[158] In the wake of Salem, such *anti*-jeremiads seemed suddenly to be the most sensible laments.

How could such admittedly imperfect fathers repair the damage they had done? It will come as no surprise that the first compensation they offered Salem's victims consisted of words. Recalling the long tradition of public apology in Puritan courts and churches, the mea culpas flowed thick and fast in the 1690s. The "jurors in court at Salem" confessed "to all in general, and to the surviving sufferers in special," that their deliberations had "been instrumental" in bringing "the guilt of innocent blood" upon New England, for which they "humbly beg[ged] forgiveness."[159] Samuel Sewall, a member of the Court of Oyer and Terminer, stood before his congregation on a fast day in January 1697 and bowed his head as Samuel Willard read aloud a detailed acknowledgment of Sewall's "Blame and Shame" in the "Guilt contracted" at Salem.[160] Cotton Mather resented that "after all my unwearied Cares and Pains to . . . disappoint the Devils in their designs," he would be "driven to the necessity of an Apologie." Yet however grudgingly, he too offered explanations (or were they justifications?) for his role in the affairs of 1692.[161] Indeed, so fashionable did unspeaking the words that had led to the Salem cataclysm become that in 1706, one of the chief afflicted accusers joined the chorus of remorse. Ann Putnam Jr., then in her mid-twenties, acknowledged "before the congregation" of Salem Village that "in the year about '92," she had been "an instrument for the accusing of several . . . innocent persons," and said that she "desire[d] to lie in the dust, and to be humbled for" her role in "so sad a calamity." Aware (perhaps newly so) of the need to preserve women's modesty, minister Joseph Green read Putnam's "confession . . . together with her relation" of conversion. With Putnam thus silently admitted to full communion in the Salem Village church, the upside-down verbal order of 1692 had come full circle.[162]

Or had it? What, we have to wonder, could words *do* in the wake of Salem? The palpable force of the witch's curse had been called into question, but so too had the credibility of her confession. The afflicted girls' "bare say so" had been exposed as satanic ventriloquy, if not deliberate fraud. But had the voices of her judges or those of the colony's spiritual leaders fared much better? What power, in short, still inhered in the act of speaking? Could the apologies of Ann Putnam and other accuser-condemners begin to compensate those whose lives and livelihoods their words had stolen?

The survivors, it seems, thought not. An apology alone could not restore the damaged names, much less the worldly estates, of their loved ones. In 1711, the General Court admitted that "some of the principal Accusers and Witnesses" in Salem had "since discovered [i.e., revealed] themselves to be persons of profligate and vicious conversation."[163] Why, then, should their retractions matter? With the currency of speech so debased, those who outlasted the trials often preferred other modes of redress. The late "Sorrowfull tryals," they insisted, had left the victims and their families "Imprison'd impared and Blasted" in their "Reputations and Estates"—that is, both socially and economically. Thus they urged the court not only to apologize, but also to "pass some sutable Acts . . . that shall (so far as may be) Restore the Reputations to the Posterity of the sufferers and Remunerate them . . . in their Estates."[164] Repaying their losses would require deeds as well as words, a settling of material accounts as well as an outpouring of sorrow. The victims of Salem had felt the malign power of speech too acutely to trust in its potential for redemption. For them, apology was simply not as good as gold.

EPILOGUE

In September 1741, minister Charles Chauncy ascended the pulpit of Boston's First Church—the oldest and still the most venerable in all New England—to inveigh against the evils of an "unbridled tongue." An account of the threat to church and society posed by those "who dont keep their tongue under due government; who allow themselves an unrestrain'd liberty in their language," Chauncy's message was in many ways a familiar one. Comments on the horrors of cursing, swearing, and *"filthy conversation"*; rebukes to those who *"speak vanity . . . with flattering lips and a double tongue"*; advice to listeners to "set a watch at the door of [their] lips"—all of these elements of Chauncy's discourse spoke to Puritans' long-standing concerns about the close bonds linking speech, piety, and power. Indeed, the sermon would have played well a century before, in the days following the banishment of Anne Hutchinson. Or still yet during the 1650s and early 1660s, when Quaker invective flooded Puritan meetinghouses. Or once again in 1692, when the words hurled by witches and their "afflicted" victims overwhelmed New England's magistrates, inducing them to turn a deaf ear to their own principles of justice.[1]

But if Chauncy's homily echoed the counsel of civil and religious authorities reaching back before the founding of Massachusetts, the world in which he uttered his message had been radically transformed. Now, as the waves of revivalism that would come to be known as the Great

Awakening broke over New England, "unbridled" speech seemed almost the norm. Now, laypeople's ecstatic tales of sin qualified not as evidence of demonic possession, but as a new brand of piety, faith expressed in an emotive style that such traditionalists as Chauncy decried as "enthusiasm."[2] Now, indeed, some of the most licentious orators were themselves preachers. And these were no closet divines, no mere private conventiclers in the manner of Anne Hutchinson. No, these latter-day prophets loosed their unrestrained tongues in the open air, upon crowds of listeners numbering in the thousands.[3] In the meetinghouses, too, the notion of a singular voice of religious orthodoxy—always contested, as we have seen, amid the spiritual fervor of early New England—had ceased to be even a plausible fiction. At the very moment Chauncy spoke, some thirty to forty other preachers—many of them "Puritans" (for whatever that meant, these days), one an Irish Presbyterian, plus a Baptist, a Huguenot, several emissaries of the once-outlawed Church of England, and a number of unaffiliated ministers-at-large—delivered *their* glosses on the Word from *their* Boston pulpits.[4] In Hutchinson's day, it had been possible to speak (as Hugh Peter had done) of an essential distinction between the "preachers," whose words governed a godly people, and their "hearers," whose duty consisted chiefly of listening. In 1741, it was hard enough to distinguish one preacher from another. Projected against the sweeping changes that had reconfigured New England's economy of communication, Chauncy's struggle with those who would *"bridle not their tongue"* was a losing battle, a rearguard action in the language wars of the previous century. For nowadays, as Chauncy himself conceded, too many people seemed "too ready to say . . . *Our Lips are our own, who is Lord over us?"*[5]

They were right; increasingly, New Englanders' "lips"—that is, their words—*were* their own. The work of governing the tongue, a task to which people at the very highest levels of colonial government had once devoted themselves, had become by the mid–eighteenth century a private matter, an exercise in self-control. Chauncy and other ministers who continued to fight for godly speech in an ever more fractious world did so without help from the numerous laws that had buttressed their message under the colony's first charter. Preachers could inspire their hearers with tales of the power of godly words. They could chasten them with descriptions of the "monstrous and ugly Spectacle" of an evil speaker *"Voiding his Excrements at his Mouth."*[6] They could even excommunicate them for sins of the tongue that threatened the peace of their congregations. But no longer could they enlist "ye edge of ye Civil sword" in the battle against "blasphemy, Cursing[,] profane swearing . . . Contentiousnesse, Ill language," and a host of other "abounding Impietyes & immoralitys."[7] Quoting from Proverbs, Charles Chauncy reminded his auditory that "Death and life are in the power of the tongue." Once upon a time in New England, his emphatic warning had the force of law behind it. But in 1741, this proverbial wisdom was no longer literally true. From an official perspective, at least, speech had ceased to be deadly.

Ann Hibbens would not have hanged in 1741, for after Salem, a supposed witch's words never again cost their speaker her life. As early as May 1693, only months after the last executions in Salem, New England courts began openly to question the diabolic power of speech. Setting aside a jury's verdict condemning Mercy Disborough chiefly on the basis of her contentious words, Connecticut magistrates belittled the impassioned testimonies they had heard against the suspect: stories of "il events after quarels or threates" and tales of the consequences of "suspitious words." These, they said, were "Common things," specious evidence that should henceforth be "discarded" and even "abominated." Reminding the jury men of "the miserable toyl they are in in the Bay for Adhereing" to such doubtful proofs, Connecticut's chief judges warned that to "make witchcraft of such things" was to "make hanging work apace."[8]

Soon enough, in fact, it would become impossible to "make witchcraft" at all in colonial courts. In the years following 1692, Massachusetts authorities tried several times to define the crime in a way that conformed both to their own shifting understandings of the witch's threat and to the laws of England, as the colony's second charter demanded. Twice, their efforts were "disallowed" by the English Privy Council, condemned for being "conceived in very uncertain and doubtful terms"—that is, for using Scripture, rather than common law, as their foundation. In 1736, the repeal of the Crown's own statute condemning Satan's familiars ended the official pursuit of witches in England and its colonies. But as Perry Miller has noted, the "very word witchcraft" had all but vanished "from public discourse" long before, in the wake of Salem.[9] When witches railed against their neighbors in the eighteenth century— as indeed they continued to do—their words would not be a matter of law, let alone a matter of life and death.[10]

For those who counted such women as Hibbens as their linguistic foremothers, the diminished price of witching words must have been a bittersweet victory, a tangle of gains and losses. To be sure, it was preferable to live with one's words than to die for them—whether literally, on the gallows, or symbolically, in one's neighborhood, where the label "witch" resulted in a kind of social death. But if women's speech was less dangerous in the eighteenth century, it was less powerful as well, particularly in the realm of law. The witch's cursing had been only the most concrete example of the many ways in which woman's word *counted* in seventeenth-century courts. Sometimes to their benefit and sometimes to their peril, women in early New England had "good reason to believe," as one legal historian recently put it, "that their voices would not be ignored" by Puritan magistrates. Whether their speech was deemed useful (as it was when they testified as witnesses, medical experts, or victims) or malign (as it was when they were haled into court for scolding, witchcraft, or heresy), New England's goodwives made themselves heard. But as men's and women's daily lives began to diverge, and as legal rhetoric itself became more formal, complex, and distinct from everyday talk, women were less often called upon to speak directly to those in power.[11] To be sure, female speech in the public sphere continued to be viewed as disruptive well into the nineteenth century, as indeed it sometimes is today.[12] But never again would women's voices be as literally credible as they had been before 1692, when it was widely supposed that as a witch "sayde so it came to pass."[13] In this sense, the reduced cost of women's words went hand in hand with their falling value.

Witches' words were not alone in their diminished cost. The price a New Englander might pay for speaking against established religion also fell at the end of the seventeenth century. As late as 1686, Massachusetts courts had followed Leviticus in invoking the death penalty for speaking against "the true God, or his Creation, or Government of the World, or . . . utter[ing] any other kind of Blasphemy."[14] But like witchcraft, this type of capital speech also struck the Privy Council as "uncertain and doubtful." And so, in 1697, the General Court officially discounted blasphemy, reducing its ultimate cost from hanging to symbolic execution (offenders were to be displayed "upon the gallows with a rope about their neck"), followed by whipping, imprisonment, or "boreing through the tongue with a red hot iron."[15] Penalties for other words against orthodoxy—from swearing, to speaking against the colony's ministers, to professing heretical opinions—diminished in turn. The price of an oath was literally halved in 1693, when the long-standing fine of ten shillings per profane utterance was slashed to five.[16] Graver statements likewise carried lesser penalties. Until 1691, one who derided "the Word Preached, or the Messengers thereof" had courted a hefty £5 fine, or the public ignominy of being made to "stand two hours openly upon a Block or Stool, four foot high, on a Lecture day, with a paper fixed on his breast, written in Capital Letters, AN OPEN AND OBSTINATE CONTEMNER OF GODS HOLY ORDINANCES."[17] A mere decade later, such an offender risked nothing—at least from the courts. After the new charter made religious toleration the law of the land, heresy all but ceased to exist as a legal entity (except, of course, where "papists" and non-Christians were concerned).[18] Which means that just as Ann Hibbens would not have been executed after 1692 for her habits of speaking, neither would Anne Hutchinson have been banished for hers.

Indeed, much more than would-be witches, the rhetorical descendants of Hutchinson and other religious dissenters came out ahead in the new verbal order of the provincial era. Particularly among evangelicals who saw religion as an affair of the heart, the prophetic style was not only tolerated, but venerated. Rejecting what they saw as the desiccated formalism of New England's orthodox churches, these revivalists sought— much as the Puritans themselves had done a century before—to imbue the spoken word with new importance. In their churches, speech again became the means and medium of godliness, the faculty that separated the pious from the pretenders. And godly speech, some of them argued, was genderless.[19]

Thus had she been born in 1691 rather than in 1591, Anne Hutchinson could have uttered her message with relative impunity. Instead of ending in exile and violent death, her story might have resembled that of Newport's Sarah Osborn. Inspired by the captivating oratory of the Great Awakening, Osborn began in the 1740s to lead interested local women in prayer. Twenty years later, her prayer group had become a virtual ministry, attended by hundreds of participants. As Osborn's meetings expanded to include men, children, and free and enslaved African Americans, some established ministers expressed concern about her increasingly "Publick Manner," and wondered if she were not going "beyond the line" of proper feminine piety. But unlike Hutchinson, Osborn was able steadfastly—and *successfully*—to defend her public voice. "Would you advise me to shut up my Mouth and doors and creep into obscurity?" she asked in a letter to Stonington's Joseph Fish.[20] Apparently, he did not; her preaching continued. And even so, when Samuel Hopkins memorialized her in 1799, he compared Osborn not to Anne Hutchinson, but rather to the virtuous woman of Proverbs, noting that the "law of kindness was in her tongue to an uncommon degree," and emphasizing that she was "careful to speak evil of none."[21] Osborn's case makes clear that for some evangelical speakers (women included) during the eighteenth century, speech might both cost less and count more.

And what of John Porter Jr.? How might we reckon the price of his invective in eighteenth-century currency? While the sharp tongues of latter-day rebellious sons surely made their parents just as miserable as the Porter household had been, provincial courts would have little to say about the kind of young man who, in the 1660s, had been counted among the colony's "vilest malefactors." Once deemed to be the pillars upon which the fifth commandment (and with it, the whole edifice of government) rested, dutiful children were neither seen nor heard in the official discourse of provincial Massachusetts—with one telling exception. Tucked into a 1699 "Act for the suppressing and punishing of . . . disorderly persons"—a motley crew of rogues, beggars, jugglers, palm readers, "pipers, fidlers, runaways," "drunkards," "nightwalkers," "pilferers," "railers or brawlers," and assorted other "wanton and lascivious persons, either in speech or behaviour"—was the law's sole injunction against "stubborn servants or children." The statute ensured that, like others who "neglect their callings, mis[s]pend what they earn, and do not provide for themselves or . . . their families," unruly children might be confined to jail or to a workhouse "until they be reduced to better order."[22] Better economic order, that is. Like the other riffraff with whom they were classed, disorderly children seem to have posed more of a mon-

etary threat than a social one; the cost of their support weighed more
heavily upon the minds of lawmakers than did the less tangible burden
of filial rebelliousness.

Who, then, were John Porter's linguistic progeny? In the strict, legal
sense, there simply *were* no John Porters in the provincial era. Increasingly, the kinds of familial disorders that had brought the Porters to court
repeatedly during the 1660s would be relegated to the widening sphere
of privacy. After nearly a century of white settlement, the voices of New
England's fathers were no longer so precarious, nor were the words of
their sons so perilous, that a household's verbal disarray could touch off
a transatlantic crisis. But in a broader cultural context, John Porter had
many rhetorical descendants, the great oratorical heroes of eighteenth-
century America among them. Soon enough, the strident cries of rebellious colonial sons against their royal father would become the founding
political discourse of the American nation.[23]

For better and for worse, then, hard words landed many fewer people
in court in the eighteenth century than they had done in earlier years.
Part of this shift was institutional, a reflection of priorities imposed by
the Crown under Massachusetts's second charter. As provincial courts
stove to adhere to English legal forms—including common-law definitions of "actionable" words—only speech that posed a tangible, immediate danger to public order was likely to be deemed criminal; magistrates
proved increasingly reluctant to prosecute run-of-the-mill misspeakers
(slighters, condemners, railers, scolds). And importantly, these highly visible changes in the law of speech mirrored subtler, more gradual shifts in
the way common men and women understood the spoken word. As the
colonial era wore on, ordinary people, too, developed thicker skins (or,
perhaps, a distaste for public remedies) where heated speech was concerned. Less and less often did verbal slights drive wounded individuals
to seek judgments of slander against their neighbors.[24]

Where early New Englanders of all ranks and sorts devoted considerable energies to protecting against the theft of their good names (which
were, after all, their stock in trade), their children's children fretted over
other forms of property. The counterfeiting of money and bills of credit
became a capital offense in Massachusetts just as blasphemy ceased to be
one.[25] The litigation of debt—the most rapidly growing segment of the
rapidly expanding court dockets of the provincial period—soon dwarfed
the volume of litigation over words. And slander suits themselves came
to focus ever more narrowly on the economic components of a (man's)
good name, the facet of reputation now deemed most worthy of official
protection.[26] Fraud and forgery, bad debts and bad bargains: these were
the larcenies of the eighteenth century. If the public fathers of Massachusetts had felt acutely vulnerable to the dangers posed by the uttering of
"false newes," leaders of the colony in later years would tend to worry
more about the "uttering of false Counterfeit money."[27]

As this last example suggests, the whole idea of dangerous "utterance" was in flux by the end of the seventeenth century. Reversing the priorities of their grandparents' day, those who continued to argue that words, in and of themselves, could undermine social order centered their attention upon printed libels rather than spoken lies. In the face-to-face milieu of seventeenth-century New England, the surest way to spread a story (or, for that matter, to retract one) had been, as the courts often said, to "publish" it "audibly"—that is, to speak it.[28] Indeed, so closely linked was "publishing" with saying that magistrates sometimes preferred a written slight to a spoken one. Samuel Shrimpton, for example, did more damage to the public face of the Massachusetts Assistants when he "denied their power" in "a loud voyce . . . in open Court" than he had done by making the same charges "in's Paper given in more silently."[29] In many settings in the early colonial world, speech was simply *louder* than print.

Now it often seemed that the reverse was true: printed "slights" lasted longer, traveled farther, and therefore hurt more than spoken ones. In the communicative economy of the provincial era, as Bradford minister Thomas Symmes noted, print was "more *extensive* and *durable*" than speech.[30] Thus the Massachusetts authorities, in their attempt to reclaim reputations damaged in Salem, devoted more energy to governing the presses than to governing the tongue. Twice in the late 1690s, they ordered that books condemning the conduct of the witch trials be publicly burned.[31] Likewise, when the colony's highest court sought in 1712 to limit the "publishing" of "wicked, prophane, impure, filthy and obscene songs," it thought not of the voice but of the page, and of the dangers posed by the "writing, printing, or publishing" of such "evil communication" through a "pamphlet," or a "libel."[32]

Even Cotton Mather, whose youthful concern with the power and danger of speech epitomized the linguistic anxieties of the seventeenth century, in later years shifted his attentions to the perils of the printed page. What could New England's ministers do, he wondered in 1717, to ensure "that the Poison" of a recently printed "Libel may have an Antidote?"[33] The answer was not immediately clear. In 1721, he urged the province's governor to "interpose" himself in order to "putt an effectual Stop to those cursed Pamphlets and Libels, wherewith some wicked Men, are endeavoring to Poison the Countrey." But although Mather continued to petition legislators for tougher sanctions against printed slights, and to exhort "the wicked Printer, and his Accomplices" to cease publication of the "vile Paper[s]" that "lessen and blacken the Ministers of the Town," no "effectual stop" was forthcoming. Several years later, he would write that stanching the wounds caused by "vile Books dispersed among our people" remained a problem worthy of "Study and Labour."[34] In 1629, Thomas Adams had warned that heated speech possessed the terrifying power of "a firebrand in a frantic hand." A century later, it seemed that only "a Libellous Book" could kindle public opinion like "*A Fire-brand thrown by a Mad-man.*"[35] Not only the price of linguistic larceny but also its very nature, its very medium, was in the process of thorough-going transformation.

These shifts in the understanding of wrongful words both reflected and helped to construct a new economy of communication in the eighteenth century. The climate of information scarcity—the keen hunger after scarce rumors—that had characterized New England in its earliest years gradually gave way to a new atmosphere of information abundance. As one writer in Boston's *New England Courant* put it in 1722, "Letters . . . grow upon us daily; we have Weekly three News-Letters, and sometimes as many little Books or Pamphlets (I don't say Sermons) published."[36] The proud editorialist certainly had his finger on the pulse of the times: since Boston's first newsletter had begun publication in 1704, it had been joined by a second in 1719, and a third (the *Courant* itself) in 1721. Another would add to the chorus of competing voices in 1727, followed by a fifth in 1731, a sixth in 1734, a seventh in 1748, and on and on through the Revolution.[37] Yet as Michael Warner has compellingly argued, this rising tide of print did not itself change New England's culture; rather, the explosion of information testified to a shift that had already taken place in the hearts and minds of ordinary men and women. The increase in the sheer volume of printed matter is thus less important than other aspects of the information revolution of the eighteenth century: the steep rise in the number of points of view represented by these works, and the changing nature of what it meant to publish and to read them. As the *Courant's* editorialist took pains to point out, sermons were no longer the sole, or even the principal, products of provincial presses. In literature as in law as in life, New Englanders were beginning to conceptualize authority less as Word delivered than as a kind of dialogue in which they, as readers and as speakers, might play a part.[38]

All of which is to say: power spoke with many voices in provincial New England. Massachusetts towns were fast becoming places where stories had meaning and momentum independent of the tongues of their tellers, places in which no single voice could claim to be *the* voice of authority. It was as if the linguistic promise of reformed Protestantism—the desire to open the lines of communication between people and their God—had borne fruits that seventeenth-century Puritans could not have predicted and would not have welcomed. In spite (or because) of their best efforts to govern the tongue, the atmosphere they bequeathed to their descendants was one of linguistic proliferation: a profusion of media, of denominations, of points of view, and, not least, of speakers. When Charles Chauncy delivered his injunctions on the dangers of unbridled speech, he was one among 160,000 souls residing in Massachusetts, some 17,000 of whom lived in Boston alone.[39] In every way, Chauncy's town was a far cry from the rude hamlet that Anne Hutchinson's voice had shaken to its just-laid foundations in the 1630s. New

England's very scale begged the question, with so many voices contending against each other, how widely could any one of them reach
through speech alone? And, in turn, how dangerous might any one of
them be? If no man in Chauncy's Boston possessed the sheer oratorical
force of a John Cotton, it was also true that no dissenter posed the grave
oratorical threat of an Ann Hibbens, an Anne Hutchinson, or a John
Porter Jr. As New England had expanded—demographically, religiously,
economically, culturally—the territory that could be effectively governed
or misgoverned by the tongue had shrunk in turn.

Of course, as Chauncy's sermon reminds us, there were many who did
not embrace this increasingly modern economy of communication in
which speech would take a backseat to print, in which words seemed
separate from (and subordinate to) deeds, and in which a plurality of
competing voices would suffocate the notion of One True Voice. But if
Chauncy did not welcome the dawning of such a world, he could see it
from where he stood: inhabiting one pulpit among many, publishing one
tract among hundreds, peddling a seventeenth-century notion of "quiet-
nesse" amid the bustling cacophony of Boston in 1741. Much as he
might struggle to maintain a rhetorical link to the era of the Puritans'
Great Migration, Chauncy was in many respects closer to the world of
1789, and the moment when "freedom of speech," enshrined in print,
would become the defining ideal of American nationhood.

IS MY STORY, then, a kind of Whig speech history: a tale in which the
secular conquers the religious, the inexorable logic of freedom trumps the
barbarism of restraint, and the thin, pure air of the modern sweeps the
cobwebs from the Puritan Mind? Should the headline read: "Puritans
Show Dangers of Repression—Don't Let This Happen to Us"? The history of speech in the United States, to the extent that it has been written at all, has largely been framed as just such a tale of contrasts, a story
in which the bad old days (accounts of their extent and duration vary)
make us grateful for the dawning of the good new ones.[40] To be sure,
this way of telling the story has its virtues. Am I glad to live in a world
where talk is cheap rather than in one where words mattered so much
that loose-tongued women faced the gallows for cursing their neighbors?
A loose-tongued woman myself, you bet I am. Yet for all their visceral
attractions, such easy comparisons between the linguistic orders of then
and now—comparisons in which "now" always comes out the winner—
ultimately obscure more than they reveal about either historical moment.
If we succumb to the temptation to cap the tangled meanings of early
American speech with a single, optimistic moral, we risk ignoring two
equally important points. First, by focusing exclusively on changes in the
meaning of speech, we gloss over the continuities between the seventeenth century and subsequent eras. In addition, by accepting the
onward-and-upward paradigm as the proper shape for a cultural history
of American speech, we turn a deaf ear to another, more complex tale:

that of the *costs* of our modern way of conceptualizing the spoken word. To dwell only upon what we believe and what the Puritans didn't dream of is to neglect what they knew about the power of the tongue that we have forgotten, sometimes to our detriment.

The main continuity between the meaning of speech in the seventeenth century and its import for succeeding generations should be obvious: people still spoke, and what they said still counted, sometimes for good and sometimes for ill. Indeed, in some contexts, speech took on heightened significance. Although they unfolded in a world saturated with print, the mass revival meetings of the 1740s and the heated political debates of the following generation were fundamentally oral-aural encounters, battles to win the public's ear.[41] And gossip, invective, and other forms of wordplay continued to shape human relations even if we less often glimpse their traces in the written records of a changing legal system. Thus if the eighteenth century was no longer the heyday of "heated" speech in New England, neither was it a silent era—nor does such a thing exist. So long as men and women used their tongues, they continued to dispute the boundaries of proper speech. They did so in their courts, where well after the Revolution, some jurists argued (albeit with declining success) that prominent individuals and even the state itself could be "criminally assaulted by mere words," true and false alike.[42] They did so in their churches, where members censured one another for speech that threatened the fabric of community, and where such preachers as Charles Chauncy warned listeners of the dangers of swearing, cursing, slandering, whispering, talebearing, backbiting, and a host of other verbal ills.[43] They did so, too, in their families, where women and children still learned that, on the whole, they were better seen than heard.[44] In all of these ways, provincial New Englanders, much like their colonial forebears, continued to connect speech with power—power that demanded restrictions, curbs, controls.

Yet as we have seen, the nature of those restrictions was transformed over the course of the eighteenth century. The mission of governing the tongue passed from the sphere of law to the sphere of etiquette, where it largely remains today. Increasingly after 1789, the proper deployment of the spoken word would be understood less as a way of dividing the saved from the damned or the criminal from the law-abiding than as a code distinguishing the refined from the vulgar.[45]

To the extent that the decriminalization of speech resulted in a greater range of permissible utterances, the free-expression Whigs are surely correct: republican speech was unquestionably freer than its Puritan counterpart. It was also cheaper. In the public life of the new American nation, the spoken word was both less costly *and less valuable* than it once had been. Speech was less fettered in early national America in part because it was believed to be less potent, less dangerous, less deserving of restriction. Eighteenth-century thinkers conceded that verbal persuasion might melt hearts and move political mountains.[46] But no longer could muttered curses devastate livestock, threaten families, or move objects through space. And no longer would insulting one's natural or public fathers call down the wrath of God. Even medical science cooperated with this revaluation—and *devaluation*—of the spoken word, explaining that speech was governed less by theology than by the laws of acoustics. As Enlightenment anatomists saw it, the ability to speak neither attested to the bonds between humans and their creator nor gave voice to their fallen state. Once thought to bubble up from the depths of the soul, modern speech came from some place altogether more superficial: from the passage of air over the vocal cords.[47] Heard with an eighteenth-century ear, once-deadly words and once-godly words were now, alike, only words. Not things. Not deeds. Saying and doing were distinct, separate—as indeed they *had* to be under the Constitution's First Amendment. For only imagine, as one postmodern theorist recently quipped, the chaos engendered by a Bill of Rights that declared, "Congress shall make no law abridging freedom of *action*."[48]

Since the eighteenth century, our belief in the power of freedom to conquer the power of words has generally increased, albeit sometimes haltingly. Particularly since the 1960s, Americans have willingly paid the tariff that guarantees ever less regulated speech: we have accepted, even embraced, the debasement of our public discourse. The slings and arrows of hard words seem a small cost for the right to unleash our own tongues. Grateful for a world in which each of us possesses, at least in theory, the kind of verbal authority that once accrued only to the likes of Cotton Mather, we choose our words less carefully, and are less wary of their consequences, than any good Puritan would have been. Mindful that restrictions on expressive liberty are always injurious to the common good, and convinced that words almost never are, we make it a civic creed that more speech, no matter what speech, is better speech. Confident that if only "everyone . . . could think, write, speak, and listen without fear of governmental repression, we could sing, dance, laugh, and persuade our way to the promised land," we have discarded the Puritans' warnings that speech was both divine and demonic, a faculty worthy of scrutiny as well as praise.[49] Indeed, the notion that something as paltry as language could damage something as mighty as freedom has come to seem almost comic. As one defender of the libertarian interpretation of free speech notes, it is hard to imagine that "the truth" is "so anemic that it requires protection from words."[50] In recent years, we have armed ourselves with little more than a proverb to counter most of the words that sting us: "Sticks and stones may break my bones, but hard words cannot hurt me."[51]

Or can they? Do "hard words" *still* inflict not only personal but also social damage? The question is again a live one, more pressing than it has been for decades. Viewed in the context of a national commitment to racial and gender equality that has deepened since the 1950s, the need to assess the relationship between words and harms, and to understand the implications of that relationship for free speech, seems as urgent to-day as it has seemed at any moment since 1692—so urgent, in fact, that debates about the meaning of speaking have lately entered the realm of popular culture.[52] Thus in December 1992, precisely three centuries after the last of the Salem witch trials, a cartoon in the *New Yorker* explored the issue. In the quickly sketched scene, a stern father warns a tearful son: "Sticks and stones may break your bones, but hate speech is action-able."[53] The gag, of course, trades on the gap between a halcyon Yester-day and a confusing Today. Until recently, the artist implies, we felt secure in the knowledge that (as the rhyme implicitly continues) words would never hurt us. Now we are not so sure. Cartoonist Lee Lorenz is hardly the only one to feel this anxiety. In various arenas of our free public discourse—in law, in literature, in commerce, in politics, even in the rarefied environs of cultural theory—we have begun to interrogate the libertarian understanding of words codified over the last two centu-ries. In so doing, critics of prevailing interpretations of free speech and its social impact are reviving modes of thinking that the Puritans would have recognized.

Cotton Mather would surely have welcomed, for example, recent at-tempts to rethink the relationship between words and things. Words, some revisionist critics argue, are not arbitrary signifiers but embodied (and malign) actors—pathogens of a sort. Unknowingly echoing early New Englanders' descriptions of the Antinomian and Quaker heresies, they describe hate speech as a plague, an "epidemic," or an "outbreak."[54] Cruel remarks are not only infectious, but also "assaultive": a "verbal slap in the face" that can "produce physical symptoms" and "real harm."[55] An advertising campaign mounted by Planned Parenthood in response to escalating violence against abortion clinics in the mid-1990s put it still more starkly: "WORDS KILL. Words are like bullets—they can be used to kill."[56] Taking their cues from ordinary-language philosopher J. L. Austin, among others, those active in the movement to silence hate speech (including pornography) decry the neat separation of our mental universe into "speech" on one side and "action" on the other. Our lived experience, writes legal scholar Mari J. Matsuda, "explodes the notions that there are clear lines between words and deeds." Once we accept that words, like actions, produce palpable results, she tells us, we will realize that *"we are not safe when these violent words are among us,"* and will take the necessary steps to control them.[57]

About the dangers of "violent words," no seventeenth-century victim of a slighter's belittling invective or a witch's discontented muttering could disagree. For like today's critics of so-called First Amendment abso-lutism, early New Englanders understood the close affinity of speech and authority, or what one critic has recently called "the relationships be-tween naming and reality, knowledge and power."[58] Would not Salem's Hugh Peter, who reminded Anne Hutchinson that preaching produced authority just as listening embodied wifely subjection, agree with critical race theorist Charles Lawrence that words are capable of constructing a world of "masters and slaves"?[59] Would not John Endecott, the Massachusetts Bay Colony governor who resorted to torture and even execution in his struggle to silence Quaker itinerants, concur with Catharine MacKinnon that "some people get a lot more speech than others," and that "the less speech you have, the more the speech of those who have it keeps you unequal"?[60] And would not Cotton Mather, mindful as he was of the godly potential as well as the diabolic tendencies of female speech, understand why I feel both sickened and silenced when confronted, through the flickering pixels of electronic "conversation," by a recently circulated list of the "top 75 reasons why women (bitches) should not have freedom of speech"?[61] Surely they would. Indeed, such ideas about the power of words, and the relationship of words to power, appear more radical at the end of the twentieth century than they would have seemed in the middle of the seventeenth.

Still, the obvious affinities between premodern and postmodern thought about language should not deafen us to the profound differences between Cotton Mather's understanding of "right speaking" and the kind of linguistic order that would be acceptable to most of us today. Just as New England's experience reminds us of the many ways that words enact power, it should alert us to the fact that notions of the good life—beliefs about the way in which power *should* operate in society—change over time. Yes, Hugh Peter might agree with Charles Lawrence that words, as much as whips, built a world of masters and slaves. But unlike Lawrence, neither Hugh Peter nor anybody else alive in the mid–seventeenth century especially objected to a world of masters and slaves. And yes, John Endecott might endorse MacKinnon's claim that speech (or the lack thereof) "keeps you unequal." But "unequal" was not a dirty word in Endecott's day. To the contrary: his was a historic moment when people assumed that, in John Winthrop's words, "as in all times some must be rich some poore, some highe and eminent in power and dignitie; others meane and in subjeccion."[62] In such a world, public speech was generally assumed to devolve upon those worthy of possessing it, those capable of controlling its powers. From the Puritan perspective, unchecked speech was dangerous chiefly because it could damage those who had (rightly) ascended to the top of a steeply vertical social order. Today's First Amendment revisionists believe just the opposite. Instead of limiting speech *against* those at the top, they seek to "lower the voices" of people with power and, symbolically, to "hand out megaphones . . . to those whose voices would not otherwise be heard in the public square."[63] In this battle, the Puritans would have been enemies rather than allies.

Does this mean that where speech is concerned, the seventeenth century was the dark ages after all? Do recent attempts to "censure the vocabulary of hate" simply represent a less evolved understanding of language, a "confusion between word and deed, between object and the name describing it that anthropologists . . . once attributed to 'savages,'" and that some today decry as "puritanical"?[64] Surely the Puritan example is more complex, more ambiguous, and more useful than such blanket dismissals allow. For if Cotton Mather would not endorse—indeed, could not comprehend—the commitment to social equality that animates so much of our public debate, he and his fellow New Englanders still have something to teach us about the place of language within it. They remind us to listen carefully to the dense counterpoint of voices that makes up our communities of discourse. They ask us to pay close attention to who is trying to silence whom, who is resisting those demands, and why. They caution us that words can destroy as well as nourish liberty, and they urge us to define that elusive point at which the freedom to speak becomes a license to wound. Only if we do so can we move forward in our own struggles with that age-old adversary and uncertain ally, the unbridled tongue.

APPENDIX

Litigation over Speech in Massachusetts, 1630–1692

TABLE A.I: Gender and Litigation over Speech, by Court

	Essex County Courts (1636–86)		Court of Assistants (1642–92)		General Court (1630–92)		Total	
	Cases	Women (%)[c]	Cases	Women (%)	Cases	Women (%)	Cases	Women (%)
Civil infractions[a]	385	32.5	—		—		385	32.5
Criminal speech[b]	651	24.6	45	6.7	128	17.1	824	22.4
Speech against authority	162	15.3	18	5.6	64	14.1[d]	244	13.5

[a]Civil slander and defamation were tried only at the county court level.

[b]Criminal speech includes blasphemy, criminal slander, cursing, lying, perjury, railing, reviling, scolding, swearing, threatening, treason, as well as speech against authority.

[c]Includes female plaintiffs and defendants, female "targets" of civil and/or criminal speech, and female "defamers." Also includes women who appeared in any of these capacities as part of a married couple or in a mixed-sex group of litigants.

[d]Seven of the eight female speakers against authority who came before the General Court were Quakers; see discussion in chapter 4.

Sources for all data: Nathaniel B. Shurtleff, ed., Records of the Governor and Company of the Massachusetts Bay in New England, 5 vols. in 6 (1854; reprinted New York: AMS Press, 1968); John Noble and John F. Cronin, eds., Records of the Court of Assistants of the Colony of Massachusetts Bay, 1630–1692, 3 vols. (Boston: Rockwell and Churchill, 1901–1928); and George F. Dow, ed., Records and Files of the Quarterly Courts of Essex County, Massachusetts, 9 vols. (Salem, Mass.: Essex Institute, 1911–1978).

TABLE A.2: Speech against Authority, by Target (Essex County Courts, 1636–86; Court of Assistants and General Court, 1630–92; Combined)

Target	Number	% of Total
Civil government (court)	113	46.3
Church/religion	67	27.5
Multiple targets[a]	31	12.7
Town[b]	24	9.8
Unknown	4	1.6
King	3	1.2
Master (of servant)	2	0.8
Total cases	244	100.0

[a]Typically, court and church ($N = 14$), or either court or church plus another target (family relation, town officer, etc.).

[b]"Town" category includes constables, prominent members of one's congregation, heads of local militia, and other local officials.

TABLE A.3: Apology[a] as a Remedy for Civil Speech Offenses, Essex County Courts, 1636–86

Total civil speech offenses	385	
less punishment unknown	(172)	
less suits withdrawn	(69)	
less plaintiffs not found guilty[b]	(43)	
Total cases with known punishments	101	

Remedies for civil speech offenses with known punishments

Apology only	37	36.6
Apology and/or fine	16	15.8
Fine only	31	30.7
Arbitration	9	8.9
Other public shame[c]	6	5.9
Appealed before sentencing	6	5.9
Bond for good behavior	6	5.9
Whipping	4	4.0
Admonishment	4	4.0
Total[d]	135	

[a]Includes compulsory acknowledgment and voluntary public confession.

[b]Includes cases where defendant prevailed, and cases dismissed, nonsuited, defaulted, or in which the bench did not accept a jury's guilty verdict.

[c]Includes time in the stocks, wearing a paper or cleft stick, etc.

[d]Total adds to more than 100% because of multiple punishments.

TABLE A.4: Apology[a] as a Punishment for Criminal Speech, by Court

	Essex County Courts 1636–86		Court of Assts. & General Court 1630–92	
Total criminal speech offenses	651		173	
less punishment unknown	(96)		(10)	
less offenders not punished	(40)		(6)	
Total cases with known punishments	515		157	
Remedies in criminal speech cases with known punishments				
Fine only	287	55.7%	53	33.8%
Apology and/or fine	56	10.9	13	8.3
Apology only	47	9.1	17	10.8
Whipping	71	13.8	40	25.5
Other public shame[b]	70	13.6	29	18.5
Admonishment	67	13.0	18	11.5
Bond for good behavior	33	6.4	11	7.0
Jail	20	3.9	22	14.0
Disenfranchisement	2	0.4	2	1.3
Appealed before sentence	1	0.2	0	0.0
Arbitration	1	0.2	0	0.0
Banishment	0	0.0	16	10.2
Total[c]	656		221	

[a]Includes compulsory acknowledgment and voluntary public confession.

[b]Includes punishments described in table A.3, plus mutilation.

[c]Total adds to more than 100% because of multiple punishments.

TABLE A.5: Apology[a] as a Punishment for Defaming Authority, by Court

	Essex County Courts 1636–86		Court of Assts. & General Court 1630–92	
Total cases defaming authority	162		82	
less punishment unknown	(22)		(5)	
less offenders not punished	(7)		(2)	
Total cases with known punishments	133		75	
Cases in which apology is remedy	53	39.9%	23	30.7%

[a]Includes compulsory acknowledgment and voluntary public confession.

TABLE A.6: Women's Participation in Speech and Silence Punishments[a] (Essex County Courts, 1636–86; Court of Assistants and General Court, 1630–92; Combined)

Type of Punishment	Total Cases	Female Offenders (%)[b]	
Compulsory acknowledgment	138	16	11.6
Voluntary confession/ petition	122	55	45.1
Pinned with paper[c]	18	8	44.4
Gagged with cleft stick	6	2	33.3
Tongue mutilated	1	0	0.0

[a]Includes all types of crime and civil litigation. For apology's special relationship to speech offenses, see tables A.4 and A.5, above.

[b]Includes women tried as part of a couple, as was often the case in fornication presentments.

[c]Offenders punished by being forced to wear a "paper" inscribed with a description of their offenses.

FIGURE A.I: Presentments for speech against authority, by decade (Essex County courts, 1636–86; General Court and Court of Assistants, 1630–92).

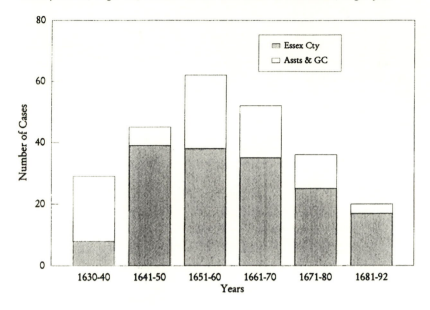

FIGURE A.2: Mandatory acknowledgments, by decade (Essex County courts, 1636–86; General Court and Court of Assistants, 1630–92).

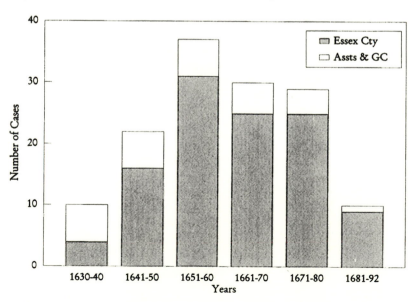

FIGURE A.3: Presentments for speech against authority and mandatory acknowledgments (all courts), by decade, per capita.

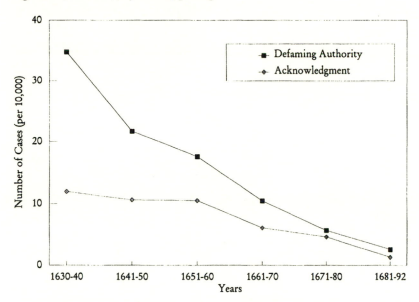

Note: Population estimates are based on Evarts B. Green and Virginia D. Harrington, *American Population before the Federal Census of 1790* (New York: Columbia University Press, 1932), 13–14. Using as end points a colony-wide population of 4,000 in 1634, and 100,000 by 1700, and assuming a linear pattern of growth, we arrive at a very rough measure of the incidence of apology per ten thousand population. Figure from county courts outside Essex would certainly increase the total number, but the percentage change would likely remain much the same.

NOTES

Introduction

1. Worthington Chauncey Ford, ed., *Diary of Cotton Mather*, 2 vols. (1912; reprinted New York: Frederick Ungar, 1957), 1: 47. On Mather's early life in general, and his stutter in particular, see Kenneth Silverman, *The Life and Times of Cotton Mather* (New York: Columbia University Press, 1985), esp. 33–42; and David Levin, *Cotton Mather: The Young Life of the Lord's Remembrancer, 1663–1703* (Cambridge: Harvard University Press, 1978), 18–105.

2. Mather, *Diary*, 1: 2–3, 19–20, emphasis original.

3. Thomas Adams, "The Taming of the Tongue" (1629), in Joseph Angus, ed., *The Works of Thomas Adams*, 3 vols. (Edinburgh: James Nichol, 1862), 3: 12. On the "infectious" nature of Hutchinson's speech, see "A Report of the Trial of Mrs. Anne Hutchinson before the Church in Boston [March 1638]," in David D. Hall, ed., *The Antinomian Controversy, 1636–1638: A Documentary History* (1968; reprinted Durham, N.C.: Duke University Press, 1990), 353.

4. Mather, *Diary*, 1: 55, 62. The theme of speaking and impediments thereto remains a frequent motif in the diary; see, e.g., 1: 35, 49–50, 52, 154, 164, 206–7, 311, 319, 333–34, 347–48.

5. Cotton Mather, *Ornaments for the Daughters of Zion* (Boston, 1692), 49; see also 5, 27–28, 50–51, and the discussion of the problematics of woman's word in chapters 3 and 6 in this book.

6. See, e.g., Cotton Mather, *Help for Distressed Parents. Or, Counsels & Comforts for Godly Parents Afflicted with Ungodly Children* (Boston, 1695), A Family

Well-Ordered (Boston, 1699), and *The Young Man's Preservative Or, Serious Advice to All, and Especially to Young People, about Their Company* (Boston, 1701).

7. Mather, *Diary*, 1: 347–48. Mather refers here to a pamphlet entitled *The Good Linguist, Or, Directions to Avoid the Sins of the Tongue* (Boston, 1700), of which no copy survives. See also Mather, *A Golden Curb for the Mouth* (Boston, 1709), and *The Right Way to Shake Off a Viper. . . . What Shall Good Men Do, When They Are Evil Spoken Of?* (Boston, 1720).

8. Cotton Mather, *The Angel of Bethesda* (1724), ed. Gordon W. Jones (Barre, Mass.: American Antiquarian Society, 1972), 167–68; see also 62–63, 226–33.

9. Brian Stross, "Speaking of Speaking: Tenejapa Tzeltal Metalinguistics," in Richard Bauman and Joel Sherzer, eds., *Explorations in the Ethnography of Speaking* (Cambridge: Cambridge University Press, 1974), 213–39, esp. 214–15.

10. The phrase "heated speech" is borrowed from Robert Blair St. George, whose pioneering work on symbolic communication, broadly defined, in early America has served as a model for other scholars seeking to apply linguistic and anthropological models to historical communities. See especially St. George, " 'Heated' Speech and Literacy in Seventeenth-Century New England," in David D. Hall and David Grayson Allen, eds., *Seventeenth-Century New England* (Boston: Colonial Society of Massachusetts, 1984), 275–322; and St. George, *Conversing by Signs: Poetics of Implication in Colonial New England Culture* (Chapel Hill: University of North Carolina Press, forthcoming).

11. William Hubbard, *The Benefit of a Well-Ordered Conversation* (Boston, 1684), 3. Confirming the connection between godly conduct and godly speech, Hubbard prefaces his sermon with a proverb stating that "Words in season are as Apples of Gold in Pictures of Silver." For a similar usage by an eighteenth-century Irish Presbyterian who was beloved by orthodox New Englanders for his opposition to the Quakers and to the Church of England, see Francis Makemie, *A Good Conversation, A Sermon Preached at the City of New York* (Boston, 1707), 8–9, 11.

12. For a review of some of the countless anthropological works on small societies, see Mary Beth Norton, "Gender and Defamation in Seventeenth-Century Maryland," *William and Mary Quarterly* (hereafter *WMQ*) 3rd ser., 44:1 (January 1987): 5, n. 5.

13. William H. Whitmore, ed., *The Colonial Laws of Massachusetts, Reprinted from the Edition of 1660, with the Supplements to 1672, Containing also the Body of Liberties of 1641* (Boston: Rockwell and Churchill, 1889), 49, 35.

14. For a list of "categories of aggressive verbal behavior" censured by Massachusetts courts, see St. George, " 'Heated' Speech," 318–19. The Essex County courts tried a total of 651 criminal-speech offenses between 1636 and 1686. See George F. Dow, ed., *Records and Files of the Quarterly Courts of Essex County, Massachusetts* (hereafter *ECR*), 9 vols. (Salem, Mass.: Essex Institute, 1911–1978); and Archie N. Frost, comp., *Verbatim Transcript of the File Papers of the Essex County Quarterly Courts, 1636–1692* (hereafter *Essex File Papers*), 75 vols. (typescript on deposit at the James Duncan Phillips Library of the Peabody-Essex Museum, Salem, Mass.; microfilm copy at Sterling Memorial Library, Yale University). The colony's higher courts, the General Court and the Court of Assistants, presided over 173 trials for deviant speech between 1630 and 1692, or an average of 2.8 per year. For detail, see appendix, table A.1, in this book.

15. An average of 7.7 cases per year represents a total of 385 suits for slander or defamation, divided evenly over the fifty years from 1636 to 1686. For detail,

see appendix, table A.1. Essex County thus exhibits roughly three times the rate of slander litigation that Cornelia Dayton finds in New Haven Colony (and then County), where the volume of cases peaked at 2.9 per year between 1639 and 1665; see Cornelia Hughes Dayton, *Women before the Bar: Gender, Law, and Society in Connecticut, 1639–1789* (Chapel Hill: University of North Carolina Press, 1995), 288–92.

16. Bernard Bailyn, ed., *The Apologia of Robert Keayne: The Self-Portrait of a Puritan Merchant* (New York: Harper and Row, 1964), 50–51, 46.

17. Presentment of Thomas Bragg and Edward Cogswell, Ipswich, 1670, *ECR*, 4: 243, *Essex File Papers*, 15: 126-1 through 127-6; presentment of Samuel Honeywell, Salem, 1683, *ECR*, 9: 164 (also 83, 163). For more examples of neighbors' endorsement of a person's "quietness" and their condemnation of idle, foolish, and nasty talk, see Jane Kamensky, "Governing the Tongue: Speech and Society in Early New England" (Ph.D. dissertation, Yale University, 1993), 72–80.

18. See the extended discussion of Hutchinson's case in chapter 3.

19. For a useful introduction, see Richard M. Rorty, ed., *The Linguistic Turn: Essays in the Philosophical Method, with Two Retrospective Essays* (1967; rev. ed. Chicago: University of Chicago Press, 1992).

20. For succinct introductions to the "linguistic turn" in historical studies, see David Harlan, "Intellectual History and the Return of Literature," *American Historical Review* (hereafter *AHR*) 94:3 (June 1989): 581–609; Joyce Appleby, "One Good Turn Deserves Another: Moving beyond the Linguistic; A Response to David Harlan," *AHR* 94:5 (December 1989): 1326–32; Joyce Appleby, Lynn Hunt, and Margaret Jacobs, *Telling the Truth about History* (New York: W. W. Norton, 1994), 195–96, 212–16, 267–68; and Lynn Hunt, ed., *The New Cultural History* (Berkeley: University of California Press, 1989), 6–7, 14, 17.

21. For introductions to this sociolinguistic understanding of linguistic competence, see Bauman and Sherzer, eds., *Explorations in the Ethnography of Speaking*; John J. Gumperz and Dell Hymes, eds., *Directions in Sociolinguistics* (New York: Holt, Rinehart and Winston, 1972); Dell Hymes, *Foundations in Sociolinguistics: An Ethnographic Approach* (Philadelphia: University of Pennsylvania Press, 1974); John J. Gumperz, ed., *Language and Social Identity* (Cambridge: Cambridge University Press, 1982); Susan U. Philips, Susan Steele, and Christine Tanz, eds., *Language, Gender, and Sex in Comparative Perspective* (Cambridge: Cambridge University Press, 1987); and Suzanne Romaine, *Language in Society: An Introduction to Sociolinguistics* (Oxford: Oxford University Press, 1994).

22. See Peter Burke and Roy Porter, eds., *The Social History of Language* (New York: Cambridge University Press, 1987), esp. 11–15; Peter Burke, *The Art of Conversation* (Ithaca, N.Y.: Cornell University Press, 1993); and William M. O'Barr, "Asking the Right Questions about Language and Power," in Cheris Kramarae, Muriel Schulz, and William M. O'Barr, eds., *Language and Power* (Beverly Hills, Calif.: Sage Publications, 1984), esp. 265–69.

23. Burke, *Social History of Language*, 2–4.

24. On the distortion that inheres in "reported" speech, see Walter J. Ong, *The Presence of the Word: Some Prolegomena for Cultural and Religious History* (New Haven: Yale University Press, 1967), 32–33, 45–47, 115–16.

25. The Puritan ethos of neighborly watchfulness is a chestnut of New England history; see especially Roger Thompson, " 'Holy Watchfulness' and Communal Conformism: The Functions of Defamation in Early New England Communities," *New England Quarterly* 56:4 (December 1983): 504–22.

26. Kimball v. Webster, Ipswich, 1681, *Essex File Papers*, 35: 16-1; present-ment of Mary Grant, Ipswich, 1681, *Essex File Papers*, 35: 65-4, and *ECR*, 8: 98.

27. Heard v. Heard, Salem, 1677, *Essex File Papers*, 26: 131-3, and *ECR*, 6: 295–96, 7: 78. For similar incidents, see also presentments of Hannah Gray, Ipswich, 1674, *Essex File Papers*, 21: 35-1 through 36-1, 36-4, and *ECR*, 5: 291; and John Pierce, Ipswich, 1673, *Essex File Papers*, 20: 96-1, *ECR*, 5: 231. For an example of overattentive listening that resulted in criminal charges, see present-ment of John England, Salem, 1638, *ECR*, 1: 7.

28. On the centrality of auditory memory in the early modern period, see St. George, " 'Heated' Speech," 315–17; and Barry Reay, ed., *Popular Culture in Seventeenth-Century England* (London: Croom Helm, 1985), 6–7.

29. Woolcott v. Atkinson, Ipswich, 1682, *Essex File Papers*, 37: 25-5, 26-1, and *ECR*, 8: 248–49.

30. See, e.g., Haseltine v. Knowlton, Ipswich, 1672, *ECR*, 5: 13–15, 38; Collins v. Needham, Ipswich, 1684, *Essex File Papers*, 42: 108-4.

31. Nathaniel B. Shurtleff, ed., *Records of the Governor and Company of the Massachusetts Bay in New England* (hereafter *Mass. Recs.*), 5 vols. in 6 (1854; reprinted New York: AMS Press, 1968), 2: 259–60; 3: 263.

32. To further this goal, the General Court ordered in 1650 that all deposi-tions be taken prior to trial, faithfully recorded, and "presented in writinge" in court, where their accuracy would be sworn to; see *Mass. Recs.*, 3: 211.

33. On legal language in England versus New England, see Dayton, *Women before the Bar*, 4, 8–10, 45–49; and William E. Nelson, "Court Records as Sources for Historical Writing," in Daniel R. Coquillette, ed., *Law in Colonial Massachu-setts, 1630–1800*, Colonial Society of Massachusetts Publications, vol. 62 (Bos-ton: Colonial Society of Massachusetts, 1984), 499–518, esp. 508–11. The "plain style" of Puritan preaching has been the subject of numerous studies. For a useful introduction, see the classic treatment by William Haller, *The Rise of Puritanism Or, the Way to the New Jerusalem as Set Forth in the Pulpit and Press from Thomas Cartwright to John Lilburne and John Milton, 1570–1643* (New York: Columbia University Press, 1938), 128–72.

34. A definitive statement of the heroic interpretation of print and literacy found in much of the scholarship on language from the 1960s and 1970s appears in Jack Goody and Ian Watt, "The Consequences of Literacy," in Goody, ed., *Literacy in Traditional Societies* (Cambridge: Cambridge University Press, 1968), 27–68. A similar understanding underlies a recent essay on the decline of reading in the United States; see Cynthia Ozick, "The Question of Our Speech: The Return to Aural Culture," in Katharine Washburn and John F. Thornton, eds., *Dumbing Down: Essays on the Strip Mining of American Culture* (New York: W. W. Norton, 1996), 69–87. For a cogent critique of these assumptions, see Jill Lepore, "Dead Men Tell No Tales: John Sassamon and the Fatal Consequences of Liter-acy," *American Quarterly* 46:4 (December 1994): 479–512, esp. 480–83.

35. This point is forcefully made by David D. Hall in *Worlds of Wonder, Days of Judgment: Popular Religious Belief in Early New England* (New York: Alfred A. Knopf, 1989), 21–70, esp. 42, and "The World of Print and Collective Mentality in Seventeenth-Century New England," in *Cultures of Print: Essays in the History of the Book* (Amherst: University of Massachusetts Press, 1996), 79–96. Hall's work is foremost among recent efforts by scholars to reconceptualize the notion of literacy, treating reading and writing as cultural practices varying by time and place, rather than as information technologies consistent in their meaning and

impact. Contrast, for example, the skills-based definition of literacy employed by Kenneth A. Lockridge, *Literacy in Colonial New England: An Enquiry into the Social Context of Literacy in the Early Modern West* (New York: W. W. Norton, 1974) with the more contextual understandings of reading and writing that characterize Roger Chartier and Alain Paire, eds., *Pratiques de la lecture* (Marseille: Rivages, 1985); Lisa Jardine and Anthony Grafton, " 'Studied for Action': How Gabriel Harvey Read His Livy," *Past and Present* 129 (November 1990): 30–78; Cathy N. Davidson, ed., *Reading in America: Literature and Social History* (Baltimore: Johns Hopkins University Press, 1989); Michael Warner, *Letters of the Republic: Publication and the Public Sphere in Eighteenth-Century America* (Cambridge: Harvard University Press, 1990), esp. 1–21; Peter Wogan, "Perceptions of European Literacy in Early Contact Situations," *Ethnohistory* 41:3 (summer 1994): 407–29; and Lepore, "Dead Men Tell No Tales."

36. On the Bible as speech, and the Puritan sermon as oral performance, see Sandra Marie Gustafson, "Performing the Word: American Oratory, 1630–1860" (Ph.D. dissertation, University of California at Berkeley, 1993), 1–27, 93–125; Harry S. Stout, *The New England Soul: Preaching and Religious Culture in Colonial New England* (New York: Oxford University Press, 1986), 19–25; Ong, *Presence of the Word*, 12–13, 184–89; and the discussion in chapter 1 in this book.

37. Mather, *Diary*, 1: 154.

38. Ong, *Presence of the Word*, 21–22.

39. Merja Kytö, "Robert Keayne's *Notebooks*: A Verbatim Record of Spoken English in Early Boston?" in Susan Herring, Pieter van Reenen, and Lene Schósler, eds., *Textual Parameters in Older Languages* (London: John Benjamins, forthcoming). The manuscript volumes of Keayne's sermon notebooks are housed in the Massachusetts Historical Society, Boston. Kytö's annotated transcription of the speech-centered portions of the notebooks will soon appear as Merja Kytö, ed., *Voices in Early Boston: Robert Keayne's Notes of the Meetings of the First Church of Boston, 1639–1646* (forthcoming). For Keayne's biography, see Bailyn, ed., *Apologia of Robert Keayne*.

40. The first recorded instance of the proverb and its variants appears in G. F. Northall, *Folk-Phrases of Four Counties . . . Gathered from Oral Tradition* (London: English Dialect Society, 1894), 23; see also Bartlett Jere Whiting, *Modern Proverbs and Proverbial Sayings* (Cambridge: Harvard University Press, 1989), 594–95. It is found in none of the numerous similar collections published earlier in the nineteenth century, nor in Morris Palmer Tilley's classic *A Dictionary of Proverbs in England in the Sixteenth and Seventeenth Centuries* (Ann Arbor: University of Michigan Press, 1950).

41. Hubbard, *Benefit of a Well-Ordered Conversation*, 45–46. The proverb disappears from common usage in the mid–eighteenth century; see Bartlett Jere Whiting, *Early American Proverbs and Proverbial Phrases* (Cambridge: Harvard University Press, 1977), 447.

42. William Perkins, *A Direction for the Government of the Tongue According to Gods Word* (1597), in [Perkins], *The Works of that Famous and Worthy Minister . . . Newly Corrected* (London, 1635), 440.

Chapter 1

1. Joseph Swetnam, *The Arraignment of Lewde, Idle, Froward and Unconstant Women* (London, 1615), 41–42. The ancient land was Egypt, where Amasis (Ah-

mose II) ruled in the fifth century B.C. See Peter A. Clayton, *Chronicle of the Pharaohs* (London: Thames and Hudson, 1994), 195–99. Although Swetnam gave his king the name of a historical figure who, according to a Tudor translation of Herodotus, had experienced the perils of "scoffing without measure," the anecdote appears to be his own invention. See Leonard Whibley, ed., *The Famous Hystory of Herodotus* (1584; reprinted New York: Alfred A. Knopf, 1924), 2: 237.

2. On the popularity of Swetnam's volume, see Angeline Goreau, *The Whole Duty of a Woman: Female Writers in Seventeenth-Century England* (New York: Dial Press, 1985), 67.

3. Thomas Adams, "The Taming of the Tongue" (1629), in Joseph Angus, ed., *The Works of Thomas Adams*, 3 vols. (Edinburgh: James Nichol, 1862), 3: 10–22, quotation from 12. Numerous other tracts echoed Adams's sense of the contradictory qualities of speech. See, e.g., Richard Allestree, *The Government of the Tongue*, 4th impression (Oxford, 1675), esp. 3, 219. On the "contradictory" qualities attributed to speech in the seventeenth century, see also Robert B. St. George, " 'Heated' Speech and Literacy in Seventeenth-Century New England," in David D. Hall and David Grayson Allen, eds., *Seventeenth-Century New England* (Boston: Colonial Society of Massachusetts, 1984), 275–322, esp. 279–80.

4. William Holder, *Elements of Speech* (1669; facsimile reprinted Menston, Eng.: Scolar Press, 1967), 5–6, 63; George Webbe, *The Arraignement of an Unruly Tongue* (London, 1619), 5.

5. Adams, "Taming of the Tongue," 12.

6. Webbe, *Arraignement of an Unruly Tongue*, 133, 11, emphasis original; see also 28–29, 75.

7. William Gouge, *Of Domesticall Duties, Eight Treatises* (London, 1634), 4. The literature analyzing notions of social order in early modern England is vast. See esp. Gordon J. Schochet, *Patriarchalism in Political Thought: The Authoritarian Family and Political Speculation and Attitudes Especially in Seventeenth-Century England* (Oxford: Basil Blackwell, 1975); Susan Dwyer Amussen, *An Ordered Society: Gender and Class in Early Modern England* (New York: Basil Blackwell, 1988); and the essays in Anthony Fletcher and John Stevens, eds., *Order and Disorder in Early Modern England* (Cambridge: Cambridge University Press, 1985).

8. The phrase is taken from Norbert Elias, *The Civilizing Process*, trans. Edmund Jephcott (1939; reprinted Oxford: Basil Blackwell, 1994), 95.

9. There is a growing literature applying anthropological insights about the politics of reputation and the invidious threat of slander to historical communities. For anthropological background, see esp. F. G. Bailey, *Gifts and Poison: The Politics of Reputation* (New York: Schocken Books, 1971). On England and Europe, see J. A. Sharpe, *Defamation and Sexual Slander in Early Modern England: The Church Courts at York* (Borthwick Institute of Historical Research, University of York, paper 58 [1980]); and Lyndal Roper, "Will and Honor: Sex, Words, and Power in Augsburg Criminal Trials," *Radical History Review* 43:1 (January 1989): 45–71. On the colonies, see St. George, " 'Heated' Speech"; Cornelia Hughes Dayton, *Women before the Bar: Gender, Law, and Society in Connecticut, 1639–1789* (Chapel Hill: University of North Carolina Press, 1995), 285–328; Mary Beth Norton, "Gender and Defamation in Seventeenth-Century Maryland," *William and Mary Quarterly* (hereafter *WMQ*) 3rd ser., 44:1 (January 1987): 3–39; Peter N. Moogk, " 'Thieving Buggers' and 'Stupid Sluts': Insults and Popular Culture in New France," *WMQ* 3rd ser., 36:4 (October 1979): 524–47; Helena M.

Wall, *Fierce Communion: Family and Community in Early America* (Cambridge: Harvard University Press, 1990), esp. 30–48; and Kirsten Fischer, " 'Kiss the Book and Tale a Hundred Lyes': Women's Speech and Resistance to Authority in Colonial North Carolina," paper presented at the IEAHC conference, Ann Arbor, Mich., June 1995.

10. Ecclesiastes 7:1. For an extended gloss on this image, see Jeremy Dyke, *The Mischiefe and Miserie of Scandalls Both Taken, and Given* (London, 1632), esp. 138–46. The image remained popular in the eighteenth century; see Joseph Butler, *Upon the Government of the Tongue* (1729), in Samuel Halifax, comp., *The Works of Joseph Butler*, 2 vols. (London: Scott and Webster, 1834), 2: 65.

11. This language is found in the lengthy subtitle of Webbe's *Arraignement of an Unruly Tongue*.

12. Allestree, *Government of the Tongue*, preface, n.p. See also Stephen Ford, *The Evil Tongue Tryed and Found Guilty, or, the Hainousness and Exceeding Sinfulness of Defaming and Back-biting Opened and Declared* (London, 1672), 16, 46–47, 60; William Perkins, *A Direction for the Government of the Tongue According to Gods Word* (1597), in [Perkins], *The Works of that Famous and Worthy Minister . . . Newly Corrected* (London, 1635), 451; "J. W.," *The Baseness and Perniciousness of the Sin of Slandering and Backbiting* (Boston, 1769), 4, 5.

13. Allestree, *Government of the Tongue*, 134. For other images of words-as-disease, see Robert Codrington, *The Second Part of Youth's Behaviour, or Decency in Conversation Amongst Women* (London, 1664), 6; "J. W.," *Slandering and Backbiting*, 19; Robert Boyle, *A Free Discourse Against Customary Swearing* (London, 1695), 110.

14. Butler, *Upon the Government of the Tongue*, 55. See also Adams, "Taming of the Tongue," 17, 19; and Allestree, *Government of the Tongue*, 47. Robert St. George points out that fire was an overdetermined image in the seventeenth century, calling to mind the flames of hell, the heat of unacceptable passions, and humoral theories of medicine; " 'Heated' Speech," esp. 283. George Webbe made the connection explicit, linking the "fire of an evill Tongue" to "the fire of hell which goeth never out." See Webbe, *Arraignement of an Unruly Tongue*, 83–84; and chapter 6 in this book.

15. The locution is a common one; see, e.g., Allestree, *Government of the Tongue*, preface, n.p. The sexual double entendre is unmistakable. On the link between the tongue and other "unruly members," see Lynda E. Boose, "Scolding Brides and Bridling Scolds: Taming the Woman's Unruly Member," *Shakespeare Quarterly* 42:2 (summer 1991): 179–213, esp. 196; and Susan Juster, *Disorderly Women: Sexual Politics and Evangelicalism in Revolutionary New England* (Ithaca, N.Y.: Cornell University Press, 1994), 147–50, 156–60.

16. Webbe, *Arraignement of an Unruly Tongue*, 28. See also 44–45, 50, 75; and Allestree, *Government of the Tongue*, 19.

17. Adams, "Taming of the Tongue," 12.

18. Adams, "Taming of the Tongue," 12, 17, emphasis mine.

19. Webbe, *Arraignement of an Unruly Tongue*, 8. Compare with Allestree, *Government of the Tongue*, 7; Swetnam, *Froward and Unconstant Women*, 1; and Ford, *Evil Tongue Tryed and Found Guilty*, 102–3.

20. See Boose, "Scolding Brides and Bridling Scolds," 185, 189, 195, 203; and David Underdown, "The Taming of the Scold: The Enforcement of Patriarchal Authority in Early Modern England," in Fletcher and Stevens, eds., *Order and*

Disorder in Early Modern England, 116–36. Underdown, mistakenly I think, attributes evidence of rising anxiety about "scolding" to an actual increase in women's anti-authoritarian behavior (see esp. 120).

On the long history of works linking women's voices with social disorder, see Katharine M. Rogers, *The Troublesome Helpmate: A History of Misogyny in Literature* (Seattle: University of Washington Press, 1966), chapter 1; and Katherine Usher Henderson and Barbara F. McManus, eds., *Half Humankind: Contexts and Texts of the Controversy about Women in England, 1540–1640* (Urbana: University of Illinois Press, 1985), part 1. For many Renaissance writers, women's mental inferiority was the root cause of female loquaciousness. On the physiological roots and intellectual ramifications of sex differences, see Ian Maclean, *The Renaissance Notion of Woman* (New York: Cambridge University Press, 1980); and Thomas Laqueur, *Making Sex: Body and Gender from the Greeks to Freud* (Cambridge: Harvard University Press, 1990).

21. Swetnam, *Froward and Unconstant Women*, 40.

22. "Word-mad" from the popular book of proverbs *The Precepts of Alfred*, quoted in Rogers, *Troublesome Helpmate*, 95; see also 93–94, 97. See also the anonymous pamphlet entitled *The Anatomy of Woman's Tongue* (1638), in *The Harleian Miscellany: Or, a Collection of . . . Pamphlets and Tracts*, 2 vols. (London, 1744), 2: 167–78.

23. John Taylor, *A Juniper Lecture* (London, 1639), 74–75.

24. John Taylor [Mary Make-peace, pseud.], *Divers Crabtree Lectures, Expressing the Severall Languages that Shrews Read to Their Husbands* (London, 1639), dedicatory letter, n.p.; and Taylor, *Juniper Lecture*, 27–28. Taylor's pseudonym is, itself, a pun on female volubility. In 1640, these two pamphlets provoked an angry response entitled *The Women's Sharpe Revenge*. See Simon Shepherd, ed., *The Women's Sharp Revenge: Five Women's Pamphlets from the Renaissance* (London: Fourth Estate, 1985); and Henderson and McManus, eds., *Half Humankind*, 305–23.

25. Taylor, *Crabtree Lectures*, 186–87; see also Taylor, *Juniper Lecture*, 27–28.

26. For other sayings and rhymes, see [Anonymous], *Anatomy of Woman's Tongue*, 172; Swetnam, *Froward and Unconstant Women*, 37; and Codrington, *Second Part of Youth's Behavior*, 224.

27. Allestree, *Government of the Tongue*, 73; see also George Webbe, *The Practise of Quietnes: Directing a Christian How to Live Quietly in this Troblesome World*, 3rd ed. (London, 1618), 108–10.

28. I Timothy 5:13; Taylor, *Juniper Lecture*, 113.

29. [Anonymous], *Anatomy of Woman's Tongue*, 170. "Gossip," in seventeenth-century parlance, referred to a person rather than a communicative act. Etymologically related to "god-parent," a gossip was a close friend—typically, though not always, female. A "gossiping" (noun) was thus a meeting with one's "gossips." See Patricia Meyer Spacks, *Gossip* (New York: Alfred A. Knopf, 1985), 25–28.

30. [Anonymous], *Hic Mulier; or, the Man-Woman* (1620), reprinted in Henderson and McManus, eds., *Half Humankind*, 265–69.

31. Taylor, *Juniper Lecture*, 111; John Wing, *The Crowne Conjugall* (1632), quoted in Frances E. Dolan, "Home-Rebels and House-Traitors: Murderous Wives in Early Modern England," *Yale Journal of Law and the Humanities* 4:1 (winter 1992): 3. On the theory of "correspondences," which posited direct analogies between family and state, see Schochet, *Patriarchalism in Political Thought*; Susan

Dwyer Amussen, "Gender, Family and the Social Order, 1560–1725," in Fletcher and Stevens, eds., *Order and Disorder in Early Modern England*, 196–217; and Patrick Collinson, *The Birthpangs of Protestant England: Religious and Cultural Change in the Sixteenth and Seventeenth Centuries* (New York: St. Martin's Press, 1988), 60–61.

32. Webbe, *Arraignement of an Unruly Tongue*, 28; see also 75.

33. On the social and literary history of ritual shrew "taming" in England, ca. 1550–1650, see Boose, "Scolding Brides and Bridling Scolds," esp. 198–212. Examples of shrew taming in contemporary literature include Swetnam, *Froward and Unconstant Women*, 40; [Anonymous], *Anatomy of Woman's Tongue*, 170; Henry Smith, *A Preparative to Marriage* (1591), quoted in Henderson and McManus, eds., *Half Humankind*, 53. On scolding as a legally and culturally acceptable justification for wife beating in seventeenth-century England, see Roderick Phillips, *Putting Asunder: A History of Divorce in Western Society* (New York: Cambridge University Press, 1988), 328–29.

34. Webbe, *Practise of Quietnes*, 69, 14–15.

35. Webbe, *Arraignement of an Unruly Tongue*, 103–4, 82.

36. Proverbs 6:16–19; 10:20, 31–32; 13:3. See also James 1:26; 3:3–10. Numerous other biblical texts, particularly in Proverbs, Psalms, Ecclesiastes, and Jeremiah, had much to say on the issue of ordering speech, and were frequently used in sermons on the subject. A lengthy, inventive, though not always persuasive reading of biblical texts on speaking and oratory is found in Sandra Marie Gustafson, "Performing the Word: American Oratory, 1630–1860" (Ph.D. dissertation, University of California at Berkeley, 1993), 29–52, 64–91.

37. Norbert Elias separates his history of manners into three phases, centering on a period of rapid and difficult change from roughly 1500 to 1700. See Elias, *The Civilizing Process*, esp. 86–98. On the rise of manuals prescribing norms for speech, see also Peter Burke, *The Art of Conversation* (Ithaca, N.Y.: Cornell University Press, 1993), 89–122. Burke argues that on the continent, the how-to manual for polite conversation emerged as a genre distinct from medieval courtesy books in the sixteenth century and remained popular through the eighteenth.

38. This ethos represents a marked contrast with the emphasis of European manuals from the same period studied by Peter Burke. Italian and French sources, unlike the English materials under study here, focused primarily on fostering conversation that was amusing and engaging, as befitted courtiers. This focus on avoiding tedium did not gain popularity in England until the mid–eighteenth century. See Burke, *Art of Conversation*, 106–7, 109–10.

39. Webbe, *Arraignement of an Unruly Tongue*, 145, 147. On the immediate and unrestrained quality of speech, see St. George, " 'Heated' Speech," 281–83.

40. Allestree, *Government of the Tongue*, 219.

41. Richard Brathwait, *The English Gentleman* (London, 1630), 83, 13.

42. These labels for strands of English "folk" culture are borrowed from David Hackett Fischer, *Albion's Seed: Four British Folkways in America* (New York: Oxford University Press, 1989).

43. Martin Elsky, *Authorizing Words: Speech, Writing, and Print in the English Renaissance* (Ithaca, N.Y.: Cornell University Press, 1989), 35–54, 74.

44. John Hewes, *A Perfect Survey of the English Tongue* (1624; facsimile reprinted Menston, Eng.: Scolar Press, 1972), X4.

45. Owen Price, *The Vocal Organ* (1665; facsimile reprinted Menston, Eng.: Scolar Press, 1970), 47. Price, whose work was intended for boys who attended country "Free-Schools," presents the alphabet and the rudiments of spelling and pronunciation through simple English rhymes rather than the traditional grammar.

46. Hewes, *Perfect Survey of the English Tongue*, X4.

47. Brathwait, *English Gentleman*, 11, 13, 87, 89.

48. Numerous scholars of literacy and the book have established that writing—as distinct from reading—was considered a skill that befitted men and was taught more to boys than girls in the early modern period. See E. Jennifer Monaghan, "Literacy Instruction and Gender in Colonial New England," in Cathy N. Davidson, ed., *Reading in America: Literature and Social History* (Baltimore: Johns Hopkins University Press, 1989), 53–80.

49. Aristotle, *Politics*, quoted in Maclean, *Renaissance Notion of Woman*, 54.

50. Richard Brathwait, *The English Gentlewoman* (London, 1631), 41, 89–90, 170. Compare with Robert Tofte, *The Blason of Jealousie* (1615), quoted in Ruth Kelso, *Doctrine for a Lady of the Renaissance* (Urbana: University of Illinois Press, 1956), 51; and Taylor, *Juniper Lecture*, 72–73, 76–77. The subtitles to Brathwait's pair of tracts are instructive: his *English Gentleman* promised "excellent rules" for deportment in "publike or private affaires," while *The English Gentlewoman* focused on female "ornaments," "attire," and "complements." For a critical bibliography of didactic material directed at women in the early modern era, see Suzanne W. Hull, *Chaste, Silent and Obedient: English Books for Women, 1475–1640* (San Marino, Calif.: Huntington Library, 1982).

51. Juan Luis Vives, *De Institutione Feminae Christianae* (1523), trans. Richard Hyrde as *Instruction of a Christian Woman* (1540), reprinted in Foster Watson, ed., *Vives and the Renascence Education of Women* (London: Edward Arnold, 1912), 55, emphasis mine. While Vives supported female learning, he also stressed the need to limit instruction to suit female gender roles. See Goreau, *Whole Duty of a Woman*, 2–3.

52. Codrington, *Second Part of Youth's Behavior*, 75.

53. Richard Allestree, *The Ladies Calling* (1673), quoted in Goreau, *Whole Duty of a Woman*, 43. See also Codrington, *Second Part of Youth's Behavior*, 33; and Brathwait, *English Gentlewoman*, 41.

54. Francesco Barbaro, *Directions for Love and Marriage* (1677), quoted in Kelso, *Doctrine for a Lady of the Renaissance*, 101. Like nakedness, Barbaro explained, indecorous female speech effectively bared "habits and emotions." Lynda Boose emphasizes the metonymy between the open-mouthed woman and the sexually "open" or "unbridled" woman; "Scolding Brides and Bridling Scolds," 196.

55. Codrington, *Second Part of Youth's Behavior*, 140.

56. Vives, *Institutione Feminae Christianae*, 94–95. "Lightness" refers both to frivolity and to sexual incontinence.

57. The application of the social-scientific notion of "double bind" to women's language appears first in a pivotal work on gender and language, Robin Lakoff's *Language and Woman's Place* (New York: Farrar, Straus and Giroux, 1975); see esp. 5–6, 62.

58. On *injuria*, see Van Vechten Veeder, "The History of the Law of Defamation," in *Select Essays in Anglo-American Legal History*, 3 vols. (Boston: Little, Brown, 1909), 3: 451–65; and Leonard W. Levy, *Emergence of a Free Press* [rev.

ed. of *Legacy of Suppression: Freedom of Speech and Press in Early American History* (1967)] (New York: Oxford University Press, 1985), xii, 89.

59. See John Lassiter, "Defamation of Peers: The Rise and Decline of the Action for *Scandalum Magnatum,* 1497–1773," *American Journal of Legal History* 22:3 (July 1978): 216–36, esp. 235–36. On truth as a defense in criminal actions, see Thomas Starkie, *A Treatise on the Law of Slander and Libel, and Incidentally of Malicious Prosecutions,* 2 vols. (Albany, N.Y.: C. Van Benthuysen, 1843), 2: 218. On prevailing notions of expressive liberty, see Frederick S. Siebert, *Freedom of the Press in England, 1476–1776: The Rise and Decline of Government Controls* (Urbana: University of Illinois Press, 1952), esp. 5–7, 21–104.

60. Statute excerpted in Veeder, "History of the Law of Defamation," 453; see also 446–66; and Lassiter, "Defamation of Peers," 216.

61. Sharpe, *Defamation and Sexual Slander,* 4–5. See also Veeder, "History of the Law of Defamation," esp. 447–48; Lassiter, "Defamation of Peers," 218–22; and Norman L. Rosenberg, *Protecting the Best Men: An Interpretive History of the Law of Libel* (Chapel Hill: University of North Carolina Press, 1986), 3–11. On common-law versus ecclesiastical jurisdiction over speech offenses, see Ronald A. Marchant, *The Church under the Law: Justice, Administration, and Discipline in the Diocese of York, 1560–1640* (Cambridge: Cambridge University Press, 1969), 16, 19–20, 61, 72–74, 192–94; and Sharpe, *Defamation and Sexual Slander,* 11–15.

62. John March, *Actions for Slaunder, Or, a Methodicall Collection Under Certain Grounds and Heads, of What Words Are Actionable in the Law, and What Not?* (London, 1647), 2, 8.

63. See March, *Actions for Slaunder,* 10–101; Starkie, *Treatise on the Law of Slander,* 1: 21, 168, 99–167; and Veeder, "History of the Law of Defamation," 458–59. On the English law of slander and libel during the seventeenth century, see also Thomas A. Green and R. H. Helmholz, *Juries, Libel, and Justice: The Role of English Juries in Seventeenth- and Eighteenth-Century Trials for Libel and Slander* (Los Angeles: William Andrews Clark Memorial Library, 1984).

64. March, *Actions for Slaunder,* 2, 9.

65. Sharpe, *Defamation and Sexual Slander,* 3.

66. Christopher Hill, *The World Turned Upside Down: Radical Ideas during the English Revolution* (New York: Viking Press, 1972), 12.

67. The debate over the degree to which New England's migrants were driven by religious imperatives has been going on for decades with no end in sight. For recent statements see David Cressy, *Coming Over: Migration and Communication between England and New England in the Seventeenth Century* (New York: Cambridge University Press, 1987), 37–106; Virginia DeJohn Anderson, "Migrants and Motives: Religion and the Settlement of New England, 1630–1640," *New England Quarterly* 58:3 (September 1985): 339–83; Anderson, *New England's Generation: The Great Migration and the Formation of Society and Culture in the Seventeenth Century* (New York: Cambridge University Press, 1991); Fischer, *Albion's Seed,* 13–54; and Jack P. Greene et al., "Forum: *Albion's Seed: Four British Folkways in America*—A Symposium," *WMQ* 3rd ser., 48:2 (April 1991): 224–308.

68. [John Field and Thomas Wilcox], *An Admonition to the Parliament* (1572), in W. H. Frere and C. E. Douglas, eds., *Puritan Manifestoes: A Study of the Origin of the Puritan Revolt* (London: Church Historical Society, 1954), 11, 9, emphasis mine. The best single-volume study of the Elizabethan settlement and its discon-

tents remains Patrick Collinson, *The Elizabethan Puritan Movement* (1967; reprinted London: Methuen, 1982).

69. [Thomas Cartwright], *A Second Admonition to the Parliament* (1572), in Frere and Douglas, eds., *Puritan Manifestoes*, 84, expounding on Jeremiah 1:7 and 26:7–11.

70. Richard Bancroft, *Daungerous Positions and Proceedings, Published and Practiced within this Iland of Brytaine, Under Pretence of Reformation* (1593; reprinted New York: Da Capo Press, 1972), 22, 2, 21, 45, 183; [Cartwright], *Second Admonition to the Parliament*, 85.

71. Percival Wilburn, *A Checke or Reproofe of M. Howlet's Untimely Screeching* (1581), 15v, quoted in Collinson, *Elizabethan Puritan Movement*, 27.

72. On "puritan" as a term of opprobrium, see Collinson, *Elizabethan Puritan Movement*, 26; [Field and Wilcox], *Admonition to the Parliament*, 6; and Geoffrey Hughes, *Swearing: A Social History of Foul Language, Oaths, and Profanity in English* (Cambridge, Mass.: Basil Blackwell, 1991), 97–99.

73. "Au commencement estoit la Parole, et la Parole estoit avec Dieu; et icelle Parole estoit Dieu"; John 1:1 as explicated in Jean Calvin, *Évangile selon Saint Jean*, vol. 2 of M. Reveillard, ed., *Commentaires de Jean Calvin sur le Nouveau Testament* (Aix-en-Provence: Éditions Kerygma, 1978), 12–15; and John T. McNeill, ed., Ford Lewis Battles, trans., *Calvin: Institutes of the Christian Religion*, 2 vols. (hereafter Calvin, *Institutes*) (Philadelphia: Westminster Press, 1960), 1: 130, emphasis mine. See also Gustafson, "Performing the Word," 93.

74. [Cartwright], *Second Admonition to the Parliament*, 91–92.

75. Calvin, *Institutes*, 1: 548.

76. John Foxe, "To the True and Faithfull Congregation of Christ's Universal Church" (1570), in T. H. L. Parker, ed., *English Reformers* (Philadelphia: Westminster Press, 1966), 80, 77; Patrick Collinson, *From Iconoclasm to Iconophobia: The Cultural Impact of the Second English Reformation* (Reading, Eng.: University of Reading, 1986), 8–25; and Collinson, *Birthpangs of Protestant England*, 94–126.

77. Calvin, *Institutes*, 1: 72.

78. See, e.g., Calvin, *Institutes*, 1: 40–41, 58–59. On Foxe's devotion to printed text see Gustafson, "Performing the Word," 95–96.

79. Collinson, *Birthpangs of Protestant England*, 99. For Collinson, printing leads to reading, a purely visual activity. In this interpretation, Collinson follows the work of theorists such as Michel Foucault, Walter Ong, and Marshal MacLuhan, who lament the imposition of a visually homogenized typographic fixity upon what they characterize as the oral-aural fluidity of the premodern world. This is, to my mind, a reductive understanding of what reading means. For insights into the ways in which reading itself is a cultural practice that varies in time, see Elizabeth L. Eisenstein, *The Printing Press as an Agent of Change: Communications and Cultural Transformations in Early-Modern Europe* (New York: Cambridge University Press, 1979), esp. 67, 130; Lisa Jardine and Anthony Grafton, " 'Studied for Action': How Gabriel Harvey Read His Livy," *Past and Present* 129 (November 1990): 30–78; and Davidson, ed., *Reading in America*. On the relationship of print to Protestantism, see Natalie Zemon Davis, "Printing and the People," in *Society and Culture in Early Modern France* (Stanford, Calif.: Stanford University Press, 1975), 189–226.

80. Cotton's habitual saying is described by his grandson: see Cotton Mather, *Magnalia Christi Americana, or the Ecclesiastical History of New England*, 2 vols. (1702; reprinted Hartford: Silas Andrus and Son, 1853), 1: 274.

81. Calvin, *Institutes*, 1: 70, 81. Passages in which Calvin focused on the orality of Scripture are legion. See also Calvin, *Institutes*, 1: 78–79, 2: 1195–96; Joseph Haroutunian, ed., trans., *Calvin: Commentaries* (Philadelphia: Westminster Press, 1958), 78–79, 82–83, 343; Calvin, *On the Christian Faith: Selections from the Institutes, Commentaries, and Tracts*, ed. John T. McNeill (New York: Liberal Arts Press, 1957), esp. 151–54, 180–81.

82. Calvin, *Institutes*, 2: 1444–45. On reformers' arguments against the errors of the Catholic mass, see also ibid., 1429–48; and Edmund S. Morgan, *Visible Saints: The History of a Puritan Idea* (Ithaca, N.Y.: Cornell University Press, 1965), 4–9. On the centrality of the sermon in Puritan life see Collinson, *Elizabethan Puritan Movement*, 358–61; Collinson, *Birthpangs of Protestant England*, 55; Harry S. Stout, *The New England Soul: Preaching and Religious Culture in Colonial New England* (New York: Oxford University Press, 1986), 23; and David D. Hall, *Worlds of Wonder, Days of Judgment: Popular Religious Belief in Early New England* (New York: Alfred A. Knopf, 1989), chapter 4, esp. 167.

83. *The Seconde Parte of a Register* (1593), quoted in Morgan, *Visible Saints*, 7.

84. Collinson, *Elizabethan Puritan Movement*, 122–33. This group included John Cotton, John Milton, William Perkins, and Thomas Wood, among others.

85. [Field and Wilcox], *Admonition to the Parliament*, 23.

86. Calvin, *Institutes*, 2: 1416.

87. Collinson, *Birthpangs of Protestant England*, 122; and Collinson, *Iconoclasm to Iconophobia*, 23. On the plain style see also William Haller, *The Rise of Puritanism Or, the Way to the New Jerusalem as Set Forth in the Pulpit and Press from Thomas Cartwright to John Lilburne and John Milton, 1570–1643* (New York: Columbia University Press, 1938), 128–72.

88. William Perkins, *A Warning Against the Idolatrie of the Last Times* (1601), in Ian Breward, ed., *The Work of William Perkins* (Abingdon, Eng.: Sutton Courtenay Press, 1970), 315.

89. Calvin, *Institutes*, 2: 852. On the sophistication that Puritan ministers cultivated in lay believers, see Stephen Foster, *The Long Argument: English Puritanism and the Shaping of New England Culture, 1570–1700* (Chapel Hill: University of North Carolina Press, 1991), 25, 39, 77–78.

90. Adams, "Taming of the Tongue," 11–12. Adams is paraphrasing Calvin: the tongue "was peculiarly created to tell and proclaim the praise of God"; *Institutes*, 2: 894.

91. Calvin, *Institutes*, 1: 55; 2: 897, 896, 868, 854. See also 2: 853–920.

92. William Perkins, *The Arte of Prophecying: Or, A Treatise of Preaching*, trans. Thomas Tuke (1592; 1st English ed. London, 1607), 133–36, 141; see also 121, 109. A similarly self-conscious version of the preacher's art is found in Niels Hemmingsen, *The Preacher* (1574; facsimile reprinted Menston, Eng.: Scolar Press, 1972), esp. fols. 17–64. For other examples drawn from English Puritan sermons, see Haller, *Rise of Puritanism*, 128–72.

93. Calvin, *Institutes*, 2: 1017–18; see also 1053.

94. Calvin, *Institutes*, 2: 1516. Calvin's anxieties over the tendency of the Protestant faithful to disorder also surface on 2: 1066 (election of ministers), and 2: 1510 (obedience to magistrates).

95. Adams, "Taming of the Tongue," 14.

96. Perkins, *Direction for the Government of the Tongue*, 440, 442, 444–45.

97. See Siebert, *Freedom of the Press in England*, 2–3, 48–63, 95–100.

98. [Cartwright], *Second Admonition to the Parliament*, 84–85. On the response to this pamphlet and the Elizabethan and early Jacobean climate for printing in general, see Siebert, *Freedom of the Press in England*, 95–97; and Collinson, *Elizabethan Puritan Movement*, 60, 118–21, 150–53.

99. On the theological differences among them, see Siebert, *Freedom of the Press in England*, 190–201; and William Haller, ed., *Tracts on Liberty in the Puritan Revolution 1638–1647*, 3 vols. (New York: Columbia University Press, 1934), vol. 1. For my purposes, their common claims for expressive liberties are more important than their diverse theologies.

100. John Lilburne, *A Worke of the Beast Or, A Relation of a Most Unchristian Censure* (1638), in Haller, ed., *Tracts on Liberty*, 2: 4, 22, 32; see also 34.

101. Lord Brooke [Robert Greville], *A Discourse Opening the Nature of that Episcopacie, Which is Exercised in England* (1642), in Haller, ed., *Tracts on Liberty*, 2: 153. Compare with speech-denying punishments described in Martin Mar-Priest [Richard Overton], *The Araignement of Mr. Persecution* (1645), in ibid., 3: 220, 251.

102. John Goodwin, *Oeomaxia; or the Grand Imprudence of Men Running the Hazard of Fighting Against God* (1644), in Haller, ed., *Tracts on Liberty*, 3: 18, 17, emphasis original.

103. John Milton, *Areopagitica: A Speech of Mr. John Milton for the Liberty of Unlicensed Printing* (1644), ed. Richard C. Jebb (Cambridge: Cambridge University Press, 1918), 52–53. Although Milton's tract is the most widely known of the reformers' statements on free expression, it was not one of the most popular in its own day. See Haller, ed., *Tracts on Liberty*, 2: 7; and Siebert, *Freedom of the Press in England*, 195–97.

104. Siebert, *Freedom of the Press in England*, 89.

105. Collinson, *Birthpangs of Protestant England*, 99. The long history of the concept of blasphemy is exhaustively treated in Leonard W. Levy, *Blasphemy: Verbal Offense against the Sacred, from Moses to Salman Rushdie* (New York: Alfred A. Knopf, 1993), esp. 3, 60–62, 73–100. See also Marchant, *The Church under the Law*, 72; George Lee Haskins, *Law and Authority in Early Massachusetts: A Study in Tradition and Design* (New York: Macmillan, 1960), 78, 89–90, 166.

106. Calvin, *Institutes*, 1: 617–18, 212.

107. Haskins, *Law and Authority in Early Massachusetts*, 145, 265–66 n. 65.

108. Collinson, *Iconoclasm to Iconophobia*, esp. 12–15.

109. Phillip Stubbes, *The Anatomie of Abuses: Contayning a Discoverie, or Briefe Summarie of Such Notable Vices and Imperfections, as Now Raigne* (1583; facsimile reprinted New York: Da Capo Press, 1972), Lv. For Jacobean statutes regulating profane speech, see 3 Jac. 1, c. 21, and 20 Jac. 1, c. 20, in Danby Pickering, ed., *The Statutes at Large, from the Thirty-Ninth Year of Queen Elizabeth, to the Twelfth Year of King Charles II, Inclusive* (Cambridge, 1763), 7: 194, 288–89.

110. Stubbes, *Anatomie of Abuses*, Piiv, R.

111. Milton, *Areopagitica*, 60. "[T]olerated popery" was Milton's prime candidate for extirpation. Significantly, one of the reasons Milton advocated relaxing restrictions on printing and publishing was to keep *verbal* "publishing" in check. Spreading one's opinion "privily from house to house" was surely "more dangerous," he wrote, than doing so "openly by writing" (47). On (mis)readings of Milton as a harbinger of modern libertarianism, see Stanley Fish, *There's No Such Thing as Free Speech . . . and It's a Good Thing, Too* (New York: Oxford University Press, 1994), esp. 103.

112. Galatians 3:28.

113. [Field and Wilcox], *Admonition to the Parliament*, 28, 26; contra Calvin, *Institutes*, 2: 1320–23.

114. John Robinson, *A Justification of Separation* (1610), quoted in Keith Thomas, "Women and the Civil War Sects," *Past and Present* 13 (April 1958): 46.

115. John Earle, *The Autograph Manuscript of Microcosmographie* (1628; facsimile reprinted Leeds, Eng.: Scolar Press, 1966), 117, 119, 120–21. On female-dominated congregations see Thomas, "Women and the Civil War Sects," 45, 50. On the implications of Protestant belief systems for women's roles more broadly, see Phyllis Mack, *Visionary Women: Ecstatic Prophecy in Seventeenth-Century England* (Berkeley: University of California Press, 1992), esp. 49–50; and Mack, "Women as Prophets during the English Civil War," *Feminist Studies* 8:1 (spring 1982): 22.

116. William Whatley, *A Bride-Bush, Or a Wedding Sermon: Compendiously Describing the Duties of Married Persons* (London, 1617), 1, 2, 7–8, 15, 10; Whatley, *A Bride-Bush, Or a Direction for Married Persons* (London, 1619), 44. See also Gouge, *Of Domesticall Duties*. There is considerable debate among historians about the novelty of the companionate ideal promoted by Puritan tract writers. For the claim that Protestant beliefs revolutionized relations between husbands and wives, see Edmund S. Morgan, *The Puritan Family: Religion and Domestic Relations in Seventeenth-Century New England* (New York: Harper and Row, 1966), 29–64; and Lawrence Stone, *The Family, Sex and Marriage in England, 1500–1800* (New York: Harper and Row, 1977), esp. 149–253. Kathleen Davies disputes this thesis, arguing that many of the "innovations" of the Puritans actually predated the Reformation; see "The Sacred Condition of Equality: How Original Were Puritan Doctrines of Marriage?" *Social History* 5 (May 1977): 563–80. Patrick Collinson, in *Birthpangs of Protestant England*, 60–93, stakes out a comfortable middle ground, arguing that Puritan concepts of marriage were novel in emphasis and degree, and also built on a longer tradition of Renaissance humanism.

117. I Corinthians 14:34–36; I Timothy 2:11–15; Ephesians 5:22–28. On the emphasis Puritan thinkers placed upon Pauline doctrine, see Rogers, *Troublesome Helpmate*, 135–37; and Mary Maples Dunn, "Saints and Sisters: Congregational and Quaker Women in the Early Colonial Period," *American Quarterly* 30:1 (winter 1978): 582–601, esp. 585–86. On the context of Pauline prescriptions for female behavior in the historical setting of the early Church in Corinth, see Constance F. Parvey, "The Theology and Leadership of Women in the New Testament," in Rosemary Radford Reuther, ed., *Religion and Sexism: Images of Woman in the Jewish and Christian Traditions* (New York: Simon and Schuster, 1974), 117–49.

118. Whatley, *Bride-Bush* (1617), 16; see also Thomas, "Women and the Civil War Sects," 42–44.

119. Whatley, *Bride-Bush* (1617), 18–19, 41, 39.

120. This mirrors the fluidity of English Puritanism as a whole—in social as well as intellectual terms. See, e.g., Foster, *Long Argument*, 3–5; and Collinson, *Elizabethan Puritan Movement*.

121. William Walwyn, *The Compassionate Samaritane* (1644), in Haller, ed., *Tracts on Liberty*, 3: 77 (see also 94–95); Gerrard Winstanley, *Truth Lifting Up Its Head Above Scandals* (1649), in George H. Sabine, ed., *The Works of Gerrard Winstanley* (New York: Russell and Russell, 1965), 145. The radical potential of

Protestant ideals is thoroughly demonstrated in Hill, *World Turned Upside Down;* and, for Quaker women, in Mack, *Visionary Women.*

122. John White, *The Planter's Plea: Or the Grounds of Plantations Examined, and Usuall Objections Answered* (1630; facsimile reprinted New York: Da Capo Press, 1968), 3, 10–11.

123. Adams, "Taming of the Tongue," 14, 18.

124. White, *Planter's Plea,* 34, 81; "General Observations for the Plantation of New England" (1629), in *Winthrop Papers,* 5 vols. (Boston: Massachusetts Historical Society, 1929–1947), 2: 115, 117.

125. Dyke, *Mischiefe and Miserie of Scandalls,* dedicatory letter, n.p., 81; John Humphrey to Isaac Johnson, 9 December 1630, *Winthrop Papers,* 2: 329–30 and notes. See also Foster, *Long Argument,* 89.

126. The actual volume that Harvard bequeathed the college perished, along with virtually the entire library, in the great fire of 1764. It has been replaced with another of the same edition and binding. On the spread and social use of small-format books in the sixteenth and seventeenth centuries, see Lucien Febvre and Henri-Jean Martin, *The Coming of the Book: The Impact of Printing, 1450–1800,* trans. David Gerard (1958; English ed. London: NLB, 1976), 87–90.

127. Dyke, *Mischiefe and Miserie of Scandalls,* 80. One measure of the cultural distance between England and New England is that Isaac Johnson, the intended recipient of the Dyke tract, was months dead by the time the package reached Boston; see *Winthrop Papers,* 2: 327 n. 2.

Chapter 2

1. To date, most local studies have been confined to the offense of slander. See especially Robert B. St. George, " 'Heated' Speech and Literacy in Seventeenth-Century New England," in David D. Hall and David Grayson Allen, eds., *Seventeenth-Century New England* (Boston: Colonial Society of Massachusetts, 1984), 275–322; Mary Beth Norton, "Gender and Defamation in Seventeenth-Century Maryland," *William and Mary Quarterly* (hereafter *WMQ*) 3rd ser., 44:1 (January 1987): 3–39; and Cornelia Hughes Dayton, *Women before the Bar: Gender, Law, and Society in Connecticut, 1639–1789* (Chapel Hill: University of North Carolina Press, 1995), 285–328. A comparative approach to the legal history of seditious speech, narrowly defined, in British North America is found in Larry D. Eldridge, *A Distant Heritage: The Growth of Free Speech in Early America* (New York: New York University Press, 1994).

2. William Bradford, *Of Plymouth Plantation, 1620–1647,* ed. Samuel Eliot Morison (New York: Alfred A. Knopf, 1952), 7.

3. John Winthrop to Margaret Winthrop, 15 May 1629, *Winthrop Papers,* 5 vols. (Boston: Massachusetts Historical Society, 1929–1947), 2: 91; see also Robert E. Moody, ed., *The Saltonstall Papers, 1607–1815,* 2 vols., in Collections of the Massachusetts Historical Society, vols. 80–81 (Boston: Massachusetts Historical Society, 1972), 1: 119, 121. For an excellent overview of the religious climate in Jacobean England, see Stephen Foster, *The Long Argument: English Puritanism and the Shaping of New England Culture, 1570–1700* (Chapel Hill: University of North Carolina Press, 1991), esp. 108–37.

4. John Davenport to Sir William Boswell, 18 March 1634, in Isabel Mac-Beath Calden, ed., *Letters of John Davenport, Puritan Divine* (New Haven: Yale

University Press, 1937), 41; Robert Ryece to John Winthrop, 1629, *Winthrop Papers*, 2: 129.

5. John Cotton, *God's Promise to His Plantation* (London, 1630), 10, 9, 4; see also 14–15. Cotton is paraphrasing Micah 2:6–11, on the culling of the saving remnant out of Israel. John Winthrop, in his letter to Margaret Winthrop, 15 May 1629 (*Winthrop Papers*, 2: 92), draws his vision of refuge from Genesis 19:17–22.

6. "General Observations for the Plantation of New England" (1629), in *Winthrop Papers*, 2: 117; see also 121, 137, 142.

7. John Smith, *A Map of Virginia. With a Description of the Countrey* (1612) and *Generall Historie of Virginia* (1624), in Lyon Gardiner Tyler, ed., *Narratives of Early Virginia, 1606–1625* (1907; reprinted New York: Barnes and Noble, 1952), 117, 295. Modern historians remain as fascinated by the tribulations of early Jamestown as the New England planters were. See esp. Edmund S. Morgan, *American Slavery, American Freedom: The Ordeal of Colonial Virginia* (New York: W. W. Norton, 1975), chapters 3 and 4; and Karen Ordahl Kupperman, "Apathy and Death in Early Jamestown," *Journal of American History* 64:1 (June 1979): 24–40.

8. "General Observations for the Plantation of New England," 117.

9. John Smith, *The Proceedings of the English Colonie in Virginia Since Their First Beginning* (1612), in Tyler, ed., *Narratives of Early Virginia*, 186–87, 191; and Smith, *Advertisements for the Unexperienced Planters of New-England, or Any Where* (London, 1631; facsimile reprinted New York: Da Capo Press, 1971), 1, 21, 3 (see also 2, 20).

10. Robert Ryece to John Winthrop, 1629, *Winthrop Papers*, 2: 131.

11. This retrospective vision of New England's mission is propounded in [Joshua Scottow], *A Narrative of the Planting of the Massachusetts Colony Anno 1628* (Boston, 1694), 23.

12. John White, *The Planter's Plea: Or the Grounds of Plantations Examined, and Usuall Objections Answered* (1630; facsimile reprinted New York: Da Capo Press, 1968), 49; Robert Ryece to John Winthrop, 1629, *Winthrop Papers*, 2: 130.

13. Cotton, *God's Promise to His Plantation*, 20, emphasis mine.

14. Nathaniel Morton, *New England's Memorial: Or, a Brief Relation of the Most Remarkable Passages of the Providence of God, Manifested to the Planters of New England* (1669), in Alexander Young, ed., *Chronicles of the Pilgrim Fathers* (New York: E. P. Dutton, 1910), 21; Edward Johnson, *The Wonder-Working Providence of Sions Saviour in New England—'History of New England'* (1650/1?), ed. J. Franklin Jameson (1910; reprinted New York: Barnes and Noble, 1959), 45.

On the climate of information scarcity in early modern England, see F. J. Levy, "How Information Spread among the Gentry, 1550–1640," *Journal of British Studies* 21:2 (spring 1982): 11–34. On the colonies, see David Cressy, *Coming Over: Migration and Communication between England and New England in the Seventeenth Century* (New York: Cambridge University Press, 1987), esp. 191–234; and Richard D. Brown, *Knowledge Is Power: The Diffusion of Information in Early America, 1700–1865* (New York: Oxford University Press, 1989), 3–41. On the absence of ritual noise, especially bells, in New England churches, see David D. Hall, *Worlds of Wonder, Days of Judgment: Popular Religious Belief in Early New England* (New York: Alfred A. Knopf, 1989), 169; and Jon Butler, *Awash in a Sea of Faith: Christianizing the American People* (Cambridge: Harvard University Press,

1990), 110–12. My understanding of sound as an important and underrecognized component of premodern life owes much to an unpublished paper by Richard Rath of Brandeis University, " 'The Sounde Forme of Words': The Aural Context of Seventeenth-Century New England Society."

15. Cressy, Coming Over, 213.

16. [Scottow], Narrative of the Planting of the Massachusetts Colony, 17, emphasis mine. Scottow is writing about letters from New England. On letters as a medium of face-to-face communication as well as a private, written form of communication, see Brown, Knowledge Is Power, 8–9, 31–32.

17. James Kendall Hosmer, ed., Winthrop's Journal, "History of New England" 1630–1649, 2 vols. (1908; reprinted New York: Barnes and Noble, 1959), 1: 70, 100. William Bradford likewise describes the cargoes of letters arriving on various ships to Plymouth; see, e.g., Bradford, Of Plymouth Plantation, 127–30, 141–42, 227–31.

18. Pynchon to John Winthrop Jr., April 1669, in Carl Bridenbaugh, ed., The Pynchon Papers, 2 vols., Colonial Society of Massachusetts Publications, vols. 60–61 (Boston: Colonial Society of Massachusetts, 1982), 1: 84; see also 29, 68, 80.

19. On the ethos of neighborly watchfulness, see Roger Thompson, " 'Holy Watchfulness' and Communal Conformism: The Functions of Defamation in Early New England Communities," New England Quarterly 56:4 (December 1983): 504–22; Hall, Worlds of Wonder, 177, 224–25; David H. Flaherty, Privacy in Colonial New England (Charlottesville: University Press of Virginia, 1972), 43–44, 74, 75, 89, 111, 169; Helena M. Wall, Fierce Communion: Family and Community in Early America (Cambridge: Harvard University Press, 1990), 13–16; and Nancy F. Cott, "Eighteenth-Century Family and Social Life Revealed in Massachusetts Divorce Records," in Cott and Elizabeth H. Pleck, eds., A Heritage of Her Own: Toward a New Social History of American Women (New York: Simon and Schuster, 1979), 111–13. Examples of inspired eavesdropping are found in Jane Kamensky, "Governing the Tongue: Speech and Society in Early New England" (Ph.D. dissertation, Yale University, 1993), 98–103.

20. Brown, Knowledge Is Power, 23. Contrast with Bill McKibben's provocative essay on the overproliferation of information in our own era, The Age of Missing Information (New York: Random House, 1992).

21. [Scottow], Narrative of the Planting of the Massachusetts Colony, 16. For examples of days of thanksgiving for good news, see Winthrop, Journal, 1: 81–82, 92.

22. John Humphrey to Isaac Johnson, December 1630, Winthrop Papers, 2: 329; William Wood, New England's Prospect (1634), ed. Alden T. Vaughan (Amherst: University of Massachusetts Press, 1977), 73–74. On the time required for overseas communication and the frequent obstacles thereto, see also Cressy, Coming Over, 222–29.

23. Karen Ordahl Kupperman, introduction to Kupperman, ed., America in European Consciousness, 1493–1750 (Chapel Hill: University of North Carolina Press, 1995), 11; see also 3, 18. For a theoretical treatment of the relationship between language and social or ethnic identity, see Dell Hymes, "Ways of Speaking," in Richard Bauman and Joel Sherzer, eds., Explorations in the Ethnography of Speaking (Cambridge: Cambridge University Press, 1974), esp. 436.

24. Anthony Pagden, The Fall of Natural Man: The American Indian and the Origins of Comparative Ethnology (New York: Cambridge University Press, 1982), 127–29; see also 16, 20–22; and Edward Gordon Gray, "Indian Language in

Anglo-American Thought, 1550–1820" (Ph.D. dissertation, Brown University, 1996), chapter 1.

25. Johannes de Laet, *New World, or Description of West-India* (1625), in J. Franklin Jameson, ed., *Narratives of New Netherland, 1609–1664* (1908; reprinted New York: Barnes and Noble, 1967), 57; see also 58–60. For other seventeenth-century references to the profusion of Indian tongues, see Johannes Megapolensis, *A Short Account of the Mohawk Indians* (1644), in ibid., 172; John Eliot, *New Englands First Fruits* (London, 1643), 1; Smith, *Advertisements for the Unexperienced Planters of New-England*, 14–15; Gray, "Indian Language in Anglo-American Thought," chapter 1; and Kathleen Joan Bragdon, " 'Another Tongue Brought In': An Ethnohistorical Study of Native Writings in Massachusett" (Ph.D. dissertation, Brown University, 1981), 18–23.

26. The notion of a "middle ground" upon which cultural exchanges between Europeans and natives took place is taken from Richard White, *The Middle Ground: Indians, Empires, and Republics in the Great Lakes Region, 1650–1815* (New York: Cambridge University Press, 1991), see esp. 50–93.

27. Stephen Greenblatt, *Marvelous Possessions: The Wonder of the New World* (Chicago: University of Chicago Press, 1991), 95; J. M. Cohen, ed., *The Four Voyages of Christopher Columbus* (New York: Penguin, 1969), 56, emphasis mine; Thomas Morton, *New English Canaan* (Amsterdam, 1637; facsimile reprinted New York: Da Capo Press, 1969), 18. See also Greenblatt, "Learning to Curse: Aspects of Linguistic Colonialism in the Sixteenth Century," in Fredi Chiapelli, Michael J. B. Allen, and Robert L. Benson, eds., *First Images of America*, 2 vols. (Berkeley: University of California Press, 1976), 2: 561–80, esp. 562–64, 571. Morton's effort to link native and classical languages follows a popular belief in the European genealogy of American natives. See Gray, "Indian Language in Anglo-American Thought," chapter 1; John Eliot, *The Indian Grammar Begun; Or, An Essay to Bring the Indian Language Into Rules* (Cambridge, 1666), reprinted in *Old South Leaflets* 3:52 (1894), 9, 11; and Megapolensis, *Short Account of the Mohawk Indians*, 172–73.

28. Isaiah 33:15, 19–20. This passage forms the epigraph to Eliot, *Indian Grammar Begun*.

29. White, *Planter's Plea*, 52–53; see also [John Eliot], *The Day-Breaking, if Not the Sun-Rising of the Gospell with the Indians in New-England* (London, 1647), in Collections of the Massachusetts Historical Society, 3rd ser., vol. 4 (1834), esp. 15. For a thoughtful comparison of Jesuit and Protestant approaches to the learning and translation of Indian languages, see Gray, "Indian Language in Anglo-American Thought," chapter 2.

30. Richard Mulcaster, *The First Part of the Elementarie* (1582), quoted in Greenblatt, *Marvelous Possessions*, 88; see also 10–12. On the association of orality with barbarism and literacy with civility, see also Pagden, *Fall of Natural Man*, 129–30, 183–90.

31. For the linguistic consequences of literacy among the Massachusett, see Bragdon, " 'Another Tongue Brought In,' " esp. chapters 5 and 6; and Jill Lepore, "Dead Men Tell No Tales: John Sassamon and the Fatal Consequences of Literacy," *American Quarterly* 46:4 (December 1994): 479–512. There is considerable debate among historians about what American natives thought of European writing systems. See, e.g., Peter Wogan, "Perceptions of European Literacy in Early Contact Situations," *Ethnohistory* 41:3 (summer 1994): 407–29; contra James Axtell, "The Power of Print in the Eastern Woodlands," *WMQ* 3rd ser., 44:2 (April

1987): 300–9. For an intriguing study of the politics of "translation" in the Spanish empire, see Vicente L. Rafael, *Contracting Colonialism: Translation and Christian Conversion in Tagalog Society under Early Spanish Rule* (Ithaca, N.Y.: Cornell University Press, 1988).

32. Samuel Purchas, *Hakluytus Posthumus, or Purchas His Pilgrimes* (1625), quoted in Greenblatt, *Marvelous Possessions*, 10.

33. Daniel Gookin, *Historical Collections of the Indians in New England. Of their Several Nations, Numbers, Customs, Manners, Religion and Government* (written 1674; published Boston, 1792), 3; see also 6, 9, 16.

34. Megapolensis, *Short Account of the Mohawk Indians*, 172–73.

35. "Letter of Reverend Jonas Michaëlius, 1628," in Jameson, ed., *Narratives of New Netherland*, 117–34, esp. 128. Compare with Wood, *New England's Prospect*, 109.

36. [Eliot], *Day-Breaking, if Not the Sun-Rising*, 6 (see also 3–5, 8, 13); and Eliot, *New Englands First Fruits*, 1–3, 23–24. On Eliot's Massachusett Bible, see Gray, "Indian Language in Anglo-American Thought," chapter 3.

Most face-to-face communication in New England, and elsewhere in the colonies, doubtless took place neither in native dialects nor in English and other European languages but rather in various European-native pidgins. For scholarship on the syntax and vocabulary of Algonquian-English pidgin, see Ives Goddard, "Some Early Examples of American Indian Pidgin English from New England," *International Journal of American Linguistics* 43:1 (January 1977): 37–41; and Kathleen Bragdon, "Linguistic Acculturation in Massachusett: 1663–1771," in William Cowan, ed., *Papers of the Twelfth Algonquian Conference* (Ottawa, Can.: Carleton University, 1981), 121–32. Transcribed examples of spoken pidgin appear relatively infrequently in the written record. For an exception, see presentment of "Nimrod" and "John," Ipswich, 1670, in George F. Dow, ed., *Records and Files of the Quarterly Courts of Essex County, Massachusetts*, 9 vols. (Salem, Mass.: Essex Institute, 1911–1978), 4: 230–32.

37. Wood, *New England's Prospect*, 88, 81–92, 112–15. "Aberginian" was Wood's generic term for the natives living in what is now northern Massachusetts and southern New Hampshire (82 n). Wood's comment on the Massachusetts' disdain for scolding is one of several instances in which English writers hinted that some natives spoke in ways that were superior to those of some English. See also, e.g., John Eliot's comment that none of the Christian Indians "slept [in] Sermon or derided Gods messenger," things that English settlers had "growne bold to doe"; [Eliot], *Day-Breaking, if Not the Sun-Rising*, 16.

38. Roger Williams, *A Key Into the Language of America* (1643; facsimile reprinted Menston, Eng.: Scolar Press, 1971), 9–10, 54–56, 61. Williams also noted the Narragansetts' *"itching desire* of hearing *Newes"*—an attribute that linked their speech order with that of the colonists.

39. See Thomas Morton, *New English Canaan*, 35–38.

40. Eliot, *New Englands First Fruits*, 2–3.

41. Wood, *New England's Prospect*, 92, 79, 77, 101.

42. Eliot, *Indian Grammar Begun*, 5; see also "Letter of Reverend Jonas Michaëlius," 128.

43. Wood, *New England's Prospect*, 101.

44. Amy Schrager Lang, ed., "A True History of the Captivity and Restoration of Mrs. Mary Rowlandson" (1682), in William L. Andrews, ed., *Journeys in*

New Worlds: Early American Women's Narratives (Madison: University of Wisconsin Press, 1990), 33; see also 37, 49, 61.

45. Greenblatt, *Marvelous Possessions,* 92.

46. Bradford, *Of Plymouth Plantation,* 79.

47. Edward Winslow, *Good News from New England* (1624), in Young, ed., *Chronicles of the Pilgrim Fathers,* 296–97.

48. Winslow, *Good News from New England,* 281; Nathaniel Morton, *New England's Memorial,* 53, 44, 50. The phrase "New World Babel" is borrowed from Gray, "Indian Language in Anglo-American Thought," chapter 2.

49. Winslow, *Good News from New England,* 301.

50. Winslow, *Good News from New England,* 276–79. The incident is also mentioned in Bradford, *Of Plymouth Plantation,* 96; and Nathaniel Morton, *New England's Memorial,* 49.

51. Winslow, *Good News from New England,* 279; [William Bradford and Edward Winslow], *Journall of the English Plantation at Plimoth* (hereafter *Mourt's Relation*) (1622; facsimile reprinted Ann Arbor, Mich.: University Microfilms, 1966), 53, emphasis mine.

52. *Mourt's Relation,* 69, 19.

53. Bradford, *Of Plymouth Plantation,* 25; *Mourt's Relation,* 69–71.

54. Nathaniel Morton, *New England's Memorial,* 21.

55. Bradford, *Of Plymouth Plantation,* 61–62.

56. "Reverend John Robinson's Farewell Letters," in Bradford, *Of Plymouth Plantation,* 368–71.

57. "Robinson's Farewell Letters," 369–70. On the voluntarism at the core of separatist theology, see Edmund S. Morgan, *Visible Saints: The History of a Puritan Idea* (Ithaca, N.Y.: Cornell University Press, 1965), 25–30. My thinking on the ambiguous and troubling nature of fraternal metaphors in seventeenth-century English writing is influenced by Michael Warner, "New English Sodom," in Jonathan Goldberg, ed., *Queering the Renaissance* (Durham, N.C.: Duke University Press, 1994), esp. 346–51.

58. Bradford, *Of Plymouth Plantation,* 58.

59. Bradford, *Of Plymouth Plantation,* 75, 76, 78. Like the documentary record of early Plymouth, the historiography analyzing the first years in the "Old Colony" remains remarkably thin. The most detailed and comprehensive modern scholarly account is found in George D. Langdon Jr., *Pilgrim Colony: A History of New Plymouth, 1620–1691* (New Haven: Yale University Press, 1966); see esp. 1–15. Charles Francis Adams, *Three Episodes in Massachusetts History,* 2 vols. (1892; reprinted New York: Russell and Russell, 1965), remains useful in many particulars; see esp. 1: 1–343. An annotated bibliography of Plymouth records, especially strong on genealogical sources, is Eugene Aubrey Stratton, *Plymouth Colony: Its History and Its People, 1620–1691* (Salt Lake City: Ancestry Publishing, 1986). H. Roger King, *Cape Cod and Plymouth Colony in the Seventeenth Century* (Lanham, Md.: University Press of America, 1994), focuses primarily on the expansion of the Old Colony into Cape Cod.

60. Adams, *Three Episodes in Massachusetts History,* 1: 48.

61. Correspondence to and from Thomas Weston is reprinted in Bradford, *Of Plymouth Plantation,* 93, 95, 100, 104. On Weston's background and behavior toward the Plymouth migrants, see ibid., 37 n; and Adams, *Three Episodes in Massachusetts History,* 1: 44–55.

62. Bradford, *Of Plymouth Plantation*, 120, 136, 135, 141; see also Winslow, *Good News from New England*, 290–91. Characteristically, Thomas Morton takes the opposite side, making Weston the aggrieved party. The Plymouth "Brethren," he argues, were happy enough to take Weston's money, but turned on him and his followers when the supplies ran out; see *New English Canaan*, 105–6, 114–15.

63. Bradford, *Of Plymouth Plantation*, 144; see also Winslow, *Good News from New England*, 356–57.

64. Bradford, *Of Plymouth Plantation*, 367; Morgan, *Visible Saints*, 58–59; Langdon, *Pilgrim Colony*, 116–17. For a detailed description, ca. 1632, of the Plymouth church's practice of disputing questions in open congregation, see Winthrop, *Journal*, 1: 94. On the colony's longing for Robinson to join them, see also Bradford, *Of Plymouth Plantation*, 93, 128, 155, 179–80.

65. Thomas Morton, *New English Canaan*, 116–17. For Bradford's comments on Morton's "scurrilous terms full of disdain," see *Of Plymouth Plantation*, 209–10, 216–17. Of course, Morton makes Bradford and his ilk the slanderers; see *New English Canaan*, 138, 183.

66. Lyford's and Oldham's stories are related at length in Bradford, *Of Plymouth Plantation*, 147–69, quotations from 147, 149, 150, 152, 158, 165. The whole matter is repeated, in language very close to Bradford's, in Nathaniel Morton, *New England's Memorial*, 71–79. The Lyford incident quickly became a subject of considerable disagreement among the chroniclers of the Old Colony; see Langdon, *Pilgrim Colony*, 20–25. Unsurprisingly, Thomas Morton was one of those who denounced the colony's treatment of Lyford. Yet even he agreed that Oldham, known for his "passionate and moody" words, was "a mad Jack"; *New English Canaan*, 118–19.

67. Nathaniel Morton, *New England's Memorial*, 196, 166; see also 158. Morton's verse paraphrases Benjamin Woodbridge's eulogy on the death of John Cotton, 1652.

68. Bradford, *Of Plymouth Plantation*, 210–11 and notes, 222–23, 292–93; see also Langdon, *Pilgrim Colony*, 117–19.

69. On images of the "reversible world," see Stuart Clark, "Inversion, Misrule and the Meaning of Witchcraft," *Past and Present* 87 (May 1980): 98–127, esp. 105–10.

70. Thomas Morton, *New English Canaan*, 164, 122–23, 173–74, 177, 188; see also 152 on Ralph Smith, whose "speciall gifts," Morton said, included abilities shocking for a separatist: "hee could wright and reade, nay more." The identity of Morton's "Bubble," if he is not purely an invention, remains uncertain. In his notes to Bradford's text, Samuel Eliot Morison speculates that Bubble was the unfortunate Mr. Rogers; see Bradford, *Of Plymouth Plantation*, 210 n. Morton's satire makes clear that Bubble's nickname refers to his speech—more particularly, to his penchant for hot air.

71. Nathaniel Morton, *New England's Memorial*, 73; Bradford, *Of Plymouth Plantation*, 150. Both chronicles are referring to Lyford's slanderous reports. For Bradford's reaction to the publication of Thomas Morton's *New English Canaan*, see *Of Plymouth Plantation*, 217.

72. Bradford, *Of Plymouth Plantation*, 129–30.

73. Bradford, *Of Plymouth Plantation*, 236.

74. Indeed, Bradford only *began* his account in 1630, completing the story to 1620 that year and adding the later years "in pieces" through 1646 or 1650; see Bradford, *Of Plymouth Plantation*, xxvi–xxvii, 351.

75. Population estimates ca. 1630 are found in Stratton, *Plymouth Colony*, 50, 51 n. 7. For reactions to the death of John Robinson—news of which, of course, reached Plymouth long after the fact—see Bradford, *Of Plymouth Plantation*, 179–80; and Winslow, *Good News from New England*, 81–82, 84–85.

76. Smith, *Advertisements for the Unexperienced Planters of New-England*, 21, 2, 29, emphasis mine.

77. Winslow, *Good News from New England*, 99; White, *Planter's Plea*, 81.

78. White, *Planter's Plea*, 59.

79. Nor, the oath continued, could they "suffer the same to be spoke or done." See David Pulsifer, ed., *Records of the Colony of New Plymouth in New England* (hereafter PCR), 12 vols. (1861; reprinted New York: AMS Press, 1968), 11: 8; see also 34, 57, 95–96, 98, 229.

80. For prosecutions of slander, contempt, swearing, etc., in Plymouth between 1633 and 1650, see PCR, 1: 12, 35, 87, 128, 132; 2: 4, 9, 12, 42, 97; 7: 9, 12, 19, 20, 39, 45, 46, 50. Even by the standards of early New England, the records of the early Plymouth courts are remarkably laconic; little can be said of these cases besides the names of the litigants, their outcome, and the level of punishment meted out.

81. Smith, *Advertisements for the Unexperienced Planters of New-England*, 35–36, 40.

82. John Winthrop, "A Modell of Christian Charity" (1630), in *Winthrop Papers*, 2: 282–95, quotation from 284.

83. Winthrop, "Modell of Christian Charity," 283, 282, 285.

84. Winthrop, "Modell of Christian Charity," 283, 295.

85. Winthrop, *Journal*, 1: 29–30; see also John Winthrop to Margaret Winthrop, April 1630, *Winthrop Papers*, 2: 228.

86. John Rogers to John Winthrop Jr., November 1630, *Winthrop Papers*, 2: 316; John Humphrey to Isaac Johnson, December 1630, ibid., 2: 328; Edward Howes to John Winthrop Jr., November 1631, ibid., 3: 54; Edward Howes to John Winthrop Jr., November 1632, ibid., 3: 94; Winthrop, *Journal*, 1: 99, 130, 64. See also Muriel Gurdon to Margaret Winthrop, April 1636, *Saltonstall Papers*, 1: 128.

87. Presentments of Thomas Fox, Watertown, March 1631; Phillip Ratliffe, Boston, June 1631; and Francis Perry, Boston, July 1631, all in Nathaniel B. Shurtleff, ed., *Records of the Governor and Company of the Massachusetts Bay in New England* (hereafter *Mass. Recs.*), 5 vols. in 6 (1854; reprinted New York: AMS Press, 1968), 1: 84, 88; and Winthrop, *Journal*, 1: 64.

88. He soon got his wish; the hapless servant and one of his compatriots drowned while gathering oysters, "an evident judgment of God upon them"; see Winthrop, *Journal*, 1: 103–4.

89. Such an incident is detailed in Winthrop, *Journal*, 1: 136–37.

90. Winthrop, "Modell of Christian Charity," 294; compare with William Whatley's description of godly marriage in *A Bride-Bush, Or a Direction for Married Persons* (London, 1619), esp. 44.

91. John Humphrey to Isaac Thompson, December 1630, *Winthrop Papers*, 2: 328.

92. On the sensitivity of leaders in New Haven to the politics of speech in the early years of that colony, see Dayton, *Women before the Bar*, 290–91.

93. See presentment of Thomas Dexter, Boston, 1633, *Mass. Recs.*, 1: 103, 97; John Endecott to John Winthrop, April 1631, *Winthrop Papers*, 3: 25.

94. Presentment of John Stone, Boston, 1633, *Mass. Recs.*, 1: 108. On Stone's fate, see also Winthrop, *Journal*, 1: 118, 140. Ludlow was a popular target of verbal abuse; see also presentment of John Lee, Boston, 1634, *Mass. Recs.*, 1: 114.

95. Presentment of Ensign William Jennison, Newtown, 1634, *Mass. Recs.*, 1: 132.

96. Presentment of Thomas Miller, Boston, 1636, *Mass. Recs.*, 1: 176. See also Winthrop, *Journal*, 1: 181; presentments of Mr. Ambros Martin, Boston, 1639, *Mass. Recs.*, 1: 252; and John Lee, Newtown, 1634, *Mass. Recs.*, 1: 132–33. For other prosecutions of high-status men for defaming authority during the 1630s, see presentment of Mr. Israel Stoughton, Newtown, 1635, *Mass. Recs.*, 1: 136; Winthrop, *Journal*, 1: 147; presentments of Mr. John Green, Boston, 1637, *Mass. Recs.*, 1: 200, 203; and Mr. Henry Sewall, Boston, 1640, *Mass. Recs.*, 1: 286. Altogether there were 24 presentments for defaming authority or seditious speech in Massachusetts before 1640, *excluding those related to the Antinomian crisis*, which is treated in chapter 3 of this book. Of the 24, 23 offenders were male, and some 15 were men of identifiably high status.

97. Winthrop, *Journal*, 1: 60, 77.

98. Winthrop, *Journal*, 1: 66, 95; see also 71, 72. On the theological background to Brown's error, see Edmund S. Morgan, *The Puritan Dilemma: The Story of John Winthrop* (Boston: Little, Brown, 1958), 98–100.

99. The "rule" is found in Matthew 18:15.

100. Winthrop, *Journal*, 1: 84–86, 91; see also 113, 114. On the substance of the dispute between the governor and his then-deputy, see Morgan, *Puritan Dilemma*, 86–87, 104–7.

101. Winthrop, *Journal*, 1: 142. On public apology as a remedy for speech crime, see chapter 5 in this book.

102. Smith, *Advertisements for the Unexperienced Planters of New-England*, 21. Smith is describing the experience of Plymouth's "humorists" with "contempt of authority."

103. The story of Williams's dissent is a famous one, much too rich in detail and import to be explored fully here. A useful introduction is found in Edmund S. Morgan, *Roger Williams: The Church and the State* (New York: Harcourt, Brace, 1967); and Morgan, *Puritan Dilemma*, 115–33. For Williams's early interactions with authorities in the Bay, see Williams to John Winthrop, July 1632, *Winthrop Papers*, 3: 86; and Winthrop, *Journal*, 1: 61–62, 116–17.

104. Winthrop, *Journal*, 1: 149, 154.

105. Presentment of Roger Williams, Newtown, 1635, *Mass. Recs.*, 1: 160–61, emphasis mine; Winthrop, *Journal*, 1: 168.

106. Winthrop, *Journal*, 1: 170.

107. Winthrop, *Journal*, 1: 170–72, emphasis mine.

108. In August 1634, Katherine Gray was ordered "whipt" for "filthy & unchast behavior"; *Mass. Recs.*, 1: 123. One Mary ———, servant to a Mr. Bartholomew, was whipped for running away from her master in September 1635; *Mass. Recs.*, 1: 154. The first woman presented in the high court for a speech crime was Elizabeth Applegate, convicted for "swearing, raileing, & revileing" in September 1636; *Mass. Recs.*, 1: 177.

109. Winthrop, *Journal*, 1: 107. Private conversion was not reserved exclusively for women, but it was certainly "marked" female, deriving its currency from Paul's rule. On the custom and its evolution in seventeenth-century New En-

gland, see Charles Lloyd Cohen, *God's Caress: The Psychology of Puritan Religious Experience* (New York: Oxford University Press, 1986), 142–44.

110. Thomas Morton, *New English Canaan*, 173.

Chapter 3

1. James Kendall Hosmer, ed., *Winthrop's Journal*, "*History of New England*" *1630–1649*, 2 vols. (1908; reprinted New York: Barnes and Noble, 1959), 1: 258–60. See also Thomas Weld's preface to John Winthrop, "A Short Story of the Rise, Reign, and Ruine of the Antinomians, Familists & Libertines" (1644), in David D. Hall, ed., *The Antinomian Controversy, 1636–1638: A Documentary History* (hereafter AC) (1968; reprinted Durham, N.C.: Duke University Press, 1990), esp. 202.

2. Thomas Morton, *New English Canaan* (Amsterdam, 1637; facsimile reprinted New York: Da Capo Press, 1969), 173.

3. "A Report of the Trial of Mrs. Anne Hutchinson before the Church in Boston [March 1638]," in AC, 382–83, 388. In addition to these surviving "transcripts," the proceedings against Hutchinson are closely narrated in Emery Battis, *Saints and Sectaries: Anne Hutchinson and the Antinomian Controversy in the Massachusetts Bay Colony* (Chapel Hill: University of North Carolina Press, 1962), 232–48.

4. John Winthrop, "A Modell of Christian Charity" (1630), in *Winthrop Papers*, 5 vols. (Boston: Massachusetts Historical Society, 1929–1947), 2: 282.

5. "Report of the Trial of Mrs. Anne Hutchinson before the Church," 384. Several recent accounts have, like this one, taken Wilson at his word and focused on the linguistic aspects of Hutchinson's challenge. Patricia Caldwell was the first to explore the reasons that "verbal behavior was what [Hutchinson's] adversaries most despised about her"; see "The Antinomian Language Controversy," *Harvard Theological Review* 69:3–4 (July–October 1976): 359. Scholars who have adopted Caldwell's emphasis on language continue to disagree about the nature of Hutchinson's verbal threat. Caldwell argues that the challenge of Hutchinson's language stemmed from her distrust of speech itself. For similar interpretations, see Sandra Marie Gustafson, "Performing the Word: American Oratory, 1630–1860" (Ph.D. dissertation, University of California at Berkeley, 1993), esp. 153–57; and Eugenia DeLamotte, "John Cotton and the Rhetoric of Grace," *Early American Literature* 21:1 (spring 1986): 49–74. Harry Stout emphasizes the link between Hutchinson's speech and the interpretive openness of the Geneva Bible; see Stout, "Word and Order in Colonial New England," in Nathan O. Hatch and Mark A. Noll, eds., *The Bible in America: Essays in Cultural History* (New York: Oxford University Press, 1982), 31–33. There has been, as yet, relatively little consideration of the link between Hutchinson's troubling voice and Puritan conceptions of femininity. For an exception, see Lad Tobin, "A Radically Different Voice: Gender and Language in the Trials of Anne Hutchinson," *Early American Literature* 25:3 (fall 1990): 253–70, esp. 263–65. For a review of feminist interpretations of the Antinomian controversy, see Mary Beth Norton, "The Evolution of White Women's Experience in Early America," *American Historical Review* 89:3 (June 1984): 593–619, esp. 599.

6. Winthrop's comment on the wish of John Cotton's wife to make a private profession of her faith appears in his *Journal*, 1: 107.

7. On the transatlantic consequences of the controversy, see Stephen Foster, "New England and the Challenge of Heresy, 1630 to 1660: The Puritan Crisis in Transatlantic Perspective," *William and Mary Quarterly* (hereafter *WMQ*) 3rd ser., 38:4 (October 1981): 624–60. For seventeenth-century reactions to the case, see Winthrop's *Journal*, 1: 195–234, 260–97; Edward Johnson, *The Wonder-Working Providence of Sions Saviour in New England—'History of New England'* (1650/1?), ed. J. Franklin Jameson (1910; reprinted New York: Barnes and Noble, 1959), 121–32, 185–86; William Hubbard, *A General History of New England from the Discovery to 1680* (1682), in Collections of the Massachusetts Historical Society, 2nd. ser., vols. 5–6 (1815), 281–85, 297; Thomas Hutchinson, *The History of the Colony and Province of Massachusetts-Bay* (1764–1768), 3 vols., ed. Lawrence Shaw Mayo (Cambridge: Harvard University Press, 1936), 1: 50–67; and the pamphlets reproduced in AC.

8. "The Examination of Mrs. Anne Hutchinson at the Court at Newtown [November 1637]," in AC, 322. *Slighting*, Zacharia Symmes did not have to point out, was more often a man's crime than a female failing, which must have made Hutchinson's transgression doubly problematic. See Jane Kamensky, "Talk Like a Man: Speech, Power, and Masculinity in Early New England," *Gender and History* 8:1 (April 1996): 22–47.

9. "Examination of Mrs. Anne Hutchinson at the Court," 322, 320; Winthrop, "Short Story," 263.

10. The following sketch of early events in the controversy draws on Battis, *Saints and Sectaries*, 3–4, 11, 58–63, 75–76; Edmund S. Morgan, "The Case against Anne Hutchinson," *New England Quarterly* (hereafter *NEQ*) 10:4 (December 1937): 635–49; Morgan, *The Puritan Dilemma: The Story of John Winthrop* (Boston: Little, Brown, 1958), 134–54; Darrett B. Rutman, *Winthrop's Boston: A Portrait of a Puritan Town, 1630–1649* (Chapel Hill: University of North Carolina Press, 1965), 72–74, 78, 81; Philip F. Gura, *A Glimpse of Sion's Glory: Puritan Radicalism in New England, 1620–1660* (Middletown, Conn.: Wesleyan University Press, 1984), 237–75; and AC, introduction, 4–10.

11. Winthrop, *Journal*, 1: 134–36.

12. "Examination of Mrs. Anne Hutchinson at the Court," 322, 338, 323; see also "Report of the Trial of Mrs. Anne Hutchinson before the Church," 370–71. For Hutchinson's church admission, see also Richard D. Pierce, ed., *Records of the First Church in Boston, 1630–1868* (hereafter *First Church Records*), Colonial Society of Massachusetts Publications, vol. 39 (Boston: Colonial Society of Massachusetts, 1961), 19. William Hutchinson, whose profession of faith apparently raised no questions, was admitted on 26 October.

13. Winthrop, "Short Story," 262. On William Hutchinson's local offices and land transactions, see Battis, *Saints and Sectaries*, 83, 86; Bernard Bailyn, *The New England Merchants in the Seventeenth Century* (Cambridge: Harvard University Press, 1955), 35, 40–41; Nathaniel B. Shurtleff, ed., *Records of the Governor and Company of the Massachusetts Bay in New England* (hereafter *Mass. Recs.*), 5 vols. in 6 (1854; reprinted New York: AMS Press, 1968), 1: 145, 149, 156, 164–65, 175, 177; and *First Church Records*, 10.

14. John Cotton, "The Way of Congregational Churches Cleared" (1648), in AC, 411–12.

15. Cotton, "Way of Congregational Churches Cleared," 412, emphasis mine.

16. Winthrop, "Short Story," 263.

17. "Examination of Mrs. Anne Hutchinson at the Court," 338.

18. On the tradition of lay prophecy among Elizabethan dissenters, see Patrick Collinson, *The Elizabethan Puritan Movement* (1967; reprinted London: Methuen, 1982), 168–76. The female prophetic mode receives it fullest treatment in Phyllis Mack, *Visionary Women: Ecstatic Prophecy in Seventeenth-Century England* (Berkeley: University of California Press, 1992).

19. Winthrop, *Journal*, 1: 116. On the mid-1630s as a moment of "hyperpuritanism" in New England, see Stephen Foster, *The Long Argument: English Puritanism and the Shaping of New England Culture, 1570–1700* (Chapel Hill: University of North Carolina Press, 1991), 138–39, 158–62. On the importance of public, verbal performance among the early New England laity, see Patricia Caldwell, *The Puritan Conversion Narrative: The Beginnings of American Expression* (New York: Cambridge University Press, 1983), esp. 90–110, 135–62.

20. "Report of the Trial of Mrs. Anne Hutchinson before the Church," 353.

21. Weld, preface to Winthrop, "Short Story," 209–10; John Wheelwright, "A Fast-Day Sermon" (1637), in AC, 163. Wheelwright loosely paraphrased Hosea 6:5. See also Gustafson, "Performing the Word," 157.

22. Johnson, *Wonder-Working Providence*, 121.

23. These efforts at private persuasion had also employed a controlled, authoritative voice against the dissenters. The ministers at first focused on defining Cotton's role in the matter, exhorting him to resolve dangerous ambiguities in his theology by responding to a series of questions. Thomas Shepard requested that Cotton deliver his answers "by way of wrighting rather then speech" so that the "clarif[ications]" would become indelible; "Letters between Thomas Shepard and John Cotton" (ca. 1635–1636), in AC, 25. See also John Cotton, "Sixteene Questions of Serious and Necessary Consequence, Propounded unto Mr. John Cotton" (1644), in AC, esp. 46.

24. Weld, preface to Winthrop, "Short Story," 213, emphasis mine. David Hall sees the synod's rhetoric as an example of a "persisting tension between academic discourse and . . . lay people's discourse," noting that the synod debates "used concepts drawn from Greek philosophy and scholasticism—'the order of nature,' 'habit,' 'essence,' 'proximate cause'—and cited books by Reformed theologians of the sixteenth century"; Hall, *Worlds of Wonder, Days of Judgment: Popular Religious Belief in Early New England* (New York: Alfred A. Knopf, 1989), 65. In addition, they call attention to the rhetorical gap separating the feminized language of prophecy and the learned, masculine style of Ramist logic.

25. Winthrop, *Journal*, 1: 232–34.

26. Winthrop, *Journal*, 1: 234, 209.

27. On the synod's accomplishments and shortcomings, see Gura, *Glimpse of Sion's Glory*, 256. The persisting tensions in the colony's churches are detailed in Winthrop, *Journal*, 1: 234–40.

28. Winthrop, "Short Story," 262.

29. Benjamin Wadsworth, *The Well-Ordered Family: Or, Relative Duties* (Boston, 1712), 34. Wadsworth is paraphrasing Proverbs 31:26. On the kind of pious feminine discourse encouraged by New England ministers, see Laurel T. Ulrich, "Vertuous Women Found: New England Ministerial Literature, 1668–1735," in Nancy F. Cott and Elizabeth H. Pleck, eds., *A Heritage of Her Own: Toward a New Social History of American Women* (New York: Simon and Schuster, 1979), 58–80.

30. Cotton Mather, *Magnalia Christi Americana, or the Ecclesiastical History of New England*, 2 vols. (1702; reprinted Hartford: Silas Andrus and Son, 1853), 2: 509; see also 516.

31. Johnson, *Wonder-Working Providence*, 131-32, 185.

32. Winthrop, "Short Story," 262-63. On Hutchinson's abuse of her proximity to women in travail, see Hubbard, *General History of New England*, 283. Reports of Hutchinson's delivery of a "monstrous birth"—resembling in its multiform shape her numerous theological errors—draw on similar rhetoric. See Winthrop, *Journal*, 1: 277; Mather, *Magnalia Christi Americana*, 2: 519; and Anne Jacobson Schutte, " 'Such Monstrous Births': A Neglected Aspect of the Antinomian Controversy," *Renaissance Quarterly* 38:1 (spring 1985): 85-106.

33. Winthrop, "Short Story," 263.

34. "Report of the Trial of Mrs. Anne Hutchinson before the Church," 353, 372. Hutchinson's alleged tie to the so-called community of women is discussed in Amy Schrager Lang, *Prophetic Woman: Anne Hutchinson and the Problem of Dissent in the Literature of New England* (Berkeley: University of California Press, 1987), 44-46. On the analogy between loose speech and loose morals, see Lynda E. Boose, "Scolding Brides and Bridling Scolds: Taming the Woman's Unruly Member," *Shakespeare Quarterly* 42:2 (summer 1991): 196.

35. Winthrop, *Journal*, 1: 299. Emery Battis accepts this version of the Hutchinsons' marriage as fact, calling William Hutchinson "Passive and imperturbable . . . quietly follow[ing] where Anne led him." See *Saints and Sectaries*, 12; also 51.

36. "Report of the Trial of Mrs. Anne Hutchinson before the Church," 371.

37. Winthrop, "Short Story," 269; see also Winthrop, *Journal*, 1: 234. On the contested meaning of the word "public" in the context of Hutchinson's trial, see Mary Beth Norton, *Founding Mothers and Fathers: Gendered Power and the Forming of American Society* (New York: Alfred A. Knopf, 1996), 359-99, esp. 381-88.

38. Winthrop, "Short Story," 268, 264.

39. Johnson, *Wonder-Working Providence*, 127.

40. This summary of Hutchinson's alleged beliefs—her eighty-two suspected "errors"—is found in Winthrop, "Short Story," 230, 203, 239 (errors 40, 1, and 74 quoted). On the meaning of "lawful" or "legal" to English Puritans, see M. van Beek, *An Enquiry into Puritan Vocabulary* (Groningen, Netherlands: Wolters-Noordhoff, 1969), 79. Historians of Puritan ecclesiology have argued, convincingly, that the substance of Hutchinson's positions were not nearly so threatening as her tactics. See, e.g., Andrew Delbanco, *The Puritan Ordeal* (Cambridge: Harvard University Press, 1989), 136-37; and Gura, *Glimpse of Sion's Glory*, 240. The positions John Cotton held on "works" versus "grace" at times seemed perilously close to those promulgated by Hutchinson. On Cotton's views, see Cotton, "Sixteene Questions," 58; Cotton, "A Conference Mr. John Cotton Held at Boston with the Elders of New England" (1646), in *AC*, 182-83; "Letters between Thomas Shepard and John Cotton," 30. Scholarship exploring Cotton's understanding of word and spirit includes DeLamotte, "John Cotton and the Rhetoric of Grace," 62, 66; Ann Kibbey, *The Interpretation of Material Shapes in Puritanism: A Study of Rhetoric, Prejudice, and Violence* (New York: Cambridge University Press, 1986); and Larzer Ziff, *The Career of John Cotton: Puritanism and the American Experience* (Princeton, N.J.: Princeton University Press, 1962), esp. 106-7.

41. Johnson, *Wonder-Working Providence*, 129.

42. Winthrop, "Short Story," 274; "Examination of Mrs. Anne Hutchinson at the Court," 336–37, 341. Hutchinson's admission on the point of revelation has typically been treated as a tactical mistake, giving the authorities evidence they needed to proceed against her but lacked at earlier points in the examination. See Morgan, *Puritan Dilemma*, 151–52. For an alternative reading, emphasizing the ritualized nature of the "show trial" and Hutchinson's limited options within the drama, see Anne F. Withington and Jack Schwartz, "The Political Trial of Anne Hutchinson," *NEQ* 51:2 (June 1978): 226–40.

43. Winthrop, "Short Story," 274.

44. On conceptions of women and the tradition of lay prophecy, see Phyllis Mack, "Women as Prophets during the English Civil War," *Feminist Studies* 8:1 (spring 1982): 19–45, esp. 23–25; and Mack, *Visionary Women*, esp. 15–86. On Hutchinson's relationship to this tradition, see Hall, *Worlds of Wonder*, 62, 67, 95–97; and Lang, *Prophetic Woman*, esp. 3–14.

45. Winthrop, "Short Story," 268 (paraphrasing Joel 2:28). The parallel passage in the trial transcript is found in "Examination of Mrs. Anne Hutchinson at the Court," 314–17. See also Hall's editorial comments in AC, 199–200, 311.

46. Patricia Caldwell emphasizes the prophetical and mystical cast of Hutchinson's language. See Caldwell, "Antinomian Language Controversy," esp. 263–66; and Tobin, "Radically Different Voice," 263. Sandra Gustafson sees Hutchinson's rhetoric as a hybrid of spontaneous prophecy and controlled ministerial oratory; "Performing the Word," 153–55, 171–72.

47. "Examination of Mrs. Anne Hutchinson at the Court," 312–13, 317–18. See also Hutchinson's attempts to force the witnesses against her (i.e., the clergy) to swear their testimony under oath (326–29, 345–46).

48. "Examination of Mrs. Anne Hutchinson at the Court," 314–16, 319; "Report of the Trial of Mrs. Ann Hutchinson before the Church," 371. For comments reducing Hutchinson's ministry to female "gadding," see Winthrop's contention that the prayer meetings she led caused "neighbours and dames" to have "neglected" their families ("Examination of Mrs. Anne Hutchinson at the Court," 316), and Cotton Mather's remarks calling her meetings "*gossippings*" of "*captive silly women*" (*Magnalia Christi Americana*, 2: 516).

49. "Examination of Mrs. Anne Hutchinson at the Court," 313, 343 (Deputy Governor Dudley is referring to Hutchinson's imitation of the disturbances caused by zealots in Münster). John Cotton was the reigning authority on the fifth commandment as a guiding principle of New England's social (and, by implication, *verbal*) order. See Cotton, *Spiritual Milk for Boston Babes* (Boston, 1656).

50. "Report of the Trial of Mrs. Anne Hutchinson before the Church," 388.

51. "Examination of Mrs. Anne Hutchinson at the Court," 348, emphasis mine. On the banishment of Hutchinson, see also Winthrop, *Journal*, 1: 264; *Mass. Recs.*, 1: 207–9, 211, 225–26.

52. Rutman, *Winthrop's Boston*, 117, 147, 161. Emery Battis places the Hibbenses in Boston "before 1634" and makes them peripheral supporters of Hutchinson; *Saints and Sectaries*, 336. The documentary record supports Rutman's estimation of late 1638: Boston's town records show William Hibbens admitted as "an Inhabitant in this Towne" on 27 May 1639; "Boston Records, 1634–1660," *Report of the Record Commissioners of the City of Boston*, 2nd ed. (Boston: Rockwell and Churchill, 1881), 2: 41. He became a freeman of the colony in September of that year; see *Miscellaneous Papers*, vol. 29 of *Records Relating to the Early*

History of Boston (Boston: Municipal Printing Office, 1900), 140; *Mass. Recs.*, 1: 254.

53. The Antinomian controversy ranked with the recently concluded Pequot War as a topic of discussion in the letters of elite men. See, e.g., Emanuel Downing to John Winthrop, 21 November 1637, *Winthrop Papers*, 3: 512. Men throughout the colonies and from London wrote to Winthrop to inquire after Hutchinson's "monstrous birth"; see William Bradford to Winthrop, 11 April 1638 (*Winthrop Papers*, 4: 23), Roger Williams to Winthrop, 16 April 1638 (4: 25), Edward Howe to John Winthrop Jr., 14 April 1639 (4: 115). Published commentary on the proceedings against Hutchinson, including John Cotton's "Conference Mr. John Cotton Held at Boston" (1646), Winthrop's "Short Story" (1644), and Cotton's "Way of Congregational Churches Cleared" (1648), would find audiences in England during the following decade.

54. *First Church Records*, 25, 26. The Widow Philip[a?] Hammond was cast out on 7 September 1639; the Hibbenses were admitted as members on 28 September 1639.

55. Winthrop, *Journal*, 1: 331; "Proceedings of the Boston Church against the Exiles" (February 1640), in *AC*, 390. Ironically, the matter of Hutchinson's behavior in exile came before the elders at the same time as Hibbens's transgressions. Hall mistakenly dates Keayne's notes on the proceedings to "early in 1639"; *AC*, 389. But the *First Church Records* (27) show that the expedition began in February 1640.

56. The First Church's proceedings against Hibbens in September 1640 and March 1641 were meticulously transcribed by Hibbens's fellow communicant, Robert Keayne. See Robert Keayne, "Note-book of John Cotton's Sermons, 1639–1642," manuscript on deposit at Massachusetts Historical Society, Boston, 161r–172r, 202v–221r. Transcriptions by Anita Rutman and Merja Kytö, used with their permission, have helped me to decipher Keayne's difficult hand. Published versions of sections of the notebook can be found in Merja Kytö, ed., *Voices in Early Boston: Robert Keayne's Notes of the Meetings of the First Church of Boston, 1639–1646* (forthcoming); and John Putnam Demos, ed., *Remarkable Providences: Readings on Early American History*, rev. ed. (Boston: Northeastern University Press, 1991), 262–82. For evidence that Keayne's notes represent "as reliable a record as can be of spontaneous spoken language of the past recorded in a fairly formal discourse situation," see Merja Kytö, "Robert Keayne's *Notebooks*: A Verbatim Record of Spoken English in Early Boston?" in Susan Herring, Pieter van Reenen, and Lene Schósler, eds., *Textual Parameters in Older Languages* (London: John Benjamins, forthcoming).

57. I have found only a single journal article devoted to Hibbens: Donald Capps, "Erikson's Theory of Religious Ritual: The Case of the Excommunication of Ann Hibbens," *Journal for the Scientific Study of Religion* 18:4 (1979): 337–49. She is most often mentioned in the historiography of New England witchcraft.

58. On Hibbens's social status, see Rutman, *Winthrop's Boston*, 232, 247. Hibbens, at one time called "secretary of Boston," received such important assignments as emissary to England; see Winthrop, *Journal*, 2: 32, 70–71, 98, 231. Hibbens's name also figures prominently in Winthrop's correspondence; see, e.g., *Winthrop Papers*, 5: 56, 122, 220, 244, 257, 258, 339.

59. William Gouge, *Of Domesticall Duties, Eight Treatises* (London, 1634), 5. Gouge argues that every member of the godly community occupies an in-between rung on the ladder of hierarchy, or, as he writes, exists in "severall places":

> The master that hath servants under him, may be under the authority of a Magistrate. . . . The wife, though a mother of children, is under her husband. The husband, though head of a family; is under publike Magistrates. Publike Magistrates, one under another, and all under the King. The King himselfe under God. . . . And Ministers of the Word, as Subjects, are under their Kings and Governours.

Women occupy a special place in this pyramid of rank. Theirs are the only *fixed* points in this constellation. Servants become masters, children become parents, men become ministers, magistrates, governors, and kings. But females remain, perpetually, either daughters or wives. For an elite woman such as Hibbens, the disjuncture between social and sexual status must have been particularly dramatic. On the liminal social position of such elite women, see also Norton, *Founding Mothers and Fathers*, esp. 147–80, 359–99.

60. See, e.g., William Whatley, *A Bride-Bush, Or a Direction for Married Persons* (London, 1619); and Kathleen M. Davies, "The Sacred Condition of Equality: How Original Were Puritan Doctrines of Marriage?" *Social History* 5 (May 1977): 563–80.

61. Keayne, "Note-book of John Cotton's Sermons, 1639–1642," 169v. On the economic duties of the "deputy husband," see Laurel Thatcher Ulrich, *Good Wives: Image and Reality in the Lives of Women in Northern New England, 1650–1750* (New York: Alfred A. Knopf, 1982), 35–50, esp. 45.

62. Keayne, "Note-book of John Cotton's Sermons, 1639–1642," 170r, 168r, 168v, 205v, 162v, 219r, 169r. The description of Hibbens's "gadding" echoes I Timothy 5:13, in which Paul decries "idle" women, "tattlers," and "busybodies" "wandering about from house to house . . . speaking things which they ought not." The issue of price gouging was very much on the minds of the colony's leaders at the time. See Morgan, *Puritan Dilemma*, 67; John Putnam Demos, *Entertaining Satan: Witchcraft and the Culture of Early New England* (New York: Oxford University Press, 1982), 87. Note taker Robert Keayne had himself been admonished for charging excessive rates; see *First Church Records*, 29.

63. Keayne, "Note-book of John Cotton's Sermons, 1639–1642," 163r, 168v, emphasis mine.

64. Keayne, "Note-book of John Cotton's Sermons, 1639–1642," 161v; see also 161r.

65. Keayne, "Note-book of John Cotton's Sermons, 1639–1642," 167r, 169r, emphasis mine.

66. Keayne, "Note-book of John Cotton's Sermons, 1639–1642," 162v, 163r.

67. Keayne, "Note-book of John Cotton's Sermons, 1639–1642," 167r. Hibbens attempted several times to commit her defense to paper, but each time the elders rejected her plea. To them, her arguments seemed disingenuous. "[S]he may as well make mention of [her reasons] by word of mouth," Brother Penn quipped, as "she Cane utter her minde well Enough" (213v).

68. Keayne, "Note-book of John Cotton's Sermons, 1639–1642," 162r, 166v, 167r. On the conventions of the ritual of public apology for speech crimes—conventions that Ann Hibbens so obviously disregarded—see chapter 5 in this book.

69. Keayne, "Note-book of John Cotton's Sermons, 1639–1642," 166v, 161v, 166r, 218r.

70. Keayne, "Note-book of John Cotton's Sermons, 1639–1642," 169v. Doubtless the "other haynous Evells that Lye upon her" mentioned early in the proceedings also concerned this transgression of womanly submission (162r).

71. Keayne, "Note-book of John Cotton's Sermons, 1639–1642," 169v, 171v; *First Church Records*, 31–32.

72. Keayne, "Note-book of John Cotton's Sermons, 1639–1642," 162r.

73. Keayne, "Note-book of John Cotton's Sermons, 1639–1642," 203v, 206v–207r.

74. Keayne, "Note-book of John Cotton's Sermons, 1639–1642," 207r–208v, emphasis mine. Compare the hair-splitting tone of Hutchinson in "Examination of Mrs. Anne Hutchinson at the Court," 324–25, 347. The elders repeatedly cued Hibbens about the kind of "penitency" they hoped she would demonstrate; see Keayne, "Note-book of John Cotton's Sermons, 1639–1642," 212r, 213v–214r, 215v.

75. Keayne, "Note-book of John Cotton's Sermons, 1639–1642," 208r–209v, 210v. Hibbens claimed that Cotton had preached a sermon "from that speech of god to Abraham [']Harken to thy wife in all that she shall say to thee['] " (quoting Genesis 16:2). Cotton denied the charge, saying he could "Confidently affirme that I never delivered any such thinge." What was more, Cotton claimed, the Scripture in question did not elevate woman's voice, but rather the voice of God speaking *through* her in the prophetic mode (210v, 211r).

76. Keayne, "Note-book of John Cotton's Sermons, 1639–1642," 214v, 213r, 215r–v.

77. Keayne, "Note-book of John Cotton's Sermons, 1639–1642," 217r, 215r, 217v.

78. Keayne, "Note-book of John Cotton's Sermons, 1639–1642," 219v, 217v–218r. In sentencing Hibbens, the elders very pointedly compared her to the biblical Miriam, who spoke against Moses and became leprous (Numbers 12:1–15); see 217v.

79. *First Church Records*, 33.

80. "Proceedings of the Boston Church against the Exiles," 390–93.

81. Winthrop, *Journal*, 1: 299, 277; 2: 7–8. See also Winthrop, "Short Story," esp. 281; Johnson, *Wonder-Working Providence*, 132; Schutte, " 'Such Monstrous Births' "; and Carol F. Karlsen, *The Devil in the Shape of a Woman: Witchcraft in Colonial New England* (New York: W. W. Norton, 1987), 15–18.

82. Hubbard, *General History of New England*, 574; Norton's remarks quoted in a letter to Increase Mather, ca. 1684, reprinted in Hutchinson, *History of Massachusetts-Bay*, 1: 160–61; *Mass. Recs.*, 4.1: 269; and Karlsen, *Devil in the Shape of a Woman*, 1–2, 28, 150–52. None of the original testimony from Hibbens's trials before the Court of Assistants or the General Court survives.

83. Both possessed more than the rudimentary literacy skills common to women in early America. Both seem to have written as well as read. Hutchinson wrote her responses to some of the allegations against her and penned her dubious recantation. See Winthrop, "Short Story," 305–6; "Report of the Trial of Mrs. Anne Hutchinson before the Church," 379–81. Although there is less evidence of Hibbens's knowledge of letters, her notions of prices, accounts, and contracts suggest extensive contact with written documents. In addition, she wrote a lengthy will in her own hand; see "Abstracts of the Earliest Wills on Record in the County of Suffolk," *New England Historical and Genealogical Register* 6 (Boston: Thomas Prince, 1852), 287–88. On patterns of female literacy in early New England, see Kenneth Lockridge, *Literacy in Colonial New England: An Enquiry into the Social Context of Literacy in the Early Modern West* (New York: W. W. Norton, 1974), esp. 38–43; Richard D. Brown, *Knowledge Is Power: The Diffusion*

of Information in Early America, 1700–1865 (New York: Oxford University Press, 1989), 11–12, 163–67; Hall, *Worlds of Wonder*, esp. 22–23, 32–34; and E. Jennifer Monaghan, "Literacy Instruction and Gender in Colonial New England," in Cathy N. Davidson, ed., *Reading in America: Literature and Social History* (Baltimore: Johns Hopkins University Press, 1989), 53–80.

84. That Hutchinson and Hibbens were excommunicated for their behavior rather than for their "opinions" is demonstrated by the choice of Pastor John Wilson (not Teacher John Cotton) to pronounce their sentences. Winthrop noted that because Hutchinson's excommunication was "for manifest evil in matter of conversation" (i.e., conduct and speech), the job of sentencing her fell to "the pastor, matter of manners belonging properly to his place"; Winthrop, *Journal*, 1: 264. On this division of roles within the Puritan ministry see also Thomas Lechford, *Plain Dealing; Or, News from New England* (1642), ed. J. Hammond Trumbull (Boston: Wiggin and Lunt, 1867), 30–31. Lechford states: "If [the excommunication] be for defaults in erroneous opinions . . . the Teacher" delivers the sentence; "If for matter of ill manners, the Pastor denounceth it."

85. Harry Stout argues that Hutchinson literally employed an old voice: an earlier and less interpretively fixed version of the Bible. He writes that Hutchinson "and her followers came from an older language and, like foreigners, spoke past their clerical opponents"; see Stout, "Word and Order," 32.

86. On the tradition of conventicles and its unsuitability to New England Puritanism, see Foster, "New England and the Challenge of Heresy"; Gura, *Glimpse of Sion's Glory*, 243–44, 248, 250; and Delbanco, *Puritan Ordeal*, 142.

87. "Examination of Mrs. Anne Hutchinson at the Court," 338.

88. Wheelwright's censure is found in *Mass. Recs.*, 1: 189, 207; Winthrop, "Short Story," 258. His letters to Cotton are shrewdly analyzed in Sargent Bush Jr., " 'Revising What We Have Done Amisse': John Cotton and John Wheelwright, 1640," *WMQ* 3rd ser., 45:4 (October 1988): 733–50, esp. 736–37, 740–41.

89. For Wheelwright's defense, see John Wheelwright Jr., *Mercurius Americanus, Mr. Welds His Antitype; or, Massachusetts Great Apologie Examined* (London, 1645), reprinted in Charles H. Bell, ed., *John Wheelwright*, Publications of the Prince Society, vol. 9 (1876), 181–228. Wheelwright's apology (and the repentances of other leading male Antinomians) is found in Winthrop, *Journal*, 2: 56, 165–67; see also Bush, " 'Revising What We Have Done Amisse,' " 734.

90. This comparison between Winthrop's tone toward Williams and his stance toward Hutchinson is suggested by Karlsen, *Devil in the Shape of a Woman*, 273 n. 64. The outlines of Williams's story are found in Edmund S. Morgan, *Roger Williams: The Church and the State* (New York: Harcourt, Brace, 1967). Decorous tones of "brotherly" exchange characterize Williams's extensive correspondence with Winthrop. See, e.g., *Winthrop Papers*, 3: 86, 298, 314–18, 410–12, 433–52, 479–80; 4: 1–2, 6–7, 15–17. On Hutchinson's "monstrous birth," see *Winthrop Papers*, 4: 25.

91. Cotton to Williams, 1636?, in Glenn W. LaFantasie, ed., *The Correspondence of Roger Williams*, 2 vols. (Providence: Rhode Island Historical Society and Brown University Press, 1988), 1: 33. This collection gives a sense of the lofty discursive circles in which Williams continued to participate after his "exile."

92. See, e.g., "Report of the Trial of Mrs. Anne Hutchinson before the Church," 370–73; Keayne, "Note-book of John Cotton's Sermons, 1639–1642," 163r, 167v, 206v, 211r.

93. On the degree to which New England women were able to converse in court about their "menfolks'" economic lives, see Cornelia Hughes Dayton, *Women before the Bar: Gender, Law, and Society in Connecticut, 1639–1789* (Chapel Hill: University of North Carolina Press, 1995), 69–104; and Jane Kamensky, "Governing the Tongue: Speech and Society in Early New England" (Ph.D. dissertation, Yale University, 1993), 119–25, 132–37.

94. See *First Church Records*, 25 (admonition), 29 (reconciliation); and Bernard Bailyn, "The *Apologia* of Robert Keayne," *WMQ* 3rd ser., 7:4 (October 1950): 568–87. Keayne filled various "responsible public positions," including selectman, representative of the General Court, and surveyor of highways.

95. See James F. Cooper Jr., "The Confession and Trial of Richard Wayte, Boston, 1640," *WMQ* 3rd ser., 44:2 (April 1987): 310–31, esp. 311.

96. Harry S. Stout, *The New England Soul: Preaching and Religious Culture in Colonial New England* (New York: Oxford University Press, 1986), 25, 19. On the emerging clerical orthodoxy, see Rutman, *Winthrop's Boston*, 126–28; and Gura, *Glimpse of Sion's Glory*, 239.

97. *A Platform of Church Discipline Gathered out of the Word of God* (Cambridge, 1649) (hereafter *Cambridge Platform*), reprinted in Williston Walker, ed., *The Creeds and Platforms of Congregationalism* (New York: Charles Scribner, 1893), 219; John Cotton, *The Keys of the Kingdom of Heaven* (1644), reprinted in Larzer Ziff, ed., *John Cotton on the Churches of New England* (Cambridge: Harvard University Press, 1968), 114, emphasis original. A detailed firsthand account of the orderly services in New England ca. 1647 is found in Lechford, *Plain Dealing*, 43–58. For a dissenting view of the changes in lay participation in the wake of Hutchinson, see James F. Cooper, "Anne Hutchinson and the 'Lay Rebellion' against the Clergy," *NEQ* 61:3 (September 1988): 381–97, esp. 392–94; and Cooper, "Confession and Trial of Richard Wayte."

98. John Cotton, "Psalm-Singing a Godly Exercise" or "Singing of Psalmes a Gospel-Ordinance" (London, 1650), in Edmund Clarence Stedman and Ellen MacKay Hutchinson, eds., *A Library of American Literature from the Earliest Settlement to the Present Time*, 11 vols. (New York: Charles L. Webster, 1892), 1: 266. By invoking I Timothy 2:13–14 to denounce women's teaching as "seducing," Cotton again links female speech to Eve's treachery. On Hutchinson's impact on Cotton's writings, particularly on his ideas about the "interpretive authority" of women, see Kibbey, *Interpretation of Material Shapes*, 116, 118.

99. Johnson, *Wonder-Working Providence*, 217. Thomas Lechford explained in 1642 that women in the Boston congregation typically made their confessions "before the Elders, in private," while those in Salem tended to "speake themselves, for the most part." But, he noted, even the unorthodox Salem church was beginning to alter this unusual practice; Lechford, *Plain Dealing*, 22–23. By 1648, the relationship between gender and public professions was so thoroughly assumed that the Cambridge synod felt no need even to mention it, instead listing only "excessive fear, or other infirmity" as conditions that would prevent godly persons from making "their *relations, & confessions* personally with their own mouth"; *Cambridge Platform*, 223. For a counterexample, see the Wenham church's decision in the matter ca. 1644, in Robert G. Pope, ed., *Notebook of the Reverend John Fiske, 1644–1675* (Salem, Mass.: Essex Institute, 1974), 4.

100. Mather, *Magnalia Christi Americana*, 1: 437, quoting Rev. Samuel Stone of Hartford. See also Caldwell, *Puritan Conversion Narrative*, 50 n. 16, 79, 144–47.

101. On the origins of the *Body of Liberties*, see Morgan, *Puritan Dilemma*, 164–67; Johnson, *Wonder-Working Providence*, 245; Winthrop, *Journal*, 1: 323–24; and William H. Whitmore, ed., *The Colonial Laws of Massachusetts, Reprinted from the Edition of 1660, with the Supplements to 1672, Containing also the Body of Liberties of 1641* (hereafter *Body of Liberties* or *Mass. Laws, 1660 Edition*) (Boston: Rockwell and Churchill, 1889), introduction. The first edition of the *Book of General Lawes and Libertyes* is reprinted in Max Farrand, ed., *The Laws and Liberties of Massachusetts, Reprinted from the Copy of the 1648 Edition in the Henry E. Huntington Library* (hereafter *Mass. Laws, 1648 Edition*) (Cambridge: Harvard University Press, 1929). See also William H. Whitmore, ed., *The Colonial Laws of Massachusetts, Reprinted from the Edition of 1672, with the Supplements to 1686* (hereafter *Mass. Laws, 1672 Edition*) (Boston: Rockwell and Churchill, 1887). On the impact of the Antinomian controversy upon Massachusetts legal institutions, see David Thomas Konig, *Law and Society in Puritan Massachusetts: Essex County, 1629–1692* (Chapel Hill: University of North Carolina Press, 1979), 33–34.

102. Hutchinson to Thomas Leverett, quoted in Samuel Groome, *A Glass for the People of New England* (1676), reprinted in *Magazine of History* 37:3, extra no. 147 (1929): 131–68, quotation from 137.

103. John Winthrop, "A Reply in Further Defense of an Order of Court Made in May 1637," in *Winthrop Papers*, 3: 465–66.

104. *Mass. Recs.*, 1: 212–13. These restrictions on contemptuous speech against civil authority remained in force through each subsequent edition of the colony's laws.

105. *Mass. Recs.*, 2: 177–79. Statute condemning so-called "WANTON GOSPELLER[S]" or "OPEN AND OBSTINATE CONTEMNER[S] OF GODS HOLY ORDINANCES" (repeat offenders) is found in *Mass. Laws, 1648 Edition*, 19–20. On private prayer, see *Body of Liberties*, 57; *Mass. Laws, 1648 Edition*, 19.

106. Winthrop, "Short Story," 259, emphasis mine. Contrast this view of the relationship between speech and conscience with Thomas Shepard's in "Examination of Anne Hutchinson at the Court," 323.

107. *Body of Liberties*, 35, 49; *Mass. Laws, 1648 Edition*, 45–46, 50, 52. As many scholars have pointed out, this degree of verbal freedom, however bounded, far outstripped prevailing English norms. See George Lee Haskins, *Law and Authority in Early Massachusetts: A Study in Tradition and Design* (New York: Macmillan, 1960), esp. 130, 196–97; and Larry D. Eldridge, *A Distant Heritage: The Growth of Free Speech in Early America* (New York: New York University Press, 1994), chapter 2. Nonetheless, it represents a compromise, tailoring the expressive liberties inherent in Puritan thought to the realities of life in New England.

108. New Haven's courts explicitly cited this biblical grounding; see Charles J. Hoadly, ed., *Records of the Colony and Plantation of New Haven, 1638–1649* (Hartford: Case, Lockwood, 1857), 1: 293. Massachusetts blasphemy law appears first in the *Body of Liberties*, 55. See also *Mass. Laws, 1648 Edition*, 5; *Mass. Laws, 1660 Edition*, 128; *Mass. Laws, 1672 Edition*, 14. For an argument that capital laws prohibiting witchcraft and filial rebellion (see *Body of Liberties*, 55; *Mass. Laws, 1648 Edition*, 5, 6; *Mass. Laws, 1660 Edition*, 128, 129; *Mass. Laws, 1672 Edition*, 14, 15) were also, in effect, laws governing the tongue, see chapters 4 and 6 in this book.

109. On lying, see *Mass. Recs.*, 2: 104–5 or 3: 18–19; *Mass. Laws, 1648 Edition*, 35–36; *Mass. Laws, 1660 Edition*, 171; and *Mass. Laws, 1672 Edition*, 90–91. On heretical speech, swearing, and cursing, see *Mass. Laws, 1648 Edition*, 24, 44; *Mass. Laws, 1660 Edition*, 154–56, 194, 219–20, 222; *Mass. Laws, 1672 Edition*, 60–63, 144–45, 235. No statute covered slanderous speech per se; actions for slander and defamation loosely followed English common-law precedent.

110. *Body of Liberties*, 33, 61, 45.

111. On the ways in which the shift from ad hoc "Puritan" jurisprudence to legal formalism acted to discourage female litigants and deponents in Connecticut courts, see Dayton, *Women before the Bar*.

112. *The Scarlet Letter*, vol. 1 of *The Centenary Edition of the Works of Nathaniel Hawthorne* (Columbus: Ohio State University Press, 1962), 48.

113. Lyle Koehler exaggerates the degree of concerted "feminist" action involved when he refers to "the rebellion of [Hutchinson's] female followers" in the years after the banishment of the Antinomians. Still, the incidents of public female misbehavior he cites are worth noting, especially in the context of the problematics of speaking. See Lyle Koehler, "The Case of the American Jezebels: Anne Hutchinson and Female Agitation during the Years of Antinomian Turmoil, 1636–1640," *WMQ* 3rd ser., 31:1 (January 1974): 55–78, esp. 69–72.

114. *First Church Records*, 37, 39, 46, 49. See also the proceedings against Ann Burden and Sister Hogg, also accused of unseemly speech (53–57).

115. Winthrop, *Journal*, 2: 126, 138; see also presentment of Lady Deborah Moody, Salem, 1642, in George F. Dow, ed., *Records and Files of the Quarterly Courts of Essex County, Massachusetts*, 9 vols. (Salem, Mass.: Essex Institute, 1911–1978), 1: 48. Moody was a cousin of Sir Henry Vane the younger, one of Hutchinson's chief supporters; see Gura, *Glimpse of Sion's Glory*, 108.

116. Newman Smyth, ed., "Mrs. Eaton's Trial (in 1644); as it Appears upon the Records of the First Church of New Haven," in *New Haven Colony Historical Society Papers* 5 (1894), 133–48, quotations from 139, 142, 147. Eaton's anabaptist heresy, the elders said, stemmed from a conversation with "Lady Moodey," thus completing the circle of threatening women's speech. On the local gossip network fueling Eaton's offenses, see Norton, *Founding Mothers and Fathers*, 165–80.

117. Winthrop, "Short Story," 308.

118. See Gura, *Glimpse of Sion's Glory*, 264–75; and Lang, *Prophetic Woman*.

119. Nathaniel Mather to Increase Mather, 31 December 1684, reprinted in David D. Hall, ed., *Witch-Hunting in Seventeenth-Century New England: A Documentary History, 1638–1692* (Boston: Northeastern University Press, 1991), 28.

120. On the gender egalitarianism of courtroom behavior in early New Haven, see Dayton, *Women before the Bar*, esp. 10–13, 32–34. On women as witnesses in New England courts, see Mary Beth Norton, "Gender, Crime, and Community in Seventeenth-Century Maryland," in James A. Henretta, Michael A. Kammen, and Stanley N. Katz, eds., *The Transformation of Early American History: Society, Authority, and Ideology* (New York: Alfred A. Knopf, 1991), 123–50.

121. "Report of the Trial of Mrs. Anne Hutchinson before the Church," 373; "Examination of Mrs. Anne Hutchinson at the Court," 322.

Chapter 4

1. Cotton Mather, *Magnalia Christi Americana, or the Ecclesiastical History of New England*, 2 vols. (1702; reprinted Hartford: Silas Andrus and Son, 1855), 1: 271–73, emphasis original.

2. John Norton, *Abel Being Dead, Yet Speaketh* (London, 1658), reprinted as Enoch Pond, ed., *Memoir of John Cotton* (New York: Saxton and Miles, 1842), 13.

3. Thomas Shepard the younger eulogized Wilson. On the deaths of Hooker, Winthrop, Shepard, Cotton, Bradford, Norton, Wilson, and others, see Nathaniel Morton, *New England's Memorial: Or, a Brief Relation of the Most Remarkable Passages of the Providence of God, Manifested to the Planters of New England* (1669), in Alexander Young, ed., *Chronicles of the Pilgrim Fathers* (New York: E. P. Dutton, 1910), 155–58, 159–60, 164–67, 178, 186, 195, 211–17.

4. Morton, *New England's Memorial*, 164–65. On the "blazing star" of 1652 and the range of "remarkables" that followed in its wake, see also Increase Mather, *Kometographia, Or, a Discourse Concerning Comets* (Boston, 1683), 111–12; and Norton, *Abel Being Dead, Yet Speaketh*, 86–87.

5. As Stephen Foster argues, we must approach the very notion of a sudden generational passage critically, for such anxieties had more basis in Puritan rhetoric than in social reality. In fact, by the 1660s, many prominent New Englanders, born in England during the 1610s or 1620s, belonged neither to the cohort sermons referred to as "our Fathers" nor to the dissolute "*Present Generation*." See Foster, *The Long Argument: English Puritanism and the Shaping of New England Culture, 1570–1700* (Chapel Hill: University of North Carolina Press, 1991), esp. 215.

6. Norton, *Abel Being Dead, Yet Speaketh*, 13, paraphrasing Hebrews 11:4.

7. Recent scholarship exploring the connection between family and state in early modern thought is vast and growing. On England, see especially Gordon J. Schochet, *Patriarchalism in Political Thought: The Authoritarian Family and Political Speculation and Attitudes Especially in Seventeenth-Century England* (Oxford: Basil Blackwell, 1975); and Susan Dwyer Amussen, *An Ordered Society: Gender and Class in Early Modern England* (New York: Basil Blackwell, 1988). On New England, see Edmund S. Morgan, *The Puritan Family: Religion and Domestic Relations in Seventeenth-Century New England* (New York: Harper and Row, 1966), esp. 17–21; John Putnam Demos, *A Little Commonwealth: Family Life in Plymouth Colony* (New York: Oxford University Press, 1970); Phillip J. Greven Jr., *The Protestant Temperament: Patterns of Child-Rearing, Religious Experience, and the Self in Early America* (Chicago: University of Chicago Press, 1977), esp. parts 1 and 2; and Mary Beth Norton, *Founding Mothers and Fathers: Gendered Power and the Forming of American Society* (New York: Alfred A. Knopf, 1996). Contemporary sources leave little doubt that "parents" often meant "fathers," just as generic "children" typically referred to "sons." See, e.g., William Gouge, *Of Domesticall Duties, Eight Treatises* (London, 1634), esp. 490–92, 494–95; and Cotton Mather, *Help for Distressed Parents. Or, Counsels & Comforts for Godly Parents Afflicted With Ungodly Children* (Boston, 1695), 8. A number of scholars have recently analyzed this point. See, e.g., Jane Kamensky, "Governing the Tongue: Speech and Society in Early New England" (Ph.D. dissertation, Yale University, 1993), 312–13; John Putnam Demos, "The Changing Faces of Fatherhood," in *Past, Present, and Personal: The Family and the Life Course in American*

History (New York: Oxford University Press, 1986), 41–67, esp. 44; and Norton, *Founding Mothers and Fathers*, 96–100.

8. Gouge, *Of Domesticall Duties*, 436–37, 440; Cotton Mather, *A Family Well-Ordered* (Boston, 1699), 60–61 (also 40–48). For similar advice in later child-rearing literature, see Benjamin Wadsworth, *The Well-Ordered Family: Or, Relative Duties* (Boston, 1712), 25, 91; and Samuel Willard, *A Compleat Body of Divinity* (Boston, 1726), esp. 601–8, 648.

9. Gouge, *Of Domesticall Duties*, 438.

10. Cotton Mather, *Help for Distressed Parents*, 40 (paraphrasing Isaiah 53:2), emphasis original.

11. Gouge, *Of Domesticall Duties*, 17.

12. See especially Foster, *Long Argument*, chapter 5. The theological and political imperatives leading up to the Halfway Covenant are summarized in Williston Walker, ed., *The Creeds and Platforms of Congregationalism* (New York: Charles Scribner, 1893), esp. 244–69. See also Edmund S. Morgan, *Visible Saints: The History of a Puritan Idea* (Ithaca, N.Y.: Cornell University Press, 1965), 113–52; Morgan, *Puritan Family*, 161–86; and Carla Gardina Pestana, *Quakers and Baptists in Colonial Massachusetts* (New York: Cambridge University Press, 1991), 47–49, 60–79.

13. Increase Mather, *Kometographia*, 112. See also John Norton, *Abel Being Dead, Yet Speaketh*, 87; and John Wilson, *A Seasonable Watch-Word Unto Christians . . . Delivered in a Sermon November 16th, 1665* (Cambridge, 1677), 4, 5.

14. Capital laws against filial rebellion first appeared in Massachusetts in 1648, Connecticut in 1652, New Haven in 1656, Plymouth in 1671, and New Hampshire in 1680; Rhode Island, as in so many matters, was an exception. See Edgar J. McManus, *Law and Liberty in Early New England: Criminal Justice and Due Process, 1620–1692* (Amherst: University of Massachusetts Press, 1993), appendix A, 187–91. The Massachusetts statute was included in John Cotton's 1634 draft of the colony's laws (see Thomas Hutchinson, comp., *Hutchinson Papers*, Publications of the Prince Society, vol. 1 [1865; reprinted New York: Burt Franklin, 1967], 183–205, esp. 198) but did not appear in the *Body of Liberties*. It entered the records of the General Court in 1646, along with several other measures restricting speech against authority; see Nathaniel B. Shurtleff, ed., *Records of the Governor and Company of the Massachusetts Bay in New England* (hereafter *Mass. Recs.*), 5 vols. in 6 (1854; reprinted New York: AMS Press, 1968), 2: 77–80, esp. 79; and Max Farrand, ed., *The Laws and Liberties of Massachusetts, Reprinted from the Copy of the 1648 Edition in the Henry E. Huntington Library* (Cambridge: Harvard University Press, 1929), 6. New England's "stubborn son" statutes were grounded in Scripture but included important extrabiblical innovations; see George Lee Haskins, *Law and Authority in Early Massachusetts: A Study in Tradition and Design* (New York: Macmillan, 1960), 145–52. No child was put to death under these laws.

15. Gouge, *Of Domesticall Duties*, 441.

16. *Probate Records of Essex County*, 3 vols. (Salem, Mass.: Essex Institute, 1920), 3: 111–18; see also George F. Dow, ed., *Records and Files of the Quarterly Courts of Essex County, Massachusetts* (hereafter *ECR*), 9 vols. (Salem, Mass.: Essex Institute, 1911–1978), 6: 233–34. For a description of Porter's house and lands, see Sidney Perley, *The History of Salem Massachusetts*, 3 vols. (Salem, Mass.: n.p., 1926), 2: 161–65, 291.

17. Perley, *History of Salem*, 2: 161, lists the younger Porter's birth date as 1618. However, two contemporary documents fix his birth somewhere between 1630 and 1635. The General Court of Massachusetts said he was "about thirty" in 1665 (*Mass. Recs.*, 4.2: 216), and Porter junior set his own age at 48 in a deposition taken in June 1678 (*ECR*, 9: 54–55). Since the elder Porter immigrated to Massachusetts around 1635, it remains unclear whether John junior was born in New England.

18. For John Porter Jr.'s inventory, see Archie N. Frost, comp., *Verbatim Transcript of the File Papers of the Essex County Quarterly Courts, 1636–1692* (hereafter *Essex File Papers*), 75 vols. (typescript on deposit at the James Duncan Phillips Library of the Peabody-Essex Museum, Salem, Mass.; microfilm copy at Sterling Memorial Library, Yale University), 40: 96-1; also *ECR*, 9: 157. Porter's estate totaled £32, 9s. His father's "33 load of hay" had an estimated value of £33.

19. For Porter's service as deputy from Hingham, see *Mass. Recs.*, 2: 66. Porter was elected deputy from Salem in 1668; *Mass. Recs.*, 4.2: 362. His frequent appearances as witness, overseer, and arbitrator are recorded in *ECR*, 1: 144, 257; 2: 136, 151, 191, 428, 429; 3: 369, 386; 4: 110, 144. For Porter as a "jury man," see *ECR*, 1: 180, 191, 229, 238; 2: 123, 157; 3: 367; 4: 143, 171. On Porter's local offices as Salem selectman and constable, see Martha O. Howes, ed., *Salem Town Records, 1659–1680*, in *Essex Institute Historical Collections* (Salem, Mass.: Essex Institute, 1896–1933), 40: 100–1, 110; 41: 131, 299; 42: 51; and Perley, *History of Salem*, 2: 291.

20. See, e.g., *ECR*, 2: 105, 218, 269, 333; 3: 32, 57, 174.

21. It is difficult to fix with precision the date of Porter's arrival in Salem. He resided in Hingham when he was chosen General Court deputy in June 1644. By June 1646, his appearance on Salem's jury of trials confirms his residence in Essex County; see *ECR*, 1: 95. The First Church heard his relation of conversion in April 1649; Richard D. Pierce, ed., *The Records of the First Church in Salem, Massachusetts, 1629–1736* (Salem, Mass.: Essex Institute, 1974), 13. On the baptism of Porter's children, see Perley, *History of Salem*, 2: 161–65. The language of Porter's will also speaks to his piety; see *Probate Records of Essex County*, 3: 111.

22. John Porter Jr., petition to the Essex County Court at Salem, 1661, *Essex File Papers*, 7: 35-1; also *ECR*, 2: 337.

23. Raye v. Rowden, Salem, 1649, *ECR*, 1: 157; no testimony from the case survives. Porter would have been between thirteen and eighteen years old at the time (see note 17 above).

24. "Narrative of the Case of John Porter, Jr.," May 1665, in *Mass. Recs.*, 4.2: 216. The elder Porter had journeyed to Barbados in 1658, as his signature on a contract arranging for the delivery of 1,225 pounds of "good dry Muscovada sugar" to a Boston merchant attests; see *ECR*, 3: 369.

25. In Andover, Massachusetts, the average age at first marriage among second-generation Englishmen was 26.7; in the brief interval between 1660 and 1664, men married significantly earlier on average. See Philip J. Greven Jr., *Four Generations: Population, Land, and Family in Colonial Andover, Massachusetts* (Ithaca, N.Y.: Cornell University Press, 1970), 34–35. On the centrality of marriage for the self-definition and economic good fortune of "middling" colonists, see Jackson Turner Main, *Society and Economy in Colonial Connecticut* (Princeton, N.J.: Princeton University Press, 1985), 88, 141–47, 372–73.

26. "Narrative of the Case of John Porter, Jr.," 216.

27. Depositions of William Dixey and William Hollingworth, Salem, 1669, *ECR*, 4: 175.

28. Burton v. Porter, Salem, 1661, *ECR*, 2: 320–22, and *Essex File Papers*, 7: 2-2 through 6-2; presentment of John Porter Jr., Salem, 1661, *ECR*, 2: 335, and *Essex File Papers*, 7: 36-1.

29. John Porter Jr. to his father, November 1661, *Essex File Papers*, 7: 34-1.

30. "Narrative of the Case of John Porter, Jr.," 216–17.

31. Morgan Jones and Joseph Porter deposition, *Essex File Papers*, 7: 36-1. Significantly, Hathorne was more than a metaphorical father to young Porter. In January 1665, John's brother Joseph married Hathorne's daughter Anne. Thus Hathorne would become young Porter's brother's father-in-law, a kinsman in fact as well as by analogy; Perley, *History of Salem*, 2: 162.

32. *Essex File Papers*, 7: 34-1, 35-1; *ECR*, 2: 336–37, 346.

33. "Narrative of the Case of John Porter, Jr.," 216–17. The court noted that during "the two last yeares, sixty two & sixty three," Porter had been particularly "vile & unsufferable."

34. Significantly, Porter's motivation for speaking as he did is never directly addressed by the court. In the eyes of Massachusetts authorities, perhaps, no cause for such behavior—short of mental incompetence—could plausibly be advanced. In their later "narrative" of Porter's case, however, the magistrates mention that he had been "prooved to be a . . . drunkard"; "Narrative of the Case of John Porter, Jr.," 216. Porter's own comments about the "many Sad disasters" that had befallen him and his desire to be "happy" in his parents' sight invite speculation about the restiveness of a wealthy but unmarried young man forced by both law and custom to live into adulthood under the confines of "family government."

35. "Narrative of the Case of John Porter, Jr.," 216; *Suffolk Court Files*, manuscript collection including papers submitted for trials before the Court of Assistants, on deposit at the Massachusetts State Archives, Boston (hereafter *Suffolk Files*), case 608, papers 2 and 5. See also John Noble and John F. Cronin, eds., *Records of the Court of Assistants of the Colony of Massachusetts Bay, 1630–1692* (hereafter *Assts. Recs.*), 3 vols. (Boston: Rockwell and Churchill, 1901–1928), 3: 138–39.

36. "Narrative of the Case of John Porter, Jr.," 216–17; *ECR*, 3: 111, 117, 227; and *Suffolk Files*, case 608, papers 1 and 3. In binding the case over to a higher court, the Salem magistrates effectively acknowledged that Porter's offenses fell under the capital law against rebellious sons.

37. Cotton Mather, *Help for Distressed Parents*, 4; "Narrative of the Case of John Porter, Jr.," 217. John Porter Sr.'s complaint against his son does not survive.

38. See, e.g., *Suffolk Files*, case 608, papers 2 and 5.

39. "Narrative of the Case of John Porter, Jr.," 217.

40. *Suffolk Files*, case 608, paper 4. Porter was also fined the heady sum of £200.

41. *Suffolk Files*, case 608, paper 5.

42. The commissioners (with the exception of Maverick, a Boston resident and longtime opponent of Massachusetts authorities) had been dispatched to New England after the Restoration to settle disputed points of sovereignty. See Thomas Hutchinson, *The History of the Colony and Province of Massachusetts-Bay* (1764–1768), ed. Lawrence Shaw Mayo (Cambridge: Harvard University Press,

1936), 1: 206-15; and James Duncan Phillips, *Salem in the Seventeenth Century* (New York: Houghton Mifflin, 1933), 206-8.

43. "The Humble Petition of John Porter Junior of Salem," 1 May 1665, from an unsigned copy filed in *Colonial Office Records, General Series 1, 1574-1690*, 69 vols. (manuscript in Great Britain, Public Record Office; microform copy on deposit at Yale University), vol. 19, doc. 42.

44. Order of Protection, 8 May 1665, *Colonial Office Records, General Series 1*, 19: 42; also reproduced in *Mass. Recs.*, 4.2: 177.

45. Response of the General Court, May 1665, *Mass. Recs.*, 4.2: 195, 146.

46. See the Commissioners' Response, 10 May 1665; the General Court's Response to the Commissioners' 10 May Response; and the Court's "Further Response" to the Commissioners. *Mass. Recs.*, 4.2: 195-97, 210.

47. See Phillips, *Salem in the Seventeenth Century*, 208; and Hutchinson, *History of Massachusetts-Bay*, 1: 215.

48. "Narrative of the Case of John Porter, Jr.," 216, 218.

49. Presentment of John Porter Jr., Salem, 1668, ECR, 4: 37, emphasis mine.

50. Howes, *Salem Town Records*, 42: 44.

51. Two cases were "withdrawn": see John Porter Sr. v. John Porter Jr. for trespass, Salem, 1670, ECR, 4: 297; and for an unspecified charge, Salem, 1672, ECR, 5: 20. John Porter Sr. lost a case against his son for forfeiture of a bond of arbitration in 1674. The court had ordered John senior to pay his son £150 in 1670, which the son refused to accept, see Porter v. Porter, Salem, 1674, ECR, 5: 345-46.

52. *Probate Records of Essex County*, 3: 111.

53. Cotton Mather, *Family Well-Ordered*, 48.

54. Cotton Mather, *Help for Distressed Parents*, 17.

55. Cotton Mather, *Family Well-Ordered*, 32. It is significant in this regard that the surviving descendants of John Porter Sr. figured prominently among the accused during the Salem witch trials; see Paul Boyer and Stephen Nissenbaum, *Salem Possessed: The Social Origins of Witchcraft* (Cambridge: Harvard University Press, 1974), esp. 110-52.

56. Porter's singularity in this regard was still remembered in the late eighteenth century; see Hutchinson, *Papers*, 1: 198 n. 148; and Hutchinson, *History of Massachusetts-Bay*, 1: 372-73 and notes.

57. John Porter Jr. to his father, November 1661, *Essex File Papers*, 7: 34-1; "Narrative of the Case of John Porter, Jr.," 216.

58. Presentment of ———— Howe for prophane swearing and other offenses, New Haven, 1651, in Franklin B. Dexter, ed., *New Haven Town Records, 1649-1662* (hereafter *NHTR*, 1) (New Haven: New Haven Colony Historical Society, 1917), 88-89. See also the presentment of Samuel Ford for "undutyfull, rebellious cariag to his mother," New Haven, 1655, *NHTR*, 1: 238-40. New Haven's statutes making such words a capital offense were published the following year; see Charles J. Hoadly, ed., *Records of the Colony or Jurisdiction of New Haven, from May, 1653, to the Union* (hereafter *NHCR*, 2) (Hartford: Case, Lockwood, 1858), 578.

59. Canterbury v. Rowden, Salem, 1658, ECR, 2: 101; 1: 426. Porter knew John Rowden and his family; he had testified against them in the county court in 1648 (see note 23 above). Rowden was one of few rebellious children who used physical force against a parent; she had been known to "sling stones at him

with great violence." For other examples, see presentment of Richard Martyn, Salisbury, 1669, ECR, 4: 186–87; presentments of Anna, Dorcas, and Mary Bessey, Plymouth, 1662, in David Pulsifer, ed., *Records of the Colony of New Plymouth in New England* (hereafter PCR), 12 vols. (1861; reprinted New York: AMS Press, 1968), 4: 10; and the conviction of Edward Bumpas "for stricking and abusing his parents," Plymouth, 1679, PCR, 6: 20.

60. Presentment of Belief Gridley, 1664, Assts. Recs., 3: 144–45. Gridley was sentenced in September 1664; Porter had been imprisoned the previous March and petitioned for his release just a month after Gridley's trial. See *Suffolk Files*, case 608, paper 4; and *Mass. Recs.*, 4.2: 137.

61. Tappan v. Hill, Salem, 1671, ECR, 4: 381; see also 6: 176–78. Hill paraphrased Proverbs 30:17. Numerous sermons and conduct manuals used the verse in their warnings to wayward children. See, e.g., Gouge, *Of Domesticall Duties*, 441; Cotton Mather, *Family Well-Ordered*, 40–48; and Increase Mather, *The Wicked Mans Portion. Or, A Sermon . . . Wherein Is Shewed That Excesse in Wickedness Doth Bring Untimely Death* (Boston, 1675), 9, 11.

62. Presentment of Elizabeth Perkins, Ipswich, 1681, *Essex File Papers*, 35: 55-1 through 56-4, 35: 66-1 (see also ECR, 8: 89–90); presentment of Hugh Hancock, Salem, 1666, *Essex File Papers*, 12: 29-3 (see also ECR, 3: 376–77).

63. Presentment of Charles Hill, Salem, 1669, ECR, 4: 200.

64. In Essex County and the higher courts of Massachusetts, roughly 13 percent of all presentments for contempt of authority included multiple "targets"; see appendix, table A.2 in this book. In addition, nearly 40 percent of speakers against authority were prosecuted for other speech offenses at some time during their lives. Among recidivist condemners (31 out of 190 individuals presented), the trend was even stronger: nearly two-thirds of the men and women charged more than once with defaming authority also had been or would be accused of other verbal transgressions.

65. I have defined speech against authority to mean words directed against individuals explicitly because of their high rank, whether as fathers or masters (by children and servants), or as ministers, magistrates, or local officials. This definition echoes English laws against *scandalum magnatum*. See John Lassiter, "Defamation of Peers: The Rise and Decline of the Action for *Scandalum Magnatum*, 1497–1773," *American Journal of Legal History* 22:3 (July 1978): 216–36; Bradley Chapin, *Criminal Justice in Colonial America, 1606–1660* (Athens: University of Georgia Press, 1983), esp. 134; and Haskins, *Law and Authority in Early Massachusetts*, 183. It is a much broader definition than that used in a recent study by Larry D. Eldridge, who considers sedition, narrowly conceived, in *A Distant Heritage: The Growth of Free Speech in Early America* (New York: New York University Press, 1994), esp. 10–14.

66. Although civil suits for slander or defamation have attracted more attention from scholars, criminal speech offenses predominated during the seventeenth century. In Essex County, Massachusetts, ca. 1636–1686, presentments for speech crimes (N = 651) outnumbered civil suits for verbal offenses (N = 385) by nearly two to one; see appendix, table A.1 in this book. On civil slander, see Cornelia Hughes Dayton, *Women before the Bar: Gender, Law, and Society in Connecticut, 1639–1789* (Chapel Hill: University of North Carolina Press, 1995), 285–328; Mary Beth Norton, "Gender and Defamation in Seventeenth-Century Maryland," *William and Mary Quarterly* (hereafter WMQ) 3rd ser., 44:1 (January 1987): 3–39; Norton, *Founding Mothers and Fathers*, 203–77; and Robert B. St.

George, " 'Heated' Speech and Literacy in Seventeenth-Century New England," in David D. Hall and David Grayson Allen, eds., *Seventeenth-Century New England* (Boston: Colonial Society of Massachusetts, 1984), 275–322.

67. The particular importance of this issue during the first years of English settlement is explored in chapter 2. On the link between public speech and Puritan conceptions of masculinity, see Jane Kamensky, "Talk Like a Man: Speech, Power, and Masculinity in Early New England," *Gender and History* 8:1 (April 1996): 22–47.

68. Female transgressors accounted for under 15 percent of those presented for speech against authority, and the predominance of men became even more pronounced in the higher courts, particularly when Quaker offenders are omitted. In contrast, in civil suits for slander and defamation, women comprised over 30 percent of the speaking "players"—plaintiffs and defendants, or offenders and targets; see appendix, table A.1 in this book. Compare with Cornelia Dayton's findings for New Haven Colony; *Women before the Bar*, 289, table 16.

69. For a sample (by no means exhaustive) of condemners of authority bearing honorific titles or holding public office, see, in *ECR*, presentments of Mr. Henry Walton (1: 59), Mrs. Samuel Hall (1: 88), Mrs. Holgrave (1: 275), Mr. Edward Woodman (4: 122–24, 350–67), Mrs. Eleanor Hollingworth (4: 269–70), Mr. Samuel Phillips (6: 267–69); in *Assts. Recs.*, presentments of Mr. Isaac Waldron (1: 88), Capt. Thomas Brattle (1: 103), Mr. William Pope (1: 104–5), Mr. Samuel Shrimpton (1: 299), [Dr.] Henry Greenland (3: 217); in *Mass. Recs.*, presentments of Capt. John Stone (1: 108), Mr. John Green (1: 200, 203), Sgt. Edward Hutchinson (1: 207), Mr. Ambros Martin (1: 252), Mr. Henry Sewall (1: 286), Deputy Bozoone Allen (3: 206–7), Mr. Richard Leader (3: 227–28), Mr. William Aubrey (4.1: 238), Lt. Robert Pike (4.1: 156–57), Sgt. William Cotton (4.2: 61), Capt. Thomas Breden (4.2: 69, 75), Maj. William Hathorne (4.2: 149), Capt. George Corwin (5: 90).

70. Mary Beth Norton finds a similar pattern in the Chesapeake; see "Gender, Crime, and Community in Seventeenth-Century Maryland," in James A. Henretta, Michael A. Kammen, and Stanley N. Katz, eds., *The Transformation of Early American History: Society, Authority, and Ideology* (New York: Alfred A. Knopf, 1991), 136. Eli Faber constructs a similar gender/status profile for condemners of high authority in Middlesex County, Massachusetts; see "Puritan Criminals: The Economic, Social, and Intellectual Background to Crime in Seventeenth-Century Massachusetts," *Perspectives in American History* 11 (1977–1978): esp. 120–22.

71. Presentment of Capt. George Corwin, 1676, *Mass. Recs.*, 5: 90. For variations in the level of contempt prosecutions by decade, see appendix, figures A.1 and A.3 in this book. A similar phenomenon obtained in England, where prosecutions for *scandalum magnatum* greatly accelerated in periods during which the peerage felt threatened; see Lassiter, "Defamation of Peers," 220–24, 233–35.

72. The function of insults as an "inverse definition" of moral goodness is discussed in Peter N. Moogk, " 'Thieving Buggers' and 'Stupid Sluts': Insults and Popular Culture in New France," *WMQ* 3rd ser., 36:4 (October 1979): 525–47, quotation from 526; see also Mary Beth Norton, "Gender and Defamation," 7. The notion that insulting speech operates under its own culturally defined syntax and vocabulary was one of the pioneering insights in the field of discourse analysis; see, e.g., William Labov, "Rules for Ritual Insults," in David Sudnow, ed., *Studies in Social Interaction* (New York: Free Press, 1972), 120–68.

73. The metaphoric use of "blot" and "blemish" in connection with reputa-

tion appears frequently in the records. See, e.g., presentments of Bozoone Allen, 1650, *Mass. Recs.*, 4.1: 25–26; Richard Stackhouse, Salem, 1659, ECR, 2: 166; and Rev. Thomas Gilbert, Ipswich, 1671, ECR, 4: 367–70.

74. Presentment of Joseph Medcalfe, Richard Swan, and William Acey, Ipswich, 1660, ECR, 2: 198. The prevalence of attacks against the ability of leading men to fulfill their offices is, in part, a matter of legal definition; English common-law constructions of "actionable" words focused heavily on such insults. See John March, *Actions for Slaunder, Or, a Methodicall Collection Under Certain Grounds and Heads, of What Words Are Actionable in the Law, and What Not?* (London, 1647). Yet colonial practice adhered only loosely to English standards of actionability. See Mary Beth Norton, "Gender and Defamation," 7–8; Dayton, *Women before the Bar*, 288 n. 5, 301. On the gendered nature of the notion of competence, see St. George, " 'Heated' Speech," 295–99.

75. Presentment of Thomas Wells, Robert Cross Sr., Stephen Cross, and Benjamin Marshall, Ipswich, 1668, ECR, 4: 78. See also presentments of John Goit, Salem, 1641, ECR, 1: 35; Joseph Armitage, Salem, 1651, ECR, 1: 244; Thomas Bishop, Ipswich, 1667, ECR, 3: 412; and Capt. George Corwin, 1676, *Mass. Recs.*, 5: 90.

76. A whole subgenre of words against the court concerned pronouncements about the validity of the statutes and charter of the colony. See, e.g., presentments of Thomas Starr, 1638, *Mass. Recs.*, 1: 220; John Hoare, 1669, *Assts. Recs.*, 3: 195–96; and Lt. Robert Pike, 1653, *Mass. Recs.*, 4.1: 156–57.

77. Attributed to Norris by Eleanor Trusler in her presentment, Salem, 1644, ECR, 1: 68; presentment of Thomas Wells et al., Salem, 1668, ECR, 4: 76–82. See also presentments of Thomas Fox, 1631, *Mass. Recs.*, 1: 84; Thomas Dexter, 1633, *Mass. Recs.*, 1: 103; John Leigh, 1634, *Mass. Recs.*, 1: 132–33; Edmund Barrington, Salem, 1649, ECR, 1: 171–72; John Webster, Ipswich, 1668, *Essex File Papers*, 13: 49-4; and Capt. Thomas Brattle, 1677, *Assts. Recs.*, 1: 103.

78. Presentment of Leonard Buttles, 1652, *Mass. Recs.*, 4.1: 97–98.

79. Presentment of Mr. Ambros Martin, 1639, *Mass. Recs.*, 1: 252; presentment of Francis Hutchinson, 1641, *Mass. Recs.*, 1: 336, 340.

80. Presentment of John Leigh, Ipswich, 1660, *Essex File Papers*, 5: 83-5, and ECR, 2: 199–202. See also presentments of William Browne, Ipswich, 1657, ECR, 2: 36–38, and *Essex File Papers*, 3: 108-113; Sarah Barnes, Ipswich, 1656, *Essex File Papers*, 3: 45-3; and Henry Kenney, Salem, 1679, ECR, 7: 248–49.

81. Presentment of Mrs. Holgrave, Salem, 1652, ECR, 1: 275 (see also 254, 261–62, 287); presentment of Andrew Moss, Salem, 1665, ECR, 3: 269–70.

82. Presentment of Mr. Henry Walton, Salem, 1643, ECR, 1: 59. The passing decades apparently failed to improve Cobbett's oratory, for, nearly forty years later, Elizabeth Perkins concurred that he was more beast than man: "more fitt to be in a houg sty then in a pulpit"; see presentment of Elizabeth Perkins, Ipswich, 1681, *Essex File Papers*, 35: 66-1, and ECR, 8: 89–91.

83. Presentment of Joseph Gatchell, Salem, 1680, ECR, 7: 407.

84. On animal insults more broadly, see St. George, " 'Heated' Speech," 294; and Edmund Leach, "Anthropological Aspects of Language: Animal Categories and Verbal Abuse," in Eric H. Lenneberg, ed., *New Directions in the Study of Language* (Cambridge: MIT Press, 1964), 23–63. For other examples from the Essex County records, see presentments of George Harding, Salem, 1649, ECR, 1: 170; Evan Morris, Ipswich, 1656, ECR, 2: 3; John Allen, Salem, 1681, ECR, 8: 128–29; and Robert Swan, Ipswich, 1686, ECR, 9: 601–4.

85. *Mass. Recs.*, 4.2: 196.

86. *Salem Town Records*, quoted in Phillips, *Salem in the Seventeenth Century*, 194; see also 219.

87. Petition of John Porter Jr., Salem, November 1661, *ECR*, 2: 337.

88. The incident is described in George Bishop, *New England Judged by the Spirit of the Lord* (1660; reprinted London, 1703), 45–46; see also Perley, *History of Salem*, 2: 244–45. The story of the Quakers' arrival in New England has been told many times, recently (and well) in Pestana, *Quakers and Baptists*, chapter 1.

89. Thomas Harris quoted in Humphrey Norton, *New-England's Ensigne: It Being the Account of Cruelty, the Professors Pride, and the Articles of their Faith* (London, 1659), 73. Similar scenes played out across New England in the late 1650s; see, e.g., Norton's description of the silencing of Sarah Gibbins and Dorothy Waugh (69–70).

90. Bishop, *New England Judged*, 46.

91. Wilson, *Watch-Word Unto Christians*, 2. On what Carla Pestana calls the "violent rhetorical style" of the Quakers, see her "The Quaker Executions as Myth and History," *Journal of American History* 80:2 (September 1993): 446–47, 450; Richard Bauman, "Speaking in the Light: The Role of the Quaker Minister," in Bauman and Joel Sherzer, eds., *Explorations in the Ethnography of Speaking* (Cambridge: Cambridge University Press, 1974), 144–60; Bauman, *Let Your Words Be Few: Symbolism of Speaking and Silence among Seventeenth-Century Quakers* (New York: Cambridge University Press, 1983), 65–75; and Phyllis Mack, *Visionary Women: Ecstatic Prophecy in Seventeenth-Century England* (Berkeley: University of California Press, 1992). On the place of Quakerism within the broad spectrum of English religious radicalism see Christopher Hill, *The World Turned Upside Down: Radical Ideas during the English Revolution* (New York: Viking Press, 1972), chapters 5–7. Stephen Foster, in *Long Argument*, chapter 5, outlines the complex links between English sectarian activity and New England politics in the 1650s and 1660s.

92. Bauman, *Let Your Words Be Few*, 9–10, 20–25.

93. The extent to which ordinary New Englanders agreed with the anti-Quaker stance of their leaders has been a matter of debate among historians. Jonathan Chu argues that common men and women generally tolerated Quakers, especially those who were native to Massachusetts; see his *Neighbors, Friends, or Madmen: The Puritan Adjustment to Quakerism in Seventeenth-Century Massachusetts* (Westport, Conn.: Greenwood Press, 1985). Carla Pestana marshals convincing evidence that such claims for neighbors' tolerance are overstated; see *Quakers and Baptists*, esp. 32, 124.

94. Bauman, *Let Your Words Be Few*, esp. 25–26.

95. Francis Howgill, *The Heart of New-England Hardened through Wickednes[s]* (London, 1659), 10, 17. For echoes of this contest between Scripture as voice and Scripture as text in Puritan critiques of Anglican practice, see chapter 1 in this book. On the tension between the "dead letter" and the "living voice" in Christian thought more broadly, see Sandra Marie Gustafson, "Performing the Word: American Oratory, 1630–1860" (Ph.D. dissertation, University of California at Berkeley, 1993), 20–23.

96. John Norton, *The Heart of New England Rent at the Blasphemies of the Present Generation* (Cambridge, 1659), 8; see also 5–9. The Massachusetts General Court commissioned Norton's pamphlet as the colony's official response to Quakerism; see *Mass. Recs.*, 4.1: 348, 381, 397.

97. Francis Higginson, *A Brief Relation of the Irreligion of the Northern Quakers* (London, 1653), in Hugh Barbour and Arthur O. Roberts, eds., *Early Quaker Writings, 1650–1700* (Grand Rapids, Mich.: William B. Eerdmans, 1973), 67, 75.

98. Humphrey Norton, *New-England's Ensigne*, 55, 101, 87, 89. For Puritan reactions to the Quaker denial of magisterial and ministerial authority, see, e.g., John Norton, *Heart of New England Rent*, 33–44; Wilson, *Watch-Word Unto Christians*, 4–5.

99. Benjamin Furly, *The World's Honour Detected, and, for the Unprofitableness Thereof, Rejected* (London, 1663), 57, 58. On the anti-intellectual strain within Quaker critiques of the established ministry, see also Bauman, *Let Your Words Be Few*, chapter 3.

100. Howgill, *Heart of New-England Hardened*, 30. New England–born Quaker converts used similar language; see the presentment of Zacheus Gould, who denounced Massachusetts preachers as "a Company of hirelings who . . . fre[e] not their mouthes" (Ipswich, 1659, ECR, 2: 152, and *Essex File Papers*, 5: 3-2 through 3-6), and presentment of Arthur Smith, who claimed that "he whom you call your minister or teacher knoweth no more . . . then this child" (New Haven, 1659, NHCR, 2: 291).

101. On the symbolic meaning of the Quakers' rejection of honorific speech and gestures, see Bauman, *Let Your Words Be Few*, 45–62.

102. Higginson, *Irreligion of the Northern Quakers*, 70. The Quakers' tolerance for public, female speech was a particular sticking point with their opponents. See Margaret Fell, *Women's Speaking Justified, Proved and Allowed of by the Scriptures* (London, 1667); Pestana, *Quakers and Baptists*, 26, 71–72; Mack, *Visionary Women*; and Mary Maples Dunn, "Saints and Sisters: Congregational and Quaker Women in the Early Colonial Period," *American Quarterly* 30:1 (winter 1978): 595–601.

103. Humphrey Norton, *New-England's Ensigne*, 59–60.

104. Humphrey Norton, *New-England's Ensigne*, 118. For uses of "publish" to mean uttered, see also presentments of Edward Lumas, Ipswich, 1672, *Essex File Papers*, 18: 91-1, sheet 3, and ECR, 5: 38–39; Ruben Guppy, Salem, 1674, ECR, 5: 355–56; and Henry Kenney, Salem, 1679, ECR, 7: 248–49. Some perpetrators of written libels were subsequently accused of further "publishing" or "reporting" their sentiments verbally. See presentments of Simon Stacey, Jonathan Lomas, and Nathaniel Warner, Ipswich, 1671, ECR, 4: 341–43; John Webster, Ipswich, 1670, ECR, 4: 232–34; and John Stowers, 1643, *Assts. Recs.*, 2: 121.

105. Quakers accused of misspeaking in "open court" include William Leddra, 1661, *Assts. Recs.*, 3: 94; Phillip Verrin, Ipswich, 1663, ECR, 3: 95, 111; and Edward Wharton, Salem, 1668, ECR, 4: 41. For those who disrupted Puritan services, see (in addition to incidents described in polemical writings) presentment of Zacheus Gould, Ipswich, 1659, ECR, 2: 152, *Essex File Papers*, 5: 3-2 through 3-6. For non-Quakers who chose similarly public spaces for their remarks, see presentments of John Tillison, Ipswich, 1650, *Essex File Papers*, 1: 117-1; Richard Hutton, Daniel Kelham, and James Bettis, Salem, 1669, ECR, 4: 97; Ezekiel Woodward, Ipswich, 1667, ECR, 3: 412; Robert Dutch, Ipswich, 1653, ECR, 1: 306; and Anabaptists Thomas Gold, William Turner, and John Farnham Sr., 1668, *Mass. Recs.*, 4.2: 373–75.

106. Presentment of John Burton, Salem, 1661, ECR, 2: 337; presentment of Eliakim Wardell, Hampton, 1663, ECR, 3: 100. See also presentments of Samuel Shattock, Salem, 1663, ECR, 3: 110; William Robinson, 1659, *Assts. Recs.*, 3:

68–70; and Anthony Emory, 1659, *Mass. Recs.*, 4.1: 407. Note the similarity to depictions of the Antinomians; see John Winthrop, "A Short Story of the Rise, Reign, and Ruine of the Antinomians, Familists & Libertines" (1644), in David D. Hall, ed., *The Antinomian Controversy, 1636–1638: A Documentary History* (1968; reprinted Durham, N.C.: Duke University Press, 1990), 209–10.

107. See, e.g., the October 1658 "Law Against the Quakers," *Mass. Recs.*, 4.1: 347; presentments of Alice Cowland and nine others, 1659, *Mass. Recs.*, 4.1: 410–11; William Leddra, 1661, *Assts. Recs.*, 3: 94; John Kitchen, Salem, 1662, *ECR*, 3: 17; and Phillip Verrin, Ipswich, 1663, *ECR*, 3: 95, 111.

108. See presentments of John Burton, Salem, 1661, *ECR*, 2: 337; Edward Wharton, Salem, 1668, *ECR*, 4: 41; and William Robinson, Marmaduke Stephenson, and Mary Dyer, 1659, *Mass. Recs.*, 4.1: 386, 387.

109. Presentment of Zacheus Gould, Ipswich, 1659, *ECR*, 2: 152.

110. Presentment of Arthur Smith, New Haven, 1659, *NHCR*, 2: 291. Francis Higginson also commented upon Quakers' "severe" expressions and fixed stares; see *Irreligion of the Northern Quakers*, 71.

111. Presentment of the wife of Robert Wilson (Deborah Buffum), Salem, 1662, *ECR*, 3: 17; presentment of Lydia Wardell, Ipswich, 1663, *ECR*, 3: 64. For a man accused of a similar transgression of public order, see presentment of Alexander Coleman, Boston, 1678, *Assts. Recs.*, 1: 127. On the symbolic meaning of "going naked for a sign," see Pestana, *Quakers and Baptists*, 39–40; and Bauman, *Let Your Words Be Few*, chapter 6.

112. Howgill, *Heart of New-England Hardened*, 28; presentment of Zacheus Gould, Ipswich, 1659, *ECR*, 2: 152.

113. Presentment of Richard Crab and his wife, New Haven, 1658, *NHCR*, 2: 242, 244. After the executions of four Quakers in 1659 and 1661, accusing the magistrates of shedding innocent blood became a favored gambit. See also presentments of Phillip Verrin, Ipswich, 1663, *ECR*, 3: 95, 111; Nathaniel Hadlock, Salem, 1668, *ECR*, 4: 74–75; Edward Wharton, Salem, 1668, *ECR*, 4: 41; and Eliakim Wardell, Hampton, 1663, *ECR*, 3: 100.

114. Frederick B. Tolles, ed., "A Quaker's Curse—Humphrey Norton to John Endecott, 1658," *Huntington Library Quarterly* 14:4 (August 1951): 420. Carla Pestana points out that the violence of this early Quaker rhetoric is largely obscured by the "quietism" emphasized in their later mythologies; see "Quaker Executions as Myth and History," 446–51.

115. The scene appears in the posthumous writings of Marmaduke Stephenson, *A Call from Death to Life, and Out of the Dark Ways and Worships of the World* (London, 1660), reprinted in Barbour and Roberts, eds., *Early Quaker Writings*, 132, 136; and in Bishop, *New England Judged*, 102–3, 450. Other examples of the mystical-prophetic rhetoric of witnessing Friends appear in the General Court's transcription of "The Examination of Quakers at the Court of Assistants in Boston, March 7, 1659–60," reprinted in Richard P. Hallowell, *The Quaker Invasion of Massachusetts* (Boston: Houghton, Mifflin, 1883), 157–61.

116. Christopher Holder, "Warninge from the Spirit of the Lord to the Governor & Magistrates & People of the Massachusetts Bay (July 1659), in *Assts.*" *Recs.*, 3: 105.

117. Cotton Mather, *Magnalia Christi Americana*, 2: 531. The insult in question, which Mather attributes to "[Samuel] Fisher the Quaker," is worth quoting in full: "Thou fiery fighter and green-headed trumpeter; thou hedge-hog and grinning dog; thou bastard that tumbled out of the mouth of the Babilonish bawd;

thou mole; thou tinker; thou lizzard; thou bell of no metal, but the tone of a kettle; thou wheelbarrow; thou whirlpool; thou whirlegig. O thou firebrand; thou adder and scorpion; thou louse; thou cowdung; thou moon-calf; thou ragged tatterdemallion; thou Judas; thou livest in philosophy and logick which are of the devil." On the incantatory, oral-poetic style of English Quakers, see Bauman, *Let Your Words Be Few*, 76–81.

118. On the tangible power of words in early modern Europe, see Keith Thomas, *Religion and the Decline of Magic* (New York: Charles Scribner, 1971), 61, 436–37, 502–7; and chapter 6 in this book.

119. Legally, the truth of one's utterances was no defense against charges of slander or sedition in seventeenth-century Anglo-America. See Eldridge, *Distant Heritage*, 23, 66; and Lassiter, "Defamation of Peers," 216–17. On the sociolinguistic analysis of cross-cultural talk, see Daniel N. Maltz and Ruth A. Borker, "A Cultural Approach to Male-Female Miscommunication," in John J. Gumperz, ed., *Language and Social Identity* (Cambridge: Cambridge University Press, 1982), 196–216; and Joel Sherzer, "A Diversity of Voices: Men's and Women's Speech in Ethnographic Perspective," in Susan U. Philips, Susan Steele, and Christine Tanz, eds., *Language, Gender, and Sex in Comparative Perspective* (Cambridge: Cambridge University Press, 1987), 95–120.

120. Humphrey Norton, *New-England's Ensigne*, 90.

121. Presentment of William Leddra, Boston, 1661, *Assts. Recs.*, 3: 94, emphasis mine.

122. Presentments of Zacheus Gould, Ipswich, 1659, *ECR*, 2: 152; and John Burton, Salem, 1661, *ECR*, 2: 337.

123. Humphrey Norton, *New-England's Ensigne*, 97. Scott was Anne Hutchinson's sister, a Quaker from Providence, Rhode Island, who journeyed to witness in Massachusetts.

124. *Suffolk Files*, case 608, paper 2.

125. On Quaker prosopography, see Chu, *Neighbors, Friends, or Madmen*, 170–73; and Pestana, *Quakers and Baptists*, 38 n. 50. Because the Quakers were a decentralized group whose religion was illegal throughout much of the seventeenth century, it is difficult to label Massachusetts inhabitants as Quakers with any degree of certainty. Short of outright confession to Quakerism or presentment for "Quaker" crimes (refusing hat honor, e.g.), indicators of Quaker tendencies include presentment for repeated absence from meeting, especially in the company of known Quakers. John Porter's name appears in none of these contexts, nor in the "Records of the Salem, Massachusetts [Quaker] Monthly Meeting" that begin in 1672 (microfilm copy on deposit at the James Duncan Phillips Library of the Peabody-Essex Museum, Salem, Mass.). But on one occasion at least, the younger Porter was willing publicly to side with a group of Salem Quakers against his father. In November 1661, Quaker John Burton brought the elder Porter to court for misappropriating one of Burton's mares. Fifteen men testified in the case, eleven of them for Burton. Only Porter's sons Joseph and Israel, and his servants Morgan Jones and William Shaw affirmed the elder Porter's claim to the horse. John Porter Jr. sided with Burton's witnesses, the great majority of whom were either known Quakers or their servants; Burton v. Porter, Salem, 1661, *ECR*, 2: 320–22, and *Essex File Papers*, 7: 2-2 through 6-2.

126. On the fate of Holder, see Bishop, *New England Judged*, 45, 75–77, 98, 113; and *Mass. Recs.*, 4.1: 391.

127. Higginson, *Irreligion of the Northern Quakers*, 71; see also presentment of Arthur Smith, New Haven, 1659, NHCR, 2: 292.

128. Justification of the capital sentences of Robinson, Stephenson, and Dyer, 1659, *Mass. Recs.*, 4.1: 389.

129. Humphrey Norton made the connection between various punishments enacted against Quakers and the suppression of their writings. He noted that he and other witnesses confined to the Boston jail were deprived of candles so that "we should not see to write, to trouble the magistrates and infect the people," and claimed that the New Haven magistrates branded his "right hand to hinder him from Writing"; *New-England's Ensigne*, 11, 105.

130. "Law Concerning Quakers," 1656, *Mass. Recs.*, 4.1: 278; "Law Concerning Quakers," 1659, *Mass. Recs.*, 4.1: 390; "Law Concerning Quakers," 1658, *Mass. Recs.*, 4.1: 321. Those caught attending Quaker meetings were fined 10 shillings per offense, while those who spoke were fined £5. It is no coincidence that laws regulating public preaching by laypeople were tightened at the same time; see *Mass. Recs.*, 4.1: 328, 372.

131. "Addition to the late lawe against entertayning Quakers," 1657, *Mass. Recs.*, 4.1: 308-9; see also the parallel statutes in New Haven (NHCR, 2: 238-41) and Plymouth (PCR, 11: 68, 100-1, 120-21, 125-26, 205-6). Only male repeat offenders faced the amputation of their ears; female Quakers under the sentence of banishment would be "severely whipt" for their first two returns to the jurisdiction. All third-time offenders, men and women alike, were to suffer tongue boring. Several Quakers lost ears and four were hanged, but only one actually suffered tongue drilling; presentment of Joseph Gatchell, Boston, 1684, *Assts. Recs.*, 1: 253-54.

132. *Mass. Recs.*, 4.1: 451. Cotton Mather connects tongue mutilation and Quaker invective in his description of the fate of Thomas Harris, who was murdered in Long Island and found with "NO TONGUE in his head, nor the least sign thereof." "This was the end of a TONGUE that was to be 'as the pen of a ready writer,' " Mather quipped; see *Magnalia Christi Americana*, 2: 530. The connection between ear cropping and hearing is less direct, but suggestive nonetheless. First officially noted in Massachusetts law as a penalty for theft committed "on the Lord's day" (see William H. Whitmore, ed., *The Colonial Laws of Massachusetts, Reprinted from the Edition of 1660 with the Supplements to 1672, Containing Also the Body of Liberties of 1641* [Boston: Rockwell and Churchill, 1889], 127; and presentment of Thomas West, Salem, 1657, ECR, 2: 48), the punishment's primary aim was lasting, visible disfigurement. And yet, beginning with the punishment of condemner Phillip Ratliffe in 1631 and continuing through the era of the Quakers, a significant number of those sentenced to lose their ears had been convicted of slighting or other speech offenses. See, e.g., presentment of Ratliffe, 1631, *Mass. Recs.*, 1: 88; and presentment of Maurice Brett, 1675, *Assts. Recs.*, 1: 57. In amputating the ears of recidivist Quaker misspeakers Christopher Holder, John Copeland, and John Rous, the Massachusetts court inadvertently followed in the footsteps of anti-Puritan judges in England; the ear cropping of English Puritan pamphleteers is described in William Haller, *The Rise of Puritanism Or, the Way to the New Jerusalem as Set Forth in the Pulpit and Press from Thomas Cartwright to John Lilburne and John Milton, 1570-1643* (New York: Columbia University Press, 1938), esp. 249, 254-56, 278. On tongue boring and ear cropping in other British colonies, see Alice Morse Earle, *Curious Punish-*

ments of Bygone Days (1896; reprinted Rutland, Vt.: Charles E. Tuttle, 1986), 138–49.

133. John Endecott to Charles II, 1660, *Mass. Recs.*, 4.1: 451.

134. Presentment of Joseph Gatchell, Salem, 1683, *Essex File Papers*, 40: 9-1, and *ECR*, 9: 82; presentment of Mary Hammond, Salem, 1682, *Essex File Papers*, 38: 58-2 (see also *ECR*, 8: 367). Gatchell had strong family connections to Salem Quakers and had been fined for condemning the executions of Robinson and Stephenson. See *ECR*, 6: 101, 117; 7: 146–47, 149. In 1684, his "horrid blasphemous speeches" finally cost him his tongue, which the court ordered "drawne forth out of his mouth & peirct through wth a hott Iron"; *Assts. Recs.*, 1: 253–54.

135. Presentment of Thomas Baker, Ipswich, 1678, *Essex File Papers*, 34: 122-2.

136. Presentment of Hannah Downing, Ipswich, 1676, *Essex File Papers*, 26: 32-1, emphasis mine; see also *ECR*, 6: 208, 237–38. Similar language is at issue in the presentment of Mary Grant, Ipswich, 1681, *ECR*, 8: 98, and *Essex File Papers*, 35: 65-4.

137. William Stoughton, *New England's True Interest Not to Lie . . . a Sermon Preached . . . April 29, 1668* (Cambridge, 1670), 20. For works that explicitly connect Quakerism with filial rebellion, see Higginson, *Irreligion of the Northern Quakers*, 77; and Wilson, *Watch-Word Unto Christians*.

138. Joshua Moodey, *An Exhortation to a Condemned Malefactor* (Boston, 1686), 87–90; Increase Mather, *Wicked Man's Portion*, 16–17. Similar language appears in a series of laws passed by the General Court against the "provoking evils" of the 1670s, the majority of which center on speech; see *Mass. Recs.*, 5: 59–64.

139. *Mass. Recs.*, 4.2: 34 (see also 2–4, 19–20, 59, 164–66); John Norton, *Heart of New England Rent*, 52. The colony's capital laws against Quakerism and filial rebellion were repealed on the same day in May 1681; *Mass. Recs.*, 5: 311–13, 321–22, 339.

140. John Endecott to Charles II, 1660, *Mass. Recs.*, 4.1: 450, 452.

141. Presentment of Humphrey Norton, New Haven, 1658, *NHTR*, 1: 342; Humphrey Norton, *New-England's Ensigne*, 50. Though the New Haven records are silent on the details of Norton's being "put to silence," the key-gag is described in numerous other Quaker polemics. See Howgill, *Heart of New-England Hardened*, 28; and Bishop, *New England Judged*, 156, 404.

142. Thomas Adams, "The Taming of the Tongue" (1629), in Joseph Angus, ed., *The Works of Thomas Adams*, 3 vols. (Edinburgh: James Nichol, 1862), 3: 18, 14. Thanks to Robert St. George for helping to "decode" this image.

143. John Cotton, *The Keys of the Kingdom of Heaven* (1644), reprinted in Larzer Ziff, ed., *John Cotton on the Churches of New England* (Cambridge: Harvard University Press, 1968), 114, emphasis original.

Chapter 5

1. Watson v. Webster, Salem, 1681, in Archie N. Frost, comp., *Verbatim Transcript of the File Papers of the Essex County Quarterly Courts, 1636–1692* (hereafter *Essex File Papers*), 75 vols. (typescript on deposit at the James Duncan Phillips Library of the Peabody-Essex Museum, Salem, Mass.; microfilm copy at Sterling

Memorial Library, Yale University), 36: 114-2; presentment of Nathan Webster, Ipswich, 1682, *Essex File Papers*, 37: 101-2, 101-3, emphasis mine. Webster countercharged his neighbors with using the same affronting vocabulary that they had attributed to him. They told him, he testified, that he "had noe more to doe to comannd [them] then the dogg had & they would not obey me nor none of my authourity"; *Essex File Papers*, 37: 103-2. See also George F. Dow, ed., *Records and Files of the Quarterly Courts of Essex County, Massachusetts* (hereafter ECR), 9 vols. (Salem, Mass.: Essex Institute, 1911–1978), 8: 212–16.

2. The origins of the metaphor and other related sayings are discussed in Morris Palmer Tilley, *A Dictionary of Proverbs in England in the Sixteenth and Seventeenth Centuries* (Ann Arbor: University of Michigan Press, 1950), entries S646–S649.

3. Laws to prevent "abuse to the authority of this country by the printing presse" appear in Nathaniel B. Shurtleff, ed., *Records of the Governor and Company of the Massachusetts Bay in New England* (hereafter *Mass. Recs.*), 5 vols. in 6 (1854; reprinted New York: AMS Press, 1968), 4.2: 62, 73, 141; 5: 4. See also statutes permitting the confiscation and destruction of Quaker books in *Mass. Recs.*, 4.1: 278. On the hierarchical character of early New England's print economy, see Richard D. Brown, *Knowledge Is Power: The Diffusion of Information in Early America, 1700–1865* (New York: Oxford University Press, 1989), esp. chapter 1.

4. Perjury was often described as "sayeing and unsayeing": the perjurer or "false swearer" testified to one thing, was believed, and then changed the story or "unsaid" it. See, e.g., presentment of James Sanders, Ipswich, 1665, *ECR*, 3: 279. The charge was leveled against Anne Hutchinson when an exasperated John Winthrop denounced the way "she doth continually say and unsay things"; "The Examination of Mrs. Anne Hutchinson at the Court at Newtown [November 1637]," in David D. Hall, ed., *The Antinomian Controversy, 1636–1638: A Documentary History* (hereafter AC) (1968; reprinted Durham, N.C.: Duke University Press, 1990), 347.

5. In civil speech cases in which the defendant received a known punishment, over half of all defendants made either a voluntary or compulsory public apology. See appendix, table A.3, in this book for detail.

6. Apology was a remedy in roughly one in five criminal speech cases (presentments for swearing, railing, cursing, lying, blaspheming, etc.) for which the punishment assigned is known. For defaming authority, the category of criminal speech offense that most closely resembles civil slander, apology was mandated nearly twice as often: in some two-fifths of known outcomes in the Essex County courts, and in nearly one-third of known outcomes in the higher courts. See appendix, tables A.4 and A.5, for detail.

7. Of a recorded total of 110 public acknowledgments demanded by the court or by civil plaintiffs in Essex County, 104 were for speech offenses, mostly slander or defaming authority. The crimes answered by the remaining 6 were breach of promise, libel, assault (3 cases), and theft. Of 28 compulsory public acknowledgments that appear in the records of the Court of Assistants and the General Court, 26 represented compensation for speech crimes, and 1 answered a written libel; the occasion of the remaining apology is unknown. Of course, confessing wrongdoing, publicly or not, was not always linked to speech crimes in Puritan culture; court records and especially the records of church disciplinary proceed-

ings instance numerous voluntary confessions for a variety of wrongs. But the correlation between formalized, court-ordered public acknowledgment and verbal failings remains unmistakable.

8. Presentment of Nicholas Upshall, 1656, *Mass. Recs.*, 3: 417–18. For others accused of expressing Quaker opinions whose apologies mitigated their punishments, see presentments of Thomas Brackett, Boston, 1659, *Mass. Recs.*, 4.1: 369; Nathaniel Hadlock, Salem, 1668, *ECR*, 4: 74–75, and *Essex File Papers*, 13: 121-2; and Joseph Gatchell, Salem, 1680, *ECR*, 7: 406–8, and *Essex File Papers*, 33: 91-1. For a case in which blasphemy, a capital offense, was remedied by apology, see presentment of Benjamin Sawser, Boston, 1654, in John Noble and John F. Cronin, eds., *Records of the Court of Assistants of the Colony of the Massachusetts Bay, 1630–1692* (hereafter *Assts. Recs.*), 3 vols. (Boston: Rockwell and Churchill, 1901–1928), 3: 34–38.

9. Presentment of Mr. Richard Leader, Boston, 1651, *Mass. Recs.*, 3: 227–28 or 4.1: 45–46. For apology-fine equivalents of £20 and more, see, e.g., presentments of John Gwin, Boston, 1643, *Mass. Recs.*, 2: 36; William Cotton, Boston, 1664, *Mass. Recs.*, 4.2: 105, 107; Nathaniel Putnam, Salem, 1669, *ECR*, 4: 92–93; Stephen Haskett, Boston, 1675, *Mass. Recs.*, 5: 68, 69; Mr. Issac Waldron, Boston, 1677, *Assts. Recs.*, 1: 88–90; Peter Golding, Boston, 1681, *Mass. Recs.*, 5: 330, 359. Similar values appear in some civil slander cases. See Mansfield v. Hathorne, appealed in Boston, 1663, *Assts. Recs.*, 3: 137; and Wells v. Mentor, Ipswich, 1673, *ECR*, 5: 225, *Essex File Papers*, 20: 80-4.

10. On the power of apology as an informal ritual in modern societies, see Erving Goffman, *Relations in Public: Microstudies of the Public Order* (New York: Basic Books, 1971), 166 and chapter 4; Hiroshi Wagatsuma and Arthur Rosett, "The Implications of Apology: Law and Culture in Japan and the United States," *Law and Society Review* 20:4 (fall 1986): 461–96, esp. 462–63; and Nicholas Tavuchis, *Mea Culpa: A Sociology of Apology and Reconciliation* (Stanford, Calif.: Stanford University Press, 1991), 1–44.

11. See Thomas Tentler, *Sin and Confession on the Eve of the Reformation* (Princeton, N.J.: Princeton University Press, 1977), chapters 1–3, esp. 12–13; Geoffrey Koziol, *Begging Pardon and Favor: Ritual and Political Order in Early Medieval France* (Ithaca, N.Y.: Cornell University Press, 1992), chapter 6, esp. 182, 185; and Mary C. Mansfield, *The Humiliation of Sinners: Public Penance in Thirteenth-Century France* (Ithaca, N.Y.: Cornell University Press, 1995), chapters 2 and 3. John Bossy contends that the introduction of the confessional box during the Reformation transformed confession into a private act; see Bossy, "The Social History of Confession in the Age of the Reformation," *Transactions of the Royal Historical Society*, ser. 5, vol. 25 (1975), 29–30. But Mansfield argues that the shift toward privacy in penance has been greatly exaggerated by medieval and early modern historians; see *Humiliation of Sinners*, 78–88, 286, 289.

12. Mansfield, *Humiliation of Sinners*, 293–98; Bossy, "Social History of Confession," 26.

13. On ritualized public confession in churches throughout England and the British colonies, see Alice Morse Earle, *Curious Punishments of Bygone Days* (1896; reprinted Rutland, Vt.: Charles E. Tuttle, 1986), 108–12.

14. David D. Hall, *Worlds of Wonder, Days of Judgment: Popular Religious Belief in Early New England* (New York: Alfred A. Knopf, 1989), 166–67 and chapter 4.

15. On the requirement that all church members experience (and profess) conversion, a condition of membership unique to New England Puritanism, see

Edmund S. Morgan, *Visible Saints: The History of a Puritan Idea* (Ithaca, N.Y.: Cornell University Press, 1965), chapter 3; and David H. Flaherty, *Privacy in Colonial New England* (Charlottesville: University Press of Virginia, 1972), 139–40. From about 1640, and sometimes before, most New England clergy argued that women's conversion relations should be delivered privately—either in writing or to a small cohort of church elders—and then repeated for the congregation by a male church officer. See Robert G. Pope, ed., *The Notebook of the Reverend John Fiske, 1644–1675* (Salem, Mass.: Essex Institute, 1974), 4, 24, and esp. 106–7; and the discussion in chapter 3 in this book.

16. On the role of open confession in church disciplinary proceedings, and especially on the distinction between public and private sins, see Flaherty, *Privacy in Colonial New England*, 152–59; Emil Oberholzer Jr., *Delinquent Saints: Disciplinary Action in the Early Congregational Churches of Massachusetts* (New York: Columbia University Press, 1956), 30–38; and *Notebook of the Reverend John Fiske*, xvi, xxxii–xxxiv, 32, 42, 56–57. The link between public sins and public confession predated New England; see Mansfield, *Humiliation of Sinners*, 22. On speech crimes as emblematic sins against the commonweal in eighteenth-century evangelical congregations, see Susan Juster, *Disorderly Women: Sexual Politics and Evangelicalism in Revolutionary New England* (Ithaca, N.Y.: Cornell University Press, 1994), 76, 88–96.

17. Bradley Chapin, *Criminal Justice in Colonial America, 1606–1660* (Athens: University of Georgia Press, 1983), 92. On the "inquisitorial" nature of justice in early New England, see John M. Murrin, "Magistrates, Sinners, and a Precarious Liberty: Trial by Jury in Seventeenth-Century New England," in David D. Hall, John M. Murrin, and Thad W. Tate, eds., *Saints and Revolutionaries: Essays on Early American History* (New York: W. W. Norton, 1984), esp. 164, 176; Gail Sussman Marcus, " 'Due Execution of the Generall Rules of Righteousnesse': Criminal Procedure in New Haven Town and Colony, 1638–1658," in Hall et al., eds., *Saints and Revolutionaries*, 99–137; and Cornelia Hughes Dayton, *Women before the Bar: Gender, Law, and Society in Connecticut, 1639–1789* (Chapel Hill: University of North Carolina Press, 1995), 28–34.

18. On punishment (especially execution) as a form of theater exhibiting the power of the state, see Douglas Hay et al., eds., *Albion's Fatal Tree: Crime and Society in Eighteenth-Century England* (New York: Pantheon Books, 1975), 17–62; Michel Foucault, *Discipline and Punish: The Birth of the Prison*, trans. Alan Sheridan (New York: Pantheon Books, 1977); Thomas W. Laqueur, "Crowds, Carnival and the State in English Executions, 1604–1868," in A. L. Beier, David Cannadine, and James M. Rosenheim, eds., *The First Modern Society: Essays in English History in Honour of Lawrence Stone* (Cambridge: Cambridge University Press, 1989), 305–55; and J. A. Sharpe, " 'Last Dying Speeches': Religion, Ideology, and Public Execution in Seventeenth-Century England," *Past and Present* 107 (May 1985): 144–67.

19. See, e.g., J. M. Beattie, *Crime and the Courts in England, 1660–1800* (Princeton, N.J.: Princeton University Press, 1986), 464–65.

20. On England, see R. H. Helmholz, ed., *Select Cases of Defamation to 1600* (London: Selden Society, 1985), xxiii; see also, xxxiii, xxxix–xl. Helena M. Wall finds a "pattern of enforced acknowledgment" in response to speech crimes in the records of New Netherland, Virginia, New Jersey, New Haven, Maine, and Delaware as well as Massachusetts. See Wall, *Fierce Communion: Family and Community in Early America* (Cambridge: Harvard University Press, 1990), 44–47, 189

n. 84; and David Thomas Konig, *Law and Society in Puritan Massachusetts: Essex County, 1629–1692* (Chapel Hill: University of North Carolina Press, 1979), 124.

21. Koziol, *Begging Pardon and Favor*, 202; Foucault, *Discipline and Punish*, 45.

22. On Porter, who was treated as a fictive dependent long after he had ceased to be a legal minor, see chapter 4.

23. For an exception, see presentment of James Sanders, Ipswich, 1665, ECR, 3: 279.

24. Richard D. Pierce, ed., *Records of the First Church of Boston, 1630–1868* (hereafter *First Church Records*), Colonial Society of Massachusetts Publications, vol. 39 (Boston: Colonial Society of Massachusetts, 1961), 53; the word "open(ly)," "free," or "public" appears in virtually every record of an acknowledgment. Other acknowledgments by men (a total of twenty-seven men apologized ca. 1632–1692—four of them twice, and one, three times) appear on 20, 27–30, 33–34, 39, 41–44, 46, 49, 54, 58–62, 64–66, 69. For women's apologies, see 28, 38–39, and 58.

Only seven of the total of thirty-six apologies recorded by the First Church covered "sins of the tongue." A similar pattern obtained in Wenham's church; for confessions by women (nearly all for speech crimes), see *Notebook of the Reverend John Fiske*, 34–35, 40–42, 119–20, 207. That the link between speech crime and speech punishment is weaker in church records than in the Massachusetts courts can be explained by the fact that congregations experienced a vastly circumscribed range of choices in assigning punishments to their members: speech (in the form of acknowledgment) and silence (in the form of excommunication) were the only sanctions that fell under the purview of church discipline.

25. Examples of female members of Boston's First Church (Hutchinson and Hibbens among them) who refused to bend their spirits and apologize before the congregation appear in *First Church Records*, 21–22, 25, 32–33, 49, 53–54, 55–56, 57, 59, 61, 62, 70, 71. Ten of these thirteen were charged with speech offenses, from "irregular prophesying," to defending Anne Hutchinson, to refusing "to heare the church," to lying, to giving "bad Language to her husband."

26. *First Church Records*, 36, 37–39, 53–54. Anne Hibbens evinced similarly improbable scruples about speaking publicly during her disciplinary hearings; see Robert Keayne, "Note-book of John Cotton's Sermons, 1639–1642," manuscript on deposit at the Massachusetts Historical Society, Boston, 163r–v.

27. The laconic records of seventeenth-century congregations tend to obscure women's roles as voting members of church polities. Women virtually never figure among those who questioned repentant sinners about the nature of their regret. But were women included in ranks of those who—under the corporate label of "the church"—"voted" a given acknowledgment "satisfactory"? Did they number among those who gave the "Joynt Consent of the Congregation," either by their voices or "by their silence"? The record remains mute. See, e.g., *Notebook of the Reverend John Fiske*, 45, 47; *First Church Records*, 22, 26. Robert Keayne, "Note-book of John Cotton's Sermons, 1643–1646," manuscript on deposit at the Massachusetts Historical Society, Boston, includes several references to women's queries in disciplinary proceedings being voiced by male elders: "Hear is . . . a sister that desiers" to know such and such (30v).

28. Men predominated in compulsory acknowledgments in Essex County and the colony's high courts to roughly the same extent as they did in the crime of defaming authority: roughly nine of every ten offenders forced to apologize pub-

licly were male; see appendix, table A.6. On the complex links between public speech and masculinity in Puritan culture, see Jane Kamensky, "Talk Like a Man: Speech, Power, and Masculinity in Early New England," *Gender and History* 8:1 (April 1996): 22–47. On face-to-face insults as gendered (masculine) crimes, see also Dayton, *Women before the Bar*, 295–97.

29. For the argument that early modern women were more likely than men to see themselves as sinful, and to testify to that sinfulness in voluntary statements of repentance, see Natalie Zemon Davis, *Fiction in the Archives: Pardon Tales and Their Tellers in Sixteenth-Century France* (Stanford, Calif: Stanford University Press, 1987), 85, 103; Dayton, *Women before the Bar*, 197–99; and Elizabeth Reis, *Damned Women: Sinners and Witches in Puritan New England* (Ithaca, N.Y.: Cornell University Press, 1997), chapters 1 and 4. On the trope of women's statements of submission in period theater, see Lynda E. Boose, "Scolding Brides and Bridling Scolds: Taming the Woman's Unruly Member," *Shakespeare Quarterly* 42:2 (summer 1991): 179–213, esp. 180; and Frances E. Dolan, " 'Gentlemen, I Have One Thing More to Say': Women on Scaffolds in England, 1563–1680," *Modern Philology* 92:2 (November 1994): 157–78.

30. Presentment of Hannah Diven, Salem, 1681, *Essex File Papers*, 36: 9-2, and *ECR*, 8: 144–45. See also presentments of William and Joanna Smith, Ipswich, 1682, *ECR*, 8: 298; Mary Ready, Ipswich, 1682, *ECR*, 8: 299; and Elizabeth Gould, Ipswich, 1682, *Essex File Papers*, 37: 113-3. Of 122 voluntary (and largely nonpublic) confessions to the Essex County courts, the General Court, and the Court of Assistants ca. 1630–1692, female offenders offered 55; see appendix, table A.6.

31. Presentment of Elizabeth Perkins, Ipswich, 1681, *ECR*, 8: 89, emphasis mine; see also presentment of Elizabeth Due, Salem, 1654, *ECR*, 1: 361–62, 380. Such punishments represented a gloss on the traditional brank or bridle used to stifle English scolds. See Boose, "Scolding Brides and Bridling Scolds"; Earle, *Curious Punishments of Bygone Days*, 96–105; and E. J. Burford and Sandra Shulman, *Of Bridles and Burnings: The Punishment of Women* (New York: St. Martin's Press, 1992), 49–61. The notion that such silent punishments were more ignominious than speaking one's own shame is borne out by the case of Ralph Fogge, who was threatened with having his offense written on a paper unless he acknowledged his misspeaking aloud; see *ECR*, 1: 185–86.

32. Presentment of John Allen, Salem, 1681, *ECR*, 8: 128–29, emphasis mine. Similar formulations begin men's apologies in James v. Glass, Ipswich, 1684, *ECR*, 9: 318–19; and Collins v. Needham, Ipswich, 1684, *ECR*, 9: 330–31.

33. Joshua Moodey, *An Exhortation to a Condemned Malefactor* (Boston, 1686), 73. The sermon continues in words that echo Tenney's: "there is a Plaister as large as the Sore, the Lord in mercy make it stick."

34. James Kendall Hosmer, ed., *Winthrop's Journal, "History of New England" 1630–1649*, 2 vols. (1908; reprinted New York: Barnes and Noble, 1959), 1: 142.

35. Keayne, "Note-book of John Cotton's Sermons, 1639–1642," 215v. "Corsive" and "corsie" were popular seventeenth-century forms of *corrosive*; see OED and Walter W. Skeet, *A Glossary of Tudor and Stuart Words* (Oxford: Clarendon Press, 1914).

36. See, e.g., the case of George Norton, whose acknowledgment the Wenham church accepted some five years after initiating disciplinary proceedings against him (*Notebook of the Reverend John Fiske*, 50–56, 57–89, 92); or the disciplining of Henry Evans, excommunicated from Boston's First Church in 1653 and

readmitted upon "his publick acknowledgment" in 1663 (*First Church Records*, 53, 59); also William Leatherland (or Lytherland), expelled in 1644 and not readmitted until he delivered "his publick acknowledgment" in 1661, "after 16 years" (*First Church Records*, 59). The path of repentance (though not its rhetoric) is analyzed in Charles E. Hambrick-Stowe, *The Practice of Piety: Puritan Devotional Disciplines in Seventeenth-Century New England* (Chapel Hill: University of North Carolina Press, 1982), esp. 80–81; and Charles Lloyd Cohen, *God's Caress: The Psychology of Puritan Religious Experience* (New York: Oxford University Press, 1986), 106–8.

37. The notion that "apology is, first and foremost, a speech act" is explored in Tavuchis, *Mea Culpa*, 22–23, 31–32, 46–47, 120–21. In public apologies, which entail what Tavuchis labels "ventilated speech" (70), the act of expression assumes even greater prominence than it does in interpersonal settings.

38. Winthrop, *Journal*, 2: 29, describing John Baker's church confession for "lying," "violent contentions," and "other evil courses." See also 1: 134, 142; 2: 165–67.

39. Knowlton v. Whittred, Ipswich, 1668, ECR, 4: 54–55; See also presentment of Mr. Edward Woodman, Ipswich, 1669, ECR, 4: 122–24, 143; and the censure of Brother Gere in *Notebook of the Reverend John Fiske*, 47.

40. Presentment of Jeremiah Watts, Ipswich, 1682, ECR, 8: 293–95. See also presentment of Mr. Samuel Shrimpton, Boston, 1684, Assts. Recs., 1: 299; and M. Halsey Thomas, ed., *The Diary of Samuel Sewall, 1674–1729*, 2 vols. (New York: Farrar, Straus and Giroux, 1973), 1: 101–2, 108–9. Slander plaintiffs who failed to accept a private apology for a private insult met with little sympathy. See, e.g., the presentment of Eleanor Jackson, Ipswich, 1660, ECR, 2: 249. Thomas Jones accused Jackson of calling his children "bastard and Tallaffast gnome and Tinckkers trull and Puncke and stue," and refused to accept Jackson's remorse "until shee would go & acknoledg" her wrong in "publicke on the Lords Daie in the meeting house." But because the "Discourses betwenne them" had been confined to "Gooddie Jacksonn on [own] house," many deemed Jones's zeal excessive; *Essex File Papers*, 6: 69-2.

41. Presentments of John Webster, Ipswich, 1668, *Essex File Papers*, 13: 47-2 and ECR, 4: 11–14; Nathaniel Putnam, Salem, 1669, ECR, 4: 92–93; and Edward Lumas, Ipswich, 1672, ECR, 5: 38–39. See also Fulsham v. Fulsham, Salisbury, 1679, ECR, 7: 273.

42. Carter v. Dutton, Boston, 1659, Mass. Recs., 4.1: 407–8. See also presentments of Ruben Guppy, Salem, 1674, ECR, 5: 355–56, 360; William Winter, Salem, 1645, ECR, 1: 92; and Edward Richards, Salem, 1645, ECR, 1: 83.

43. Presentment of Mr. Richard Leader, Boston, 1651, Mass. Recs., 3: 227–28; Tomlins v. Pickering, Salem, 1640, ECR, 1: 22.

44. Presentment of Nathaniel Putnam, Salem, 1669, ECR, 4: 92–93; see also presentment of Henry Kenney, Salem, 1668, ECR, 4: 93.

45. Vinson et al. v. Marshall, Ipswich, 1653, ECR, 1: 301, 325, and *Essex File Papers*, 2: 112-5.

46. Presentment of Nathaniel Putnam, Salem, 1669, ECR, 4: 92–93; Carter v. Dutton, Boston, 1659, Mass. Recs., 4.1: 407–8; presentment of Mr. Richard Leader, Boston, 1651, Mass. Recs., 3: 227–28; also Gerrish v. Woodbridge, Salem, 1676, ECR, 6: 162. Harsh weather could occasion rare delays; see Lee v. Gifford, Salem, 1677, ECR, 6: 368, 418–19. See also Tavuchis, *Mea Culpa*, 87–88.

47. Tentler, *Sin and Confession*, 107, quoting Aquinas, *Summa Theologica*. Such verses—Tentler points out that this one rhymes in Latin—served as mnemonics for unlettered parishioners. Alternatively, medieval confessors structured their recitations around categories such as the seven deadly sins or their activities on saints' days (117–24).

48. The notion that "body glosses" are essential to the "reading" of remedial exchanges is discussed in Goffman, *Relations in Public*, 122–37; see also Jan Bremmer and Herman Roodenburg, eds., *A Cultural History of Gesture* (Ithaca, N.Y.: Cornell University Press, 1992). Historians, particularly those of us who study long-dead actors, have only the slenderest access to this gestural repertoire; written records obviously privilege the verbal over the visual.

49. Winthrop, *Journal*, 2: 12–14; Underhill's earlier, unsuccessful attempts at confession appear on 1: 275–76, 329. See also Hall, *Worlds of Wonder*, 173–74. Manly tears of sorrow appear quite frequently in Winthrop's *Journal*; see, e.g., the apologies of Nathaniel Eaton (1: 310–14), Robert Keayne (1: 316–17), John Baker (2: 29–30), and Steven Batchelor (2: 45).

50. Keayne, "Note-book of John Cotton's Sermons, 1639–1642," 77r, describing Richard Wayte's first apology in April 1640.

51. Winthrop, *Journal*, 2: 13.

52. The exceptions are petitions and so-called free confessions, which, although clearly shaped by stylistic and legal conventions, were composed by offenders. It is also difficult to determine who recited many of these statements: whether offenders read their texts aloud, or had their apologies read for them by a court officer.

53. This line of argument is heavily indebted to Davis, *Fiction in the Archives*, esp. chapters 1 and 2.

54. This facet of an "unsaying" involved what Erving Goffman calls "self-splitting": a display of respect for the rules through an admission of past disregard for those same rules; *Relations in Public*, 113.

55. Presentments of Simon Tuttle, Ipswich, 1664, *ECR*, 3: 141–43; Thomas Miller, Boston, 1636, *Mass. Recs.*, 1: 178; Arthur Mason, Boston, 1671, *Assts. Recs.*, 3: 207; and Benjamin Sawser, Boston, 1654, *Assts. Recs.*, 3: 36.

56. *Notebook of the Reverend John Fiske*, 71. What was called for, in short, was an "account" rather than an "excuse." On the difference, see Goffman, *Relations in Public*, 109–13; and J. L. Austin, "A Plea for Excuses," in J. O. Urmson and G. J. Warnock, eds., *J. L. Austin Philosophical Papers*, 2nd ed. (New York: Oxford University Press, 1970), 175–204.

57. Presentments of George Norton, Salem, 1649, *ECR*, 1: 156; and Joseph Rowlandson, Ipswich, 1651, *Essex File Papers*, 2: 18-3.

58. See presentments of William Horsham, Salem, 1684, *ECR*, 9: 287–88; Benjamin Sawser, Boston, 1654, *Assts. Recs.*, 3: 36; and John Davis, Salem, 1680, *Essex File Papers*, 33: 89-2, and *ECR*, 8: 400, 420.

59. Presentments of Mr. William Snelling, Ipswich, 1652, *Essex File Papers*, 2: 28-2; and Mr. Phillip Nelson, Ipswich, 1686, *ECR*, 9: 595–96, emphasis mine.

60. General Court's order for the acknowledgments to be made by seventy-seven men disarmed as followers of Anne Hutchinson, 1637, *Mass. Recs.*, 1: 212. See also presentments of George Norton, Salem, 1649, *ECR*, 1: 156; Joseph Miles, Salem, 1678, *Essex File Papers*, 29: 61-1, and *ECR*, 6: 227, 7: 68; and Douton v. Neale, Salem, 1685, *ECR*, 9: 472–73.

61. *Notebook of the Reverend John Fiske*, 128.

62. Presentments of Peter Golding, Boston, 1681, *Mass. Recs.*, 5: 359; Joseph Rowlandson, Ipswich, 1651, *Essex File Papers*, 2: 18-3; and Arthur Mason, Boston, 1671, *Assts. Recs.*, 3: 207. See also presentment of John Putney Sr., Ipswich, 1683, *ECR*, 9: 95, 96.

63. Presentment of Thomas Miller, Boston, 1636, *Mass. Recs.*, 1: 178.

64. Presentments of John Porter Jr., Salem, 1661, *Essex File Papers*, 7: 34-1, and *ECR*, 2: 335–38, 346; 3: 111, 117, 227; and Joseph Rowlandson, Ipswich, 1651, *Essex File Papers*, 2: 18-3.

65. *Notebook of the Reverend John Fiske*, 64, 60, 63, 62; see also 40.

66. Robert B. St. George, " 'Heated' Speech and Literacy in Seventeenth-Century New England," in David D. Hall and David Grayson Allen, eds., *Seventeenth-Century New England* (Boston: Colonial Society of Massachusetts, 1984), esp. 293.

67. Presentment of Walter Lewis, Salem, 1672, *Essex File Papers*, 32: 68-3; see also presentment of John Davis, Salem, 1680, *Essex File Papers*, 33: 89-2. Lewis's case is one of very few in the records of early Massachusetts in which English definitions of legally "actionable" words—the imputation of an infectious, and particularly a sexual, disease prominent among them—applied.

68. James v. Glass, Ipswich, 1684, *ECR*, 9: 318–19.

69. Presentment of Hugh Glanfield, Salem, 1678, *Essex File Papers*, 30: 64-4, 65-1. Glanfield had accused Hamons of treachery during her Indian captivity, and some of his allegations were gripping indeed. He had spread the rumor, for example, that "when Mrs Hamans was in Captivitie I was with her and two English Children being sick of ye flux I heard ye sayd Elizabeth Hamans Say unto ye Indians [']why doe you nott knock outt theire Braines[?'] and that ye Indians knockt outt theire Braines & some of theire Braine fell upon My clothes."

70. Presentment of Elizabeth Legg, Salem, 1654, *ECR*, 1: 378; presentment of Robert Swan, Ipswich, 1686, *ECR*, 9: 601–2.

71. Reprinted from *Newton [Massachusetts] Tribune* in *New Yorker*, 5 August 1996, 28. Likewise, NBC's celebrated on-air apology to General Motors in February 1993 for showing "unscientific demonstrations" (fictional re-creations) of crash footage did not replay the inflammatory images; *New York Times*, 12 February 93, A14. Of course, even today, every apology involves a certain degree of reiteration. But if, as Nicholas Tavuchis argues, contemporary sorry-sayers must affirm that, " 'Yes, this is what happened,' " they do so in considerably less detail than their seventeenth-century predecessors; *Mea Culpa*, 57.

72. Presentment of Mr. Edward Woodman, Mr. Richard Dummer, and William Titcomb, Ipswich, 1671, *ECR*, 4: 364; see also 350–67. This aspect of public confession evinced a widely held belief in the power of unmasking sin: the desire "to bring out in the open what was hidden"; see Hall, *Worlds of Wonder*, 173–76.

73. Presentments of John Putney Sr., Ipswich, 1683, *ECR*, 9: 95, 96; and John Hoare, Boston, 1669, *Assts. Recs.*, 3: 195, emphasis mine. See also presentments of Nathaniel Hadlock, Salem, 1668, *ECR*, 4: 74–75; and Simon Tuttle, Ipswich, 1664, *ECR*, 3: 141–43. On images of high and low in the medieval discourse of repentance, see Koziol, *Begging Pardon and Favor*, 45–48.

74. Presentments of William Barber and his wife, Salem, 1674, *ECR*, 5: 376; and John Gamage, Ipswich, 1685, *ECR*, 9: 598.

75. Presentment of Nathaniel Hadlock, Salem, 1668, *ECR*, 4: 74–75; presentment of John Hoare, Boston, 1669, *Assts. Recs.*, 3: 195.

76. Presentment of Simon Tuttle, Ipswich, 1664, *ECR*, 3: 141–43; Browne v. Smith, Salem, 1672, *Essex File Papers*, 19: 6-2.

77. On apology as a ritual that privileges community values over individual rights, see Wagatsuma and Rosett, "Implications of Apology," 464–65. Some early New England petitions can be read as deliberate attempts to disavow "rights talk." Consider, e.g., John Gamage's statement: "I am sorry I should speak of appealing the sentence being soe Just"; *ECR*, 9: 598.

78. Presentment of Nathaniel Hadlock, Salem, 1668, *ECR*, 4: 74–75; petition of Arthur Mason, Boston, 1671, *Assts. Recs.*, 3: 207.

79. Presentment of John Davis, Salem, 1680, *Essex File Papers*, 33: 89-2.

80. Smith v. Goodall, Salem, 1672, *Essex File Papers*, 18: 118-1, emphasis mine, and *ECR*, 5: 52–55. Similar language appears in presentment of Samuel Moses, Ipswich, 1684, *Essex File Papers*, 41: 67-1, and *ECR*, 9: 221.

81. An overview of contemporary debates about the history and efficacy of such punishments is found in John Braithwaite, *Crime, Shame, and Reintegration* (New York: Cambridge University Press, 1989), esp. 4, 9–10, 12, 72–73. On the reintegration of "deviants" as a goal of justice in early New England, see Eli Faber, "Puritan Criminals: The Economic, Social, and Intellectual Background to Crime in Seventeenth-Century Massachusetts," *Perspectives in American History* 11 (1977–1978): 83–144, esp. 137–42; Konig, *Law and Society in Puritan Massachusetts*; Dayton, *Women before the Bar*, chapter 1; and George Lee Haskins, *Law and Authority in Early Massachusetts: A Study in Tradition and Design* (New York: Macmillan, 1960), 210–11.

82. "A Report of the Trial of Mrs. Anne Hutchinson before the Church in Boston [March 1638]," in *AC*, 379. On the dangerous fluidity of public punishment, see Laqueur, "Crowds, Carnival and the State," 319–20; Beattie, *Crime and the Courts*, 466–68; Koziol, *Begging Pardon and Favor*, chapter 9; and Michael Meranze, *Laboratories of Virtue: Punishment, Revolution, and Authority in Philadelphia, 1760–1835* (Chapel Hill: University of North Carolina Press, 1996), 19–48.

83. John Winthrop, "A Short Story of the Rise, Reign, and Ruine of the Antinomians, Familists & Libertines" (1644), in *AC*, 300, 304–6; see also Winthrop, *Journal*, 1: 263–64.

84. Keayne, "Note-book of John Cotton's Sermons, 1639–1642," 161r.

85. *Notebook of the Reverend John Fiske*, 53, 66. By this point, Norton had already offered three failing apologies (59, 61, 63–64).

86. *Notebook of the Reverend John Fiske*, 64, 62; see also 69.

87. Keayne, "Note-book of John Cotton's Sermons, 1639–1642," 208v, 166v.

88. Gilbert v. John and Sarah Gould, Ipswich, 1671, *ECR*, 4: 419–20; see also presentment of Thomas Gilbert, Ipswich, 1670, *ECR*, 4: 244–50.

89. Lampson v. Sandy, Ipswich, 1681, *Essex File Papers*, 35: 28-2, and *ECR*, 8: 75.

90. Presentment of Edmund Bridges and Francis Ussleton, Ipswich, 1660, *ECR*, 2: 245.

91. *Notebook of the Reverend John Fiske*, 72, 81.

92. "Report of the Trial of Mrs. Anne Hutchinson before the Church," 361.

93. *Notebook of the Reverend John Fiske*, 62, 85; see also 76.

94. "Report of the Trial of Mrs. Anne Hutchinson before the Church," 377.

95. Winthrop, "Short Story," 306; "Report of the Trial of Mrs. Anne Hutchinson before the Church," 377 (see also 384–86).

96. Winthrop, *Journal*, 2: 46.

97. *Notebook of the Reverend John Fiske*, 62.

98. Presentment of Joseph Medcalfe, Richard Swan, and William Acey, Ipswich, 1660, *ECR*, 2: 198, 242, emphasis mine. See also presentment of Edmund Farrington, Salem, 1649, *ECR*, 1: 171–72; and Potter v. Ordway, Ipswich, 1684, *ECR*, 9: 188.

99. Presentment of Richard Leader, Boston, 1651, *Mass. Recs.*, 3: 227–28. The record does not indicate whether the magistrates found the apology satisfactory.

100. Presentment of Henry Sewall, Ipswich, 1651, *ECR*, 1: 220.

101. Nothing, that is, beyond the fact that with this joke, Atkinson forfeited his bond of arbitration; Merrick v. Atkinson, Salem, 1682, *ECR*, 8: 419–20. Henry Needham used a similar gambit; Collins v. Needham, Ipswich, 1684, *ECR*, 9: 325–26, 330–31.

102. "Report of the Trial of Mrs. Anne Hutchinson before the Church," 382–83.

103. The notion that moments of festive inversion both reinforce and subtly challenge hierarchies is presented in Natalie Zemon Davis, "Women on Top," in *Society and Culture in Early Modern France* (Stanford, Calif.: Stanford University Press, 1975), 124–51, esp. 142–50.

104. This point is compellingly made by Hiroshi Wagatsuma, who sees the American obsession with the earnestness of an apology as an impediment to the ritual's efficacy in the present-day United States. In Japan, he argues, sincerity is irrelevant to an apology: the affirmation of hierarchy is "sincere" whether or not the speaker's sorrow is. See Wagatsuma and Rosett, "Implications of Apology," esp. 471–73, 492; and Tavuchis, *Mea Culpa*, 71–72, 109, 117.

105. Acknowledgment of William Hathorne, Boston, 1665, *Mass. Recs.*, 4.2: 149. See also presentments of Bozoone Allen, Boston, 1650, *Mass. Recs.*, 3: 206–7 or 4.1: 25–26; and Thomas Wheeler, Salem, 1653, *ECR*, 1: 286–87.

106. Presentment of William Leddra, Boston, 1661, *Assts. Recs.*, 3: 94.

107. William G. McLoughlin and Martha Whiting Davidson, eds., "The Baptist Debate of April 14–15, 1668," in *Proceedings of the Massachusetts Historical Society* 76 (1964), 123; and Carla Gardina Pestana, *Quakers and Baptists in Colonial Massachusetts* (New York: Cambridge University Press, 1991), 52–53.

108. Presentment of Mr. Isaac Waldron, Boston, 1677, *Assts. Recs.*, 1: 90.

109. *Notebook of the Reverend John Fiske*, 86.

110. The fullest treatment of this shift in colonial law and society appears in Dayton, *Women before the Bar*, 284–328. On the declining real numbers of compulsory apologies ca. 1636–1686, see appendix, figures A.2 and A.3, in this book.

111. Harrison first was formally accused of witchcraft in Connecticut in May 1669, and was convicted in October of that year. Her execution was delayed, and she was ordered to depart the colony in May 1670, at which point she took up residence in Westchester, New York. There she was again tried and acquitted of being a witch. On Harrison's history, see Carol F. Karlsen, *The Devil in the Shape of a Woman: Witchcraft in Colonial New England* (New York: W. W. Norton, 1987), 84–89. For excerpts from the records of her trials for witchcraft, see David D. Hall, ed., *Witch-Hunting in Seventeenth-Century New England: A Documentary History, 1638–1692* (Boston: Northeastern University Press, 1991), 170–84; and "The Cases of Hall and Harrison," in George Lincoln Burr, ed., *Narratives of the Witchcraft Cases, 1648–1706* (New York: Charles Scribner, 1914), 44–52.

112. Harrison's confession, dated August 1668, is found in the manuscript collection entitled "Crimes and Misdemeanors, 1662–1789," ser. 1, pt. 1, doc. 35, on deposit at the Connecticut State Archives, in the Connecticut State Library, Hartford.

Chapter 6

1. Cotton Mather, *Ornaments for the Daughters of Zion* (Boston, 1692), 49–51, emphasis original. The section Mather devotes to speech, one of the longest passages on any single aspect of feminine deportment in the entire text, echoes Psalms 39:1 and Proverbs 10:20 and 31:30.

2. On the date of the first issue of *Ornaments for the Daughters of Zion*, see Thomas James Holmes, *Cotton Mather: A Bibliography of His Works*, 3 vols. (Cambridge: Harvard University Press, 1940), 2: 774–75. Subsequent editions appeared in London in 1694, and in Boston in 1741.

3. The tumultuous political, racial, and military climate of the early 1690s has long been interpreted as a proximate cause of the Salem witch trials. See, e.g., David Thomas Konig, *Law and Society in Puritan Massachusetts: Essex County, 1629–1692* (Chapel Hill: University of North Carolina Press, 1979), 158–85; and Richard Godbeer, *The Devil's Dominion: Magic and Religion in Early New England* (New York: Cambridge University Press, 1992), 182–98. Peter Hoffer notes the connection between sociopolitical disorder and a climate of rumor; see *The Devil's Disciples: Makers of the Salem Witchcraft Trials* (Baltimore: Johns Hopkins University Press, 1996), 55–58. For an account that deems this "traditional explanation centering on political and social turmoil . . . plausible but not satisfying," see Bernard Rosenthal, *Salem Story: Reading the Witch Trials of 1692* (New York: Cambridge University Press, 1993), 4.

4. Here and throughout this chapter, I use the label "witch" to indicate suspected or accused witches rather than to affirm the existence of witches-in-fact.

5. Deodat Lawson, *Christ's Fidelity the Only Shield Against Satan's Malignity* (1693), excerpted in Paul Boyer and Stephen Nissenbaum, eds., *Salem-Village Witchcraft: A Documentary Record of Local Conflict in Colonial New England* (hereafter *SVW*) (1972; rev. ed. Boston: Northeastern University Press, 1993), 124–25; and "Records of the Salem-Village Church from November 1689 to October 1696, as Kept by the Reverend Samuel Parris," in *SVW*, 278. The most careful narratives of the events unfolding in Salem Village in 1692 are found in Rosenthal, *Salem Story*; and Paul Boyer and Stephen Nissenbaum, *Salem Possessed: The Social Origins of Witchcraft* (Cambridge: Harvard University Press, 1974).

6. William Perkins, *A Direction for the Government of the Tongue According to Gods Word* (1597), in [Perkins], *The Works of that Famous and Worthy Minister . . . Newly Corrected* (London, 1635), 451; George Webbe, *The Arraignement of an Unruly Tongue* (London, 1619), 22, emphasis original (see also 83–84, 125, 133, 160); and Webbe, *The Practise of Quietnes: Directing a Christian How to Live Quietly in this Troblesome World*, 3rd ed. (London, 1618), 68. On the mouth as an entry point for the devil, see also Robert B. St. George, " 'Heated' Speech and Literacy in Seventeenth-Century New England," in David D. Hall and David Grayson Allen, eds., *Seventeenth-Century New England* (Boston: Colonial Society of Massachusetts, 1984), 281–83; and Keith Thomas, *Religion and the Decline of Magic* (New York: Charles Scribner, 1971), 524.

7. Webbe himself noted that women's tongues were believed to be particularly difficult to govern; see *Arraignement of an Unruly Tongue*, esp. 8, 11, and *Practise of Quietnes*, 108–10.

8. On the links between gender and witchcraft or possession in New England, see Carol F. Karlsen, *The Devil in the Shape of a Woman: Witchcraft in Colonial New England* (New York: W. W. Norton, 1987), esp. 47–51, 224; Elizabeth Reis, *Damned Women: Sinners and Witches in Puritan New England* (Ithaca, N.Y.: Cornell University Press, 1997); John Putnam Demos, *Entertaining Satan: Witchcraft and the Culture of Early New England* (New York: Oxford University Press, 1982), 60–62; and Godbeer, *Devil's Dominion*, 20–21. On England and the continent, see Alan Macfarlane, *Witchcraft in Tudor and Stuart England: A Regional and Comparative Study* (New York: Harper and Row, 1970), 160; and Brian P. Levack, *The Witch-Hunt in Early Modern Europe* (New York: Longman, 1987), 124. On the important conceptual distinction between witchcraft and demonic possession, see David Harley, "Explaining Salem: Calvinist Psychology and the Diagnosis of Possession," *American Historical Review* (hereafter AHR) 101:2 (April 1996): 307–30.

9. Heinrich Kramer and James Sprenger, *Malleus Maleficarum* (1486), trans. Montague Summers (1928; reprinted London: Arrow Books, 1971), 112, 116, 117, 119, 120. The impact of the *Malleus* on early modern notions of witchcraft is discussed in Levack, *Witch-Hunt in Early Modern Europe*, 49, 52. As Carol Karlsen has pointed out, reformed Protestants made efforts to distance themselves from the overt misogyny of such works; *Devil in the Shape of a Woman*, 159–65. Still, English tracts on witchcraft often echoed the *Malleus* directly. Alexander Roberts, for example, claimed that most witches were female because women "are of a slippery tongue, and full of words"; *A Treatise of Witchcraft* (1616), quoted in Frances E. Dolan, *Dangerous Familiars: Representations of Domestic Crime in England, 1550–1700* (Ithaca, N.Y.: Cornell University Press, 1994), 198.

10. [Anonymous], *The Anatomy of Woman's Tongue* (1638), in *The Harleian Miscellany: Or, a Collection of . . . Pamphlets and Tracts*, 2 vols. (London, 1744), 2: 171.

11. Bartlett Burleigh James and J. Franklin Jameson, eds., *Journal of Jasper Danckaerts, 1679–1680* (1913; reprinted New York: Barnes and Noble, 1959), 290.

12. Edward Johnson, *The Wonder-Working Providence of Sions Saviour in New England—'History of New England'* (1650/1?), ed. J. Franklin Jameson (1910; reprinted New York: Barnes and Noble, 1959), 132. See also James Kendall Hosmer, ed., *Winthrop's Journal, "History of New England" 1630–1649*, 2 vols. (1908; reprinted New York: Barnes and Noble, 1959), 1: 266–68; 2: 7–8.

13. John Hale, *A Modest Inquiry into the Nature of Witchcraft* (1702), in George Lincoln Burr, ed., *Narratives of the Witchcraft Cases, 1648–1706* (New York: Charles Scribner, 1914), 408; Winthrop, *Journal*, 2: 344–45.

14. Increase Mather, *An Essay for the Recording of Illustrious Providences* (hereafter referred to by its popular title, *Remarkable Providences*) (Boston, 1684), 140. He is describing the torments of Elizabeth Knapp, later classified as a demoniac.

15. Cotton Mather, "A Brand Pluck'd Out of the Burning" (1693), in Burr, ed., *Narratives*, 267; Mather, *Memorable Providences, Relating to Witchcrafts and Possessions* (1689), in Burr, ed., *Narratives*, 100, 119.

16. On witchcraft as a reversal of right order, see Stuart Clark, "Inversion, Misrule and the Meaning of Witchcraft," *Past and Present* 87 (May 1980): 98–127, esp. 105, 110; and David D. Hall, *Worlds of Wonder, Days of Judgment:*

Popular Religious Belief in Early New England (New York: Alfred A. Knopf, 1989), 167–68.

17. On witch-hunting as a way of maintaining boundaries between deviant and acceptable behavior, see Kai T. Erikson, *Wayward Puritans: A Study in the Sociology of Deviance* (New York: John Wiley and Sons, 1966); and Richard Weisman, *Witchcraft, Magic, and Religion in Seventeenth-Century Massachusetts* (Amherst: University of Massachusetts Press, 1984). On village and town boundaries, see Boyer and Nissenbaum, *Salem Possessed*; and Demos, *Entertaining Satan*, part 3. On gender boundaries, see Karlsen, *Devil in the Shape of a Woman*; Dolan, *Dangerous Familiars*, chapter 5; and Lyle Koehler, *A Search for Power: The "Weaker Sex" in Seventeenth-Century New England* (Urbana: University of Illinois Press, 1980), 264–300, 383–417.

18. Cotton Mather, "Brand Pluck'd Out of the Burning," 267.

19. This is the generic language of legal indictment for witchcraft; see, e.g., the 1650 indictment of Joan and John Carrington of Connecticut in David D. Hall, ed., *Witch-Hunting in Seventeenth-Century New England: A Documentary History, 1638–1692* (Boston: Northeastern University Press, 1991), 27. On the witch among her neighbors as a kind of "supernatural criminal," see Karlsen, *Devil in the Shape of a Woman*, 4–9; and Demos, *Entertaining Satan*, esp. chapters 3 and 6.

20. Overviews of this debate appear in Godbeer, *Devil's Dominion*, 9–16; Levack, *Witch-Hunt in Early Modern Europe*, chapters 2–4; and Clive Holmes, "Popular Culture? Witches, Magistrates, and Divines in Early Modern England," in Steven L. Kaplan, ed., *Understanding Popular Culture: Europe from the Middle Ages to the Nineteenth Century* (New York: Mouton Publishers, 1984), 85–111. Competing positions are staked out in Thomas, *Religion and the Decline of Magic*, 428–58, 636–40; Weisman, *Witchcraft, Magic, and Religion*, chapters 3 and 4; Jon Butler, "Magic, Astrology, and the Early American Religious Heritage, 1600–1760," *AHR* 89:2 (April 1979): 317–46; and Hall, *Worlds of Wonder*.

21. Cotton Mather, *Wonders of the Invisible World: Being an Account of the Tryals of Several Witches, Lately Executed in New-England* (1693; facsimile reprinted London: John Russell Smith, 1862), 193; Paul Boyer and Stephen Nissenbaum, eds., *The Salem Witchcraft Papers: Verbatim Transcripts of the Legal Documents of the Salem Witchcraft Outbreak of 1692* (hereafter SWP), 3 vols. (New York: Da Capo Press, 1977), 1: 79, 98, 318.

22. Jeanne Favret-Saada, *Deadly Words: Witchcraft in the Bocage*, trans. Catherine Cullen (New York: Cambridge University Press, 1980).

23. William Rowley, Thomas Dekker, John Ford, et al., *The Witch of Edmonton* (1658), in Peter Corbin and Douglas Sedge, eds., *Three Jacobean Witchcraft Plays* (Manchester, Eng.: Manchester University Press, 1986), 159, 162. The "tragicomedy" was based on the 1621 trial of Elizabeth Sawyer. On the depiction of the witch in Renaissance drama, see Dolan, *Dangerous Familiars*, 210–36.

24. Demos, *Entertaining Satan*, 246, 273.

25. See Demos, *Entertaining Satan*, appendix and chapter 8.

26. Presentment of Jane James, Salem, 1639, in George F. Dow, ed., *Records and Files of the Quarterly Courts of Essex County, Massachusetts* (hereafter ECR), 9 vols. (Salem, Mass.: Essex Institute, 1911–1978), 1: 11, 84.

27. James v. Pitford, Ipswich, 1650, ECR, 1: 199, 108, 204; and Archie N. Frost, comp., *Verbatim Transcript of the File Papers of the Essex County Quarterly Courts, 1636–1692* (hereafter Essex File Papers), 75 vols. (typescript on deposit at the James Duncan Phillips Library of the Peabody-Essex Museum, Salem, Mass.;

microfilm copy at Sterling Memorial Library, Yale University), 1: 71-1; James v. Gatchell, Salem, 1651, ECR, 1: 229. The court found for James in both cases.

28. James v. Rowland, Salem, 1667, ECR, 3: 413.

29. Crawford v. Ashby, Salem, 1667, ECR, 3: 420–21. Tellingly, Crawford failed to prove her claim of slander against Ashby.

30. SWP, 2: 443. In this instance, the deponents testified that even their special scrutiny of Elizabeth How over many years had failed to turn up any irregularities.

31. See Willard's anonymous pamphlet, published at the height of the Salem trials, Some Miscellany Observations on Our Present Debates Respecting Witchcrafts, in a Dialogue between S[alem] & B[oston] (Philadelphia, 1692), 4, 2; see also 13.

32. SWP, 3: 880. See also Vinson, Evans, and Dutch v. Marshall, Ipswich, 1653, ECR, 1: 301, 325, and Essex File Papers, 2: 112-5; and Karlsen, Devil in the Shape of a Woman, 38, 104.

33. SWP, 2: 399, 397. For another case in which current fears reanimated old rumors, see depositions against executed Salem witch Elizabeth How, esp. SWP, 2: 438, 451.

34. These alleged "last dying words" of a woman falsely accused who then falsely confessed, in Lauder, Scotland, in 1649, appear in Increase Mather, Cases of Conscience Concerning Witchcrafts and Evil Spirits Personating Men (1692), reprinted in Cotton Mather, Wonders of the Invisible World, 278.

35. Mary Beth Norton, Founding Mothers and Fathers: Gendered Power and the Forming of American Society (New York: Alfred A. Knopf, 1996), 248.

36. Rowley et al., Witch of Edmonton, 188; see also Thomas Heywood, The Late Lancashire Witches (1634), in The Dramatic Works of Thomas Heywood, 6 vols. (1874; reprinted New York: Russell and Russell, 1964), 4: 167–260.

37. [Anonymous], The Wonderful Discovery of the Witchcrafts of Margaret and Philippa Flower . . . Executed at Lincoln March 11, 1618 (1619), in Katherine Usher Henderson and Barbara F. McManus, eds., Half Humankind: Contexts and Texts of the Controversy about Women in England, 1540–1640 (Urbana: University of Illinois Press, 1985), 372, 373.

38. Reginald Scott, Discoverie of Witchcraft, quoted in Samuel G. Drake, ed., The Witchcraft Delusion in New England: Its Rise, Progress, and Termination, 3 vols. (Roxbury, Mass.: Elliot Woodward, 1866), 1: xlv–xlviii. On the connection between witchcraft and scolding in England and on the continent, see also Thomas, Religion and the Decline of Magic, 530; David Underdown, "The Taming of the Scold: The Enforcement of Patriarchal Authority in Early Modern England," in Anthony Fletcher and John Stevens, eds., Order and Disorder in Early Modern England (Cambridge: Cambridge University Press, 1985), 117, 119–21; and the examples compiled in G. J. Davies, ed., Touchying Witchcrafte and Sorcerye, Dorset Record Society Publications 9 (Dorchester, Eng.: Dorset Record Society, 1985), esp. 31–32, 49–51.

39. Karlsen, Devil in the Shape of a Woman, 118.

40. See Demos, Entertaining Satan, 77–78.

41. Cole's choice of insult is ironic: by calling Thing a "saucebox," defined by the OED as "a person addicted to making saucy or impertinent remarks," she implies that he is the one speaking out of turn. See also Thomas Wright, comp., Dictionary of Obsolete and Provincial English (London: Henry G. Bohn, 1857).

42. Hall, Witch-Hunting in Seventeenth-Century New England, 213–29, esp. 214, 222, 227, 225. Cole had a record for misspeaking long before witchcraft

accusations surfaced against her; see her presentments for slander in Salisbury, 1645 (*ECR*, 1: 88), and in Norfolk, 1660 (Hall, *Witch-Hunting in Seventeenth-Century New England*, 217). See also the presentment of Cole for defaming authority, Ipswich, 1647, *ECR*, 1: 129, 143, and *Essex File Papers*, 1: 93-1. Further analyses of Cole's case appear in Karlsen, *Devil in the Shape of a Woman*, 52–57, 77–78, 107; and Demos, *Entertaining Satan*, 319–29.

43. On masculine conventions of speech among the Puritans, see Jane Kamensky, "Talk Like a Man: Speech, Power, and Masculinity in Early New England," *Gender and History* 8:1 (April 1996): 22–47.

44. Presentment of Nicholas Bayley and wife, New Haven, 1655, in Franklin B. Dexter, ed., *New Haven Town Records, 1649–1662* (hereafter *NHTR*, 1) (New Haven: New Haven Colony Historical Society, 1917), 245–46; see also 256.

45. *SWP*, 1: 79–80. See similar charges against Susannah Martin, executed at Salem, in Bartlett v. Martin, Hampton, 1669, *ECR*, 4: 184; *SWP*, 2: 561. Like so many accused witches, Martin was also a frequent subject of others' slanders; see, e.g., Martin v. Sargent, Salisbury, 1669, *ECR*, 4: 129.

46. *SWP*, 2: 368–69, emphasis mine.

47. Presentment of Bridget Oliver, Salem, 1678, *ECR*, 6: 386–87; *SWP*, 1: 97–99. Similar accusations surfaced in the cases of Sarah Good and Sarah Cole. See *SWP*, 2: 357; 1: 231, 233.

48. *SWP*, 2: 632–33. Boyer and Nissenbaum misidentify the Goody Parker in Samuel Shattock's deposition as Andover's Mary Parker; for a convincing argument that it was, in fact, Salem's *Alice* Parker, see Rosenthal, *Salem Story*, 75, 167, 169, 235 n. 25, 254–55 nn. 38–40. For Sarah Bibber, see *SWP*, 1: 79.

49. Rougly half of all male "witches" were linked, via social or kin networks, to women accused of the same crime, making them what John Demos has called "secondary suspects." See Demos, *Entertaining Satan*, 57, 60–62; and Karlsen, *Devil in the Shape of a Woman*, 47.

50. The documents relating to the Parsons's case are reprinted in Hall, *Witch-Hunting in Seventeenth-Century New England*, 25–60. For Mary Parsons's suspicions of her husband, see 33, 41–42, 45–48, 53.

51. Hall, *Witch-Hunting in Seventeenth-Century New England*, 43, 41, 35.

52. Hall, *Witch-Hunting in Seventeenth-Century New England*, 41, 32, 53, 35–37, 55. See also similar exchanges concerning other male suspects: Godfrey v. Symonds and Symonds, Salem, 1659, *ECR*, 2: 157–60, and *Essex File Papers*, 5: 8-1; presentment of John Godfrey, Boston, 1666, in John Noble and John F. Cronin, eds., *Records of the Court of Assistants of the Colony of Massachusetts Bay, 1630–1692* (hereafter *Assts. Recs.*), 3 vols. (Boston: Rockwell and Churchill, 1901–1928), 3: 151–63; Demos, *Entertaining Satan*, esp. 41, 43, 52–56; and Hall, *Witch-Hunting in New England*, 168.

53. Joseph Swetnam, *The Arraignment of Lewde, Idle, Froward and Unconstant Women* (London, 1615), introductory epistle, A2v.

54. Thomas Adams, "The Taming of the Tongue" (1629), in Joseph Angus, ed., *The Works of Thomas Adams*, 3 vols. (Edinburgh: James Nichol, 1862), 3: 10–22, quotation from 17; see also Webbe, *Practise of Quietnes*, 175–81, 257–61.

55. Adams, "Taming of the Tongue," 17; John Aylmer, *An Harborowe for Faithfull and Trewe Subjectes* (1559), quoted in Katharine M. Rogers, *The Troublesome Helpmate: A History of Misogyny in Literature* (Seattle: University of Washington Press, 1966), 137.

56. *SWP*, 2: 636; 1: 80.

57. Favret-Saada, *Deadly Words*, 144, 113; see also 9, 198. On the history of charms, curses, and other speech acts in which words are invested with power in and of themselves, see Macfarlane, *Witchcraft in Tudor and Stuart England*, 201; Thomas, *Religion and the Decline of Magic*, 61, 182–83, 436–37, 502–9. For a useful anthropological analysis of the ways in which magical speech is distinct from everyday utterances, see S. J. Tambiah, "The Magical Power of Words," *Man* n.s. 3:2 (June 1968): 175–208. The notion that promises are both speech and acts is explored in J. L. Austin, *How to Do Things with Words* (1955; reprinted New York: Oxford University Press, 1976).

58. Ellenwood v. Ellenwood, Salem, 1682, *Essex File Papers*, 38: 15-2.

59. Hall, *Witch-Hunting in Seventeenth-Century New England*, 101–2.

60. *SWP*, 2: 400; 1: 189.

61. *SWP*, 2: 558.

62. *SWP*, 2: 375.

63. NHTR, 1: 252; see also Charles J. Hoadly, ed., *Records of the Colony and Plantation of New Haven, from May, 1653, to the Union* (Hartford: Case, Lockwood, 1858), 2: 29–36, 152.

64. Samuel Martin Sr., deposition, May 1669, Samuel Wyllys Collection, Records of Trials for Witchcraft in Connecticut, manuscript on deposit at the Connecticut State Library, Hartford (hereafter Samuel Wyllys Collection/CSL), docs. 13, 11–12, 7. See also Wyllys Papers—Records of Trials for Witchcraft in Connecticut, manuscript on deposit at the Annmary Brown Memorial, Brown University Library, Providence, R.I. (hereafter Wyllys Papers/AMBL), doc. W-11; Demos, *Entertaining Satan*, 290–91, 355–65; and Karlsen, *Devil in the Shape of a Woman*, 84–89.

65. *SWP*, 2: 567–68. Cotton Mather thought the incident worth retelling; see *Wonders of the Invisible World*, 143–44.

66. Examination of Mercy Disborough, June 1692, Wyllys Papers/AMBL, W-33. For Parsons, see Hall, *Witch-Hunting in Seventeenth-Century New England*, 52.

67. *SWP*, 1: 189; also 190, 192–93. See also the misdated file papers on the matter in *Essex File Papers*, 13: 28-4, and ECR, 3: 471–72.

68. *SWP*, 2: 369; 1: 301–2; Thomas Bracy deposition against Katherine Harrison, August 1668, Wyllys Papers/AMBL, W-10.

69. She was also heard to say that a farmer's "cattell could be much scattered in the Summer but it might be we might finde them up againe about Michaeltyde," an eventuality that would seem almost an inevitable part of the seasonal rhythms of dairying. See presentment of the wife of Henry Batchelor, Ipswich, 1667, *Essex File Papers*, 12: 4-1, 6-1; ECR, 3: 403–4.

70. *SWP*, 3: 702; 2: 635.

71. *Records of the Town of East-Hampton, Long Island, Suffolk County, New York*, 5 vols. (Sag Harbor, N.Y.: John H. Hunt, 1905), 1: 132, 129, 135. See also ibid., 139–40; and Demos, *Entertaining Satan*, chapter 7. Sarah Bibber was also called "double-tongued"; see *SWP*, 1: 79. For a rare instance of a male suspect accused of fawning, see testimony against Salem merchant Phillip English, *SWP*, 1: 318–19.

72. Swetnam, *Froward and Unconstant Women*, 11, 15, 39, 12.

73. On the gendered nature of the linguistic double bind, see Robin Lakoff, *Language and Woman's Place* (New York: Farrar, Straus and Giroux, 1975), 6, 62.

74. *SWP*, 2: 440–41. Despite seven such depositions on her behalf, How hanged on 19 July 1692. See also similar language in testimony for Sarah Buck-

ley, *SWP*, 1: 146–47; and Ellenwood v. Ellenwood, Salem, 1682, *Essex File Papers*, 38: 15-4, 16-1.

75. *SWP*, 1: 118. Bradbury was surely calling attention to the difference between his wife's feminine decorousness and the too-free speech of her accusers in Salem.

76. *SWP*, 2: 636.

77. Heywood, *Late Lancashire Witches*, 178, 183; see also 188, 227–28, 236.

78. This wonderfully evocative request came from the specter of suspect Elizabeth Clawson to her bewitched victim, servant Katherine Branch, who fulfilled the plea by turning cartwheels in her master's parlor; see deposition of Sgt. Daniel Wescott, May 1692, Wyllys Papers/AMBL, W-19, sheet 3. A similar image of inversion appears in an anonymous tract entitled *A Narrative of the Planting of the Massachusetts Colony Anno 1628* (Boston, 1694), presumed to have been written by Joshua Scottow. Declension from the colony's founding ideals, Scottow says, had turned Massachusetts "topsy turvy," as if "heads and Heels have changed places" (46).

79. Godbeer, *Devil's Dominion*, 158–59. Godbeer's conviction rate of 26.2 percent is based only upon the number formally presented as witches; adding those informally suspected (as reflected in slander suits, e.g.) would reduce the rate of conviction considerably. For comparisons to England and Europe, see Macfarlane, *Witchcraft in Tudor and Stuart England*, esp. 57; and Levack, *Witch-Hunt in Early Modern Europe*, chapter 3. For a compilation of statutes defining witchcraft in New England, see Hall, *Witch-Hunting in Seventeenth-Century New England*, 315–16.

80. William Perkins, *A Discourse of the Damned Art of Witchcraft* (ca. 1600), in Ian Breward, ed., *The Work of William Perkins* (Abingdon, Eng.: Sutton Courtenay Press, 1970), 581–609, quotations from 601–4. It is no coincidence that Perkins was New England's leading authority both on witchcraft and on the power and the perils of speech; see, e.g., Perkins's treatise on preaching, *The Arte of Prophecying: Or, A Treatise of Preaching*, trans. Thomas Tuke (1592; 1st English ed. London, 1607); and Perkins, *Direction for the Government of the Tongue*.

81. Cotton Mather, "Brand Pluck'd Out of the Burning," 261; also 262. Reviews of the vast demonological literature published in England and on the continent are found in Godbeer, *Devil's Dominion*, 55–85; Levack, *Witch-Hunt in Early Modern Europe*, chapters 2 and 4; and Stuart Clark, "Protestant Demonology: Sin, Superstition, and Society (c. 1520–c. 1630)," in Bengt Ankarloo and Gustav Henningsen, eds., *Early Modern European Witchcraft: Centres and Peripheries* (Oxford: Clarendon Press, 1990), 45–81.

82. Perkins, *Discourse of the Damned Art*, 595, 596. On Puritan beliefs in the special vulnerability of the female soul to the devil's snares, see Reis, *Damned Women*, chapter 3.

83. Karlsen, *Devil in the Shape of a Woman*, 48; see also 49–50. These fourteen presentments include three for John Godfrey, who was never convicted; see Godbeer, *Devil's Dominion*, 235–37. Both of the men convicted, John Carrington and Nathaniel Greensmith, were executed along with their wives, who were the primary suspects.

84. Perkins, *Discourse of the Damned Art*, 590, 600. The term "antisociety" is borrowed from Levack, *Witch-Hunt in Early Modern Europe*, 37, 46.

85. Perkins, *Discourse of the Damned Art*, 593, 600.

86. Samuel Willard, "A Brief Account of a Strange and Unusual Providence of God Befallen to Elizabeth Knapp of Groton" (1672), in John Putnam Demos, ed., *Remarkable Providences: Readings on Early American History*, rev. ed. (Boston: Northeastern University Press, 1991), 426. The nature and implications of this diabolic covenant are explored in Godbeer, *Devil's Dominion*, 85–121; and Reis, *Damned Women*, chapter 4.

87. Cotton Mather, *Memorable Providences*, 103. The term "antilanguage" is Peter Burke's; see his "Languages and Anti-Languages in Early Modern Italy," *History Workshop Journal* 11 (spring 1981): 24–32.

88. Thomas Hooker, *The Soules Humiliation*, 3rd ed. (London, 1640), 36–37, emphasis mine.

89. Prefatory letter to Cotton Mather, *Memorable Providences*, 95–96.

90. Hale, *Modest Inquiry into the Nature of Witchcraft*, 412–13; John Gaule, *Select Cases of Conscience Touching Witches and Witchcraft* (London, 1646), Il2v, quoted in Dolan, *Dangerous Familiars*, 203.

91. Hall, *Worlds of Wonder*, 189–90.

92. Cotton Mather, *Memorable Providences*, 103–4.

93. Hall, *Witch-Hunting in Seventeenth-Century New England*, 152; Increase Mather, *Remarkable Providences*, 137–38.

94. As David Harley points out, "bewitchment" (through the agency of a witch) and "possession" (through the direct agency of the devil) were treated as distinct entities in early modern learned writings; see Harley, "Explaining Salem," esp. 311–13. Yet the two often overlapped in practice. Describing Martha Godwin's affliction, for example, Cotton Mather credited the malefic agency of "witch" Goody Glover *and* the torments authored by "Devils," "Demons," "unseen Fiends," and "Evil spirits" after Glover's death, the symptoms of which torments he labels "Demonstrations of an Enchantment growing very far towards a Possession"; *Memorable Providences*, 107, 108, 121–22. A similar confusion of categories appears in numerous other New England writings on the subject. On the age and sex of "possessed" victims, see Karlsen, *Devil in the Shape of a Woman*, 223–24.

95. Cotton Mather, "Brand Pluck'd Out of the Burning," 267, 275.

96. Willard, "Brief Account," 422, 423, 426; Cotton Mather, *Memorable Providences*, 107. For an astute psychodynamic analysis of Knapp's "diabolical distemper," see Demos, *Entertaining Satan*, 97–132.

97. Willard, "Brief Account," 423.

98. Cotton Mather, *Memorable Providences*, 112–13 (see also 101); Mather, "Brand Pluck'd Out of the Burning," 272 (see also 279, 262); Willard, "Brief Account," 434 (see also 426).

99. Kramer and Sprenger, *Malleus Maleficarum*, 467, 479. Kramer and Sprenger recommend judicial torture as an effective antidote. Silence assumes a similar power in Quaker conceptions of speech; see Richard Bauman, *Let Your Words Be Few: Symbolism of Speaking and Silence among Seventeenth-Century Quakers* (New York: Cambridge University Press, 1983), chapter 2. On the connections between Quakerism and witchcraft, see Christine Leigh Heyrman, "Specters of Subversion, Societies of Friends: Dissent and the Devil in Provincial Essex County, Massachusetts," in David D. Hall, John M. Murrin, and Thad W. Tate, eds., *Saints and Revolutionaries: Essays on Early American History* (New York: W. W. Norton, 1984), esp. 48–49, 52–54, 68.

100. Increase Mather, *Remarkable Providences*, 137 (see also 170–71); Cotton Mather, *Memorable Providences*, 103, 104–5, 119–20. Jane Hawkins, midwife and supporter of Anne Hutchinson, was similarly reputed to "utter many speeches in the Latine Tongue"; see Johnson, *Wonder-Working Providence*, 132. On the occult phenomenon of speaking in tongues or glossolalia, see Thomas, *Religion and the Decline of Magic*, 478.

101. Cotton Mather, "Brand Pluck'd Out of the Burning," 267–68, 275; Mather, "Another Brand Pluckt Out of the Burning," printed in Robert Calef, *More Wonders of the Invisible World* (1700), in Burr, ed., *Narratives*, 316. The echoes of Anne Hutchinson here are unmistakable.

102. Cotton Mather, "Brand Pluck'd Out of the Burning," 271–72; Mather, *Memorable Providences*, 110, 112–13.

103. Willard, "Brief Account," 432–33.

104. Worthington Chauncey Ford, ed., *Diary of Cotton Mather*, 2 vols. (1912; reprinted New York: Frederick Ungar, 1957), 1: 171–72, emphasis original.

105. Cotton Mather, "Brand Pluck'd Out of the Burning," 262.

106. Cotton Mather, "Brand Pluck'd Out of the Burning," 267; Mather, *Memorable Providences*, 95–96.

107. Willard, "Brief Account," 433; Cotton Mather, "Another Brand Pluckt Out of the Burning," 321–22.

108. Willard, "Brief Account," 422–23, 435; see also Cotton Mather, "Another Brand Pluckt Out of the Burning," 312–13. On alternative explanations for possession, see Harley, "Explaining Salem," 311–13; and Rosenthal, *Salem Story*, 39–40.

109. Cotton Mather, "Brand Pluck'd Out of the Burning," 276; Mather, *Diary*, 1: 172. In this diary entry describing his conduct during Margaret Rule's possession, Mather responds defensively to accusations that he has failed to exercise such checks on the speech of "the afflicted young Woman."

110. Samuel Willard, *Useful Instructions for a Professing People in Times of Great Security and Degeneracy* (Cambridge, 1673), 33. Willard's concern for spreading the story of Knapp's possession is evident throughout *Useful Instructions*, a series of sermons he preached on Groton's diabolical torments. Although he centers his message on the case, he writes of it obliquely, referring only to Groton's "common sickness and calamity," and to the "stupend Judgement of God which is among us" (32). Neither does he ever use Knapp's name, speaking instead of the devil's "Instruments" (31), of "this poor creature" (34), and more generally of those "who are *spiritually possesst by Satan*" (41). See also Cotton Mather, "Brand Pluckt Out of the Burning," 276.

111. Willard, "Brief Account," 431.

112. On the narcissism of the possessed, see Demos, *Entertaining Satan*, 117–18, 128–31.

113. Willard, *Useful Instructions*, 33.

114. Increase Mather, *Cases of Conscience*, 253, paraphrasing Malachai 2:7.

115. In early modern parlance, the ventriloquist was known as "one that has an evil spirit speaking in his belly," an image often gendered female by reference to the Bible's "Witch of Endor" (I Samuel 28:6–7). See Thomas Blount, *Glossographia: Or, a Dictionary Interpreting All Such Hard Words . . . as Are Now Used in Our Refined English Tongue*, 2nd ed. (London, 1656); Joseph Glanvil, *Saducismus Trimphatus: Or, Full and Plain Evidence Concerning Witches and Apparitions*,

2nd ed. (London, 1688), esp. 36–37; and Steven Connor, *Ventriloquies: A Cultural History of the Dissociated Voice* (Oxford: Oxford University Press, forthcoming).

116. Willard, "Brief Account," 435, 432.

117. Increase Mather, *Remarkable Providences*, 140–41, emphasis mine (see also 171, 196); Cotton Mather, *Memorable Providences*, 121; Willard, "Brief Account," 432, 433, emphasis mine. See also Cotton Mather, "Brand Pluck'd Out of the Burning," 262. The OED suggests that "grum," a seventeenth-century neologism, represented a "blended reminiscence of words like grim, glum, gruff, grumble."

118. Willard, "Brief Account," 435, 427. On Knapp's happy ending, see Demos, *Entertaining Satan*, 114.

119. John Cotta, *The Triall of Witchcraft* (London, 1616), quoted in Increase Mather, *Cases of Conscience*, 258, 259; see also 256.

120. Konig, *Law and Society in Puritan Massachusetts*, esp. 168–73.

121. Rosenthal, *Salem Story*, 7. On the scale of the Salem trials as compared to earlier outbreaks, such as that in Hartford in the early 1660s or those in Essex County, England, see ibid., 213–15; and Godbeer, *Devil's Dominion*, 179–82.

122. Hale, *Modest Inquiry into the Nature of Witchcraft*, 400. The Salem hanged included five men, a former minister of the village among them. In addition to the nineteen people executed, one suspect (Giles Corey) was pressed to death, and four died in prison; see Godbeer, *Devil's Dominion*, 238–42. The story of Salem is too familiar—and too intricate—to bear a full retelling here. Excellent narrative treatments are found in Rosenthal, *Salem Story*, and Boyer and Nissenbaum, *Salem Possessed*, from which many of the details of the following account are taken.

123. "Records of the Salem-Village Church," 270, emphasis mine.

124. Increase Mather, *A Further Account of the Tryals of the New-England Witches* (London, 1693), 6; Deodat Lawson, *A Brief and True Narrative of Some Remarkable Passages Relating to . . . Witchcraft, at Salem Village* (1692), in Burr, ed., *Narratives*, 154–55, 160, 161. The sermon Lawson attempted to preach that day was later published as *Christ's Fidelity the Only Shield Against Satan's Malignity*. Hartford's Ann Cole was likewise said to have caused "disturbance" in the meetinghouse there in 1662; see Hall, *Witch-Hunting in Seventeenth-Century New England*, 149.

125. Calef, *More Wonders of the Invisible World*, 343. Lawson, *Brief and True Narrative*, 155, estimated that "many hundred people" attended the examination of Martha Corey and others on 21 March.

126. John Cotton, *The Keys of the Kingdom of Heaven* (1644), reprinted in Larzer Ziff, ed., *John Cotton on the Churches of New England* (Cambridge: Harvard University Press, 1968), 114, emphasis original; Calef, *More Wonders of the Invisible World*, 343; SWP, 2: 357.

127. See, e.g., SWP, 1: 185, 250, 253 and 2: 372–73, 389, 390, 420, 434–35; Lawson, *Brief and True Narrative*, 155–58; and Calef, *More Wonders of the Invisible World*, esp. 355.

128. SWP, 1: 84.

129. SWP, 2: 646; 3: 747. See also 1: 59–61, 65–69, 73–76, 113–14, 134–35, 139–40, 213–14, 227–28, 279–82; 2: 405–13, 615–17, 643–44, 647–48; 3: 741–43, 746–55.

130. Rosenthal speculates that the accusers' shift to targeting men was one of the major breaking points in the trials; see *Salem Story*, 108–15.

131. Boyer and Nissenbaum, *Salem Possessed*, 32. For Alden's age at the trials, see Sidney Perley, *The History of Salem Massachusetts*, 3 vols. (Salem, Mass.: n.p., 1926), 3: 293.

132. *SWP*, 1: 51–53. For Alden's accusers, see *SWP*, 1: 173, 183; 3: 871. For the basis of these slanders, see Konig, *Law and Society in Puritan Massachusetts*, 166.

133. *SWP*, 1: 53–54. When the court apprehended and retried him the following April, he was "cleared by Proclamation, none appearing against him." Alden's case became a favorite among those arguing, retrospectively, against the conduct of the Salem trials; see, e.g., Calef, *More Wonders of the Invisible World*, 353–55.

134. [Willard], *Miscellany Observations on Our Present Debates*, 15.

135. This breach in the meaning of confession, Perry Miller noted, "nearly wrecked" the entire "intellectual structure" of covenant theology; see Miller, *The New England Mind: From Colony to Province* (Cambridge: Harvard University Press, 1953), 192, 197–98, 205–7. See also Hall, *Worlds of Wonder*, 196; and Rosenthal, *Salem Story*, 42–55, 125.

136. Hale, *Modest Inquiry into the Nature of Witchcraft*, 423.

137. Calef, *More Wonders of the Invisible World*, 360, 367–68; *SWP*, 1: 303. Lest we dismiss Calef's descriptions as after-the-fact martyrology, Samuel Sewall mentioned Burroughs's speech in his diary, noting that the condemned man's words "did much move unthinking persons"; M. Halsey Thomas, ed., *The Diary of Samuel Sewall, 1674–1729*, 2 vols. (New York: Farrar, Straus and Giroux, 1973), 1: 294.

138. Hale, *Modest Inquiry into the Nature of Witchcraft*, 424.

139. Calef, *More Wonders of the Invisible World*, 358.

140. The role of Good's curse in the death of Noyes was a "tradition among the people of Salem"; see Thomas Hutchinson, *The History of the Colony and Province of Massachusetts-Bay* (1764–1768), 3 vols., ed. Lawrence Shaw Mayo (Cambridge: Harvard University Press, 1936), 2: 41 n. For the role of Good's speech in the bewitchment of Mercy Short, see Cotton Mather, "Brand Pluck'd Out of the Burning," 260.

141. Calef, *More Wonders of the Invisible World*, 299; [Scottow], *Narrative of the Planting of the Massachusetts Colony*, 49.

142. John Winthrop, "A Modell of Christian Charity" (1630), in *Winthrop Papers*, 5 vols. (Boston: Massachusetts Historical Society, 1929–1947), 2: 295.

143. "Records of the Salem-Village Church," 295, 298–99.

144. "Records of the Salem-Village Church," 302, 296, 295; Petition of John Tarbel, Samuel Nurse, Joseph Putnam, and Daniel Andrew, July 1697, in Charles W. Upham, *Salem Witchcraft*, 2 vols. (1867; reprinted New York: Frederick Ungar, 1978), 2: 497–98.

145. On the circumstances of Parris's departure from the Salem Village church, see Boyer and Nissenbaum, *Salem Possessed*, 69–79.

146. [Willard], *Miscellany Observations on Our Present Debates*, 11.

147. "Letter of Thomas Brattle, F.R.S., 1692," in Burr, ed., *Narratives*, 172.

148. Hale, *Modest Inquiry into the Nature of Witchcraft*, 425. See also Increase Mather, *Cases of Conscience*, 255; Calef, *More Wonders of the Invisible World*, esp.

304–5; "The Apology of the Members of the Jury" (n.d.), in Upham, *Salem Witchcraft*, 2: 474; and "Letter of Thomas Brattle," 175, 177.

149. See, e.g., the caution Mather recommends in *Wonders of the Invisible World* (esp. 15–16), "Brand Pluck'd Out of the Burning" (274–76), and "Another Brand Pluckt Out of the Burning" (311, 321), and his defensive tone in an unpublished exchange with his critic Robert Calef; Worthington Chauncey Ford, ed., "Mather-Calef Paper on Witchcraft," in *Proceedings of the Massachusetts Historical Society* 47 (1914), 248–68.

150. "Letters of Governor Phips to the Home Government, 1692–1693," in Burr, ed., *Narratives*, 199.

151. Hale, *Modest Inquiry into the Nature of Witchcraft*, 423.

152. Cotton Mather, *Wonders of the Invisible World*, 15.

153. [Willard], *Miscellany Observations on Our Present Debates*, 7–8; Calef, *More Wonders of the Invisible World*, 298–99, 344; "Mather-Calef Paper on Witchcraft," 261 n. 2, 266 n. 2, 249 n. 5. See also "Letter of Thomas Brattle," 188. In the late eighteenth century, Thomas Hutchinson argued for deliberate fraud as a cause of the Salem hangings; see Hutchinson, *History of Massachusetts-Bay*, 2: 45–47. For a strong, recent argument on behalf of this now-unfashionable explanation, see Rosenthal, *Salem Story*, esp. 32–39, 184–201.

154. Calef, *More Wonders of the Invisible World*, 331, 380, 327, 342.

155. SWP, 1: 250. See also Calef's paraphrase of Corey's remark; *More Wonders of the Invisible World*, 346.

156. "Letter of Thomas Brattle," 173, 174; see also 180–81, 189. Some critics applied their reassessment of witches' confessions to the past, suggesting that earlier suspects, too, had been "poor despised crazy" women who effectively committed suicide with the help of colonial magistrates; see, e.g., Robert Calef's marginalia in "Mather-Calef Paper on Witchcraft," 264–65 n. 5.

157. "Letter of Thomas Brattle," 169–70.

158. Hale, *Modest Inquiry into the Nature of Witchcraft*, 431. For Hale's depositions against several accused women, see SWP, 1: 95; 2: 397–99; 3: 810.

159. Upham, *Salem Witchcraft*, 2: 474–75.

160. Sewall, *Diary*, 1: 366–67; see also 2: 947–48. The General Court's call for a fast to expiate the sins of Salem is reprinted in Upham, *Salem Witchcraft*, 2: 473–74.

161. Cotton Mather, "Another Brand Pluckt Out of the Burning," 319–20.

162. The acknowledgment/profession of faith of Ann Putnam Jr. appears in Upham, *Salem Witchcraft*, 2: 510.

163. SWP, 3: 1016.

164. SWP, 3: 972.

Epilogue

1. Charles Chauncy, *An Unbridled Tongue a Sure Evidence, that Our Religion is Hypocritical* (Boston, 1741), 13–16, 25, emphasis original. Chauncy paraphrases such earlier Puritan works as Thomas Adams, "The Taming of the Tongue" (1629), in Joseph Angus, ed., *The Works of Thomas Adams*, 3 vols. (Edinburgh: James Nichol, 1862), 3: 10–22, esp. 14–15.

2. On the comparison between the rhetorics of witchcraft and revivalism, see Laurel Thatcher Ulrich, *Good Wives: Image and Reality in the Lives of Women in Northern New England, 1650–1750* (New York: Alfred A. Knopf, 1982), 224–25;

Carol F. Karlsen, *The Devil in the Shape of a Woman: Witchcraft in Colonial New England* (New York: W. W. Norton, 1987), 255; and Paul Boyer and Stephen Nissenbaum, *Salem Possessed: The Social Origins of Witchcraft* (Cambridge: Harvard University Press, 1974), 215–16.

3. For a concise survey of the events and issues in the New England awakenings of the 1740s, see Harry S. Stout, *The New England Soul: Preaching and Religious Culture in Colonial New England* (New York: Oxford University Press, 1986), 185–211.

4. On the growth and diffusion of Boston's congregations, see Alexander McKenzie, "The Religious History of the Provincial Period," in Justin Winsor, ed., *The Memorial History of Boston*, 4 vols. (Boston: James R. Osgood, 1882), 2: 187–248. Many thanks to Mark A. Peterson for this reference, and his thoughts on this point in general. On denominationalism in the colonies more broadly, see Jon Butler, *Awash in a Sea of Faith: Christianizing the American People* (Cambridge: Harvard University Press, 1990), 98–128.

5. Chauncy, *Unbridled Tongue*, 12, 5.

6. Cotton Mather, *A Golden Curb for the Mouth* (Boston, 1709), 6.

7. "A Memoriall to ye Great and Generall Court of Massachusetts Bay offered in ye name & behalfe of ye ministers of ye Province" (May 1696), in *The Acts and Resolves, Public and Private, of the Province of the Massachusetts Bay* (hereafter *Massachusetts Acts and Resolves*), 21 vols. (Boston: Wright and Potter, 1869), 7: 539–40.

8. "Reasons for Reprieve," 12 May 1693, Wyllys Papers—Records of Trials for Witchcraft in Connecticut, manuscript on deposit at the Annmary Brown Memorial, Brown University Library, Providence, R.I.; W-36, sheets 2–3.

9. *Massachusetts Acts and Resolves*, 1: 55–56, 90–91; Perry Miller, *The New England Mind: From Colony to Province* (Cambridge: Harvard University Press, 1953), 191. On shifts in English law concerning witchcraft, see Keith Thomas, *Religion and the Decline of Magic* (New York: Charles Scribner, 1971), 443; and Brian P. Levack, *The Witch-Hunt in Early Modern Europe* (New York: Longman, 1987), 217. On the relationship between English law and colonial practice, see David Thomas Konig, *Law and Society in Puritan Massachusetts: Essex County, 1629–1692* (Chapel Hill: University of North Carolina Press, 1979), 186–87; and Sanford J. Fox, *Science and Justice: The Massachusetts Witchcraft Trials* (Baltimore: Johns Hopkins University Press, 1968), 36–37.

10. On the persistence of informal, neighborhood sanctions against witches in the eighteenth and early nineteenth centuries, see Richard Godbeer, *The Devil's Dominion: Magic and Religion in Early New England* (New York: Cambridge University Press, 1992), 223–27; and Peter Benes, ed., *Wonders of the Invisible World, 1600–1900*, Dublin Seminar for New England Folklife Annual Proceedings, 1992 (Boston: Boston University Scholarly Publications, 1995), esp. 86–148.

11. Cornelia Hughes Dayton, *Women before the Bar: Gender, Law, and Society in Connecticut, 1639–1789* (Chapel Hill: University of North Carolina Press, 1995), 32; see also 10–13, 60–64.

12. On this point see Dana Rose Comi, " 'They've Mounted the Rostrum': The Problem of Women's Public Speech in Antebellum America," unpublished essay, Brandeis University, 1996.

13. Presentment of the wife of Henry Batchelor, Ipswich, 1667, in Archie N. Frost, comp., *Verbatim Transcript of the File Papers of the Essex County Quarterly*

Courts, 1636–1692, 75 vols. (typescript on deposit at the James Duncan Phillips Library of the Peabody-Essex Museum, Salem, Mass.; microfilm copy at Sterling Memorial Library, Yale University), 12: 4-1; and George F. Dow, ed., *Records and Files of the Quarterly Courts of Essex County, Massachusetts* (hereafter ECR), 9 vols. (Salem, Mass.: Essex Institute, 1911–1978), 3: 403–4.

14. William H. Whitmore, ed., *The Colonial Laws of Massachusetts, Reprinted from the Edition of 1672, with the Supplements to 1686* (hereafter Mass. *Laws, 1672 Edition*) (Boston: Rockwell and Churchill, 1887), 14.

15. *Massachusetts Acts and Resolves*, 1: 55–56, 297, 553. The last sanction was never applied. Indeed, Leonard W. Levy argues that although blasphemy statutes remained in force in many North American colonies, "In the eighteenth century . . . blasphemy all but disappeared as an offense that was actually prosecuted"; see Levy, *Blasphemy: Verbal Offense against the Sacred, from Moses to Salman Rushdie* (New York: Alfred A. Knopf, 1993), 264–71, quotation from 267.

16. *Massachusetts Acts and Resolves*, 1: 151, 679; compare with Mass. *Laws, 1672 Edition*, 144–45, 235.

17. Mass. *Laws, 1672 Edition*, 44–45; see also 60–63 on heresy.

18. *Massachusetts Acts and Resolves*, 1: 14, 423–24.

19. Susan Juster, *Disorderly Women: Sexual Politics and Evangelicalism in Revolutionary New England* (Ithaca, N.Y.: Cornell University Press, 1994), esp. 14–45. Juster argues that the genderless evangelical rhetoric that characterized the Baptists at midcentury was later undermined by the Revolution (108–79).

20. Osborn's correspondence with Fish is quoted in David Grimsted, "Anglo-American Racism and Phillis Wheatley's 'Sable Vein,' 'Lengthened Chain,' and 'Knitted Heart,' " in Ronald Hoffman and Peter J. Albert, eds., *Women in the Age of the American Revolution* (Charlottesville: University of Virginia Press, 1989), 376–77; and Mary Beth Norton, *Liberty's Daughters: The Revolutionary Experience of American Women, 1750–1800* (Boston: Little, Brown, 1980), 131. For a review of Osborn's career, along with the text of one of her letters to Fish, see Mary Beth Norton, " 'My Resting Reaping Times': Sarah Osborn's Defense of Her 'Unfeminine' Activities, 1767," *Signs: Journal of Women in Culture and Society* 2:2 (winter 1976): 515–29.

21. Samuel Hopkins, *Memoirs of the Life of Mrs. Sarah Osborn* (Worcester, Mass., 1799), 75.

22. *Massachusetts Acts and Resolves*, 1: 378.

23. On the cultural value of rebellious children, especially brothers, in the age of the Revolution, see Jay Fliegelman, *Prodigals and Pilgrims: The American Revolution against Patriarchal Authority, 1750–1800* (New York: Cambridge University Press, 1982); and Lynn Hunt, *The Family Romance of the French Revolution* (Berkeley: University of California Press, 1992), esp. chapters 1 and 2.

24. See, e.g., Dayton, *Women before the Bar*, 284–328; Norman L. Rosenberg, *Protecting the Best Men: An Interpretive History of the Law of Libel* (Chapel Hill: University of North Carolina Press, 1986), 16–27; and Larry D. Eldridge, *A Distant Heritage: The Growth of Free Speech in Early America* (New York: New York University Press, 1994), esp. 65–66, 75–77, 114–31.

25. *Massachusetts Acts and Resolves*, 1: 70–71, 741; see also 53–54, 629–30 on fraud and forgery.

26. Dayton, *Women before the Bar*, 45, 78–79, 91, 285–87, 304–5. On the relationship between economic and moral issues in eighteenth-century jurisprudence, see also Hendrik Hartog, "The Public Law of a County Court: Judicial

Government in Eighteenth-Century Massachusetts," *American Journal of Legal History* 20:4 (October 1976): 282–329, esp. 300–1; and Cornelia Hughes Dayton, "Taking the Trade: Abortion and Gender Relations in an Eighteenth-Century New England Village," *William and Mary Quarterly* (hereafter *WMQ*) 3rd ser., 48:1 (January 1991): 19–49.

27. The General Court first enacted a statute against the spreading of false news in 1645, and similar laws remained in force into the eighteenth century. See Nathaniel B. Shurtleff, ed., *Records of the Governor and Company of the Massachusetts Bay in New England* (hereafter *Mass. Recs.*), 5 vols. in 6 (1854; reprinted New York: AMS Press, 1968), 2: 104–5; *Mass. Laws, 1672 Edition*, 90–91; *Massachusetts Acts and Resolves*, 1: 53; and chapter 2 in this book. For counterfeiting as the uttering of false money, see presentment of Martin Williams, Boston, 1691, in John Noble and John F. Cronin, eds., *Records of the Court of Assistants of the Colony of Massachusetts Bay, 1630–1692* (hereafter *Assts. Recs.*), 3 vols. (Boston: Rockwell and Churchill, 1901–1928), 1: 359–60. Williams was convicted, and sentenced to be exhibited in Boston's pillory on "three severall Lecture dayes . . . with a Paper signifying his Crime."

28. See, e.g., presentment of Nathaniel Putnam, Salem, 1669, *ECR*, 4: 92–93; presentment of Edward Lumas, Ipswich, 1672, *ECR*, 5: 38–39.

29. Presentment of Mr. Samuel Shrimpton, Boston, 1686, *Assts. Recs.*, 1: 299; M. Halsey Thomas, ed., *The Diary of Samuel Sewall, 1674–1729*, 2 vols. (New York: Farrar, Straus and Giroux, 1973), 1: 101–2.

30. Thomas Symmes, *A Discourse Concerning Prejudice in Matters of Religion* (Boston, 1722), i–ii; see also Michael Warner, *Letters of the Republic: Publication and the Public Sphere in Eighteenth-Century America* (Cambridge: Harvard University Press, 1990), 22–23.

31. A pamphlet entitled *Truth Held Forth and Maintained* (New York, 1695), by Quaker merchant Thomas Maule, was burned in Boston in December of that year; see the documents compiled in John Edward Maule, *Better That 100 Witches Should Live: The 1696 Acquittal of Thomas Maule* (Villanova, Pa.: Jembook Publishing, 1995). In 1700, Increase Mather allegedly supervised the burning of Robert Calef's *More Wonders of the Invisible World* (1700) in Harvard Yard. See John Eliot, *A Biographical Dictionary, Containing a Brief Account of the First Settlers* (Boston: Edward Oliver, 1809), 95; Samuel Eliot Morison, *Harvard College in the Seventeenth Century* (Cambridge: Harvard University Press, 1936), 496–98.

32. The remedy for such violations, too, was written rather than spoken. Instead of being asked to recite his shame, the convicted offender was to be displayed "with an inscription of his crime, in capital letters, affixed over his head"; *Massachusetts Acts and Resolves*, 1: 682. See also *OED* for changes in the meaning of the word "publish," which took on its current identification with print in the early eighteenth century.

33. Worthington Chauncey Ford, ed., *Diary of Cotton Mather*, 2 vols. (1912; reprinted New York: Frederick Ungar, 1957), 2: 450; see also 327. The libel in question was Ipswich minister John Wise's *A Vindication of the Government of New-England Churches* (Boston, 1717). On Wise and his reception among the Massachusetts clergy, see Miller, *New England Mind from Colony to Province*, 288–302.

34. Mather, *Diary*, 2: 605, 663, 716.

35. Adams, "Taming of the Tongue," 17; [Anonymous], *Some Few Remarks Upon a Scandalous Book, Against the Government and Ministry of New England*

(Boston, 1701), 5, emphasis original. *Some Few Remarks* was written to defend the Mathers against the aspersions Robert Calef had spread, in print, in his *More Wonders of the Invisible World.*

36. *New England Courant,* 12 March 1722, quoted in Warner, *Letters of the Republic,* 44.

37. Delano A. Goddard, "The Press and Literature of the Provincial Period, 1692–1770," in Winsor, ed., *Memorial History of Boston,* 2: 387–403.

38. Warner, *Letters of the Republic,* 1–72; see also Richard D. Brown, *Knowledge Is Power: The Diffusion of Information in Early America, 1700–1865* (New York: Oxford University Press, 1989), chapters 1 and 2.

39. Evarts B. Greene and Virginia D. Harrington, *American Population before the Federal Census of 1790* (New York: Columbia University Press, 1932), 13–19, 22.

40. Compare, e.g., Leonard W. Levy's *Emergence of a Free Press* [rev. ed. of *Legacy of Suppression: Freedom of Speech and Press in Early American History* (1967)] (New York: Oxford University Press, 1985); and Eldridge, *Distant Heritage.* Where Levy contrasts the glories of unfettered expression in modern life with the repressive climate of pre- and post-Revolutionary America, Eldridge—whose monograph is framed as an explicit challenge to Levy's paradigm—succeeds only in pushing this vaunted evolution back in time. The bad old days, he argues, were really getting much better by 1660 or so. Moreover, as Michael Warner points out, such "libertarian laments" over the shortcomings of the framers' visions share the root assumptions about the emancipatory character of free public discourse of the older, Whig histories they seek to supplant; see *Letters of the Republic,* 49–50.

41. Historians continue to debate the relative importance of orality and print during the Great Awakening and the American Revolution. Michael Warner's insistence upon the primacy of print *(Letters of the Republic)* has recently been challenged by scholars insisting upon the continued "salience" of "vocal utterance." See, e.g., Christopher Looby, *Voicing America: Language, Literary Form, and the Origins of the United States* (Chicago: University of Chicago Press, 1996), esp. 2–3; Sandra Marie Gustafson, "Performing the Word: American Oratory, 1630–1860" (Ph.D. dissertation, University of California at Berkeley, 1993); and Jay Fliegelman, *Declaring Independence: Jefferson, Natural Language, and the Culture of Performance* (Stanford, Calif.: Stanford University Press, 1993), all of whom build upon the earlier work of Rhys Isaac, *The Transformation of Virginia, 1740–1790* (Chapel Hill: University of North Carolina Press, 1982); and Harry S. Stout, "Religion, Communications, and the Ideological Origins of the American Revolution," *WMQ* 3rd ser., 34:3 (July 1977): 519–41. For a sensible middle ground, which emphasizes the marketing and advertising of evangelical orality by means of print, see Frank Lambert, " 'Pedlar in Divinity': George Whitefield and the Great Awakening, 1737–1745," *Journal of American History* 77:3 (December 1990): 812–38, esp. 824.

42. Levy, *Emergence of a Free Press,* xii. As Levy notes, eighteenth-century juries challenged magistrates' continued adherence to this central tenet of the common-law definition of seditious libel (119–229).

43. On disputes over speech in eighteenth-century evangelical sects, see Juster, *Disorderly Women,* 76, 88–96, 156–60. In addition to Chauncy's *Unbridled Tongue,* published eighteenth-century sermons on speech include Samuel Willard, *The Fear of an Oath Or, Some Cautions to Be Used About Swearing* (Boston,

1701); William Shewen, *A Brief Testimony Against Tale-bearers, Whisperers, and Back-biters* (Philadelphia, 1701); "J. W.," *The Baseness and Perniciousness of the Sin of Slandering and Backbiting* (Boston, 1769); and several works by Cotton Mather: *Golden Curb for the Mouth, The Good Linguist, Or, Directions to Avoid the Sins of the Tongue* (Boston, 1700; no extant copy), and *The Right Way to Shake Off a Viper. . . . What Shall Good Men Do, When They are Evil Spoken Of?* (Boston, 1720).

44. See, e.g., Benjamin Wadsworth, *The Well-Ordered Family: Or, Relative Duties* (Boston, 1712), 29–30, 34, 40, 91; and [Anonymous], *The School of Good Manners* (Boston, 1772), 5–10, 17–21.

45. On the relationship of speech to status and gentility in the late eighteenth and early nineteenth centuries, see Kenneth Cmiel, *Democratic Eloquence: The Fight over Popular Speech in Nineteenth-Century America* (New York: William Morrow, 1990), esp. chapters 1 and 2.

46. See Fliegelman, *Declaring Independence*, 35–62.

47. On changes after the sixteenth century in medical beliefs about the origins of speech, see Ynez Violé O'Neill, *Speech and Speech Disorders in Western Thought before 1600* (Westport, Conn.: Greenwood Press, 1980), esp. 178–215; and Robert B. St. George, *Conversing by Signs: Poetics of Implication in Colonial New England Culture* (Chapel Hill: University of North Carolina Press, forthcoming), esp. part II, "Embodied Spaces."

48. Stanley Fish, *There's No Such Thing as Free Speech . . . and It's a Good Thing, Too* (New York: Oxford University Press, 1994), 105, emphasis mine.

49. Mary Ellen Gale, "First Amendment But . . . On Curbing Racial Speech," *The Responsive Community: Rights and Responsibilities* 1:1 (winter 1990–1991): 48. A succinct summary of First Amendment jurisprudence and scholarship in recent years appears in Owen M. Fiss, *The Irony of Free Speech* (Cambridge: Harvard University Press, 1996).

50. Richard Dooling, *Blue Streak: Swearing, Free Speech, and Sexual Harassment* (New York: Random House, 1996), 165.

51. The now-familiar saying was first recorded in the 1890s, appearing in G. F. Northall, *Folk-Phrases of Four Counties . . . Gathered from Oral Tradition* (London: English Dialect Society, 1894), 23. See discussion in the introduction to this book.

52. On the differences between today's challenges to the First Amendment and other historical threats to free speech (notably during the McCarthy era and the Vietnam War), see Fiss, *Irony of Free Speech*, esp. 2, 9–13. For a liberal rejoinder that attempts to take account of First Amendment revisionists' arguments and move beyond them, see the essays collected in Henry Louis Gates et al., eds., *Speaking of Race, Speaking of Sex: Hate Speech, Civil Rights, and Civil Liberties* (New York: New York University Press, 1994), especially Gates, "War of Words: Critical Race Theory and the First Amendment," 17–58.

53. Cartoon by Lee Lorenz, *New Yorker*, 7 December 1992, 96. For another example of merrymaking about the notion that speech can harm, see James Barron, "Up against the Wall in a No-Curse Zone," *New York Times*, 16 October 1994, sec. 4, 2.

54. See, e.g., Mari J. Matsuda, Charles R. Lawrence, Richard Delgado, and Kimberlé Williams Crenshaw, *Words That Wound: Critical Race Theory, Assaultive Speech, and the First Amendment* (Boulder, Colo.: Westview Press, 1993), 1, 83. On the Puritan rhetoric of speech as infection, see chapters 3 and 4 in this book.

55. Charles R. Lawrence, "If He Hollers, Let Him Go: Regulating Racist Speech on Campus," in Matsuda et al., *Words That Wound*, 68, 72-73; and Richard Delgado, "Words That Wound: A Tort Action for Racial Insults, Epithets, and Name-Calling," *Harvard Civil Rights–Civil Liberties Law Review* 17:1 (spring 1982): 135-43.

56. Printed nationally, including *New York Times*, 5 January 1995, A17.

57. Mari J. Matsuda, "Public Response to Racist Speech: Considering the Victim's Story," in Matsuda et al., *Words That Wound*, 23, 38, emphasis mine; see also Catharine A. MacKinnon, *Only Words* (Cambridge: Harvard University Press, 1993), 30-31, 48. For a description of the prevailing legal understanding of "speech" and a reaffirmation of the distinction between speech and action, see Fiss, *Irony of Free Speech*, 13-15.

58. Matsuda et al., *Words That Wound*, 5.

59. Lawrence, "If He Hollers, Let Him Go," 87.

60. MacKinnon, *Only Words*, 72; see also 31-33.

61. Electronic communication circulated via WHIRL-Net, 4 December 1995.

62. John Winthrop, "A Modell of Christian Charity" (1630), in *Winthrop Papers*, 5 vols. (Boston: Massachusetts Historical Society, 1929-1947), 2: 282.

63. Fiss, *Irony of Free Speech*, 18, 4.

64. Dooling, *Blue Streak*, 178. For the charge that anti-pornography feminism, for example, is "puritanical," see "Political Correctness and the Assault on Individuality," *The Heritage Lectures* (Heritage Foundation Reports), 29 January 1993; and John Irving, "Pornography and the New Puritans," *New York Times Book Review*, 29 March 1992, 25-26.

INDEX

CPSIA information can be obtained at www.ICGtesting.com
Printed in the USA
LVOW10s0915280914

406234LV00003B/602/P